Names & Nicknames
of Places & Things

Names & Nicknames of Places & Things

LAURENCE URDANG

GRAFTON BOOKS
A Division of the Collins Publishing Group

LONDON GLASGOW
TORONTO SYDNEY AUCKLAND

Grafton Books
A Division of the Collins Publishing Group
8 Grafton Street, London W1X 3LA

Published by Grafton Books 1987

British Library Cataloguing in Publication Data
Names and nicknames of places and things.
　1. Names, Geographical　　2. Nicknames
　I. Urdang, Laurence
　910′.014　　　　　G105

ISBN 0-246-13246-9

Printed in Great Britain by
St Edmundsbury Press, Bury St Edmunds, Suffolk

Foreword

It will not surprise readers to learn that there are many thousands of everyday words—perhaps *designations* is the proper term—that are omitted from general dictionaries. Many of these, though spelt with capitals, are legitimate candidates for reference books on the grounds that they are genuine lexical elements of English and, indeed, occur with greater frequency in ordinary speech and writing than a large percentage of the words that are listed in dictionaries. There is a tradition that has developed in lexicography to omit such entries from *dictionaries* because they are encyclopaedic and belong, more properly, in *encyclopaedias*. Yet, if one examines the average dictionary, he finds a curious mixture of metaphors, eponyms (proper names that became generic, like *denim* from *serge de Nîmes*), and many other categories of word information, some of it denotative, some of it connotative.

Names & Nicknames of Places & Things is an attempt to describe the associations that many people share but that, because of differences of age, education, location, and other factors may be unfamiliar to other speakers of English. For instance, to anyone in Britain *the North, the South, the Midlands,* and other terms of that type are familiar; but in his reading he may encounter American references to *the Midwest, the (Deep) South, New England,* and so forth that are meaningless without definitions. But definitions are not always enough. It is not sufficient, say for the American, to know the geographical area included—even roughly—in *the North*: to *understand* what is meant by reference to *the North* he must know the connotations of the term, matters of accent, stereotyped prejudice, social classes, and other factors that give weight and substance to the reference. *The North* means something different in the United States, where overtones and undertones of the War Between the States still influence the feelings of many, especially those in *the South*. Thus, the use of these terms depends to a large extent on one's point of view, yet, till *Names & Nicknames...*, the connotations have, with a few exceptions, gone unnoticed in reference books. A notable exception appears in Samuel Johnson's *Dictionary*, in which there appears this definition of *oats*:

> A grain, which in England is generally given to horses, but in Scotland supports the people.

For the most part, however, we can learn little about how lexicographers and others actually feel about the material they process from the books they produce, and one of the functions of *Names & Nicknames...* is to document, not the sentiments of its editor and contributors but of those who use the language.

Another purpose of this book is to provide straightforward information of the kind that is not readily accessible or needs some fleshing out to be meaningful and to be used meaningfully. What are, for example, the similarities and differences between, say, *Piccadilly Circus* and *Times Square*? between *West End* and *Park Avenue* or *Fifth Avenue*? The entries for all of these are long enough to provide the reader with a reasonably good idea of how they fit into their respective cultures and, hence, what they really mean to those who use them.

Other places and things described in *Names & Nicknames...* include shops, restaurants, streets, neighbourhoods, neuroses (*Scarsdale syndrome*), railway stations, etc. Not all of these are still in existence (e.g., *Shepheard's Hotel in Cairo, Black Hole of Calcutta*), but most are, and all can appear at any time in ordinary conversation and writing.

It may seem that there are not many entries in this book, but reference should be made to the Index, where all items are listed that are mentioned in the text. Still, *Names & Nicknames...*, in this first British Edition, only scratches the surface of a vast area of common knowledge and information that could be greatly expanded. The Editor would be grateful for suggested additions, changes, corrections, and other comments sent in care of the publishers.

I should like to express my gratitude for all of the help given me by various members of the American Name Society for entries dealing with American names, to George Turner, of Adelaide, for help with Australian entries, to Eric Cumine, of Hong Kong, for help with entries dealing with that city and the Far East, and especially to John Ayto without whose help on British and European entries those coverages would have been sparsely treated. Finally, my thanks to Jacquelyn Goodwin for helping to shepherd the manuscript through all its phases, from start to finish.

Laurence Urdang

Aylesbury, Buckinghamshire
May 1987

NAMES & NICKNAMES

A

AAA, the
An abbreviation for the Agricultural Adjustment Administration, established in the United States in the 1930s to administer measures for soil conservation and for the relief of farmers, as provided for by the Agricultural Adjustment Acts of 1933 and 1938.

Aardvark
The nickname of the F-111, a United States fighter-bomber aircraft, prior to its being fitted with infrared targeting and a laser guidance bombing system.

Abbey Road
A road in the St John's Wood area of London which contains the EMI Recording Studios. It achieved wider fame when the Beatles gave its name to one of their albums (1969).

Abercrombie & Fitch
A department store, formerly headquartered at 45th Street and Madison Avenue, in New York City, known mainly for its sporting goods and, especially, for having fitted out a number of safaris and polar expeditions. It went bankrupt in 1977; its name was bought by another company, which opened twenty-five new stores and established a mail-order catalogue division.

Abu Simbel
A set of three temples to sun-gods, hewn out of sandstone cliffs in the time of Ramses II in about 1250 B.C. On the west bank of the Nile at Aswan (ancient Nubia), they are known chiefly for four 65-foot-high

colossi of the king. The entire site was threatened in the late 1960s by the creation of a huge reservoir, resulting from the construction of the Aswan Dam; in response to a drive by UNESCO, sufficient funds were raised to pay for the cutting of the colossi from the cliff face and their relocation on a 200-foot cliff above.

Abyssinia
A former name for Ethiopia, a country in northeastern Africa. As a word, the name enjoyed a certain vogue in the 1930s as a jocular farewell, based on its phonetic similarity to 'I'll be seeing you'.

Academy, the
A public pleasure-ground on the Cephissus, about one mile northwest of ancient Athens, on land said to have belonged, in the time of the Trojan War, to the hero Academus. It was surrounded by a wall by Hipparchus and further adorned by Cimon, the son of Miltiades, who bequeathed it to the citizens of Athens. It was the resort of Plato, who taught in its groves (the **Groves of Academe**) for nearly fifty years, till his death in 348 B.C., and gave its name to the Platonic school of philosophy.

Acadia
A former French colony in Canada, covering an area approximately that of modern Nova Scotia. Settled by France in 1604, except for Cape Breton Island, it was ceded to Great Britain by the Treaty of Utrecht (1713). Cape Breton Island was a French possession till 1763. The British deported the French in 1755, an event that was the theme of the poem *Evangeline* (1847), by Henry Wadsworth Longfellow.

accidental war, the
A nickname for World War I, so called because the German high command, obsessed with what analysts have called the 'cult of the offensive' (in contrast with the 'power of a strong defence'), misinterpreted the mobilization by Russia following the assassination of the Archduke Franz Ferdinand of Austria-Hungary by a Serbian extremist on June 28, 1914, at Sarajevo, and attacked and overwhelmed Belgium. Had Germany seen the event in its proper context of a minor political disturbance, the war, in which eight million were killed, could probably have been avoided. Also called **the war to end war, the war to end all wars, the war to make the world free for democracy** (Woodrow Wilson), (facetiously) **the war to make the world free for the Democrats,** (in Britain) **the Great War.**

Acemannes burh
An Old English name, meaning 'sick man's town', for Bath, England. An ancient Roman road connecting Bath with London is called Akeman Street.

Addled Parliament
A nickname of the second Parliament of James I (April–June 1614). It was dissolved without having passed any acts when it refused to grant supplies till the king's imposition of customs and till the restoration of the nonconforming Anglican clergy ejected in 1604 had been considered.

Adelphi, the
A former fashionable area of London between the Strand and the River Thames, designed in neoclassical splendour by Robert Adam and his brothers in 1768. Its elegant terraces housed many glitterati of the times, including the actor David Garrick, the caricaturist Thomas Rowlandson, and, later, the authors Thomas Hardy and Sir James Barrie; it was demolished in 1936.

Adonai
The name used by the Jews in place of the ineffable name Yahveh, or Jehovah (from YHWH), wherever it occurs in the Scriptures.

Adventure
The name of Captain Kidd's pirate ship.

Aetolia
An ancient district of Greece, bounded by Epirus and Thessaly on the north, Doris on the northeast, Locris on the east and southeast, the Corinthian Gulf on the south, and Acarnania on the west.

Aganippides, the
An alternate name for the Muses of ancient Greek mythology, so called because the fountain Aganippe, near Mount Helicon, in Boeotia, was sacred to them.

Agora, the
A large irregular area in ancient Athens, part of which was a marketplace, part an area for political meetings.

AIPS
A nickname for AIDS-Induced Panic Syndrome, coined by scientists to dispel fears of the contagious nature of AIDS (Acquired Immune Deficiency Syndrome) by casual social contact.

Alamo, the
The name of a former mission church in San Antonio, Texas, that served as the site in 1836 of what is considered to be one of the most heroic of U. S. military battles, although none of the Texan defenders survived and the battle was lost. Texan settlers living in Mexican territory decided to sever their relations with Mexico because of dissatisfaction with the Mexican government. About 150 men, under William Barret Travis, and including James Bowie and Davy Crockett, retreated to the Alamo at the unexpected arrival of Mexican General Antonio López de Santa Ana with an army of about 5,000 men. After ten days of siege, the Texans ran low on ammunition, Santa Ana was able to scale the walls, and the battle was over. 'Remember the Alamo' became a battle cry and enabled General Sam Houston to gather troops; two months later he defeated Santa Ana at San Jacinto and forced him to sign a treaty granting Texas its independence.

Alamo City
A nickname of San Antonio, Texas. See also **Alamo.**

Albany
An exclusive apartment building in Sackville Street, in the Piccadilly area of the West End of London. It was converted from Melbourne House, the London residence of the Duke of York, in 1802, and in its early years Lord Byron and Thomas Macaulay, George Canning, and W. E. Gladstone lived there. Its fashionable heyday was probably in the Edwardian era; at that time its tenancies were still restricted to bachelors, and one of its most noted (fictional) occupants was Raffles, the celebrated gentleman burglar. It used to be a touchstone of high caste to know that to say 'the Albany' was decidedly Non-U, a sure sign that one was not quite top-drawer.

Albany doctor, the
A refreshing sea breeze in Albany, Western Australia.

Albany Regency
A clique of New York politicians who controlled the Democratic Party in
New York State from about 1820 to about 1854. Among its members
were Martin Van Buren (president of the United States 1837–41), John A.
Dix, and William L. Marcy.

Albion
A poetic term for England, cited as early as Pliny (*Natural Histories*) IV.
102, (ca. A.D. 77), popular particularly from the 16th to the 18th centuries—William Blake, for example, often used it. The word may be a
reference to the white cliffs that fringe much of the southeast corner of
England, *albus* being the Latin word for 'white'. Nowadays it crops up
only in 'perfidious Albion' (a French view) and, curiously, in the names
of English soccer clubs, such as Brighton and Hove Albion, and West
Bromwich Albion.

Al Borak
A legendary animal, between a mule and an ass in size, with two wings
and of great swiftness, on which Muhammad is said to have made a
nocturnal journey to the seventh heaven.

Alcan Highway
A highway, about 1600 miles long, built in 1942–43, between Dawson
Creek, British Columbia, and Fairbanks, Alaska.

Alcatraz
An island in San Francisco Bay, site, from 1934 to 1963, of a federal
prison known for its security: it is said that in its entire history only one
convict escaped from there. The prison became well known especially
during the 1930s mainly through a number of Hollywood movies dealing
with crime and prisons, and in the ensuing years it became a symbol of
the harsh severity that awaited evil-doers. The island was named by the
Spaniards for its large colony of pelicans (*alcatraz* means 'pelican' in
Spanish), the name stemming originally from Arabic *al qädäs* 'bucket of
a water wheel'. For a short time after the closure of the prison, Alcatraz
Island served as the site of a hippie commune (in the 1960s) but has been
largely deserted since the early 1970s.

Aldebaran

The ancient name for the red first-magnitude star alpha Tauri, forming the eye of the bull.

Aldermaston

A village in Berkshire, to the west of London, which is the home of the Atomic Weapons Research Establishment, an obvious target for anti-nuclear demonstrators. It became famous for giving its name to the 'Aldermaston marches'. At Easter, 1958, under the aegis of the so-called 'Committee of 100', protesters marched in strength from London to Aldermaston, and for some years subsequently the annual event was a familiar part of the British Easter scene. In 1959 the route was reversed, starting at Aldermaston and ending with a big rally in Trafalgar Square. In its early years it never failed to draw enthusiastic support; however, as the '60s wore on, public concern dwindled, the number of participants fell away, and finally the march was discontinued altogether.

Aldershot

A town in northeastern Hampshire, about 34 miles southwest of London; the site of a large military camp since 1855 and thoroughly imbued with the traditions and lore of the army. It figures in the opening lines of Rudyard Kipling's poem, *Gunga Din*:

> You may talk o' gin and beer
> When you're quartered safe out 'ere,
> An' you're sent to penny-fights an' Aldershot it. . . .

Alexiad, The

A biography of Alexius I (Comnenus) (1048-1118), Byzantine emperor (1081-1118), written by Anna Comnena (1083-1148) and covering the period from 1069 to 1118.

Alhambra

A Moorish citadel and palace on the outskirts of Granada, Spain, built during the 13th and 14th centuries by the Moorish kings. Its name means simply 'red' in Arabic and, from the exterior, it appears to be a solid fortress of red brick. The interior, however, is a maze of alcoves, halls, archways, and courtyards with pools and fountains, all entirely covered with intricately carved and polychromed stucco decorations. The beauty of the palace captured the imagination of Washington Irving who, as a diplomatic attaché in Spain, lived in part of the building and wrote *The Alhambra*, a collection of tales of medieval Moorish Spain.

Alice Springs
A town in the southern part of the Northern Territory of Australia. It began as a telegraph station set in a wilderness, and resembles in many ways the frontier towns of America during the 19th century. The Alice, as it is frequently referred to, tends to be dry and dusty, its wooden houses roofed over with galvanized corrugated iron. Although there are no springs, as such, and water is not abundant during most of the year, it is nonetheless available from wells. It is named after the wife of Sir Charles Todd, Superintendent of Telegraphs, for whom the Todd River, dry for most months, was named. See also **Centre.**

Alligator Alley
The nickname for the west-east section of the Tamiami Trail (US 41), which runs from Tampa to Miami, in Florida, so named because it passes through parts of the Everglades that are infested with alligators.

Ally Pally
A nickname for Alexandra Palace, an imposing Victorian structure built on an eminence to the north of London. It was erected in 1873, 'to refine and elevate the public taste', but only sixteen days after its opening it burned down; nothing daunted, the builders built anew. It was put to considerable use for exhibitions, but it really came into its own and began to acquire its nickname, from 1936 onwards, when the BBC used it as Britain's first television studios. Although the last entertainment programme was broadcast from there in 1954, it continued to be used for news broadcasts for a further quarter of a century. It partly burned down again in 1980, but lavish plans were thereafter formulated to rebuild it as an arts, sports, and exhibition centre.

Alsatia
An area of medieval and early modern London that was off limits to those who wished to remain sound of body and purse. Situated between Fleet Street and the River Thames, it retained until 1697 the power of the former Whitefriars monastery to grant sanctuary. It consequently acted as a magnet for all the rogues and felons in London, who turned it into a notorious "rookery"—a maze of disreputable tenements, dives, and brothels. Its name comes from Alsace, a border area between France and

Germany which was famous for harbouring the disaffected. See also **Whitefriars**.

Amazonia

A name applied to the Amazon basin, the vast (about 1.5 million square miles) plain in Brazil through which the River Amazon flows to the sea. Most of it is occupied by huge tracts of tropical rain forest, although many areas are now being cleared, causing concern to environmentalists. The river itself got its name from some long-haired warlike tribesmen encountered on its banks by early Spanish explorers, who evidently thought they had met with the legendary Amazons, fierce female warriors.

Amen Corner

The nickname given by W. J. Chamberlain of the *New York Sun* to that part of the main corridor of the Fifth Avenue Hotel in New York City where the managers of the Republican Party met (1859-1908) to discuss plans and platforms. In churches, it refers to the section near the altar where the devout sit and shout 'Amen!' in approval of what the preacher is saying.

American Nile, the

A nickname of the St John's River in northeastern Florida, so called because the reeds and tropical vegetation growing along its banks resemble those along the Nile.

American Workhouse, the

An ironical nickname coined by London taxi drivers for the Park Lane Hotel, with reference to wealthy American tourists' predilection for its luxurious appointments.

America's Cup

A racing trophy, first given in 1851 to the *America*, a yacht owned by J. C. Stevens. In recent times, the class of yachts allowed to compete, called '12-metre', has drawn entrants from France, Australia, and other countries; all the races, which are held every two to four years, now organized as sedate affairs around a closed triangular course, had been won by the American vessel till 1983, when the Australian yacht, *Australia II*, with a uniquely designed hull, captured the huge silver trophy which, in arrogant confidence, had been 'permanently' bolted into its display case at the New York Yacht Club, on West 44th Street, in New York City. The 12-metre class is established by a complex measuring rule, its name having little to do with over-all length, beam, waterline length, sail area, or any of the other individual dimensions customarily used in naming classes of racing boats. The competing boats are usually built by a syndicate of wealthy yacht racing enthusiasts, because their cost, maintenance, and crewing are far too expensive for any one aficionado, no matter how fervent or wealthy. Although the vessels' sponsors regard the quadrennial competition as a national symbol, because yacht racing is scarcely a spectator sport and because the costs of participation are so far outside the reach of any but a handful of avid millionaires, the average person's association with the event is quite remote. Formerly held at Newport, Rhode Island, the race is officially held at the port designated by the winning team, and in 1987 the venue was Perth, Western Australia. In 1989, the United States having regained the trophy, the race is expected to be held in Hawaii.

Anatolia

An oblong plateau of mountainous land bounded on the north by the Black Sea and on the south by the Mediterranean. Anatolia forms the Asian part—and indeed by far the major part—of Turkey. The European part, on the far side of the Bosporus, is only about three per cent of the total area of the country. In ancient times, Anatolia was the same as Asia Minor.

anatomist's snuffbox

The small hollow formed on the back of the hand at the root of the thumb when the thumb is bent back strongly, so called because those who take snuff use it as a temporary repository before sniffing it up the nose.

Andersonstown

A district on the western edge of Belfast, Northern Ireland, at the western end of the **Falls Road** (*q.v.*). It is a major stronghold of the IRA, but also saw the founding of the Peace People movement in 1976.

Angel, the

A road junction in northeast London, where the City Road meets Pentonville Road and Islington High Street. It is named after a famous former coaching inn on the site.

Angora
Before 1930 Ankara, the Turkish capital, was known as Angora; today the name survives only as a designation for certain long-haired breeds of rabbits, cats, and goats.

Angostura
From 1764 to 1846 the name of Ciudad Bolívar, a town in Venezuela. Angostura bark, from certain South American trees, provided some of the secret ingredients of Angostura bitters, an astringent potion first concocted in the 19th century as a stimulant for people suffering from loss of appetite, but now much used for adding bite to mixed drinks.

Antipodes, the
Antipodes comes from a Greek word meaning 'with feet opposite', and so literally refers to areas on the opposite side of the world—that is, where people 'stand on their heads'. The word became particularly popular with British speakers to refer specifically to Australia and New Zealand, which are almost diametrically opposite Britain on the globe. See also **down under**. In addition, *the Antipodes* is the official designation of a small group of uninhabited islands to the southeast of New Zealand.

Aotearoa
A poetic name for New Zealand, often quoted in an English version as 'The Land of the Long White Cloud'. If the Maori name consists of three words, *ao* could mean 'cloud', 'dawn', 'daytime', or 'world'; *tea* could mean 'white', 'clear', or 'bright'; while *roa* means 'long' or 'tall'. The usual explanation is that when the first Maoris arrived by canoe, they saw a long cloud over the land. An alternative possibility is that the name is connected with *Aotea,* one of the first Maori canoes to reach New Zealand. The name originally applied to the North Island only.

Appalachia
A name that immediately calls to mind great poverty and an almost total lack of hope. It refers to that part of the Appalachian Mountains in West Virginia, Tennessee, and Kentucky, where the terrain is too steep and rocky for farming or for road, highway, or airport construction, and where mountain streams often flood valley settlements. Coal mining was the major industry, but many mines have closed because the stringent enforcement of anti-pollution laws has reduced the use of coal, leaving most of the area's inhabitants with no alternative means of employment.

Appalachian Mountains
Named after the Apalachee Indians, these mountains are the oldest in
North America and the second largest after the Rockies. They extend
about 1500 miles from the Gaspé Peninsula in Quebec, Canada, to Birmingham, Alabama. They include the Notre Dame mountains in Quebec,
the White Mountains in New Hampshire, the Green Mountains in Vermont, and the Catskill Mountains in New York. Southwest of the Hudson River Valley they divide into three main sections: the Blue Ridge,
which extend into Alabama; the Great Valley, from Pennsylvania to
Tennessee; and to their west, the Ridge-and-Valley Province which, in
turn, is bordered on their west by the Cumberland and Allegheny mountains. These last, together with the Blue Ridge and Great Smoky mountains make the Appalachians one of the great divides in North America,
separating rivers that empty into the Atlantic Ocean from those that flow
into the Gulf of Mexico.

Appalachian Trail, the
A two-thousand-mile-long footpath through the Appalachians from
Mount Katahdin, Maine, to Springer Mountain, Georgia. It passes
through fourteen states, two national parks, and eight national forests.

Apple Isle, the
A nickname given by Australians to Tasmania; apples are the mainstay of
the island's agricultural production.

Arabia
A huge peninsula in the shape of an axe-head, at the southwest corner of
Asia. To its west is the Red Sea, to its east the Persian Gulf; and its vast,
almost trackless interior, the Arabia Deserta of the ancients, is a burning
desert beneath which repose highly lucrative reserves of oil. It is comprised of the modern states of Saudi Arabia, Yemen, South Yemen,
Oman, Bahrein, Qatar, and the United Arab Emirates. Less specifically,
Arabia has in the past been used as a term for the Arab world generally,
much as we might use Middle East today. Shakespeare no doubt had its
oriental mystery in mind when he wrote 'All the perfumes in Arabia will
not sweeten this little hand' (*Macbeth*, V.i.). The archaic, poetic version
Araby (as in *The Sheik of Araby*) has the same associations.

Aragon Ballroom

A slightly shabby Chicago dancehall that, in its glory days beginning in the late 1920s, and continuingly popular during the 1930s and '40s, was a picturesque mecca for couples and singles eager to socialize and appreciative of the big-name bands that often played there. Located in the North Side's Uptown area, near Lake Michigan, the Aragon in its prime was noted for its grandly romantic decor, a heavily Hollywood-influenced imitation of Moorish architecture. Radio 'remotes'—on-location broadcasts—helped spread the ballroom's fame across the Midwest and a fair portion of the rest of the country. Perhaps best known of those who broadcast from there were Wayne King, 'The Waltz King', and singer/bandleader Eddy Howard. With the advent of television and changing musical tastes, the Aragon began a long decline through a series of such dubious reincarnations as a psychedelic disco, a rock-band auditorium, a boxing-match arena, and, most recently, as the occasional host to Latino 'salsa' bands.

Arcadia

An area in southern Greece. In modern times it is officially a Greek department in the central Peloponnese, but its fame rests firmly on its reputation as a paradisiac land of pastoral peace and revelry—a reputation incongruous in the light of the bleakness and mountainousness of its actual terrain. It was the ancient Greek poet Theocritus, echoed later in Virgil's *Eclogues*, who first peopled the landscape with amorous shepherds and nymphs; but the setting was eagerly seized on during the Renaissance by revivers of classical bucolics, who created anew the never-never land of *Arcady* (as they called it) and filled its long golden afternoons with lovesick Elizabethan swains. The most famous example of the genre is probably Sir Philip Sidney's long prose romance, *Arcadia*. A more chilling use of the name is in the tombstone inscription *Et in Arcadia ego* (literally 'I, too, in Arcadia'), not uncommon in medieval and early modern times; its import is enigmatic, but it may mean 'Even in Arcadia death is present'.

Archway

An area in London, to the northwest of Hampstead Heath. Through the middle of it runs Archway Road, which gets its name from a large viaduct, razed in 1900. When a London Underground station was opened nearby in the early 20th century it was called Archway station, and, as very often happened in such cases, the station's name became established for the surrounding district.

Arctogaea
In the scientific study of the distribution of animal species around the world, the name given to the vast landmass that includes Europe, Asia, and Africa, with the addition of North America. Compare **Neogaea, Notogaea**.

Arden
An area in the western part of Warwickshire, once part of a large forest that may have extended from the Severn to the Trent across the English Midlands. In English literature of the 16th and 17th centuries, it was often used as the scene of pastoral revels in shade-dappled glades and sylvan grottoes, and large parts of Shakespeare's *As You Like It* are set there. The association with Shakespeare, strengthened by the fact that his mother's maiden name was Arden, has led to a well-known modern edition of his works being called the *Arden Shakespeare*.

Army & Navy Stores
Originally an outlet for surplus army and navy goods and apparel, today a large department store, in Victoria Street, in London (with other branches elsewhere), known as outfitters for safaris and explorers and, formerly, for those posted to colonies in India, Africa, etc.

Ascot
A village in Berkshire, to the west of London, famed for its racecourse on Ascot Heath. The race meeting held there every June, known as Royal Ascot, was founded by Queen Anne in 1711; it is one of the focal points of the summer season in British high society. Competition is keen, not to say ruthless, for places in the Royal Enclosure that afford an opportunity to mingle, or at least seem to mingle, with such royalty as is present. It is a bonanza for couturiers, whose talents provide ammunition for a spectacular display of ladies' high fashion. Gentlemen turn up more soberly and uniformly attired in morning coat and topper, sometimes set off with a species of cravat known as an ascot.

Ashes, the
The name given to the trophy awarded to winners of an England-Australia test cricket series. It is in fact a rather insignificant-looking little urn,

but its emotional importance to English and Australian cricket enthusiasts far outweighs its actual size. It gets its name from a mock obituary of English cricket published in the *Sporting Times* in 1882, when Australia had beaten England on English soil for the first time. It read:

> In Affectionate remembrance of English Cricket
> which died at The Oval, 29th August, 1882. Deeply
> lamented by a large circle of sorrowing friends and
> acquaintances. R.I.P.   N.B. The body will be
> cremated and the Ashes taken to Australia.

The following Australian summer a bail used in an England-Australia match was ceremonially burned and the ashes placed in an urn, and ever since this has been the coveted prize in the oldest of all test series (although it never actually leaves **Lord's**).

Ash Wednesday fires
The name given to disastrous bushfires that took place in South Australia on Ash Wednesday, 1980, and (especially) in South Australia and Victoria on Ash Wednesday in 1983.

Asia Minor
A now rather dated or literary name for **Anatolia** (*q.v.*), the part of Turkey that is in Asia.

Atchison, Topeka, & Santa Fe
The name of a major transcontinental railway, between Chicago and the southwestern states of the U. S. (though it never passed through Santa Fe); it followed generally the old Santa Fe Trail.

Athenaeum, the
A London club, founded in 1824, situated in a large, white, Greek Revival building in Waterloo Place, just off Pall Mall (in **Clubland**, *q.v.*). In 1830, the members passed the following Resolution:

> The Athenaeum was instituted in 1824 for the association of
> individuals known for their scientific or literary attainments,
> artists of eminence in any class of the fine arts, and
> noblemen and gentlemen distinguished as liberal patrons of
> science, literature or the arts.

As the Committee acknowledges, 'over the years these categories have been considerably widened and now extend to persons of attainment in any field where their work is of an intellectual nature and of substantial value to the community'. This presumably accounts for the abundance of bishops among the membership, which is limited to about 2000.

Athens of America, the
A nickname of Boston, Massachusetts, so called after its many educational, literary, and cultural institutions.

Athens of the North, the
Edinburgh, the capital of Scotland, acquired this epithet in the 18th and early 19th centuries, when it was the centre of a great cultural and literary flowering, fostered by such distinguished citizens as James Boswell, David Hume, Sir Walter Scott, and Thomas Carlyle. But it could almost as well have been inspired by the elegant Georgian buildings of the New Town, which are of an Athenian refinement.

Atlantic Provinces, the
A name for the four Canadian provinces of Newfoundland, New Brunswick, Nova Scotia, and Prince Edward Island, though the last three are sometimes called the Maritime Provinces. They have been a major fishing centre since the 1400s, providing more than three-quarters of Canada's fish, and include the Grand Banks, southeast of Newfoundland, one of the world's richest fishing grounds.

Atlantic States
A nickname for those states south of New England which border on the Atlantic ocean or are economically tied to it. The Middle Atlantic States are New Jersey, New York, and Pennsylvania; the South Atlantic States are Delaware, Florida, Georgia, Maryland, North and South Carolina, and Virginia, though West Virginia is sometimes included.

Atlantis
A legendary island in the Atlantic Ocean, just beyond the **Pillars of Hercules** (*q.v.*), mentioned by Plato in the *Timaeus* and the *Critias* as a major power in the entire Mediterranean area; it was destroyed by a cataclysm and sank beneath the sea thousands of years ago. Throughout history, similar legends pervaded the European cultures. Attempts to rationalize the existence of Atlantis have persisted to the present, the most

recent theory placing its site on the island of Santorini (modern Thera), in the Aegean Sea, which evidence shows disappeared beneath the sea as a result of a gigantic eruption of a volcano in the 15th century B.C., obliterating all but traces of the Minoan Cretan colony that flourished there. Although such a theory is not impossible, it would place Atlantis thousands of miles east of its legendary site; besides, it is well known that there were many active volcanoes in the Mediterranean (and there still are—Vesuvius, Etna, Stromboli, etc.)—so there is no necessary justification to identify Atlantis with Santorini.

Auld Reekie
A nickname given in former times to Edinburgh, Scotland, on account of the pall of smoke, or 'reek', that hung above the city in the days before clean-air legislation. *Auld* represents the Scottish pronunciation of 'old'.

Auntie
A nickname for the British Broadcasting Corporation, coined in a spirit of exasperated affection. It refers to the BBC's attitude towards its audience, and towards its employees, which is seen as being kindly but often fussy and old-fashioned. Compare **Beeb, Portland Place.**

Australasia
A vague collective term incorporating an indefinite number of territories in the southwest Pacific Ocean. In its most restricted use, it can refer simply to Australia and New Zealand, although it usually includes the nearby islands of Melanesia. It can also, however, embrace the farther-flung islands of Micronesia and Polynesia, when it becomes almost a synonym for Oceania. In addition, it is often used to refer to the British Commonwealth countries of the area: Australia, New Zealand, Fiji, and Western Samoa. See also **Oceania.**

Avebury
A village in Wiltshire, England, site of one of the most extensive ceremonial locales in Europe, encompassing more than 28 acres. The ceremonial structures are, in some respects, similar to those at **Stonehenge** (*q.v.*); on the other hand, the area is much larger than Stonehenge and involves structures that, successively, span more than 2000 years, up to the end of the Bronze Age, or about 1000 B.C.

Avenue of the Americas
The official name given to Sixth Avenue, in New York City, in the 1940s
to honour the Latin American countries. Few New Yorkers use the name,
which is inconveniently long for a people who are always in a hurry, and
(as in this book) it is habitually referred to as Sixth Avenue. Its southern
end is at Canal Street; its northern terminus at 59th Street, where it ends
at Central Park. During the past three decades, since the removal of the
elevated 'subway' that blighted most of its length, the upper part, from
40th Street northwards, has seen a revitalization through the erection of
modern office buildings, some of which are part of **Rockefeller Center**
(*q.v.*). **Radio City Music Hall** (*q.v.*) stands at the corner of Sixth Avenue
and 50th Street.

Ayers Rock
A huge, red sandstone rock, about 1100 feet high, two miles long, and
eight around, situated in the southwestern part of the Northern Territory
of Australia, southwest of Alice Springs. Long a favourite of rock-climb-
ers and vacationers, the caves at its base were long the habitation of
aborigines, and rock paintings can be seen there. The nearest towns are
some distance away, and Ayers Rock is regarded as being beyond the
frontiers of civilization.

Azania
A name given by African nationalists to the territory occupied by the
Republic of South Africa. It was applied to a fictitious African nation by
the English writer Evelyn Waugh in his novel, *Black Mischief* (1932).

Aztec State, the
A nickname of Arizona, so called after the old ruins erroneously believed
to have been built by the Aztecs because they had Aztec names.

B

B, the
A nickname for Bridewell, the former London prison, closed in the mid 19th century; it has become a metonym for prison in general, especially in Liverpudlian slang.

Babylon
The capital of ancient Mesopotamia, and a name that has come to be used symbolically for the corruption and depravity of great metropolises. In Protestant polemic of the Reformation and later times it was applied to Rome and to the Roman Catholic church in general, and more recently it has been adopted by the Rastafarians to refer to the oppressiveness and wickedness of western (white) society.

Baby State, the
A former nickname of Arizona, so called because until the 1959 entry of Alaska and Hawaii, it was the last state to join the Union (1912).

Back Bay
The name of the area west of downtown Boston along the Charles River from the Public Garden west to the suburb of Brookline, where until the 1920s lived the wealthiest families, often referred to as the *Boston Brahmins* (from *Brahmin caste*, the highest class in the Hindu religion). When they began to move to the suburbs in the 1920s, the long rows of beautiful townhouses on tree-lined streets were converted into apartments, which are now occupied by college students and young, upwardly mobile, white-collar workers. Many of Boston's finest stores and best restaurants are to be found here, as well as the Museum of Fine Arts, the Institute of Contemporary Art, Symphony Hall, the New England Conservatory of Music (the country's oldest music school), and Fenway Park, home of the Boston Red Sox baseball team. Two modern high-rise complexes are also here: Prudential Center has apartment buildings, a hotel, a civic auditorium, many shops, and the 52-story Prudential Tower Office building; in Copley Square, a few blocks northeast, is the tallest building in New England, the 60-story John Hancock Tower, in the glass sides of which are reflected Trinity Church and the main branch of the Boston Public Library, which has over 3½ million volumes.

Backbone of England, the
An epithet for the Pennines, in England, a range of hills from the Cheviot
Hills, near Scotland at the north, to the Trent, the main river in the
Midlands.

Backbone of the Confederacy
A nickname of the Mississippi River during the Civil War when most of
the supplies for the Confederate forces had to be shipped on it, through
the port of New Orleans, after Union ships blockaded the east coast.

Backs, the
A series of lawns running down to the River Cam in the centre of Cambridge, on the opposite bank of the river from Queens', King's, Clare,
Trinity, and St John's Colleges. Particularly attractive in Spring, they
offer an unrivalled vista of many of Cambridge's finest buildings; the view
of King's College Chapel is especially famous.

Bad Lands, the
A depressingly grim region of southwestern South Dakota, extending into
northwestern Nebraska, that is the result of deforestation and natural
erosion.

Bagshot
Perhaps it is the connotations of the name—bagging anything that moves
within the sights of one's shotgun—but the town of Bagshot inevitably
suggests peppery comic-strip retired colonels, moustaches abristle. This
part of Surrey, southwest of London, is indeed army country, with
Camberley (home of the Royal Military Academy) just a few miles down
the road.

Bakerloo
One of the lines of the London Underground. When it was opened in
1906 it ran only between Baker Street and Waterloo—hence its name,
originally a nickname—but it has since been extended out to Watford in
the north and **Elephant and Castle** (*q.v.*) in the south.

Baker Street
A large thoroughfare in central London that leads down from Regent's
Park to Oxford Street. It is a rather drab, nondescript street, its most
noteworthy building probably being the monolithic headquarters of

Marks and Spencer, one of Britain's leading department stores. But its most famous address does not exist and never existed: 221B, fictional address of the rooms let by Sherlock Holmes, the paragon of literary detectives. Here he would meet his clients and conduct experiments, and from here he would sally forth with Dr. Watson in pursuit of murderers, jewel thieves, kidnappers, and spies, or deploy his band of 'Baker Street irregulars', young street urchins, in search of clues. It is no doubt more than a coincidence that his creator, Arthur Conan Doyle, a doctor, once had his consulting rooms in Devonshire Place, off Harley Street, not far from Baker Street.

Balkans, the
The area occupied by the countries of the mountainous Balkan peninsula in southeastern Europe: in the present day, Yugoslavia, Rumania, Albania, Bulgaria, the European part of Turkey, and Greece (although many people would feel that only the northern and northeastern parts of Greece—Macedonia and Thrace—are truly Balkan). Until the early 20th century, however, the region was divided into a far larger number of states, including Bosnia, Herzegovina, Serbia, Montenegro, Croatia, Moldavia, and Transylvania. As the area where the Turkish, Russian, and Austro-Hungarian empires jarred against each other, the Balkans became one of the great political flashpoints of the later 19th century, and many statesmen and diplomats retired defeated by the famously irresoluble 'Balkan problem'.

Balmoral Castle
A residence of the British royal family, in Aberdeenshire, Scotland, built in 1856 on the site of a former, smaller castle, which had belonged originally to the Farquharsons. Prince Albert acquired it in 1847. It is today occupied by the Queen during the summer months; it is rumoured that the other members of the royal family dislike Balmoral, but the Queen insists. . . .

baloney dollar
The nickname of the devalued dollar when the U. S. went off the gold standard in 1933, so called because no matter how thin baloney is sliced, it still retains its basic characteristics.

Baltic States
Three states, Estonia, Latvia, and Lithuania, bordering the east coast of
the Baltic sea and part of the Soviet Union. Prior to becoming independent countries in 1918, they had been ruled variously by the Danes,
Swedes, Poles, Germans, and Russians and were part of the Russian
czar's empire before World War I. In 1940 they were annexed by Russia.

Bamboo Curtain, the
A name used to characterize the ideological and cultural barrier between
Communist China and its satellites, and the West. It was coined in imitation of the Iron Curtain, the boundary of East European Communism,
and was used particularly in the 1950s and '60s, when China pursued a
policy of hostile insularity. Compare **Iron Curtain**.

Bananaland
A jocular nickname for Queensland, Australia. Its residents may be called
Bananalanders or *Banana-benders* and live behind the *Banana Curtain*.
In fact, more bananas are produced in northern New South Wales than in
Queensland.

banana republic
A derisive nickname, infrequent in current usage, for any of several
Central or South American countries. The name was used especially in
reference to those countries that were under the economic influence
(hence, political control) of the United Fruit Company of the USA, a
combine that purchased much of the produce of those nations.

Banbury Cross
The original of the nursery rhyme that begins, 'Ride a cockhorse to
Banbury Cross', was destroyed by Puritans in 1602; it was replaced in
1859. The town of Banbury, in northern Oxfordshire, England is known
mainly for its spiced currant cakes but also for its ale and cheese.

Bank, the
A road junction at the very heart of the City of London, which takes its
name from the **Bank of England** (*q.v.*), on its north side. Also to be
found here are the Royal Exchange and the Mansion House, official
residence of the Lord Mayor of London. Seven heavily congested roads
converge on the Bank's triangular space, including Threadneedle Street,
Cornhill, Lombard Street, and Poultry.

Bank of England, the
The central bank of England and Wales, which acts as the British government's bankers and helps to implement many aspects of its fiscal policy. It was founded in 1694, and nationalized in 1946. It is lodged in a suitably monolithic building in the City of London, on the north side of the Bank; particularly impressive and evocative of hoarded bullion is its massive blank outer wall, through which no ray of light or prying eye can penetrate. See also **Old Lady of Threadneedle Street.**

Bankside
In the late 20th century, this road, on the south bank of the Thames in London, just across the river from St Paul's cathedral, is probably best known for its power station, which dominates the surrounding scene. But it was once much more lively. In Elizabethan times and later, Bankside was a bustling, thriving area that teemed with slightly disreputable joie de vivre; there were taverns, theatres (including Shakespeare's *Globe*), gardens, brothels, and abundant public entertainments of the bull- and bear-baiting variety. (A lane nearby is still called Bear Gardens.) In those days, prostitutes were often known as 'sisters of the Bank'.

Banzai Pipeline
A tube-like configuration of a large, slow-breaking wave at the beach at Waikiki, in Hawaii, regarded as an idyllic opportunity for surfing enthusiasts. The name *banzai* comes from a cry (meaning 'ten thousand years') used by Japanese attacking soldiers in World War II. The association is between their reckless, suicidal spirit and the extreme danger in surfing through the Pipeline.

Barbary Coast, the
A historical name for the Islamic lands along the north coast of Africa, from the Egyptian border to the Atlantic. The Barbary States were Tripolitania, Tunisia, Algeria, and Morocco. The Barbary Coast was notorious in ancient and medieval times as a haunt of pirates. The name comes from the same source as the word *barbarian*, since the Saracens who lived there were regarded by Christians as heathens.

barber, the
The chilly, cutting wind that is typical in Greymouth, New Zealand.

Barbican, the
A site in the City of London, to the northeast of St Paul's Cathedral. The
area lies just outside the site of the ancient city walls (part of the original
Roman wall is on display there), and the name *Barbican* comes from a
word meaning 'watchtower or gateway in a wall'. In the 19th century it
was London's garment district. Devastated by bombing in World War II,
extensive postwar redevelopment plans led first to a grouping of luxury
apartment blocks and finally to the Barbican Centre, an amalgam of
theatres, cinemas, galleries, and a concert hall, opened in 1982. This
building, usually known simply as *the Barbican*, was derided initially for
its mazelike complexity, but quickly established itself as an essential part
of London's cultural scene.

Barefoot Cantonese
The spoken vernacular used as a lingua franca in Hong Kong.

Barrio, the
The name given to any American city neighbourhood the residents of
which are mainly Hispanic, especially Puerto Rican.

Barset
Also known as Barsetshire, it is probably the most famous fictional
county in English literature. Anthony Trollope wrote a series of novels in
which it is featured, from *The Warden* (1855) to *The Last Chronicle of
Barset* (1867), many of which are concerned with back-stairs ecclesiastical
intrigue in the cathedral city of Barchester (modelled on Winchester).

Bart's
A nickname given to St Bartholomew's Hospital and Medical School, in
the City of London to the south of Smithfield. It was founded in 1123 and
is the oldest hospital in London still on its original site.

Battersea
An inner-city suburb of London, on the south bank of the Thames,
opposite Chelsea to the north. It has a rather grimy image, probably
because it is firmly linked in the public imagination with Battersea Power
Station (see **Nine Elms**), a powerful icon of urban industrialization; but in
fact in the 1980s it is something of an up-and-coming area, with people
moving in and renovating. Other well-known Battersea landmarks are the

Funfair, which opened in 1951 as part of the Festival of Britain celebrations but no longer survives, and Battersea Dogs' Home, London's main dog pound.

Battle above *or* in the Clouds
Lookout Mountain, the site of the Battle of Chattanooga in 1863, is so high that it was said the soldiers were obscured by the clouds.

Battlebridge
Until the 1830s, the name for the area of north London now known as King's Cross. It is preserved in *Battle Bridge Road*, near King's Cross Station. See also **King's Cross, 1.**

Battleground of Freedom, the
A nickname of Kansas, so called in reference to the ten years of arguments, after passage of the Kansas-Nebraska Bill in 1854, as to whether slavery would be permitted.

Bay, the
A nickname for Sydney's maximum security prison, Long Bay Gaol.

Bayreuth
A city in Bavaria where, in the mid 18th century, the Margravine Wilhelmine, sister of Frederick the Great of Prussia, sponsored the building of a magnificent opera house as a focal point for her interest in the arts. The composer Richard Wagner (1813–83) settled there in 1872 and was present at the dedication of the Festival Theatre. In 1876, the first complete performance of *The Ring* was given there, and 1882 saw the first performance of *Parsifal*. In the past century, Bayreuth has become firmly associated with Wagner, and his music and operas are performed there regularly, attended by devotees from all over the world.

Bay Street
The name for the financial district of Toronto, Canada.

Bayswater
A district in west London, to the north of Kensington Gardens and the west of Paddington. Like Earl's Court to the south, this is essentially bed-sitter-land, with a largely floating population of young people starting out on city life, and it has an appropriate air of slightly scruffy liveliness and

impermanence. The grand houses of former generations are dowagers in decline.

Beachy Head

A 575-foot chalk cliff near Eastbourne, on the south coast of England, atop which is a favourite area for picnics when the weather permits. Its name comes from the French *beau chef* 'beautiful headland' and was spelt *Beuchef* in the 13th century.

Beacon Hill

North of Boston Common rises a hill where beacon fires were lit in the 1600s to signal ships, and which, since the 1700s, has given its name to a fashionable neighbourhood of narrow cobblestoned streets, brick sidewalks, and gaslights. The first white settler in Boston, William Blackstone, was the first to build a home there in 1620. Its elegant brick townhouses are home to some of Boston's oldest and most distinguished families. The State House is located on the southern edge, and brick apartment buildings line the northern slope.

Bean, L. L.

See **L. L. Bean**.

Beantown

A nickname of Boston, Massachusetts.

Bearsden

A neat upmarket commuter suburb of Glasgow. Situated to the northwest of the city, it is officially part of the Bearsden and Milngavie District.

Bedlam

In 1247 the priory of St Mary of Bethlehem (or Bedlam, as it was often known then) was founded in the Bishopsgate area of the City of London. As early as 1402 it is mentioned as being used as a lunatic asylum. It was burnt down in the Great Fire of 1666, and in 1676 a new Bedlam asylum was built a few streets away to the west. Finally, in 1815, it was moved south of the Thames to Lambeth. It has long since given place to more enlightened institutions (its former buildings now house the Imperial War Museum), but echoes of the chaos and terror that prevailed in mental hospitals of the not so distant past remain in the current application of the term *bedlam* to any scene of noisy confusion.

Bedloe's Island
From 1758 the name of the twelve-acre island in Upper New York Bay southwest of Manhattan Island (since 1956 officially named Liberty Island), on which the Statue of Liberty stands. The land was privately owned until 1800 when it was given to the U. S. government; in 1841, a fort with the plan of an eleven-point star was built there and named Fort Wood, after an officer killed in the War of 1812. The foundations of the fort are the base on which the statue stands. The island was named after Isaac Bedloe, its first owner.

Beeb, the
A nickname for the British Broadcasting Corporation, based on the pronunciation of its initial letters, BBC. Compare **Auntie, Portland Place.**

Beehive State, the
The official nickname of Utah.

Belgravia
A fashionable residential area in the West End of London, to the south of Hyde Park. It was laid out in 1825 on land owned by the Grosvenor family, whose country estate in Leicestershire is called Belgrave. It assumed its position as the high-rent place to live in London as **Mayfair** (*q.v.*) was given over more and more to commerce, and it continues to hold its place, even though in the 1980s one's neighbour is more likely to be an Arab oil merchant than an English duke. See also **Sloane Square.**

Belisha beacon
A black-and-white-banded pole topped with a yellow glass globe which is placed on both sides of pedestrian ('zebra') crossings in England as a warning to motorists. It was introduced during the mid 1930s by Leslie Hore-Belisha, the Minister of Transport.

Bellevue
A major hospital of the City of New York, situated below 34th Street on First Avenue. Although it is a large general hospital, it is best known for its psychiatric ward where violent psychotics, would-be suicides, and intransigent criminals are taken, often under restraint by the police, for confinement and treatment. Its name has become a symbol of uncontrollable behaviour and insanity and has given rise to expressions like, 'You're ready for Bellevue'. See also **Bloomingdale's.**

Benelux
In 1948 three northwest European states, Belgium, the Netherlands, and Luxembourg, formed a customs union to which the name *Benelux* was given. In 1960 this was expanded to a more general economic union, allowing free circulation of people, goods, money, etc., among all three, and over the years they have come to be known collectively as the *Benelux countries*. Compare **Low Countries**.

Berkeley Square
A square in Mayfair, in the West End of London, to the southeast of Grosvenor Square. In former times it contained many elegant town houses, but since World War II several of these have been replaced by rather bleak modern office blocks. There are still trees in the square, but in the 1980s it is less likely than ever that a nightingale would ever sing there.

Berlin Wall, the
In August 1961, the German Democratic Republic (East Germany) erected a barrier, then a concrete wall six feet high, with barbed wire on top, to seal off the part of Berlin it had occupied since the end of World War II from that occupied by the Federal Republic of Germany (West Germany). Prior to that, millions of people from Soviet-controlled countries had passed through Berlin to settle in the West. After the Wall was completed, such passage from east to west was virtually brought to a halt, and it was not uncommon for those who attempted it to be shot dead by the guards who man the turrets set above the Wall. Officially, East Berlin did not become a part of East Germany till 1966.

Bermondsey Market
A street market, formerly the Caledonian Market, now officially the Bermondsey and New Caledonian Market, situated in Bermondsey Street, on the south bank of the Thames, near Tower Bridge, in London. All sorts of wares are sold in its stalls, mostly antique and rummage, and it is open only on Fridays. There is also a large indoor area of stalls. See also **Caledonian Market**.

Bermuda Triangle, the
A roughly triangular area of the western North Atlantic Ocean, off the eastern seaboard of the U. S., that is notorious for the unexplained disappearance of planes and ships that venture into it. It covers a very

large extent of sea (about one and a half million square miles in total, with its three corners at the tip of Florida, just below New York, and a point to the east of the island of Bermuda), and records of ships missing there or being mysteriously abandoned by their crews stretch back to the mid 19th century. Since that time about fifty vessels and twenty aircraft have been reported as the Triangle's victims. Perhaps the most celebrated case is that of five bombers that set out from Fort Lauderdale Naval Air Station, Florida, in 1945: after radioing back that they were lost, they were never seen or heard of again.

Bernese Oberland, the
The foothills and lower northern slopes of the Alps in south-central Switzerland, to the south of Interlaken. It is the quintessential Switzerland of mountain chalets, cowbells, alpenhorns, Emmenthaler cheese, and edelweiss. It lies mostly in the southern part of the canton of Bern.

Bessarabia
A region at the extreme southwest of the Soviet Union, on the borders of Romania. As a frontier area it was long the subject of disputes between the Russians and the Ottoman Empire, changing hands several times during the 19th century, until at the end of World War I it was occupied by Romania. It was ceded to the Soviet Union in 1947 and is now mostly in the Moldavian Soviet Socialist Republic.

Bethnal Green in the Sun
A humorous nickname given to Marbella, on the **Costa del Sol** (*q.v.*) in southern Spain. It refers to the large influx of the British criminal fraternity in the 1960s and '70s (see under **Costa del Crime**), many of whom came from Bethnal Green and nearby areas of East London.

Beverly Hills
A small city (1980 population 32,367) surrounded by Los Angeles. Mostly a low-density residential area with large houses on large lots, it has a commercial area in the southern part along and near Wilshire Boulevard. The population was only 674 in 1920, but it grew 250% in the next decade as it became a favoured residence of people associated with the motion-picture business in nearby Hollywood. The relative affluence and notoriety of its citizens have given it a worldwide fame out of all proportion to its size.

Beverly Hills Hotel
The name of a hotel located in the heart of the residential area of Beverly Hills, California, on Sunset Boulevard. One of its dining rooms, the Polo Lounge, is a favourite haunt of people in the entertainment business at breakfast and lunch.

Bhopal
A city in the heart of India, the capital of the huge state of Madhya Pradesh, which lurched into unwanted fame in December 1984 when a calamitous leak from a tank of methyl isocyanate in the Union Carbide chemical plant there brought death and suffering to many thousands of its inhabitants. From being a pleasant but anonymous industrialized city, Bhopal turned overnight into a symbol of the uncaring exploitation of cheap Third World labour by rapacious Western capitalists—or of the ramshackle safety procedures in Indian factories, depending upon one's point of view. Compare **Flixborough.**

Bible Belt, the
An area of the United States, chiefly in the South and Southwest and including Tennessee, parts of Kentucky, Arkansas, Oklahoma, Texas, etc., characterized by fervid religious fundamentalism. Its name derives from the success of itinerant Bible salesmen in the region.

Big Apple, the
A nickname of New York City.

Big Australian, the
A nickname of the Broken Hill Proprietary Company Ltd, usually known as BHP Ltd, originally a silver-lead-zinc mining company which has become Australia's largest manufacturing organization and one of its largest mineral and energy producers. Its early mining operation was at Broken Hill in western New South Wales.

Big Bang, the
A nickname given to the deregulation of the Stock Exchange in the City of London, which took place in October 1986. The far-reaching changes included the abolition of the distinction between stock brokers and job-bers (so that the former could for the first time actually deal in shares directly) and the removal of the ban on foreign organizations being members of the Stock Exchange. It resulted in a massive realigning of the

City's financial institutions, with banks and stock brokers joining forces to take advantage of the anticipated bonanza, and in the payment of stratospheric salaries to thrusting young marketmakers. After the hype came the shakeout, however; before six months had passed several companies found that they had burned their fingers, and instituted a strategic withdrawal.

Big Ben
As most British schoolboys know, Big Ben is not really the gothic clock tower at the northern end of the Houses of Parliament in London; it is the huge 13-ton bell that hangs inside it and rings out the hours after the famous Westminster chimes. It was installed in 1859 and gets its name from the nickname of Sir Benjamin Hall, who was Commissioner of Works at the time. Gradually over the years the tower, a potent symbol of parliamentary democracy around the world, has taken over the bell's name.

Big Bend
The epithet for the extreme western portion of Texas, so called because its southern and western boundaries are formed by a natural bend in the Rio Grande, which separates Texas from Mexico.

big Bertha
The nickname of a World War I German long-range gun, a reference to the daughter of the manufacturer, Friedrich Alfred Krupp.

Big Board, the
The nickname for the listing of companies with stocks sold on the New York Stock Exchange, especially in contradistinction to the listings of the American Stock Exchange and other stock exchanges in New York and elsewhere.

Big D
A nickname for Dallas, Texas.

Big Dipper
An American name for the constellation Ursa Major, so called from the outline formed by its stars.

Big Hole, the
The nickname of a huge, funnel-shaped crater, some 1500 feet in diameter, situated at Kimberley, South Africa. Its core was formerly a diamond-bearing volcanic plug, or pipe, of kimberlite, the portion above ground called *Colesberg Kopje*, or *Colesberg Hill*. Mining removed the core to a depth of 3600 feet and yielded three tons (14,504,375 carats) of diamonds. The crater served as a place of refuge during the siege of Kimberley; since 1921 it has been used as a reservoir.

Big Inch
A pipeline for conveying natural gas from Texas to the Northeast, constructed in the 1950s and actually 24 inches in diameter.

Big Mac, the
The nickname for a hamburger-shaped formation of quasars, discovered through the four-metre mapping telescope at Pisco Elqui, Chile, by Arturo Gómez. Its formal name is the Gomez Object, and it is so referred to in scientific journals.

Big Run, the
The Victoria River Downs station on the Victoria River in the Northern Territory, southwest of Katherine, is said to be the biggest cattle-run in the world. Before its subdivision it had an area larger than that of Belgium, but with one millionth the population. It still has an area of almost one and a quarter million hectares and runs a total of some 75,000 cattle.

Big Tex
The nickname of a statue, some eighty feet tall, used at the annual Texas State Fair, held in October at Dallas. Dressed in western attire, Big Tex is wired to speak greetings to fair visitors.

Big Town
A former nickname of Chicago.

Billingsgate
London's largest fish market, which took its name from one of the old gates of the City of London. It was formerly situated in Lower Thames Street, near the Tower of London, but in 1982 it moved to a new site

further east, on the Isle of Dogs, near the old West India Docks. Billingsgate porters were famous for the colourfulness of their language. This led to *billingsgate* being used as a synonym for 'coarse abuse': 'We disapprove the constant billingsgate poured on them officially', wrote Thomas Jefferson in 1799. The word is now used infrequently.

Billy Goat Tavern
A short-order café and bar in Chicago just north of the Loop, popular with newspaper people who work nearby. The Billy Goat's colourful owner, Sam Sianis, recently achieved national celebrity of a sort as the model for a character portrayed on television by the late comedian John Belushi; although neither the Billy Goat nor its owner was referred to by name, to patrons the setting and the distinctively accented calls for a 'chizzborger, chizzborger' were unmistakable references.

Biograph Theater
A classic 'Art Deco' moviehouse on the Near North Side of Chicago, famous for having been patronized on July 22, 1934, by 'Public Enemy Number One', bankrobber John Dillinger, just before dying in a volley of FBI bullets, in an alley a few yards south. Dillinger had been hiding out nearby in the apartment of Anna Sage—the notorious 'Lady in Red'—who, with another woman, had accompanied him to the Biograph after first alerting the FBI, which had then set up an ambush. (The film that Dillinger and his companions saw was *Manhattan Melodrama* starring Clark Gable, William Powell, and Myrna Loy.)

Birdland
A nightclub theatre, opened in 1948 on Broadway, in New York City, mainly to provide a setting for bebop, the style of jazz then in its emergent phase. It was named after Charlie 'Bird' Parker, the saxophonist regarded, along with Dizzy Gillespie and others, as a chief proponent of the genre.

Birmingham of America, the
A nickname of Pittsburgh, Pennsylvania.

Birthplace of American Liberty, the
A nickname claimed by Lexington, Massachusetts, and Philadelphia, Pennsylvania. The first battle of the Revolutionary War was fought on the Lexington Commons by the Minute Men in 1775 ('the shot heard

round the world'), while Philadelphia is the location of Independence Hall, the seat of the Continental Congress, and the site of the signing of the Declaration of Independence.

Birthplace of Aviation, the
A nickname of Dayton, Ohio, so called because it was the home of Wilbur and Orville Wright. See also **Cradle of Aviation.**

Birthplace of Baseball
A nickname of Cooperstown, New York, based on an erroneous belief that it was the site of the first baseball diamond designed by Abner Doubleday in 1839. Nevertheless, Doubleday Field there is baseball's official home, and the Baseball Hall of Fame is there.

Blackbird
A United States spy plane capable of flight at Mach 3 at extremely high altitudes.

Black Country, the
In the 19th century, the southern part of Staffordshire, to the northwest of Birmingham in the West Midlands of England, was a concentrated centre of coalmining and iron-founding. The noise and smell of heavy industry were ever present, and the resulting slow drizzle of soot built up a black patina on the Victorian buildings of Wolverhampton, Wednesbury, Walsall, Dudley, and West Bromwich that gave the area its name. More ecologically acceptable light industry has since moved in, but the Black Country is still far from being one of England's beauty spots.

Black Death, the
An epidemic, probably of bubonic plague, that killed about one third of the population of Europe, Asia, and north Africa in the middle of the 14th century and is generally regarded as the greatest disaster ever to have affected western Europe.

Black Diamonds
A nickname for coal.

Black Forest, the
A mountainous area east of the Rhine, in Germany. Its name, translated from German *Schwarzwald*, derives from those regions covered with

dense forests of pine trees. In western lore, it is associated with cuckoo clocks (which are, indeed, made there, along with toys and other products) and with Black Forest cake, a rich chocolate layer cake made with cherries (which is probably named for its colour rather than its place of origin).

Blackfriars

An area of central London on the north bank of the Thames, to the south of the eastern end of Fleet Street. From 1276 to 1538 the Dominicans (or Black Friars) had a monastery here, and since at least the 16th century their name has been applied to the district. Shakespeare refers to it in *Henry VIII.* It is the site of a busy rail terminus bringing commuters from the southern suburbs to work in the City. Compare **Whitefriars.**

Black Friday

1. In England, December 6, 1745, when a financial panic was caused in London on the news that Charles Edward Stuart ('Bonnie Prince Charlie' or 'the Young Pretender') had marched into Derby.
2. In England, May 11, 1866, when the failure of Overend and Gurney, a London banking house, occasioned financial panic.
3. In the United States, September 24, 1869, when a panic in the securities market in New York was brought about by the government's release of gold bullion into the market, which Jay Gould and James Fisk were illegally trying to corner. That day, the price of $100 in gold dropped from $163½ to $133 in paper money, wiping out many speculators.

Black Gold

A nickname for oil.

Black Hills, the

A mountain range in eastern Wyoming and western South Dakota, so called because its forested slopes have a dark appearance when viewed at a distance. It is an area rich in minerals.

Black Hole (of Calcutta)

A barracks room about 14 by 18 feet at Fort William, in Calcutta, India, where 146 Europeans were incarcerated by the Nawab of Bengal, on June 20, 1756. It was reported that by the following morning only twenty-three had survived but later research showed that only forty-three were unaccounted for. Ever since, however, the name has been used as a metaphor for a confining, dark, dungeon-like place.

Blackpool

The quintessential seaside resort of northern England, on the Lancashire coast. From Victorian times onwards it was working people's great vacation magnet. Its attractions have become almost proverbial: donkey rides along the seven miles of sand; amusement arcades on the Golden Mile; the Tower built in 1895 in imitation of the Eiffel Tower, with the ballroom below it; variety shows; and of course the famous Blackpool illuminations, a spectacular display of coloured lights in various fanciful patterns representing anything from animals and birds to spacecraft. With the increasing cheapness of foreign travel after World War II, Spain's **Costa Brava** (*q.v.*) and **Costa del Sol** (*q.v.*) began to replace Blackpool as a holiday mecca, but the English resort retains its position in Northern folklore.

Black Stump, the

In Australia, a mythical marker of remoteness, a last post of comparative civilization, usually in the phrase 'beyond the black stump'. There have been properties called 'The Black Stump', but the phrase may well be older than these names.

blackthorn winter

An English nickname for a period of cooler than normal weather in May, associated with the days of the 'ice saints', Mamertus, Pancras, and Gervais, on May 11, 12, and 13, respectively.

Blackwall Tunnel

A vehicular tunnel beneath the Thames, east of London, recently connected with the M-25, an orbital motorway around the city. It is known as the site of frequent traffic jams.

Bleeding Kansas

A nickname for Kansas in the mid 19th century, when it became a battleground between Abolitionists and pro-slavery partisans. The Abolitionist stronghold of Lawrence was attacked in 1855 and 1856 (when some important buildings were burnt), and again in 1863, when William

Quantrill led a raid in which the men were massacred and many buildings were destroyed.

Blenheim Palace

A magnificent palace in Oxfordshire given by the Parliament of Great Britain to the Duke of Marlborough in gratitude for his victory at Blenheim, August 13, 1704, on the Danube, in Bavaria, defeating the Bavarians and the French in a decisive battle of the War of the Spanish Succession. It is said that the arrangement of the trees in the park of the palace match the formation of the troops at the battle.

Blighty

A slang term used by British servicemen abroad to refer to Britain. It originated with the British army in India, and comes from the Hindi word *bilyati* 'foreign land'. It is associated particularly with World Wars I and II, but remains in use in the second half of the 20th century.

Block, the

The name given to a central city area in Melbourne or Sydney. In the 1860s to *do the Block* was to 'saunter or parade in the fashionable part of the city'.

Blood Alley

The name of a short street in Shanghai with bars and brothels cheek by jowl its entire length. Frequented by European and American servicemen, its native name is Rue Chu Pao-San.

Bloomie's

A nickname for Bloomingdale's department store, between 59th and 60th streets and Lexington and Third avenues, in New York City. Formerly, just another large department store, it recast its image entirely in the 1950s by an extensive programme of interior redecoration and by promoting itself as the 'in' place to shop for a new generation of the young at heart and the upscale in pocket. During the 1960s, when the upwardly mobile were moving into the new apartment buildings sprouting up along upper Third Avenue and the side streets of the **Upper East Side** (*q.v.*), it acquired its affectionate nickname. Any associations its formal name might have had with **Bloomingdale's** (*q.v.*) belongs to a generation long gone.

Bloomingdale's
A former lunatic asylum at 116th Street near the Hudson River in New
York City, replaced in part by Columbia University when it moved from
50th Street and Madison-Fifth avenues to its present site early in the 20th
century. Widely known at the time, the asylum gave rise to expressions
like, 'You're ready for Bloomingdale's'. See also **Bellevue.**

Bloomsbury
An area in central London, to the northeast of Oxford Street, in which
the British Museum and many of the buildings of London University are
situated. At its northeast corner is Gordon Square, where in 1904 the
novelist Virginia Woolf and her sister Vanessa Bell came to live. The
coterie of writers and artists that gathered around them in the ensuing
years has become universally known as the Bloomsbury Group, an avant-
garde assault on Victorian stuffiness in art and morality that stressed
above all else the search for the good, the true, and the beautiful. It
included, among many others, the essayist Lytton Strachey, the novelists
E. M. Forster and David Garnett, the painters Roger Fry and Duncan
Grant, and the economist John Maynard Keynes.

Bluegrass State
The official nickname of Kentucky, so called because of the abundant
grass of that type on which their Thoroughbreds thrive.

Blue Hen State, the or **Blue Hen's Chickens State**
A nickname of Delaware, so called in reference to an incident during the
Revolutionary War: two game cocks of a blue hen that belonged to a
Captain Caldwell, of Kent County, fought so furiously and courageously
that one of the Captain's men cried, 'We're sons of the Old Blue Hen and
we're game to the end'. Thereafter, the regiment was known as 'Blue
Hen's Chickens'.

blue laws
Originally, a series of stringent regulations, printed on blue paper, imposed on the citizens of some New England colonies in the 17th century
by the Puritans based at New Haven, Connecticut. From a history of the
state published in 1781, the laws seem unduly harsh in terms of today's
standards, e.g.:

The judge shall determine controversies without a jury.
Married persons must live together or be imprisoned.
A wife shall be good evidence against her husband.

But it must be remembered that contemporary laws (in England) provided
for amputation of the hand upon conviction of the theft of a loaf of
bread. The term *blue law* has come into modern use in America to
designate any regulation felt to be unwarrantedly strict or severe.

blue-light district
In Cartagena, Colombia, the name for the 'red-light' district.

Blue Ridge Mountains, the
The main eastern range of the Appalachian Mountains that runs from
southern Pennsylvania to northern Georgia, their name deriving from the
blue tone that their forested slopes have when seen at a distance. The
most famous section is in Virginia, separating the Shenandoah Valley
from the Piedmont region. The outstanding beauty of their high peaks
and valleys attracts thousands of tourists every year, and they are immortalized in the song *The Trail of the Lonesome Pine*, by Ballard MacDonald and Harry Carroll (1913), which begins, 'In the Blue Ridge Mountains
of Virginia . . .'

Boardwalk, the
A 60-foot-wide, wooden platform built several feet above the sand alongside the Atlantic Ocean in New Jersey, stretching for 4½ miles along the
beach at Atlantic City and a further two miles along that in Ventnor.
Originally constructed in 1870, the present one was completed in 1896. It
borders the entrances to many of the hotels and of the casinos that have
sprung up since the state enacted legislation allowing gambling, in 1976.
Atlantic City has long been a favourite holiday spot, especially during the
1920s and '30s, and the Boardwalk, a focal point for amusement, entertainment, shopping, and eating, formed a promenade along which
generations of visitors have been wheeled in the traditional high-back
chairs, once pushed by hand, now usually pedaled or powered by battery.
The inventor of the popular board game, Monopoly, came from Atlantic
City and named the positions on the board after streets and places in the
city. As all players of the American version know, 'The Boardwalk' is the
most expensive 'property' in the game, and an opponent whose token
lands on the Boardwalk must pay the highest 'rent'.

Bodleian Library

A major resource library at Oxford University, named for its founder, Sir Thomas Bodley (1545-1613) who, after his retirement from foreign service, devoted his efforts and his fortune to the expansion of the library, which had been established in 1327 but almost ruined under Edward VI by those bent on university 'reform'.

Bognor Regis

A salubrious seaside resort on the Sussex coast of England, to the west of Brighton. Its heyday was probably in the late 18th century, when it was a favourite watering-place of the aristocracy. Its splendour has faded since then, particularly with the decline of the Great British Seaside Holiday, but it retains its fair share of retirement bungalows (see **Costa Geriatrica**). Its title *Regis* 'King's' was conferred on it in 1929 by a grateful King George V after convalescing there, but it seems his private view of the place was not always so charitable: a few years later, when he was in fact in his last illness, a courtier, thinking to cheer him up, remarked, 'If your Majesty continues to make such excellent progress, he will soon be able to enjoy a few weeks' holiday at Bognor'; muttered the king, under his breath: 'Bugger Bognor!'

Bohemia

An area in central Europe, which now forms the Czech-speaking part of western Czechoslovakia. In the early Middle Ages it was an independent kingdom; then in 1526 it became absorbed into the Hapsburg Empire, and remained in German hands until World War I. Its name has come to be used, without a capital letter, for a resort of the artistic and unconventional because in former times the gypsies, who had a rather vagabondish reputation, were thought to come from Bohemia.

Bondi Beach

Australia's most famous beach, on the Pacific coast of New South Wales, to the south of Sydney. Always crowded, it is a mecca for surfers.

Bond Street

A road in the West End of London, running north and south between Oxford Street and Piccadilly. The southern section is known as Old Bond Street, the northern part New Bond Street. Often nicknamed *the high street of* **Mayfair** (*q.v.*), it is proverbial around the world for its dazzling array of exclusive and expensive boutiques, art dealers' galleries, jewellers, and perfumers. Indeed, it seems that any establishment that wishes to be fashionable only has to add *of Bond Street* to its name to achieve instant cachet.

boomer
A nickname for a submarine equipped with rocket-propelled missiles.

Boot Hill
The name of a hill in Dodge City, Kansas, so called because only people who were killed in gunfights were buried there, said to have 'died with their boots on'.

Border, the
In Britain, an epithet conventionally used for the boundary between England and Scotland. *North of the Border* is understood to mean Scotland; *South of the Border*, England. In addition, the hilly area of Scotland contiguous with the boundary is generally known as *the Borders*. The name was made official in 1975 when the Borders region was formed from the former counties of Berwick, Peebles, Roxburgh, Selkirk, and parts of Midlothian. The area's literary fame rests on the *Border Ballads*, a collection of local songs and verses compiled by Sir Walter Scott in the early 19th century; Scott also set many of his novels here. Compare **Marches**.

Border Town
A nickname of Rye, New York, so called because it was founded (1660) on the border of what are now Connecticut and New York, and for many years controversies moved it between the two states.

Borough, the
The familiar name for the former south London borough of Southwark, particularly the part of it immediately to the south of London Bridge. (The new London borough of Southwark, created in 1965, covers a far larger area.) It is mainly a commercial and industrial area, much damaged by bombing during World War II, but it is relieved by some attractive Georgian squares. Through the middle of it runs Borough High Street, a gateway to southeast England and the Continent, especially in the Middle

Ages. The area was crowded with inns to accommodate travellers, including the Tabard, where Chaucer's Canterbury pilgrims lodged. See also **Old Kent Road**.

borrowing days
An English nickname for a period of colder than normal weather in April.

Borscht Circuit
Collectively, a nickname for the resort hotels in the Catskill Mountains, about 100 miles north of New York City, that have been popular with mainly Jewish guests since the 1920s; many of the guests were of eastern European origin, hence the 'Borscht'. The other part of the appellation, 'Circuit', reflects the viewpoint of entertainers—singers and singing groups, dancers, comedians, and other performers who were hired to amuse the guests and who combined bookings at several hotels in one tour. Another nickname for the area is **Borscht Belt**, but that does not emphasize the entertainment aspect.

Boston Common
The name for the oldest public park in the United States, covering 45 acres in downtown Boston. It was originally set aside in 1634 as a military training field and public cattle pasture. In the 1600s women found guilty of witchcraft were hanged here; today it is a favourite spot for open-air political rallies and is much used and enjoyed by those escaping city noise and heat.

Boston Post Road
An old road, stretching from New York City about 250 miles to Boston, Massachusetts, originally developed for the transportation of mail and people via coach. For many years, until the opening of the New England Thruway (US I-95) in the 1960s, it was the main road through coastal New England and, as it passed through a large number of cities, towns, and villages, became the Main Street of many of them. Along most of its length it is largely commercial, with filling stations, retail shops of every description, eating places, and (latterly) office buildings abounding. The first major road in America, as a federal highway it was designated 'US1', and, as such, it extends south from New York to Key West, Florida, and north into Maine, a total length of almost 1500 miles.

Botany Bay

An inlet to the south of Sydney, Australia, discovered by Captain James
Cook in 1770 and named for the variety and profusion of plant life he
found there. Because of its notorious penal colony (which was, in fact, a
little further north at Port Jackson), Botany Bay became synonymous in
the 19th century with transportation, and many a British felon feared
being *sent to Botany Bay* scarcely less than the death sentence.

Bourget, le

The name of the small airport which was the first place in Europe where
Charles A. Lindbergh set down his *Spirit of St Louis* in his record-
breaking, single-handed transatlantic flight from New York, in 1927. It is
the site of an aeronautical museum, and now serves private planes only.

Bourke

The name of a town in northwestern New South Wales, situated on the
Darling River, which has legendary associations with the outback. The
phrase *back of Bourke* indicates extreme remoteness, and a *Bourke
shower* (like a *Bedowrie shower* or a *Wilcannia shower*) is a dust-storm.
Bourke has literary associations, notably as a place from which Henry
Lawson set out on his tramp round the outback.

Bournemouth

A seaside resort in Dorset, England, on the English Channel, with about
six miles of beach and a promenade. Popular as a middle-class retirement
retreat, it is associated mainly with the elderly, who now live there all year
round. See also **Torquay.**

Bourneville

A suburb of Birmingham, in the West Midlands of England, which is
intimately associated in the British public's imagination with chocolate,
particularly plain chocolate. The district was laid out to provide houses
for the workers in Cadbury's chocolate factory in the 1870s. The name
was coined because it sounded French, French chocolate possessing a
particular cachet.

Bow

An area of the East End of London, to the north of Limehouse. It has no
connection with the famous Bow Bells, which are to be found in the

church of St Mary-le-Bow (often also known as Bow Church) in the City of London.

Bowery, the

A broad avenue between the Canal Street area to East 14th Street, where it meets Third Avenue, on the lower east side of New York City. As its name ('Bouwerie'), bestowed by Dutch settlers in the 17th century when the city was still called New Amsterdam, suggests, it was once a farm; later it became a tree-lined thoroughfare, which was till the late 19th century, a major attraction for the promenaders and boulevardiers of the time. It was the subject of a song, popular at the time and since then a traditional air, the opening lines of which are:

> The Bowery, The Bowery
> They do strange things and they say strange things
> On The Bowery, The Bowery,
> I'll never go there anymore.

About the turn of the century, it became rather run-down and has never since recovered from its decline. Its condition was not improved by the construction of the Third Avenue elevated railway, originally a steam train, which created a noisy, dark, sooty, and dingy atmosphere in the street below. The 'el' was torn down in the 1940s; but today, as for the past fifty years or so, The Bowery has remained a skid row, the haunt of down-and-outers known as Bowery bums, who panhandle from passersby and offer, for a handout, to 'clean' the windscreens of the cars of embarrassed motorists who have been 'trapped' in their domain by a traffic light. Most are men who live in 'flophouses' and in 'shelters' that are operated by church groups and the Salvation Army, which also provide free meals for the indigent. However, because there are so many of them, a lack of facilities forces some to sleep in doorways or on the sidewalk gratings, through which heat rises from below. Although The Bowery is a blight that could be renovated by the City, it is low on the list of priorities if only because its drifting inhabitants might be left with no place to go.

Bowie State

A nickname of Arkansas, so called because during its early days many of the residents carried a bowie knife. See also **Toothpick State**.

Bow Street
A street in the West End of London, just to the east of Covent Garden. It has always had close associations with the administration of the law; in the present day it contains a police station and the Bow Street Magistrates' Court, the chief magistrates' court of the Metropolitan Police area, and in former times it housed the headquarters of the famous 'Bow Street Runners', who preceded the modern police, and functioned from 1749 to 1829.

Boystown
The nickname of West Hollywood, California, where a large number of homosexuals have settled from various parts of the United States. Incorporated in 1984, the city in 1985 became the first in the U. S. to elect a city council a majority of which was openly gay or lesbian.

Bozeman Trail
A trail begun in 1863 by John M. Bozeman and used by travellers to reach the gold fields in Montana and Idaho. It ran for about 600 miles between what are now Fort Laramie, Wyoming, and Virginia City, Montana. The Sioux Indians continually attacked its travellers because the trail crossed their main hunting grounds, and it was finally closed in 1868. However, in 1877, the Indians having been subdued, Texas ranchers opened it again to move their cattle into Montana and Wyoming.

Bray
A village on the Thames River in Berkshire, to the west of London. It is famous for its former vicar, immortalized in an anonymous 18th-century song, who boasted of having held on to his job through the reigns of five different monarchs, from Charles II to George I, which involved his having to switch from the Catholic persuasion to the Protestant twice, and back again in the other direction twice. Thanks to the legend of this enterprising parson, the name of Bray evokes the notion of timeservery.

Brenner Pass
The name of the most accessible pass through the Alps, crossing the border of Italy and Austria and linking the Mediterranean region with the northern part of Europe. It begins near Bolzano, Italy, and descends to Innsbruck, Austria. The ancient Romans used it; the Teutons crossed it in the 6th century to invade Italy; medieval traders used it to carry products

from the Near East and India; and the U. S. Army crossed it in 1945, during World War II.

Brickfielder
Originally a wind blowing dust from Brickfield Hill in Sydney, this nickname was later applied to any dusty wind.

Bride of the Sea
A nickname of Venice, Italy.

Bridge of Sighs
1. The name for a bridge built about 1600 that crosses the canal in Venice between the Doges' Palace and the state prison, so called because of the sighs of prisoners who had to cross it. It is probably best known from Byron's poem, *Childe Harold's Pilgrimage*.
2. In New York City, the nickname for a covered bridge-like structure between the Tombs prison and the former criminal courts building across Centre Street. It was used so prisoners could be taken directly to courtrooms out of the view of the public.
3. In Cambridge, England, the nickname given to a bridge over the Cam River; it connects one building of St John's College with another containing the dining room.
4. A nickname of a bridge in Oxford, England, that connects two buildings of Hartford College, so called because it resembles the bridge in Venice.

Brigalow, the
A name given to an area in Queensland where a thick bluish scrub of brigalow (*Acacia harpophylla*) is the chief vegetation.

Brighton
A large seaside resort in Sussex, on the south coast of England. It first achieved popularity in the late 18th century, when it became a favourite watering place of the Prince of Wales, later George IV; his patronage led to its being frequented by fashionable society. When, in the 19th century, the railway reached the town, it became instantly accessible to ordinary working people and has never really looked back as a popular destination for day-trippers and vacationers alike. Its heyday was perhaps in the 1930s, and since World War II the expansion in the foreign holiday trade has meant that its amusement gardens, piers, and pebbly beaches are no

longer so claustrophobically crowded in summer as they were; but it makes up the numbers with the conference trade and English language students from abroad, and it remains the quintessential coastal holiday resort in southern England. Its proximity to and easy accessibility from London have contributed a lot to a rather risqué reputation it has gained as a venue for dirty weekends, much frequented by businessmen and their secretaries (or 'secretaries'). See also **Dr. Brighton, Kemp Town, Lanes.**

Britain

The standard everyday name for the country formally called the United Kingdom of Great Britain and Northern Ireland. Some British people are slightly squeamish about the term Great Britain, feeling that it sounds immodest, but in fact it arose originally in order to distinguish Britain from Little Britain, a name used in medieval times for Brittany (in those days Britain and Brittany were frequently spelt identically). It began to take on new significance in the 16th century, as moves for the unification of Scotland with England and Wales got under way; in this context it is intended to denote the entire country, in contrast with individual bits of it, in much the same way as Greater London refers to the whole area. It first came into official use with the union of Scotland with England and Wales in 1707, and for a time after that England and Scotland were referred to in Acts of Parliament as South Britain and North Britain, respectively. The other main constituent of the British Isles, Ireland, was sometimes humorously known as *West Britain*. Of the three names, only *North Britain* survived for any length of time. See also **England, United Kingdom.**

Brixton

A district of south London, to the south of Lambeth. It is a downtrodden working-class residential area, and has a rather negative image; its most famous building and institution is probably Brixton Prison, and it rose to notoriety in 1981 when tensions between the police and the local population, a large proportion of which is of West Indian origin, erupted into violence on the streets. Since then Brixton has been synonymous with racial riots.

Brizzie

A colloquial abbreviation of Brisbane.

Broad, the
Just as Oxford's High Street is known as *the High*, Broad Street is usually
called *the Broad*. Amongst its occupants are Trinity and Balliol Colleges,
the Sheldonian Theatre, and Blackwell's bookshop. See also **High**.

Broad Acres, the
A now rather clichéd epithet for Yorkshire, the largest county in England.
In the popular imagination, Yorkshire may conjure up chiefly industrial
rather than rural scenes—in particular, the soot-grimed towns and cities
around the River Aire such as Leeds, Bradford, and Huddersfield, that
were once at the heart of the mighty woollen industry, and further south
the steel-making area centred on Sheffield—but in fact large areas of
unspoiled countryside still exist. As the name *Broad Acres* implies, this is
open, rolling, large-scale country, from the beautiful but sometimes bleak
North York Moors to the Dales that extend away to the south and west.
See also **Ridings.**

Broads, the
Just below the northern shoulder of the bulge of East Anglia in eastern
England stretches a low-lying area of watery land, where reedy swamps
give place to quiet stretches of open water, which are in turn succeeded by
grazing pastures. These are the Norfolk Broads, 50,000 acres of wetland
crisscrossed by six rivers that open out into 52 shallow lakes, or *broads*,
that give the area its name. They owe their existence to peat diggings that
were begun by the Saxons in the 9th century and were flooded 600 years
later when the sea level changed. Since Victorian times they have been a
very popular venue for boating holidays, but more recently, with both
commercial over-exploitation and changing agricultural techniques, including extensive drainage, there is concern for their survival as both a
place of outstanding beauty and a home for many rare species of animals
and plants.

Broadway
1. Said to be the longest street in the world, New York City's Broadway
extends from Bowling Green, at its southerly terminus, the site where
17th-century Dutch burghers played at bowls when the City was New
Amsterdam, north into Yonkers and, some maintain, beyond, a distance
of more than twenty miles. At its lower end it is a focus of the financial
world, associated with nearby Wall Street; like a river that has eroded its
way into a canyon between walls of tall office buildings, it passes through

commercial areas of a characterless nature, past Union Square, Madison Square, and Herald Square (where it borders Macy's), to emerge at Times Square, where it acquires a tawdry dignity because of its long traditional association with the world of entertainment—vaudeville, the legitimate theatre, and the not-so-legitimate theatre, once represented by burlesque, now by the sleazier bars, dance-halls, massage parlours, and 'private' clubs that offer the voyeur, the depraved, and the lustful topless and/or bottomless dancers and waitresses. Broadway's passage through Times Square, though brief, has provided it with much of its reputation. Even though there are few legitimate theatres actually on Broadway—most are on the side streets, east and west of Times Square—'Broadway' *means* the theatre world to most people, both in and out of the profession. It also symbolizes brash promoters in loud suits and boasts a variegated, floating population of drifters, grifters, runaways, panhandlers, conmen, pimps, prostitutes, vendors of corsages and of every other conceivable item, gofers, tourists from far away who speak little English, tourists from nearby whose English is difficult to understand (even for a native speaker), and a cadre of indigenous people, mostly men, who just 'hang out'. It is always crowded, and at times of a special event, like V-E day, V-J day, or any New Year's Eve, its traffic is closed off and the density of population increases to about one person per square foot. Before it was closed by Mayor Fiorello H. La Guardia, in the mid 1930s, burlesque flourished along Broadway, especially at the Gaiety Theatre, near 46th Street. Across Duffy Square (the official name for the north end of Times Square, where Seventh Avenue has already crossed over to the east of Broadway) stands the Palace Theatre, renowned as the place where a performer can realize the zenith of his ambition for recognition by his peers and receive the accolades of an adoring public. The Palace in the mid 1980s was a legitimate theatre. This image of Broadway has been sustained through songs that remain ever popular ('Give My Regards to Broadway'), associated with songwriters and performers whose legends never die (George M. Cohan), and through the perpetual romanticization of the theatre by Hollywood, especially in musical comedies produced during the late 1920s, and in the 1930s and '40s. Broadway became the centre of first-run motion-pictures in New York, and huge theatres catered to enormous crowds during the 1930s and '40s when the Paramount, Strand, Capitol, Rivoli, and other cinemas flourished. Many of these offered stage shows as well, with 'Big Bands' and singers of great fame: headliners in those days were Frank Sinatra, who was besieged by thousands of screaming bobby-soxers when he appeared at the Paramount; Vaughn Monroe; Benny Goodman; Spike Jones; Artie Shaw; Tommy Dorsey; Glenn Miller; and other bandleaders, including Phil Spitalny and his all-girl orchestra. Always gaudy, Broadway and Times Square turn night into day by means of huge neon and incandescent extravaganzas; not only are the streets lit up by the coursing, flashing lights of the theatre marquees, but enormous electrical billboards—some a full city block in length—burst forth their colossal displays to create a glow over the area that is visible from miles away. Totally brazen and indecorous, these gigantic displays move, flash on and off, scintillate, blow smoke rings, and perform in the most incredible ways to engage the attention of passersby: atop a clothing store, there were even two huge, seemingly nude statues of a man and a woman separated (at a distance of about 150 feet) by a genuine waterfall, about thirty feet high. Broadway does not run parallel to the other north-south thoroughfares in Manhattan, and at those avenues it crosses 'squares' are created, like Union, Madison, and the others mentioned. After it wends its way north of Times Square, it crosses Eighth Avenue (which then becomes Central Park West) at Columbus Circle (59th Street), the site of the New York Coliseum, a major convention centre. At 65th Street, it crosses Ninth Avenue (which becomes Columbus Avenue) and forms Lincoln Square, where the Metropolitan Opera House, Symphony Hall, the Juilliard School, the New York City Ballet, the New York City Opera, and other public entertainment facilities form Lincoln Center. Finally, it crosses Tenth Avenue (which becomes Amsterdam Avenue) at 72nd Street. North of Lincoln Center, Broadway acquires the character of the main street of the many neighbourhoods it traverses, with wall-to-wall retail shops, restaurants, cinemas, and the like along its entire length. These establishments are set into the ground floors of apartment houses and, occasionally, hotels. Except for an area several blocks north of 114th Street, where the brick and granite buildings of Columbia University offer relief from the commercial atmosphere, this character remains unrelieved for the rest of its length. At 125th Street, it passes west of Harlem; north of 135th Street through the western reaches of Spanish Harlem; above 155th Street through a mixed neighbourhood, Washington Heights, which was once settled mainly by Jews and, after the mid 1930s, by Jewish refugees from Europe; it crosses the Harlem River at 225th Street (at Spuyten Duyvil Creek), where it is joined by the elevated subway that goes as far as 242nd Street, runs alongside Van Cortlandt Park in The Bronx, and on to the

City line at 260th Street. Beyond that point it remains 'Broadway' technically, but its association with New York City is lost. From **Columbus Circle** (*q.v.*) north to 168th Street, it is a roadway divided by a central mall which once offered trees and a grassy lawn to relieve the unremitting atmosphere of asphalt and concrete. In recent years, owing to neglect, it has more closely resembled a rubbish dump than the elegant greensward its designers intended. Over its entire length of some twenty miles, Broadway's reputation derives mainly from the short stretch between 42nd and about 50th streets.

2. A section of San Francisco, centred on Broadway, characterized by cabarets, bars, and theatres featuring nude women and by its honky-tonk atmosphere.

3. A village in the county of Hereford and Worcester, in the west of England. It is perhaps the most celebrated of the Cotswold villages, its wealth of Tudor, Jacobean, and Georgian buildings in the glowing local stone having appeared on countless calendars and chocolate boxes.

Brocken
The highest peak (3746 feet) in the Harz Mountains in East Germany. Legend has it that witches danced here on Walpurgisnacht (1st May). It has given its name to the 'Brocken spectre', a phenomenon observed in mountainous areas when there is a mist and the sun is low: if someone stands with his back to the sun, he can see the greatly enlarged shadow cast on the mist.

Brooklyn
A borough of New York City on Long Island, south of Queens. After New York City (Manhattan) itself, it is probably the best known part of New York, having figured widely in national and world culture, especially as the result of books (*A Tree Grows in Brooklyn*, by Betty Smith) and dozens of films in which people from Brooklyn have been characterized mainly as being fervently, uncompromisingly loyal to their home county (technically called Kings) and to their (former) baseball team (the Brooklyn Dodgers, whose home was Ebbetts Field). Natives of Brooklyn are somewhat caricatured for their accent, which, in fact, carries traces of an earlier pronunciation of English in New York City, still heard among the older residents, with slight remnants of Dutch, especially in the pronunciation of certain vowels. Thus, the caricatured pronunciation of 'Third Avenue and 33rd Street' as 'Toid Avenya 'n' Toidy-Toid Street', heard less often than formerly, is actually a simulation of a pronunciation in

which the vowels of 'Third' and 'Thirty' are uttered closer to the front than the back of the mouth. Like the other boroughs of New York City (The Bronx, Manhattan, Queens, and Staten Island), Brooklyn is an agglomeration of neighbourhoods, some of which are well known to non-natives. Brooklyn Heights, south of the eastern tower of the Brooklyn Bridge and overlooking the East River and lower Manhattan, was once occupied by writers and artists, but, as typical elsewhere in the City, most of them have been driven out by the increased rents in recent years, to be replaced by upper-middle-class residents who have bought the pretty, quaint old townhouses and reconverted many of them from small apartment houses back to single-family dwellings. Coney Island, a famous amusement park along an ocean beach, has, in later years, become known for its gaudy, raucous atmosphere; Flatbush, an area in the southern part of Brooklyn, was long (and incorrectly) identified with the Brooklyn Dodgers baseball club, which is associated with Ebbetts Field, actually to the northwest; the Williamsburgh section is known chiefly as an area inhabited by a large colony of Hasidic Jews; and Park Slope, once a wealthy neighbourhood near Prospect Park, went through a long decline only to be revitalized, beginning in the 1960s, by young, upwardly mobile middle-class residents who have bought the old Victorian houses and have restored them to their former elegance. At its eastern end, near the Atlantic Ocean, is the huge John F. Kennedy Airport, formerly called Idlewild. The Brooklyn Dodgers have long since moved their baseball club to Los Angeles, and Ebbetts Field has been demolished. Yet the firmly incised impressions of Brooklyn linger on, little changed from years ago, and many people, though they may never have ventured there, retain for it a vicarious nostalgia.

Brooklyn Bridge

A suspension bridge linking lower Manhattan Island with Long Island, at Brooklyn. It was designed by John A. Roebling and completed in 1883 by William A. Roebling after the death of his father and at the cost of permanent injury incurred during a fire in one of the caissons while he was working on the foundation. Aside from its industrial beauty, somewhat marred by the later construction of a steel-trussed roadway, it figures in the folklore of New York in a number of tales. One centres on Steve Brody, a brawling resident of Irish descent, who is said to have won a bar wager that he would survive a leap from the bridge into the East River below; the other concerns the 'sale' of the bridge by confidence men who dupe naive visitors to the city.

Brooks Brothers
A department store at 44th Street and Madison Avenue, in New York City, known chiefly for its conservative men's wear. Never renowned as a style-setter, Brooks has outfitted business executives in traditional clothing—narrow-lapel suits, button-down collars, and striped 'old-school' ties—and was for many years (before the trend changed to blue jeans) supplier of clothing to the ivy-league college crowd.

Brother Jonathan
The first known nickname for Americans, used derisively by British soldiers and Tories during the American Revolution. It later became a comic Yankee figure in plays and gradually came to symbolize simplicity, forthrightness, honesty, and common sense. The original Jonathan is thought to have been Governor Jonathan Trumbull of Connecticut, whom George Washington frequently consulted because of his solid common sense. A study of the American character by that name, written by Joan Neal, published in 1825 and intended primarily for foreign consumption, emphasized the alleged vulgarity of New York, the greed of New England, and the ignorance of the Quakers. See also **Uncle Sam.**

Brown Bess
The nickname, referring to its colour, for an 18th-century British army flintlock musket, still in use at Waterloo in 1815.

brownstone
Literally, a reddish-brown sandstone, widely used in New York City as a facing on private dwellings built in the late 19th century. It became (and remained) so prevalent throughout the city that the name has become generic for private homes of a particular design: typically, the brownstone has a high exterior brownstone staircase (called a *stoop*) leading upwards from the sidewalk to the parlour floor; a semi-sunken ground floor below that is reached by a door that is below the top landing of the exterior stairs. These homes, usually four storeys tall, were built on the standard 20' x 100' city lot, usually to a depth of 50' with a garden at the rear. Thousands of almost identical houses of this design were built in rows along the side streets of the residential areas of Manhattan and Brooklyn, especially. The increased property values and the construction of apartment buildings that characterized the development of residential housing in New York City after the turn of the century made private homes too expensive to maintain, and most brownstones were converted to small

apartments and rooming houses. By the 1940s, the neighbourhoods—chiefly the side streets where these houses were numerous—had deteriorated, and, in the poorer sections of the city, had become slums. The real estate boom following WW II and the subsequent housing shortages of the 1950s and '60s prompted many middle-class families to purchase old brownstones and renovate them, returning a large number of them to single-family occupancy. In wealthy neighbourhoods, such houses cost about $75,000 in the 1950s; by the 1980s, renovated, modernized brownstones brought prices in the millions. Despite the fact that the truly luxurious townhouses, especially in Manhattan, are faced with limestone, the term *brownstone* has become generic for all such houses.

Brum

A nickname for Birmingham, Britain's second largest city; the local people are known as *Brummies*. The word is a shortened version of Brummagem, itself a local dialect variation, no longer much used, of *Birmingham*. In the 19th century the city gained such a reputation for the vast production of cheap manufactured goods, especially knickknacks and jewellery, that *brummagem* became a synonym for 'tawdry' or 'tatty'. The tower of Birmingham Council House is known by the local nickname *Big Brum*, in mock imitation of Big Ben.

Bubbling Well

A district in Shanghai named after a well that bubbles constantly. Bubbling Well Road is the focus of a wealthy residential area.

Buckeye State, the

The official nickname of Ohio, so called in reference to the buckeye tree (*Aesculus glabra*) and to an Indian nickname for a Colonel Sproat who impressed them as he led the settlers into the first court session held there (1788).

Buck House

A disrespectful but on the whole affectionate nickname for Buckingham Palace, the official London residence of British monarchs since 1837. It was built in 1703 for the Duke of Buckingham and Chandos, when it was in fact called Buckingham House; George III bought it in 1761, and since then it has been much added to and enlarged.

Bughouse Square
A park on the Near North Side of Chicago, and the locale for numerous political and philosophical debates, particularly during the 1920s and '30s, when speakers espousing primarily radical causes would stand on boxes or crates in order to be better seen and heard above the heads of the many listeners and participants who gathered about. Though the tradition of these debates has survived, their former frequency and passion are things of the past. Washington Square Park, the official name, is rarely used.

Bulli
The name of a town south of Sydney, applied to a rain-resistant type of soil used in cricket pitches.

Bullion State, the
A nickname of Missouri, so called after the sobriquet, 'Old Bullion' of Senator Thomas Hart Benton, for his defence of the use of gold and silver in preference to paper currency.

Bullring, the
A huge multi-level shopping area in the centre of Birmingham, in the West Midlands of England. It is on a 23-acre site, and includes markets, restaurants, car parks, and a bus station.

Bunker Hill
The site of one of the most important battles in the American War of Independence, which took place (depending on the source) either on Bunker Hill or Breed's Hill on June 17, 1775. Both hills are in Charlestown, across the Charles River from the north shore of Boston, and it was here that the colonists repelled three British attacks in a bloody battle to defend Boston. The colonists lost the battle and were forced to flee, exhausted and without ammunition or reinforcements; but their fighting ability so raised the spirits and confidence of the Americans that in March of the following year George Washington and his troops were able to rout the British from Boston and the harbour. A memorial commemorating the battle was erected some fifty years later on the site.

Burbank
A city in California located within the Los Angeles metropolitan region at the eastern end of the San Fernando Valley. Because the largest concentration of film and television studios is now found in and around Burbank, the city is frequently mentioned, often in a derisive or deprecatory manner, on television talk shows or comedies: the phrase 'beautiful downtown Burbank' was often heard on the Rowan and Martin 'Laugh-In' show in the late 1960s, and more recently, Johnny Carson has poked fun at Burbank on his 'Tonight Show'.

Burlington House
A grand edifice in Victorian-renaissance style, in Piccadilly, London, the home of the Royal Society, the Royal Academy (of Arts), and several other organizations. The nearby Burlington Arcade, an attractive regency covered promenade extending from Piccadilly to Burlington Gardens, has many fine shops known for the luxury of their wares.

Burma Road, the
A highway 2100 miles long from Lashio, northeast of Mandalay in Burma, to Chungking in southern China, which was used by the Allies from 1940 to 1942 to supply military equipment to Chiang Kai-shek, whose forces were fighting the Japanese.

Burton-upon-Trent
A town in Staffordshire, in the West Midlands of England. The water of the Trent River is said to be particularly suitable for the making of fine beer, and over the centuries Burton became known as the brewing capital of Britain. In the 19th century there were forty breweries there, and Burton became synonymous with beer: 'Burton and biscuit and cheese he had, which indeed, is Burton in its proper company', as H. G. Wells wrote. Many of the Victorian breweries have since closed down or been amalgamated with others, but beer continues to be produced there in substantial quantities. In the days of biplanes and dogfights, when an RAF pilot was killed or went missing in action he was euphemistically said to have *gone for a Burton*—that is, gone out to get a drink of beer. The phrase later passed into general use in British English, meaning 'to be broken or ruined'.

Bush House
A huge office block in Aldwych, at the eastern end of the Strand in central London. It houses the external services of the BBC, which broadcast to other countries around the world, and has come to be used as a synonym for them. Built in 1931, it was named after the American businessman, Irving T. Bush.

C

Cabbage Patch, the
An old nickname for Victoria, Australia.

Cabrini-Green Public Housing Project
America's first high-rise public housing complex, on the Near North Side of Chicago, commonly known as, simply, 'Cabrini-Green'. Gang-ridden, beset by a high crime rate, and with many of its 14,000 predominantly black residents on welfare and unemployment, the project constitutes a stark contrast to the affluent dwellings of the **Gold Coast** (*q.v.*), slightly over a mile away.

Caledonia
The Roman name for Scotland, much used in neoclassical poetry but today surviving virtually only in its adjectival form, as in the *Caledonian Canal*, a canal linking the Atlantic and the North Sea through the north of Scotland, and *British Caledonian*, an airline.

Caledonian Market
A street market, formerly held off Caledonian Road, southeast of Hampstead, north London. It has been moved to Bermondsey Street, on the south bank of the Thames, near Tower Bridge. See also **Bermondsey Market**.

Camargue, the

A desolate triangle of marshy land that forms the delta of the River
Rhone on the southern coast of France. It is famous for its beef cattle,
herded by lance-carrying cowboys on horseback, and for its abundance of
waterbirds, particularly flamingos. It used to be sheep country, too, but
much of its brackish water has been drained and replaced by fresh for the
large-scale production of rice, and the sheep have been edged out.

Camberley

A genteel military town set amongst the sandy heaths and pinewoods of
west Surrey. Its development started in the early 19th century, when the
Royal Military Academy was set up at nearby Sandhurst; it aimed to
attract army families and retired officers to its salubrious villas, and
succeeded so well that it is now pigeonholed as the haunt of bristly
colonels and their sporty daughters. Its original name was Cambridge
Town, but this seems to have caused a certain amount of confusion, and
in 1877 the new name of Camberley was found for it, invented by a
certain Dr. Atkinson.

Cambodia

A state in Southeast Asia that has had something of an identity crisis in
the latter part of the 20th century. With shifts of political status have
gone many changes of name: in 1970, when the former monarchy was
ousted and a republic declared, it became the Khmer Republic; then in
1975 its name was officially declared to be Democratic Kampuchea; and in
1979, when the blood-soaked Pol Pot regime came to an end, it metamor-
phosed again into the People's Republic of Kampuchea. Over and above
these events it has continued to be widely known by its original name of
Cambodia.

Cambria

The Roman name for Wales. In modern times it is preserved in the
Cambrian Mountains, a range which runs north and south along mid
Wales, and in the names of ancient geological eras: the Cambrian Period
is so called because its characteristic rocks and fossils were first described
from specimens found in Wales. The name *Cambria* derives ultimately
from Welsh *Cymry* 'Welshmen'.

Camden Lock
An open-air market situated where Chalk Farm Road crosses Regent's Canal, in north London. All sorts of merchandise—jewellery, clothes, hardware, antiques, crafts, etc.—are sold here on Saturdays and Sundays.

Camden Town
A district in north London, to the northeast of Regent's Park. From being rather a poor area before World War II, with many Greek and Irish immigrants, it has moved steadily upmarket until in the 1980s it is a very fashionable and expensive place to live. In its midst, Camden Lock, part of the Regent's Canal, is at the centre of a well-known artists' colony, with many trendy and rather high-priced craft shops. Its name is easily confused with Camden, a new London borough formed in 1965, which covers a very large area from Holborn in the south to Hampstead in the north and includes Camden Town. Nor is it to be confused with Camden Passage, well known for its antiques shops, which is further east, in Islington.

Camelot
1. The town where, according to Arthurian legend, the court and castle of King Arthur were situated. It has been identified with an array of real places in England, most of them in the Southwest: Sir Thomas Malory, the most famous of Arthurian authors, thought it was in Winchester, Hampshire; Camelford, South Cadbury, and Queen's Camel, all in Somerset, have been candidates; and the 20th-century Arthurian scholar R. S. Loomis suggested that its name was an amalgamation of Avalon, legendary site of Arthur's last battle, and Caerleon in South Wales.
2. A nickname given to the White House during the presidency of John F. Kennedy, mainly because of the charismatic behaviour of the president, the king-like power he exercised, and the queen-like beauty of his wife, Jacqueline.

Camino Real, el
'The Royal Road', running from Chihuahua, Mexico, to Santa Fe, New Mexico, was first used in 1581, making it the oldest road in the United States. It is now US 85. The name is roughly equivalent to 'Main Street' (q.v.) and is used in many places in the southwestern and western United States that were originally settled by Spanish speakers.

Campagna, the

A plain, about 800 square miles in extent, surrounding Rome. In classical times it was a rich and fertile area, and many ancient monuments remain to bear witness to its former glories. In the Dark Ages it declined to a malaria-infested wilderness, but in the 20th century much land reclamation has taken place.

Camp David

An area in the Catoctin Mountains of Maryland, about seventy miles from Washington, D. C., established as a retreat in 1942 by President Franklin Delano Roosevelt to allow him relief from the un-airconditioned summers in the capital, and which he named Shangri-La. It became the president's official retreat under Harry S. Truman. The scene of a number of important conferences between world leaders, including Roosevelt's meeting with Winston Churchill in 1943 and President Dwight D. Eisenhower's meeting in 1959 with Nikita S. Khrushchev, the Premier of the Soviet Union, it is especially noted for the talks President Jimmy Carter organized between President Anwar el-Sadat of Egypt and Prime Minister Menachem Begin of Israel, which resulted in a major peace agreement between their two countries, referred to as the Camp David Accords. See also **Shangri-la, 3.**

Canary Islands

A group of thirteen mountainous islands belonging to Spain in the Atlantic ocean about sixty miles off the coast of northwest Africa. The people of Gomera, one of the islands, are famous for their ability to communicate over large distances with a whistled language that imitates spoken Spanish. Although canaries were first discovered in the islands, its name comes not from birds, but from Latin *canis* 'dog', because the ancients found fierce, large dogs there.

Cape, the

A nickname for Cape Cod, a hundred-mile-long narrow peninsula that sticks out eastward into the Atlantic Ocean like a beckoning finger. Properly part of Massachusetts and lying at its southeast corner, it is situated due east of Rhode Island. The towns of Woods Hole, site of a world-renowned oceanographic institute, and Hyannisport are on its south shore, on Vineyard Sound; Cape Cod Bay is formed on its northern and western shores by the crook of the finger; Chatham is at its southeasternmost point. Cape Cod may, technically, begin at Hyannisport, but many natives consider it as reaching northwards from Chatham, where it is little more than a narrow sandbar, fringed by dunes, vegetated by razorgrass and by low, scrub-like trees and shrubs, and populated, except in the summer season, by more seagulls than people. At its very tip is Provincetown, in some respects a free-swinging beach resort town, in others, especially during the winter, a New England village. Provincetown is well known for being an artists' and writers' colony and almost equally famous for its open morality, a place where visitors of every sexual persuasion can enjoy themselves and each other unfettered by restraint. Once an area of quiet retreat for Bostonians and other New Englanders, the Cape has become, since World War II, a resort for those who enjoy long, open stretches of ocean beaches that are occupied only by the inhabitants of the relatively few homes scattered along its length. In the 1950s, it was designated a National Seashore by the U. S. government, a move that restricted the building of houses, hotels, and other facilities and, by that token, effectively increased the property values substantially.

Cape Cod turkey
A sobriquet for codfish. Also called **Marblehead turkey.**

Capital of the Highlands, the
Epithet for Inverness, in the north of Scotland, the chief town of the Scottish Highlands. See also **Highlands**.

Capital of the World, the
A nickname of New York City.

Capitoline, the
The most important of the Seven Hills of ancient Rome. In earliest times (when it was known as the Saturnine or Tarpeian Hill) the Roman citadel was built on its northern summit. Subsequently the main national temple of Rome, dedicated to Jupiter, was erected on its southern summit; this temple was known as the *Capitol* (Latin *caput* 'head' or 'summit'), and eventually gave its name to the hill. The term has passed down the centuries to the building, itself on a hill, occupied by the U. S. Congress for its sessions.

Capricornia
A fictitious name for the Northern Territory, scene of Xavier Herbert's novel, *Capricornia*. *Port Zodiac* in the novel represents Darwin, and even Melbourne gets a disguise as *Batman*.

Carey Street
A street to the north of the Strand in London, once the location of the Bankruptcy Department of the Supreme Court. Hence the now rather dated British slang expression *be in Carey Street*, meaning 'have no money'.

Carfax, the
A crossroads in the centre of Oxford where four roads meet: Cornmarket Street, Queen Street, St. Aldate's, and High Street (see **High**). The name derives from Latin *quadrifurcus,* 'four-forked'.

Carlton Club, the
A club in London, founded in 1831 by Conservative Members of Parliament and their supporters. Occupying a building of some architectural importance, its name is often used metonymically for the Conservative Party.

Carnaby Street
A road in the West End of London, to the east of and parallel to Regent Street. It leapt to fame in the mid 1960s, when boutiques sprang up there selling the products of the booming British teenage fashion industry, and the road became strongly associated with the culture of the 'swinging '60s'. In the 1980s the action has moved elsewhere, but Carnaby Street remains a popular tourist attraction and is still lined with clothing shops. Compare **King's Road**.

Casa Oscar Romero
A sanctuary sponsored by the Roman Catholic church in San Benito, Texas, about fifteen miles from the Mexican border. Named for an archbishop who was assassinated while saying Mass in El Salvador in 1980, it offers temporary sanctuary to those fleeing Central America and is thought by many to serve as an underground railway helping refugees to enter the United States illegally.

Castro, the
An area in San Francisco typically frequented by homosexuals.

Cathay
In medieval and early Renaissance times China was known in the West as *Cathay*. The name survives today only as an archaic or poetic term—with associations of Oriental mystery and remoteness, penetrated by the daring Marco Polo—and in the name of Hong Kong's airline, *Cathay Pacific*.

Cat Street
An area in Hong Kong comprising Upper and Lower Lascar Row and part of Hollywood Road. Its name, now formalized, comes from a particular street so called because it was a red-light district, frequented at the turn of the century by camp followers resettled from the Philippines after the Spanish-American War and characterized by its many brothels (cathouses).

Causeway Bay
A teeming shopping area in downtown Hong Kong offering a diverse variety of wares in stalls as well as in modern department stores, like Lane Crawford's, Daimaru, and Mitsukoshi.

Celestial Empire, the
A name used in former times for China. It is a translation of one of the many epithets the Chinese themselves used for their empire. Compare **Middle Kingdom**.

Centennial State, the
The official nickname of Colorado, so called because its entry into the Union (1876) occurred one hundred years after the signing of the Declaration of Independence.

Centre, the
A name given to the arid, desolate plains that cover more than half the continent of Australia and particularly to the area in the middle surrounding Alice Springs. The flat desert of the outback supports little life and is only occasionally relieved by hilly outcrops and salt lakes. The area is also known as the Red Centre, from the predominant colour of the sand and rocks, and as the Dead Heart, a name taken from J. W.

Gregory's book *The Dead Heart of Australia* (1906). In former times the
name Centralia was coined, but it never really caught on.

Centre Point
A 33-story office building in central London, at the junction of Tottenham Court Road and **Oxford Street** (*q.v.*). It was erected in the mid
1960s, in the confident expectation that it would become a symbol of the
age of thrusting new technology. However, the office space proved to be
too expensive at the time of its completion, and its owners gained considerable financial advantage, through tax relief, by refusing to rent out
smaller units. Derelicts and tramps began to take it over for nighttime
accommodation, and it rapidly achieved a dubious celebrity as a white
elephant.

Ceylon
A large island at the southern tip of India. The nation which occupies it
has been officially known as Sri Lanka since 1970. The ancient Arabic
name for the island is Serendip, from which we get the word *serendipity*,
meaning 'the knack of making fortunate discoveries'; the connection is
that this was an aptitude possessed by the heroes of the Persian fairy tale,
The Three Princes of Serendip.

Champs Élysées, the
Probably the most famous street in Paris, and one of the most renowned
in the world, the Avenue des Champs-Élysées sweeps majestically up
from the Place de la Concorde at its southeastern end towards the Arc de
Triomphe, presenting a tree-lined vista that never fails to take one's
breath away. At its northwestern end it is lined with shops, offices, cinemas, and pavement cafés ideal for sitting and observing the passing scene.
Not far away, at the southeastern end, is the Élysée Palace, official home
of the French president; *Élysée* is frequently used as a shorthand name for
the French government.

Chancery Lane
A street in central London, which runs north and south between Holborn
and Fleet Street. Its name is firmly linked with the legal profession. It
houses the Public Record Office, the headquarters of the Law Society,
and many offices and shops connected with the law: patent agents, for
example, and law stationers. Just to the west is Lincoln's Inn, one of
London's Inns of Court (societies of lawyers), and turning right at the

foot of Chancery Lane one comes to the Law Courts. See also **Inns of Court and Chancery.**

Channel, the

To an Englishman, the Channel, pure and simple, is always the English Channel, that narrow stretch of water that separates the British Isles from the continent of Europe (see also **Continent**). The French call it *la Manche* (literally, 'the sleeve'), while the Germans are content with *der Kanal*. Traditionally viewed as a powerful bastion of defence against potential invaders from Europe (although the idea didn't work out too well in 1066), the Channel has increasingly come to be seen as symbolic of the gulf in understanding between Britain and its supposed partners in the European community. 'Europe' starts on the other side of the Channel, and significantly none of the projects to link the two sides physically has yet come near completion (see **Chunnel**). Bridging the gap continues to be left to the Channel swimmers, who crawl or dog-paddle along in ever greater numbers in the wake of Captain Matthew Webb, who first made it to the other side in 1875. Scores now have a go every year, and a record of 7 hours 40 minutes for the 21 miles was set in 1978 by Penny Dean. The Channel has witnessed some of the most notable episodes in the island's history, from that typically British glorious defeat, the evacuation from Dunkirk, in 1940, to a genuine naval victory over the Spanish Armada, in 1588.

Channel country

A nickname for an area of southwest Queensland where there are three rivers, the Georgina, the Diamantina, and Cooper's Creek.

Chappaquiddick

A tiny island, part of the island of Martha's Vineyard, Massachusetts. A more or less exclusive summer resort, it sprang into national—even international—prominence in 1969 when Senator Edward Kennedy, brother of the late president John F. Kennedy and U. S. Attorney General Robert F. Kennedy, was involved in an accident in which a young woman, Mary Jo Kopechne, was trapped and drowned when the car he was driving ran off a small bridge. There was an attempt, at first, to conceal the entire episode, and, although Kennedy was exonerated at an inquest in January, 1970, from which the press was barred and the testimony of which was sealed, the presiding magistrate, in April 1970, released the transcripts with a report in which he stated that he could not accept as truth key parts of Kennedy's testimony: he concluded there was probably cause to believe Kennedy had been driving negligently and had contributed to Miss Kopechne's death. The Massachusetts attorney general's office declined to prosecute and said the matter was legally at an end. But many still felt that the entire event was whitewashed because of Kennedy's social and political power. For many years, the name Chappaquiddick continued to crop up in oblique references to Kennedy as well as in macabre, black humour, and there is no doubt that the publicity surrounding the incident effectively stymied his aspirations for the presidency of the United States.

Charing Cross

1. A small triangular open space at the northern end of Whitehall in central London, forming the southern part of Trafalgar Square. The area was originally called Charing; the *cross* part of its name comes from the so-called Eleanor Cross erected here in 1291, the last of a series put up by Edward I to mark the funeral procession of his wife Eleanor from Nottingham to Westminster Abbey. In 1675 it was replaced with a statue of Charles I. Charing Cross is officially at the centre of London; distances from the capital are measured from it. To the north runs Charing Cross Road, well known for its secondhand book shops. Charing Cross is also the name of a major rail terminus here, from which trains go to the southeast of England. The local Underground station used to be called *Trafalgar Square*, but is now *Charing Cross*; confusingly, the station that used to be called *Charing Cross* is now known as *Embankment*. **2.** Charing Cross is also the name of an important crossroads near the centre of Glasgow, Scotland. Like its London counterpart, it, too, gives its name to a railway station.

Charles's Wain

A British name for Ursa Major, so called from the outline formed by its stars.

Charter Oak City, the

A nickname of Hartford, Connecticut, so called after the tree in which the early settlers hid the Charter of the Colony of Connecticut in order to avoid surrendering it to King James II.

Checkpoint Charlie
A famous crossing point between the West and East zones of Berlin, situated on the Friedrichstrasse. It has been the scene of some brave escapes to the West.

Cheddar
The production of hard tangy Cheddar cheese has now spread around the world, far from the little Somerset village of Cheddar where it first started. Less susceptible to exportation is the spectacular Cheddar Gorge, a popular tourist spot with its series of limestone cliffs that rise to more than 450 feet.

Chelm
An imaginary town of eastern European folklore, peopled by foolish citizens who do outlandish things. See also **Gotham, Kocourkov, Mistelbach.**

Chelsea
1. An area in west London, on the north bank of the Thames, the status of which has undergone a cyclical change. In the 17th and 18th centuries it was a fashionable residential district, and many attractive streets and squares from the period help to give it its character. From the mid 19th century onwards it became something of an artists' quarter: J. M. W. Turner lived there in his later years, and after him Dante Gabriel Rossetti, James McNeill Whistler, Wilson Steer, Augustus John, and John Singer Sargent. By the early 20th century it had acquired a distinctly bohemian reputation, but as property prices moved relentlessly upwards, impecunious artists could no longer afford a Cheyne Walk address; they moved out westward, and the area reverted to fashionable society. Its slightly raffish air has never completely left it, however; its main street is the trendy King's Road, and its occupants have always tended to be younger and livelier than those of the more staid Kensington to the north (with the exception, that is, of the celebrated Chelsea Pensioners, red-coated British Army veterans who occupy Chelsea Royal Hospital). Chelsea is famous for its buns (first referred to in 1711), its boots (a sort of elastic-sided shoe), and its porcelain (first manufactured in the 18th century). But perhaps most of all it is known for the sort of youthful lightheartedness and high spirits typified by the annual Chelsea Arts Club Ball, a lively

frolic at which London's *jeunesse dorée* lets its hair down: it was discontinued at one point for being too rowdy, but in the 1980s has been revived. See also **Royal Borough**.
2. A nondescript area on the West Side of New York City, bounded roughly by 14th and 34th streets on the south and north, and Fifth and Tenth avenues on the east and west. It is mainly commercial, from the large office building at Fifth Avenue and 24th Street, where the toy business is centred, to the flower mart in the mid 20s west of Sixth Avenue. There are some Greek and Armenian restaurants, some featuring belly-dancers, along Eighth Avenue, and what residential neighbourhoods exist are largely run down. The Chelsea Hotel, a baroque residential hotel on 23rd Street, once figuring in the reminiscences of the writers and artists who lived there during their years of penury, remains more as an architectural landmark than as a focal scene of the arts.

Cheltenham
A town in Gloucestershire, in the West of England. It first rose to fame in the early 19th century as a spa town, where fashionable folk came to take the waters. As the century progressed it came increasingly into vogue as a place of retirement for crusty old colonels and others whose livers and tempers had been impaired by prolonged service in Britain's tropical colonies. As a result, the town achieved, and has retained, something of a reputation as a redoubt of conservatism. Part and parcel of its image is Cheltenham Ladies' College, a famous private girls' school founded by the formidable Miss Beale, a model of forceful Victorian womanhood.

Chiltern Hundreds, the
In former times, most English counties were divided up into areas known as *hundreds*, for the purpose of judicial administration. The Chilterns, an area of wooded hills in Oxfordshire and Buckinghamshire, to the northwest of London, comprised eight such hundreds. The manorial rights of three of these, Stoke, Desborough, and Burnham, all in Buckinghamshire, belonged to the Crown, which meant that the king or queen appointed stewards or bailiffs over them. Since 1707 it has been forbidden for a British Member of Parliament to hold an office of profit under the Crown: to do so brings instant disqualification. And herein lies a neat solution to a curious anomaly of Parliament, namely, that members are not allowed to resign from it. The Stewardship of the Chiltern Hundreds is such an office of profit, so any MP appointed to it immediately ceases to be an MP. To *apply for the Chiltern Hundreds* is therefore now the

standard way for a member to leave Parliament if he or she does not wish to wait for a dissolution. The Stewardship is a purely nominal office, with no duties, and the holder resigns it immediately in order to leave it open for the next applicant.

Chimneyville

A nickname of Jackson, Mississippi, so called because nothing was left but the chimneys after a fire burned the city to the ground during the Civil War.

Chinatown

1. The name given to the section of any large western city occupied entirely or largely by Chinese. Most of the large cities of the western world have a Chinatown, notably San Francisco, whose Chinese inhabitants settled during the late 19th century, imported mainly to construct the railways in the western United States. Typically, in addition to living quarters, such districts have retail shops and restaurants, owned and operated by Chinese, and many visitors are attracted by the exotic wares and foods offered. There is a large Chinatown in New York City, on the Lower East Side, just east of Foley Square and the court buildings on Centre Street and extending north to Canal Street. In a whimsical mood, the telephone company has installed in the streets public telephone booths that have pagoda-shaped roofs.

2. London's original Chinatown was in Limehouse, the Dockland district to the east of the Tower of London. It came into being as Chinese sailors who had worked in the tea trade began to settle in the area. The oriental community here flourished in the 19th century, albeit under the cloud of opium trafficking and rumours of mysterious secret societies, which fuelled fears of the 'yellow peril'; and up until World War II it was all but an autonomous enclave. At its centre was the small road known as Pennyfields, but some of the surrounding streets give the flavour of the area better: Oriental Street, Canton Street, Ming Street, and Pekin Street. In the 1980s Soho, and particularly the area around Gerrard Street, house London's chief Chinatown, but Limehouse still contains some of the best Chinese restaurants in London.

Chisholm Trail

An important route between San Antonio, Texas, and Abilene, Kansas. The original Trail, laid out by Jesse Chisholm (*ca* 1805–68) in 1832, was a wagon road between Fort Smith, Arkansas, and Fort Towson, in Indian

Territory (later Oklahoma). In the mid 1860s, it was the main road for transport of goods and cattle to Abilene, the nearest station of the Kansas Pacific Railroad. Today, US 81 follows the route of the old Trail.

Christiana

A self-governing section of Copenhagen, consisting of a block of abandoned government buildings around what was previously a parade ground. It is occupied by about 1,000 people who deal openly in hashish and other hard drugs, though its residents maintain that users among them are exiled till cured of their habit. Regarded by many as a "free city", its inhabitants have adamantly refused to comply with government offers to rehabilitate the area, a sentiment in which they are supported by a majority of Danes.

Christ of the Andes

The name given to a bronze statue, 26 feet tall, that symbolizes peace between Argentina and Chile. At the conclusion of a treaty in 1902 that established their common border, money was raised by popular subscription for the statue. Created by Argentine sculptor Mateo Alonzo, it was cast from ancient cannons and erected in 1904 at the summit of Uspallata Pass, between Mendoza, Argentina, and Santiago, Chile, 12,674 feet above sea level. The left hand holds a cross and the right is raised in blessing. In 1937 a tablet was affixed to its pedestal which translates 'Sooner shall these mountains crumble into dust than Argentinians and Chileans break the peace sworn at the feet of Christ the Redeemer'.

Chrysler Building

A New York City skyscraper office building, completed in 1930, and, for the brief time till the opening of the Empire State Building, in 1931, the tallest building in the world. Situated at Lexington Avenue and 42nd Street, it is a notable example of architectural design in the Art Deco style: the first few floors are faced with black marble decorated with aluminium window frames, and the tower, which comes to a sharp spire, is also decorated with aluminium. There are stylized decorative gargoyles projecting from corners at various setbacks.

Chunnel, the

The name Chunnel, a blend of *Channel* and *tunnel*, is first recorded in 1928, but the idea of linking Britain and France with a tunnel under the English Channel goes back much further in time. It was first proposed by a French engineer as long ago as 1802, but, with the lethargy that has overcome all Chunnel projects, no one actually started digging a hole until 1880. Shortly afterwards, British interests backed away from the project, apparently for security reasons, so the scheme was cancelled. Interest began to revive in the 1950s, and by 1964 it had been agreed to construct a railway tunnel between Folkestone and Calais. After nine years a treaty to this effect was signed, only for Britain to pull out again, in 1975, because of rising costs. The idea of a Channel tunnel never seems to die completely, though: in 1986, the governments of Britain and France announced plans for a joint project to construct a dual railway tunnel, to be completed by 1993.

Cincinnati oyster
An American nickname for a pig's foot, used as food.

Cinque Ports, the
In medieval times, before England had a navy, five southeastern harbour towns were charged with the defence of the realm against attack from the sea. In return for this responsibility, these Cinque Ports (from the French *cinq* 'five') were granted considerable privileges, including complete jurisdiction over the southeast coast of England. To the original five, Hastings, Sandwich, Dover, Romney, and Hythe, were later added Rye and Winchelsea. Evolution both in methods of coastal defence and in the actual physical nature of the coastline (although Dover is still a thriving port, the others are now silted up, and Rye and Winchelsea are two miles from the sea) has removed the Cinque Ports' role and with it their historic privileges, but they are proud to retain the title.

City, the
The City of London is the germ from which the sprawling modern metropolis grew. In location and extent it more or less corresponds to the walled city of Norman London. In the present day, sandwiched between the West End and the East End, it is still a self-governing administrative unit, run by the Corporation of the City of London, which is presided over by the Lord Mayor. It is always familiarly known as *the City*, but this name has particular overtones; it refers especially to the eastern part of the area, which is one of the world's major banking and financial centres. It contains the Bank of England, the Stock Exchange, the headquarters of the British clearing banks, Lloyd's, and the offices of many other insurance companies and of all the main merchant bankers, foreign

banks, and of other financial and commercial institutions. Those legendary accoutrements of the "City gent", the bowler hat and the tightly
furled umbrella, are no longer much in evidence on the streets; in the
1980s when the City has become computerized and high-rise buildings
prevail, during working hours, at least, there is little time for superannu-
ated traditions. See also **Square Mile**.

City College, the
An ironical nickname in former times for Newgate Prison (demolished
1902), on the site of the present **Old Bailey** (*q.v.*) in the City of London.
It was London's principal prison, and doubtless many received a compre-
hensive criminal education within its walls.

City of Brotherly Love, the
A nickname of Philadelphia, Pennsylvania, a loose translation of its
Greek name.

City of David, the
A name given in the Bible to Jerusalem, in allusion to King David.

City of Dreaming Spires
A somewhat idealistic nickname for Oxford, based on the line from
Matthew Arnold's poem 'Thyrsis' (1866): 'that sweet city with her dreaming spires'. The skyline of Oxford is dotted with the steeples, towers, and
cupolas of churches, chapels, and colleges. The adjective *dreaming* may
also suggest a certain self-absorbed detachment.

City of Firsts
A nickname of Kokomo, Indiana, so called because it was the first to
introduce the mechanical corn-picker, the push-button car radio, the
commercially built car, and canned tomato juice.

City of Five Flags
A nickname of Mobile, Alabama, so called because it was in territory
under the successive sovereignty of France, Spain, Great Britain, the
Confederate States, and, finally, the United States.

City of Isms
A nickname of Syracuse, New York, so called because in its early days it
was the meeting place of abolitionists and reformers.

City of Kind Hearts, the
A nickname of Boston, Massachusetts, so called by Helen Keller because her teacher, Anne Mansfield Sullivan, and many of those who helped and inspired her were from there.

City of Light, the
A nickname sometimes given to Paris, France.

City of Lilies, the
A name given to Florence, Italy, which includes lilies in its coat-of-arms.

City of Magnificent Distances, the
A nickname of the District of Columbia, given to it in 1816 by the Portuguese Minister to the United States, José Correa da Serra, a jocular reference to the proposed distances between public buildings, parks, and avenues.

City of Masts, the
A former nickname given to London when it was the world's leading port. In the days of sail a vista of the Thames at the **Pool of London** (*q.v.*) was of a defoliated pine forest.

City of the Midnight Sun, the
A former nickname given to London, with reference to its reputation as a centre for nocturnal pleasures.

City of Palaces, the
A sobriquet conferred initially on ancient Rome in the period of the Empire. The Roman historian Suetonius wrote that Marcus Vipsanius Agrippa, who undertook many public works during the reign of Augusta, converted it from 'a city of brick huts to one of marble palaces'. The name has also been applied to Calcutta, India, and to St Petersburg (now **Leningrad** (*q.v.*)), among whose notable palaces are the Winter Palace and, just outside the city, Catherine the Great's summer palace at Tsarskoye Selo.

City of Refuge, the
A name given by Muslims to Medina, the city (now in Saudi Arabia) to which the Prophet Muhammad fled in 622, having been driven from Mecca by conspirators. See also **City of the Prophet.**

City of St Michael, the
A nickname of Dumfries, a city in the Dumfries and Galloway region of Scotland. Its patron saint is St Michael.

City of Saints, the
A nickname given to Montreal, Canada, on account of the large number of its streets that are named after saints. It is in the French Catholic province of Quebec.

City of the Prophet, the
A name given by Muslims to Medina, the city (now in Saudi Arabia) in which the Prophet Muhammad died and is buried. See also **City of Refuge.**

City of the Seven Hills, the
A nickname for Rome. See also **Seven Hills.**

City of the Sun, the
A name given to several cities in the ancient world, on account not of their ideal climate, but of their citizens' worship of the sun: Baalbec in ancient Syria (modern Lebanon) was a centre of sun-worship; the island of Rhodes had Apollo as its tutelary deity; and Heliopolis, which in Greek means 'city of the sun', in Egypt had a Temple of the Sun.

City of Witches
A nickname of Salem, Massachusetts, a reference to the twenty people executed there for witchcraft in 1692.

Clapham
A district in southwest London that has three main claims to fame: its station, Clapham Junction, which is at the centre of a criss-cross of railway tracks from the South and Southeast of England, distributing them to the London termini; it gave its name to the Clapham Sect, a 19th-century group of highly evangelical Anglicans who were filled with missionary zeal; and perhaps most notably, the 'man on the Clapham omnibus', often cited as the type of the ordinary English person with average

opinions and tastes. Like many another formerly grimy inner-city area in London, Clapham has seen the process of gentrification well under way in the 1980s.

Clink Street
A street in London on the south bank of the Thames, just to the west of London Bridge. In former times a prison stood here—hence the dated British slang expression *in the clink* for 'in prison'. In the Middle Ages and on into Tudor and Stuart times this was the centre of a celebrated red-light district known as the Liberty of the Clink.

Clinton's ditch
A derisive nickname given to the Erie Canal that De Witt Clinton advocated building from lakes Erie and Champlain to the Hudson River, which was completed in 1825 during his term as governor of New York.

Clock at the Astor/Biltmore
A once-elegant, latterly commercial hotel, the Astor formerly stood on the west side of Times Square, between 44th and 45th streets, in New York City. In its Art Deco, black-glass-and-chrome lobby was a wall-mounted clock, where people often met by appointment before going on for an evening's entertainment. On the East Side of New York City, the Biltmore Hotel stands at 44th Street and Madison Avenue. It, too, had a clock where couples would meet. In the early 1980s, the Biltmore clock was removed during a general renovation of the hotel, and many thought it had gone the way of the Astor clock. But the hotel owners returned it, fully refurbished, when the renovation was completed, and people can again meet 'under the clock at the Biltmore'.

Clubland
1. Not so much a specific location as a general term for London's gentlemen's clubs and their members, Clubland is to be found in the St James's and Pall Mall areas of the West End. Here and nearby are such august institutions as White's and the Carlton, the Reform, the Athenaeum, the Savage, Boodle's, and Pratt's. Traditionally they have provided facilities for professional men and men about town to meet, dine, or perhaps simply sit in a comfortable armchair with a newspaper, all in a congenial atmosphere of quiet elegance.
2. Northern England has a Clubland, too. Throughout the industrial areas of the North, a tradition has built up of working men's clubs, where

after a hard day at work the lads repair to hoist a few glasses of ale, play darts or dominoes, and perhaps be entertained by a singer or comic. Many of these clubs have grown to such an extent that they provide a full cabaret, and the Clubland circuit has replaced the defunct music halls as a tough proving-ground for aspiring entertainers.

Clydeside
The area on the banks of the Clyde River, southwest Scotland, particularly the industrial and shipbuilding territory from Glasgow westwards towards Greenock. Its name is sometimes confused with Clydebank, which is a town in its own right, now virtually a western suburb of Glasgow.

Coat Hanger, the
An Australian nickname for Sydney Harbour Bridge, based on its distinctive shape.

Cobble Hill
A section of Brooklyn, near Brooklyn Heights. A residential neighbourhood, its buildings are mainly 19th-century brownstones which were renovated during the 1960s and '70s when the area became an important adjunct to Brooklyn Heights, which had become too expensive for many to afford. It is bounded by Atlantic Avenue on the north, Court Street on the east, the Brooklyn-Queens Expressway on the west, and (roughly) Union Street on the south.

Cockade City
A nickname of Petersburg, Virginia, so called after the cockades worn by the soldiers recruited there during the War of 1812. See also **Cockade State**.

Cockade State, the
A nickname of Maryland, so called after the cockade worn by the soldiers of the Old Line during the American War of Independence. See also **Cockade City**.

Cockpit Country, the
An area of desolate limestone plateau in the northern central part of the island of Jamaica. It is riddled with caves and hollows and striated with

fissures and ridges. Behind its forbidding barriers live the Maroons, descendants of fugitive slaves of the Spanish. They are a law unto themselves, and Jamaican officialdom largely leaves them alone. In former times their reputation was such that any government officers entering the Cockpit Country rode back to back to guard against ambush, whence the area's nickname, the *Land of Look Behind*.

Cockpit of Europe, the

A nickname given to Belgium because its exposed position as a buffer between France and Germany has so often led to its being turned into a battlefield—from Ramillies in 1706, through Waterloo in 1815, Mons and Ypres in World War I, to the German invasion of World War II. The term *cockpit* refers to the sense of 'a place where cockfights are staged'.

Collins Street

The name of a street in central Melbourne associated with financial and commercial interests. It gives its name to the *Collins Street Grazier* or *Farmer,* a businessman who owns farm property as an investment and a tax deduction. The Sydney equivalent is the *Pitt Street Farmer*; in Queensland it is the *Queen Street Bushie.*

Colossus of Rhodes

One of the Seven Wonders of the World, this bronze statue of the god Helios was said to have been more than 100 feet tall and to have been built from bronze weapons and armour left behind by the army of Demetrius I of Macedon when they lost their siege of Rhodes. It was designed by Charus of Lindus (a city on the island of Rhodes) and erected at the harbour between 292 and 280 B.C. It is traditionally believed that ships could sail between its legs. An earthquake in 224 B.C. destroyed it and in the 8th century A.D. the bronze fragments were sold to the Saracens. The publicist's word *colossal* is said to derive from this gigantic figure.

Columbus Circle

A junction, at 59th Street and the southwest corner of Central Park, in New York City, where Broadway, 59th Street, and Eighth Avenue cross, the last to continue northward as Central Park West. At its centre is a circular plaza with a fountain and a tall pedestal from the top of which Christopher Columbus gazes down on the frequent traffic jams below. Its west side is dominated by the Coliseum, a large convention centre; at its south side stands the marble-faced New York City Visitors Center, formerly the repository of the Huntington Hartford collection of art, one of the least imposing agglomerations of some of the worst work by the best artists ever to have been accumulated in one place. Over its north rim towers the Gulf & Western building, a modern monolith to multinational conglomerates. It is, generally, a characterless area, though many years ago a nearby barber shop, at 58th Street, offered 'Physiognomical Haircutting', perhaps the only distinctive feature seen for blocks around. It is said that Columbus Circle is the benchmark for all road distances shown on signs approaching the city.

Combat Zone
A nickname for an area in downtown Boston, bounded, roughly, on the west by Tremont Street, on the south by Boylston Street, on the east by Washington Street, and on the north by Temple Place. It is a section of theatres, but its name derives essentially from its unsavory atmosphere, created by sleazy bars, 'adult' book and porn shops, 'adult' cinemas, and the patrons and people associated with them. It has assumed the character and function of the former Scollay Square (q.v.).

Commonwealth
Only four states of the fifty in the United States call themselves a commonwealth rather than a 'state': Kentucky, Massachusetts, Pennsylvania, and Virginia. Puerto Rico is officially designated as one but in this case it is a description of its status as a self-governing territory associated with the United States.

Connecticut Avenue
An attractive, wide street in Washington, D.C., where many of the embassies of foreign countries are situated. Most of them are large mansions, some in a park-like setting with iron fences about them, giving the area an air of sedate opulence, which, in time of international stress, belies the skulduggery assumed to be plotted behind the ivied walls.

Constable Country
A name given to Dedham Vale, the valley of the lower Stour on the borders of Essex and Suffolk, in East Anglia. The landscape around here was immortalized by the painter John Constable (1776– 1837), and has changed very little since he put it on canvas. Places particularly associated with him are East Bergholt, where he was born, and Flatford, which

figures in some of his most famous paintings, including 'Flatford Mill' and 'The Haywain'.

Constitution State, the

The official nickname of Connecticut, so called because Fundamental Orders were drawn up there (1639) that are believed to be the first constitution written by the people. They were largely the work of Thomas Hooker. The Constitution of the United States is said by some to be more nearly like this constitution than that of any of the other colonies.

Continent, the

The British Isles are technically part of the continent of Europe, but when Britishers speak of *the Continent*, they do not include themselves in it. A 'continental holiday', for example, definitely involves going abroad. The usage arose at a time when continent meant 'mainland', as opposed to any islands near its shores, but there is no doubt that nowadays it is reinforced by the British people's feeling of separateness from the rest of Europe. In spite of Britain's joining the European Economic Community in 1973, the English Channel still represents a considerable cultural gulf. See also **Channel**.

Continental Divide, the

The main ridge of high land in North America that separates waters flowing into the Atlantic Ocean and the Gulf of Mexico from those flowing into the Pacific. In the Rocky Mountains, it crosses New Mexico, Colorado, Wyoming, Idaho, Montana, British Columbia, and Alberta. In Canada it joins the Height of Land and separates Pacific and Arctic Sea drainage on the west from the Arctic and Atlantic drainage on the east. It also runs through Mexico and Central America. Also called **the Great Divide.**

Continental Shelf

A geological configuration along the shores of continents, where the water is somewhat shallower before dropping off to the greater ocean depths.

Coonskin Library

The nickname given to those books in the Ames, Ohio, library that were obtained from Boston in exchange for racoon and other animal skins.

Copacabana
1. A great sweep of silvery-white sand that constitutes the main beach of
Rio de Janeiro, Brazil. Overlooked by the Sugar Loaf Mountain and the
gleaming white tower blocks of the city, it is a magnet particularly to
foreign tourists; the local smart set tend to prefer the beach at nearby
Ipanema.
2. A nightclub in New York City, on 60th Street between Fifth and
Madison Avenues. Operated for many years by the showman and impre-
sario, Billy Rose, it featured a small chorus line of girls, selected for their
height as well as their beauty, and advertised as 'Billy Rose's Long-
stemmed American Beauties'.

Copper Belt, the
A region of central Africa containing vast deposits of copper. Most of it
is in north-central Zambia, but it also stretches across the border into
Zaire. Its mining provides the mainstay of the economy of Zambia, the
world's third largest copper producer.

Cornish Riviera, the
Situated at the very southwestern tip of the country, and warmed by the
Gulf Stream, Cornwall has the mildest climate in England. The long
sandy beaches, the little harbour towns, and the frequently luxuriant
subtropical vegetation have combined with the balmy weather to suggest
the name *Cornish Riviera* for the stretch of southern coastline roughly
between Falmouth and Looe. Like its inspiration, the French and Italian
rivieras, it is a favourite vacation area. In spirit it extends further east
along the coast as far as the elegant resort of Torquay; but this is actually
in Devon, and the area is more correctly known as the *Devon Riviera*. See
also **French Riviera, Italian Riviera**.

Coromandel Coast, the
The southeast coast of India, from Point Calimere in the south (just to
the north of Sri Lanka) to the mouth of the Krishna River in the north.
Its fame is due not least to its identification as the home of the Yonghy-
Bonghy-Bo by the 19th-century English nonsense poet, Edward Lear, but
more probably to Coromandel work, a style of decoration consisting of
black-lacquered wood, incised and painted gold or other colours, and
frequently inlaid with semi-precious stones, mother-of-pearl, or porcelain. Though made in northern or central China, in the late 17th and early
18th centuries, it was transshipped from the Coromandel coast to Europe

by merchants of the French and English East India companies. It is also
called Bantam work because Dutch traders transshipped from Bantam in
Java. Compare **Malabar Coast.**

Costa Blanca
A stretch of Mediterranean coast in eastern Spain, extending from Cartagena to Cape La Nao. It challenges the Costa del Sol as a vacation area;
the resorts of Alicante and, in particular, Benidorm attract countless
visitors every year.

Costa Brava, the
A stretch of Mediterranean coast in northeastern Spain, extending from
Barcelona to the French border; the name means literally 'wild coast'. Its
attractions were first 'discovered' in the 1920s, and it played an early and
leading role in the postwar boom in which Spain became northern Europe's vacation playground, providing guaranteed sunshine at bargain
prices. Resorts, such as Lloret de Mar, with their rows of concrete hotel
blocks, dot the coastline here, and although the Costa del Sol, the Costa
Blanca, and Majorca have since come on the holiday scene, the Costa
Brava, with its chip shops, fake pubs, and 'afternoon teas' that pander to
the British holidaymakers' desire to avoid foreignness, remains quintessential 'packaged Spain' in most people's imagination.

Costa del Crime
A humorous nickname applied by Britons to the **Costa del Sol** (*q.v.*). It
derives from the large numbers of British criminals who in the 1960s and
'70s took advantage of the lack of an extradition treaty with Spain to
escape the attentions of the police in the UK and set up home, often in
some luxury, in and around Marbella. Recent changes in the Spanish law
now threaten their precarious immunity.

Costa del Sol
A stretch of Mediterranean coast in southern Spain, extending eastward
from Gibraltar to Málaga. It is popular as a vacation destination among
British sunseekers, and many of the resorts there, such as Marbella,
Torremolinas, and Fuengirola, have become so anglicized, with their
pubs and chip shops, that only the climate reminds one that this is not
Brighton or Blackpool.

Costa Geriatrica, the

A humorous nickname for the coast of southeast England, and particularly of Sussex, coined because of the large number of elderly people who tend to retire to seaside bungalows in the resorts there. Worthing, to the west of Brighton, is probably the quintessential senior-citizen territory, though Eastbourne shares the same character.

Costa Smeralda

A stretch of sybaritic vacation territory along the northeast coast of the island of Sardinia, centred on the resort of Porto Cervo. The name (*smeralda* is Italian for 'emerald') reflects the glinting colours of the Mediterranean that laps against the many bays and inlets of the coastline, but may also contain a passing reference to the proverbial wealth of the Aga Khan, who took a leading part in developing tourism there.

Côte d'Azur

The Mediterranean coast of France east of Marseilles; English speakers generally refer to it as the French Riviera. The name *Côte d'Azur*, which so aptly suggests the colour of the Mediterranean, was coined in 1887 by the poet Stephen Liégeard.

Côte d'Or

A name (French 'golden slope') given to a thirty-mile eastward-facing strip of hillside in eastern France, from Dijon in the north to Santenay in the south, on which the finest red and white wines of Burgundy are produced. The northerly vineyard area is called the Côte de Nuits, centred on the commune of Nuits Saint-Georges; the southerly area is the Côte de Beaune.

Cottonopolis

A 19th-century nickname for Manchester, a city in northwestern England. It was the hub of the Lancashire cotton industry, which in those days earned Britain more in exports than any other product, and consequently brought much wealth and power into Manchester.

Country of the Thousand Lakes

An epithet for Finland (which has some 60,000).

Covent Garden

An open space in the centre of London, to the north of the Strand, which has long been famous for two things: fruit and vegetables, and opera. There was a market on the site, for the sale of fruit and vegetables, and later flowers, from 1661 to 1974, when it was moved south of the Thames, to Nine Elms. The old market buildings have subsequently been restored to create an attractive pedestrian precinct, with many cafés and shops, and the new Jubilee Market has been opened, featuring craft stalls and a variety of street entertainments. In the 1980s it is one of the liveliest centres of London's city life. Just to the north is the Royal Opera House, familiarly known as *Covent Garden*, or, to initiates, simply as *the Garden*. There has been a theatre on this site since the 1730s, and it is now the prestigious flagship of opera and ballet in Britain. Originally, this area was a garden belonging to the monks of Westminster and was known as Convent Garden. In the mid 17th century an elegant housing project was built here by Inigo Jones, in the central square of which the market was first held.

Coventry

A city in Warwickshire, in central England, well known in legend and, more recently, in fact. The legend goes back to the 11th century, when Lady Godiva, wife of Leofric, rode naked through the streets of the town on her palfry to protest against a punishing tax that her husband had imposed on the people. As the story goes, all averted their eyes as she passed save for one voyeur, 'Peeping' Tom, whose eponymic fame is scarcely exceeded by that of the object of his gaze. Coventry also figures in the idiom, chiefly British, *send to Coventry*, 'to ignore; refuse to have anything to do with'; if the speculators are right, this phrase had its origin some 600 years later, when the Royalists were incarcerated by Cromwell at the Coventry Gaol, essentially putting them out of commission for a considerable period. Coventry again emerged some three centuries later, when it was almost entirely destroyed in a bombing raid by the Nazis, in 1940, during the Battle of Britain. As the British high command had knowledge of the impending attack, it is said that the citizens could have been warned and many lives saved. To have issued the warning would have revealed that the intelligence had been received by the breaking of the code of the Enigma machine, a Nazi coding device, and it was not deemed expedient to let that be known by the enemy. Modern Coventry is best known for its ultra-modern cathedral, designed by Sir Basil Spence and completed in 1962, built to replace the ancient one that was devastated in the 1940 air raid.

Cowes Week
The first week in August, when the Royal Yacht Squadron, which is headquartered at Cowes, Isle of Wight, England, joins with other local yacht clubs for an annual regatta.

Cracker State, the
A nickname of Georgia. There are three versions of the origin of this nickname: the sound made by the whips that the early settlers snapped over their mules; a shortening of *corncracker,* since the poorer settlers subsisted mainly on corn; and their dialect, which sounded to some like something being cracked.

Cradle of Aviation
A nickname of Hammondsport, New York, so called because of the pioneering aviation work done there by Glenn Hammond Curtiss. See also **Birthplace of Aviation.**

Cradle of Civilization, the
A nickname of Greece.

Cradle of Liberty, the
A nickname of Boston, Massachusetts.

Crescent City
A nickname for New Orleans, Louisiana, commonly used within that area. It came from the location of the city on the Mississippi River where a series of river bends gave the community a crescent shape. It is reflected in the badge of the New Orleans Police Department, which consists of a crescent positioned above a star.

Crewe
A town in Cheshire, in Northwest England. Its reputation rests mainly on its status as a railway junction. Lines converge on it from all points of the compass, and it figures largely in many rail journeys: 'Change at Crewe' is a familiar watchword.

Crystal Palace
A district in southeast London which gets its name from the Crystal Palace, a huge metal and glass pavilion originally put up in Hyde Park in 1851 for the Great Exhibition. It was re-erected here in 1854, and eventually burned down in 1936, but not before the name had attached itself to the area (reinforced, no doubt, by the fact that the well-known local soccer team is called Crystal Palace).

Cumberland
In the Northwest of England, a former county on the Scottish border. In the local government reorganization of 1974 it became part of Cumbria.

Cumberland Gap
The name of a high pass through the Appalachian Mountains, near the junction of the boundaries of Tennessee, Virginia, and Kentucky, known as 'the gateway to the West' to many early pioneers.

D

Dakota
1. A former American term for 'any very remote place', akin to the use of *Siberia* today.
2. **The Dakota.** A luxurious cooperative apartment building on Central Park West from 72nd to 73rd streets in New York City. Built in the early 20th century by William Randolph Hearst as an investment for his mistress, Marion Davies, it became a cooperative after World War II. Till about 1965, several tennis courts were maintained for the tenants who more recently included the Beatle, John Lennon, and other famous people. It was so named because at the time of its construction, its site was considerably remote from any other major buildings—residential or otherwise—in the city. (See definition 1, above.)

Dales, the
Dale is a poetic word for 'a valley', but in Britain *the Dales* has a very specific meaning. A series of rivers drain from the Pennine Hills through Yorkshire to the North Sea, and the valleys they flow through are known as *the Dales*. They range from Teesdale in the north, through Swaledale, Wensleydale (where a famous cheese is produced), Wharfedale, and Nidderdale to, just northwest of Leeds, Airedale. The Dales carve their way through a starkly beautiful landscape of craggy fells and high moors, most of which has been turned into a national park, known as the Yorkshire Dales.

Dallas Book Depository
A warehouse in Dallas, Texas, where, it was determined, Lee Harvey Oswald took up his position with a rifle and assassinated President John F. Kennedy, on November 22, 1963, as his motorcade passed nearby.

Dalmatia
The coastal area of Jugoslavia that borders on the Adriatic Sea.

Dark and Bloody Ground State, the
A nickname of Kentucky (said by some to be a literal translation of its Indian name), so called in reference to the battles fought there between the Indian tribes of the north and south.

Dark Continent, the
An old nickname for Africa, evocative of a 19th-century colonialist attitude towards the continent as a relatively unexplored and mysterious place whose inhabitants were dark-skinned. It first seems to have been used by H. M. Stanley in the title of his book *Through the Dark Continent* (1878). Twelve years later he wrote *In Darkest Africa*.

Dartmoor
A wild, desolate area in Devonshire, England, the site of England's main prison (since 1850) for long-term convicts.

Davy Jones's locker
A nickname for the sea, used by sailors, a reference to the final resting-place of the dead, possibly from the biblical story of Jonah and the whale.

Deccan, the
A vast plateau which occupies much of India to the south of the northern
plains. Beginning at the Narmada River (which is roughly on the same
line of latitude as Calcutta), it extends southward in an ever-narrowing V
as far as the Nilgiri hills and Ootacamund.

Deep South, the
In the United States, an area encompassing those states in the southeastern part of the country that were generally associated with a slave economy before the Civil War, namely, South Carolina, Tennessee,
Louisiana, Mississippi, Alabama, and Georgia. Compare **South, 1.**

Delmarva Peninsula
The name for that part of the Atlantic Coastal Plain that juts south about
180 miles between Chesapeake Bay on the west and the Atlantic Ocean on
the east, so called because it consists of parts of the states of Delaware,
Maryland, and Virginia.

Derry
A city and county in Northern Ireland. Since 1613 they have been officially known as Londonderry, because in that year the city and surrounding district was given to the City of London as a place for English people
to go and settle. Not surprisingly, the new name has never been particularly popular with the locals, and since the resurgence of Nationalist
feeling in the late 1960s resistance has grown. In the 1980s, therefore, the
old name of *Derry* has been approved for use again by the Post Office.

Deux Magots, les
A café, or brasserie, on the Left Bank, in Paris, on the Boulevard St
Germain. It has long been a popular lounging- and meeting-place of the
writers and artists who frequent or inhabit the area.

Devil's Island
A small island off the coast of French Guiana, South America, (one of a
group of three, known as the Îles du Salut) which achieved notoriety as a
French penal colony of proverbial severity. In earlier times it had been a
leper colony, but its isolated position made it an ideal prison, and its
function was changed in the late 19th century. Its most famous occupant
was probably Alfred Dreyfus, and it is memorably described in the novels

Dry Guillotine, by René Belbenoit, and *Papillon*, by Henri Charrière. It ceased to be a prison in 1938.

Devils Nest
An area of wild terrain in the United States covered by a forest on the Nebraska side of the Missouri River between the towns of Crofton and Niobrara. Robbers, outcasts, Indians, trappers, and outlaws lived in the draws between the top of the very high hills and the river front.

Diamond City
A nickname of Amsterdam, the Netherlands.

Diddy wa Diddy
A name for a legendary place of abundance, superficially of food but essentially of all good things, notably of sexual fulfilment. The term stems from the Black culture of blues and early jazz musicians; though no reliable etymology is available, it might have originated in an African language.

dinosaur of darkness
A nickname given to a prehistoric reptile of Antarctica, fossil evidence for which was discovered in 1986.

Dismal Swamp, the
One of the largest swamps in the United States, covering about 750 square miles, in southeastern Virginia and northeastern North Carolina, in which black bears, wildcats, a multitude of fish and other wildlife exist amidst a tangle of vines and a variety of valuable trees. Part of it has recently been cleared for farming. In 1974 Congress established a section of it as the Great Dismal Swamp National Wildlife Refuge. It is part of the Atlantic Inter-Coastal Waterway, but droughts in the late 1970s and '80s have made it unnavigable.

Disneyland
A large (184-acre) amusement (or 'theme') park in Orange County in southern California, opened in 1955. Developed under the direction of Walt Disney (1901–1966), who had gained fame and fortune with his animated cartoons of Mickey Mouse, Donald Duck, and other characters, Disneyland was an immediate commercial success, and it has been widely imitated. Its focal point is a large 'castle', which is modelled after

the folly built by ('Mad King') Otto I of Bavaria in the mountains of his desmesne, and which is similar to a structure at Disneyworld, Disney's other 'theme' park, in Orlando, Florida. The amusements, rides, exhibits, and other activities presented are of interest to adults as well as children, though some cynics view Disneyland as symptomatic of the false values placed on popular culture in America.

District of Columbia
A federal district in the eastern United States that contains (and is coextensive with) Washington, the federal capital. Situated on the boundary between Virginia and Maryland and having an area of 69 square miles, it is not part of any individual state.

Dixie
The words *Dixie* and *Dixieland*, referring to the southern states of the USA, is said by some to come from the Creole pronunciation of the name of Jeremiah Dixon, who, with another astronomer, Charles Mason, were hired to survey the border between Pennsylvania and Maryland. See also **Mason-Dixon Line.**

Dockland
London probably owes its existence to its potentialities as a port. It is the first place upstream where the Thames is bridgeable, and its tidal waters there are deep enough to have served as a harbour for merchant vessels in Roman times. Seaborne trade lay at the heart of London's development over the best part of the next two millennia, culminating in the building of a vast 700-acre series of docks from about 1800 onward. Behind high prison-like walls, they occupied the area stretching eastward from the Tower of London, mainly on the north bank; this is London's Dockland, which for nearly two centuries provided a livelihood for a significant proportion of East Enders (see **East End**). Furthest upstream is St Katherine's Dock, a small dock almost in the shadow of the Tower; next door, in Wapping, came London Dock, noted particularly for its huge bonded warehouses and vaults for the storage of liquor, tobacco, etc.; then, on the peninsula called the Isle of Dogs, came the East and West India Docks and the Millwall Docks; and furthest east lay the enormous Royal Docks, comprised of the Royal Victoria, Royal Albert, and King George V Docks, the last built as recently as 1921. On the south bank of the Thames, between London Dock and the Isle of Dogs, were the Surrey Commercial Docks, a great

centre for timber importation. For more than a century and a half
Dockland throbbed with life—improvements were being made to it up
until the late 1930s—but then in the 1960s, with the advent of con-
tainerization, a sudden and drastic decline began; not deep enough to
accommodate the new generation of merchant ships, by 1981 the last of
the docks had closed down. Redevelopment in the area has been rapid,
much of it under the aegis of the London Docklands Development
Corporation: St Katherine's has become a noted tourist attraction, with
a popular exhibition of ships; London Dock has disappeared, and
amongst the tenants of its site are the new headquarters of *The Times*
newspaper; much of the Surrey Docks area, too, has been filled in and
used for housing; ambitious plans are afoot for development of the Isle
of Dogs site as an upmarket residential area, for various recreational
and commercial activities, and, not least, as an overspill area for the
financial institutions of the City; and part of the huge acreage of the
Royals may be put to use as a STOL airport. So although its role as a
port has now been taken over by Tilbury, 26 miles downstream, Dockland remains a buoyant part of London's life. See also **Pool of London**.

dog days
A period of extreme heat and humidity in the temperate latitudes, in
August, usually about the middle of the month, so called because they
were attributed to the rising of Sirius, the Dog Star, which occurs at that
time.

Dog Fence, the
An unbroken barrier of wire netting, about two metres high, extending
for more than 8000 kilometres through South Australia, along the South
Australia-New South Wales and New South Wales-Queensland borders
and through part of Queensland. It is designed to protect sheep from the
ravages of dingoes. Also called **the Wire Marvel.**

Dog Star
A name for the star Sirius.

Doldrums, the
An area of the world's oceans around the equator, characterized by light
variable winds and long periods of flat calm. It is a sort of corridor
between the trade winds, which blow towards it from north and south,
and it was responsible for becalming many a vessel in the days of sail. A

doldrum was originally a fit of depression; only later did it come to mean the state of being becalmed, hence a region where this was likely to happen. See also **Horse Latitudes.**

Domus Aurea

Literally, the 'Golden House', a palace built by Nero in a park-like setting of about 200 acres, in the centre of Rome, after the great fire of A.D. 64. In its grounds were pavilions, fountains, an artificial lake where the Colosseum later stood, and a 120-foot-tall bronze statue of the emperor.

Donner Pass

The name of a pass, 7088 feet above sea level, through the Sierra Nevada Mountains in eastern California, much used by westward migrating pioneers. It is named after George and Jacob Donner who led a party of 82 settlers through it in the winter of 1846–47 and became snowbound for three months; only forty settlers survived. According to some accounts, the survivors resorted to cannibalism to remain alive. In 1869, the first transcontinental railway system went through the Pass, and it is now a national historic landmark.

doodlebugs

A jocular nickname used by the British during World War II to offset the terror and devastation of the German V-1 flying bombs. Their passage could be tracked by the sound of their motors; when the noise ceased, those below knew the eerie silence meant the bomb was dropping towards them. Also called **buzz bomb.**

Dormitory of New York, the

A nickname of Brooklyn, New York, so called because many of the people who work in Manhattan live there.

Dorset

A county in southwest England, along the English Channel. It is known mainly as the setting of the 19th-century novels of Thomas Hardy (1840–1928) in which the area was called Wessex after the Anglo-Saxon kingdom in the same general area.

double nickel
A scornful nickname for the 55-mile-per-hour speed limit imposed nationally in the United States at the beginning of the petroleum shortage in 1974.

Dover
A town and seaport in Kent, in southeast England. It commands the Straits of Dover, the narrowest section of the English Channel, and since earliest times has been England's gateway for traffic to and from the continent of Europe. Its artificial harbour is one of the largest in the world. See also **White Cliffs**.

Down East
A New England term for Maine. The 'East' is obvious, as Maine is the easternmost part of the United States; the 'Down' part probably comes from sailors' talk: first, because examination of a sailing chart that is not constructed on a Mercator projection shows Maine to be more easterly than its northerly appearance on conventional maps; second, because the prevailing winds along the Atlantic coast are westerlies, allowing a sailing vessel to go 'easting down' (the *down* meaning 'downwind'); and third, because the shortest route (on a great circle) to northern Europe would take a vessel along the New England coast, past Labrador and Newfoundland.

Downing Street
A street in central London, a turning to the left off Whitehall from Parliament Square. It contains the British Prime Minister's official London residence, and like **Number 10** (*q.v.*) itself has become synonymous with the office of Prime Minister, or indeed with the British government as a whole.

downtown
A general designation in the United States for the busy, commercial hub of a city, often where the entertainment facilities are centred. See also **uptown**.

down under
A colloquialism for 'in Australia and New Zealand,' with reference to their position almost diametrically opposite to Western Europe on the

globe. It is used mostly in the northern hemisphere, but occasionally in those countries, too. See also **Antipodes**.

Drain, the
A derogatory nickname for the Waterloo and City Line, an underground railway linking Waterloo station with Bank station on the London Underground. Built between 1894 and 1898, it is the oldest of London's 'tubes'. It operates only on weekdays, when countless thousands of commuters are conveyed by it to and from the City.

Dr. Brighton
A nickname for Brighton popularized in the Regency period, in the early 19th century, when the seaside town was celebrated as a health resort with seawater that had a most salubrious effect.

Drury Lane
A road in the West End of London, linking High Holborn with the Aldwych, just to the north of the Strand. It contains Drury Lane Theatre (officially called the Theatre Royal, Drury Lane), and with many other theatres in the streets around it, it is at the heart of London's theatrical district.

D.S.N.C.O.
An acronym used for designating the towns of Duberger, Les Saules, Neufchâtel, and Charlesbourg-Ouest, which were annexed to the city of Quebec, Canada, in the 1970s.

Dukeries, the
In the 18th and 19th centuries no fewer than four dukes bought estates in the northern part of Sherwood Forest, including Wellbeck Abbey, Thoresby Hall, and the Duke of Newcastle's place at Clumber Park; this part of Nottinghamshire has been known as the Dukeries ever since.

dundrearies
A nickname for side-whiskers down to the chin, worn (1858) by the British actor Edward A. Sothern (1826–81) as Lord Dundreary in *Our American Cousin,* by Tom Taylor. Also called **Piccadilly weepers, weepers**.

Durgin Park
A well-known, popular restaurant in Faneuil Hall, Boston, famous for its generous portions, especially of roast-beef dinners, its informal, family-style service and plain decor, and its gruff waitresses.

dusky diamonds
A nickname for coal.

dust bowl, the
The name given to the area severely affected by drought during the 1930s, west of the Mississippi River to the Rockies, and south of Canada to the Mexican border.

Dynamite Decade
A nickname given by the French to the 1890s, so called because anarchists often threw bombs into cafés in Paris.

E

Ealing
A suburb of London towards the west, identified mainly with the film studio established there and with the kinds of film produced, typically *The Lavender Hill Mob*, comedy productions starring Alec Guinness, Alastair Sim, etc.

Earl's Court
A district in west London, to the west of Chelsea. It is an area of bed-sitters whose occupants quickly come and go but give it a lively cosmopolitan feel. It is particularly popular with Australians—hence its nickname, Kangaroo Valley. It also contains Earl's Court Exhibition, a huge concrete building which houses several national exhibitions and shows every year.

East, the
1. In the United States, an area encompassing those states in the north-eastern part of the country, namely, Maine, New Hampshire, Vermont, Massachusetts, Rhode Island, Connecticut, New York, Pennsylvania, and New Jersey, as well as the District of Columbia. Compare **Deep South, Midwest, New England, South.**
2. Geographically, the term *the East* is all-embracing but vague. In broadest terms it is synonymous with Asia, or at least the more southerly and easterly portions of that continent; many people would feel Soviet western and central Asia to be excluded from the notion of *the East*. It cannot be said to be the sum of its parts—the Near, Middle, and Far East—for the Near East teeters on the brink of Europe and Africa, and even the Middle East is perhaps a little too far west to be wholeheartedly the East nowadays. What can be stated with certainty is that the Far East is the East, and that the Indian subcontinent is included in that category too; these are the areas for which anyone going 'out East' in colonial times was destined. In more romantic or literary contexts they are re-ferred to as the Orient. Paradoxically, Australia and New Zealand, which are as far or further east than Asia, are usually not thought of as belong-ing to the East. This may arise from some overlap of the geopolitical connotations of *the East*. In this context it refers to the Communist countries of the world—the Eastern bloc, or Communist bloc—and par-ticularly perhaps those in the Soviet rather than the Chinese sphere of influence: "East-West talks" essentially involve the USSR and the USA. In this sense Japan, confusingly, belongs to the West, even though geo-graphically it is in the East.

East Africa
An area of eastern Africa occupied by the states of Kenya, Uganda, and Tanzania. In 1967 they combined to form the East African Community, which was designed to foster closer economic and social links between them, but it was dissolved ten years later.

East Anglia
A region of eastern England that in broad terms occupies the rounded bulge of land at the lower right-hand corner of the country. It contains the counties of Norfolk and Suffolk, the northern part of Essex, and the eastern part of Cambridgeshire. Its name can be traced back to the 6th century, when the Angles founded their kingdom there, and has contin-ued in use since, without the need for an artificial or literary revival

(unlike, for example, Wessex or Mercia). It is used in certain official designations; the local area of the National Health Service, for example, is known as the *East Anglia Region*.

East End
An epithet for the eastern part of London, north of the Thames. Its exact boundaries are vague, but its western edge is probably marked by a line going north from the Tower of London, and it extends eastward through Whitechapel, Spitalfields, Shoreditch, Mile End, Stepney, Bow, Limehouse, Poplar, Millwall, and Canning Town out towards West Ham and Plaistow. Throughout London's history this area has been the home of the working masses and of the poor, although the term *East End* does not appear before the early 19th century. The powerful image remains of Victorian slums huddled round the teeming docks (see **Dockland**), of cheerful Cockneys making light of the Dickensian squalor of their surroundings, of the low life recorded by Henry Mayhew in his *London Labour and the London Poor* (1849–64) and by Gustave Doré in his drawings. But in fact much of this was obliterated by bombing in World War II. The slums have been replaced by high-rise blocks of flats and the docks by light industry; but the chirpy spirit of the East Enders remains undulled. Compare **West End**.

East Indies, the
A dated term for the islands of the Malay Archipelago, including Java, Sumatra, Borneo, Sulawesi (Celebes), Timor, usually the Philippines, and hundreds of smaller islands. As a name, *East Indies* recalls the days when most of the area was colonial territory controlled by the Netherlands, Britain, and Germany; not surprisingly, in an era of new independent states like Indonesia and Malaysia, its continued use is not encouraged. In earlier days still, its use was less specific: the *East Indies*, or *the Indies*, as they were often simply called, frequently meant the same as East India, the eastern part of the Indian subcontinent, and Southeast Asia, with which the famous East India Company traded.

East Midlands, the
The eastern part of the Midlands, in England, including Lincolnshire, Leicestershire, Northamptonshire, and the southern part of Nottinghamshire. It is not the legal name of a specific area, with its own local authority, in the way that the West Midlands is, but it is used as part of more or less official designations: for example, the airport serving the

region, which is situated just to the southwest of Nottingham, is called East Midlands Airport.

East River

The swift-flowing river that separates Manhattan Island, on the west, from Long Island, with Brooklyn, at the south and Queens at the north, below **Hell Gate** (*q.v.*). See also **Harlem River.**

East Side

In New York City, the East Side is, technically, the part of Manhattan lying to the east of Fifth Avenue. It is more commonly associated, however, with the area south of 96th Street to 14th Street and east of Fifth Avenue. Its eastern boundary is the East River. The northern part of this district, especially that north of 46th Street along the river and north of 57th Street a few avenues further west, is usually referred to as the 'Upper East Side' (see also **Lower East Side**) and is characterized by luxurious town houses and expensive apartments, especially those between Fifth and Lexington avenues and along the East River. Below east 57th Street lies Sutton Place, a short street with houses and apartments which, if anything, are even more expensive than those elsewhere in the area. The nickname of this part of the city has long been the 'Silk Stocking District' from those pre-nylon days when only the wealthy women wore silk stockings. Its main thoroughfare is Park Avenue, beneath which rumble the trains arriving at and departing from Grand Central Terminal, at 42nd Street. Between 46th and 60th streets, Park Avenue once boasted fine apartment houses and residential hotels, like the Marguery. As elsewhere in New York City, after World War II the vast increases in property values caused these to be replaced by high-rise office buildings, notably Lever House, at 53rd Street and Park Avenue, the first 'glass skyscraper' to be seen in the city, and, later on, the nearby Seagram Building, also largely of glass with continuous bronze mullions, designed by Ludwig Mies van der Rohe. At 50th Street, occupying an entire city block, is the Waldorf-Astoria Hotel, with its Waldorf Towers, where a suite may cost thousands of dollars a day. Overlooking the East River at 54th Street stands River House, a prime example of luxurious living. See also **Fifth Avenue, Grand Central, Lower East Side, Park Avenue.**

East Village, the

A neighbourhood on the Lower East Side in New York City, roughly north of Houston Street, east of Second Avenue, and south of 14th

Street, with its eastern boundary more or less at Avenue B. For many years it was a slum, which became only slightly improved in the 1950s when those who were displaced or put off by the higher rents in the West Village (see **Greenwich Village**) rented apartments there. The more adventurous bought the small, unpretentious houses that are characteristic of the area and renovated them. These aspiring 'new bohemians', many of whom, though writers, artists, and other professionals, were essentially from the middle class, succeeded in making changes along the western reaches of the district, but Tompkins Park, the focal point of the East Village, remained a barrier beyond which few ventured eastward into the still dangerous slums. Vandalism, drug trafficking, and other crimes continued to dominate these slums, often spilling over into the more genteel streets west of Tompkins Park. By the mid 1970s, many of the pioneers of the 1950s, now twenty years older, tired of the continuing struggle to improve the neighbourhood and moved away.

E-boat alley
A World War II nickname for the shipping lanes off the east coast of England where cargo ships were prime targets of German E-boats, which carried torpedoes as well as guns.

Eddystone Light
A lighthouse on the Eddystone rocks in the English Channel, about 12 miles from Plymouth. Built in 1698, it was the first such offshore structure, and it became legendary, memorialized in the folksong, 'The Keeper of the Eddystone Light'.

Edgbaston
A salubrious suburb of Birmingham, in the West Midlands of England, whose spacious boulevards belie the city's image of conurbated blight. Situated to the west of the city centre, it contains Birmingham University; but it is perhaps best known for the Edgbaston cricket ground, headquarters of Warwickshire County Cricket Club, where test matches are played.

Egypt
A nickname of Illinois, so called because Cairo (pronounced KAY-ro) was named after the city in Egypt, and because since the northern part was settled after the southern, the settlers would say, 'We must go down into Egypt to buy corn'.

Eire

The Gaelic name for the Republic of Ireland. It was officially introduced as the name of the country in 1937, replacing the Irish Free State. See also **Erin**.

Eisenhower Platz

A nickname given in World War II to Grosvenor Square, in the West End of London, where the American embassy is situated. During the war years most of the other buildings on the square housed the headquarters of the American military forces in Europe, which were commanded by General Dwight D. Eisenhower.

El Dorado

A mythical city or country in South America sought by the Spanish explorers of the 16th century for the fabulous wealth in gold and precious stones it was supposed to contain. Its name, which in Spanish means 'the gilded one', has since come to be used to characterize any place or situation that holds out the (perhaps illusory) promise of great riches.

Elephant and Castle

A working-class district in southeast London, to the south of London Bridge. Despite attempts to show that it is named after the Infanta de Castile, the simple explanation is that its name comes ultimately from that of a pub. There has been a tavern called the Elephant and Castle in the area since at least the 16th century, having as its sign an elephant surmounted by a *howdah*, or 'castle'. This is the crest of the Cutler's Company, a medieval trade association of those who made knives and similar implements and used a lot of ivory in the process. From the inn, the name has been transferred to the nearby crossroads, now a busy road junction, and finally to the surrounding area.

Embankment, the

All along its course through London, the banks of the Thames are shored up against possible flooding at high tide, and many stretches have broad thoroughfares along them, called embankments—Chelsea Embankment, for example, and Albert Embankment. Mention 'the Embankment', however, and it will be generally assumed that reference is to the Victoria Embankment, which runs along the north bank from the Houses of Parliament eastward to Blackfriars Bridge. Its abbreviated name is in such common usage that the former Charing Cross Underground station

is now officially called *Embankment Station*. About halfway along the
Embankment is the well-known London landmark, Cleopatra's Needle.

Embarcadero, the
The name for the waterfront in San Francisco. See also **Fisherman's Wharf.**

Embassy Row
A section of Massachusetts Avenue, between Sheridan and Observatory
Circles, in Washington, D. C., where many foreign embassies are situated.

Emerald Isle, the
A poetic name for Ireland, referring to the perennial lushness of its
pastures and woodlands. It is first recorded in *Erin* by William Drennan
(1754–1820), who later claimed to have invented it.

Empire City
A nickname of New York City.

Empire State, the
The official nickname of New York.

Empire State Building
A skyscraper office building at 34th Street and Fifth Avenue, in New York
City. It was completed in 1931 and was for many years, at 1250 feet with
102 stories, the tallest building in the world, surpassing in height the
recently opened Chrysler Building. As 1931 was the depth of the Great
Depression, there were few tenants for many years, whence its nickname,
the 'Empty State Building'. It was originally planned to use it for moor-
ing dirigibles, an idea that was never greeted with much favour for reasons of safety, especially after the Hindenburg disaster. It figured in the
climax of the motion picture, *King Kong* (1933), in which the gigantic ape
climbed to the top only to be shot down and killed by a squadron of U. S.
Army fighter planes. In 1945 a U. S. bomber crashed into the 86th floor
killing 13. A television tower, 200 feet tall, was added to it in 1950, but
the building later lost its record for height to the Sears Tower, in Chicago,
which is 1454 feet tall. A number of people have attempted suicide by
leaping from its upper floors, but only a few have succeeded. In the 1970s

a man who jumped was blown onto a setback below by a strong wind with injuries no more severe than a broken leg. See also **Sears Tower.**

Empty Quarter, the
A name given, especially in former times, to the desolate area of sand dunes, barren plateaus, and low arid plains that together constitute the southern part of the Arabian peninsula. Its Arabic name is Rub' al Khali, and in English it is usually known as the Great Sandy Desert.

England
England stops about 30 miles north of Hadrian's Wall. It is not the same as Scotland; nor does it include Wales. British people tend to get slightly miffed when foreigners refer to Britain as *England*; the Scots and Welsh get absolutely furious when the English do so. See also **Britain, United Kingdom.**

Epsom
A town in Surrey, in southeast England, which is noted chiefly for its racecourse on Epsom Downs, where the Derby and other famous races are run. It has also given its name to Epsom salts, a preparation of magnesium sulphate, much used in former times as a laxative and naturally occurring in mineral springs which rise near Epsom.

Equality State, the
The official nickname of Wyoming, so called because it pioneered in women's suffrage.

Erechtheum
A temple to Athena on the Acropolis in Athens. Built about 400 B.C., it is known chiefly for its Ionic columns and for a porch, on the south side, with a roof supported by caryatids, which are relatively rare (compared with atlantes). Also, **Erechtheon.**

Erin
A poetic name for Ireland, taken from Gaelic and most often encountered in the motto, *Erin go bragh* 'Ireland forever'.

Eternal City, the
An ancient epithet for Rome, first used in classical times by such authors as Ovid and Tibullus.

Eton

Properly, *Eton College*, an internationally famous school for boys (founded 1440) in the town of Eton, Berkshire, to the west of London. See also **Harrow**.

Etruria

A district of Stoke-on-Trent, in the Potteries in the West Midlands of England. Josiah Wedgwood had a pottery works there (established in 1769), and built houses for his workers in the surrounding area; the name chosen for it was an allusion to Etruria in Italy, where the ancient Etruscans lived and produced their celebrated pottery.

Eucliffe

A palatial residence, in Scottish Renaissance style, Eucliffe was built at Repulse Bay, Hong Kong, by Eu Ton-sen, a tycoon.

Eurasia

A portmanteau word used for the continents of Europe and Asia considered as a single landmass. The term was coined in the 19th century, and is used chiefly in scientific contexts. In addition, *Eurasian* is a dated word for someone of mixed European and Asian blood, particularly in India.

Eureka Stockade

A name given to an armed clash on 3 December 1854 between gold-diggers and the Victorian police and military forces. The diggers had built a stockade on the Eureka claim on the Ballarat gold-fields and defied the authorities who had ordered a check of licences. The ensuing conflict resulted in some thirty deaths. The grievances of the diggers were complex and their stand led to some reforms. The episode has become legendary in Australia, whether for those who admire resistance to the police or for those who resent taxation. The blue *Eureka flag,* adorned with the stars of the Southern Cross, is often seen flying from construction sites.

European Economic Community, the

The official name for an association of Western European countries formed in 1958 to promote economic cooperation between its members. It is usually used in its abbreviated form, *EEC*, or simply referred to as 'the Community'. Of alternative, unofficial, names, the *Common Market*, once very widespread, is no longer so much in favour except in America, and *Euromarket* is seldom heard. There has always been a certain tendency to refer to it by the number of its members: thus, at its inception it was *the Six* (Belgium, France, Italy, Luxembourg, the Netherlands, and West Germany); in 1973 Denmark, Ireland, and the United Kingdom joined, and it became *the Nine*; with the advent of Greece in 1981 it expanded to *the Ten*; and it became *the Twelve* in 1986 when Portugal and Spain came in.

F

Falkland Islands, the
A group of islands in the South Atlantic, about 400 miles northeast of Cape Horn. A British colony, they are also claimed by Argentina, and the Argentinian invasion and subsequent British recapture of the islands in 1982 gave prominence to their alternative Spanish name, *Islas Malvinas*.

Falls Road
A main thoroughfare of Belfast, Northern Ireland, which runs west from the city centre to **Andersonstown** (*q.v.*). The area around it is the chief Catholic district of Belfast, and the IRA draws much of its support from there. The road runs parallel to the Protestant **Shankill Road** (*q.v.*) to the south, and the two are separated by the so-called Peace Line or Orange-Green Line, erected after the 1969 riots.

Faneuil Hall
A public market and meeting-place in downtown Boston, built in 1742. Often called the *Cradle of Liberty* because of the many meetings held and inspired speeches given by colonists before the War of Independence, it now houses, in addition to its restaurants and shops, historical paintings, a library, and a military museum. Its giant grasshopper weathervane is a landmark. Also called **Quincy Market.**

Fannie Mae
A nickname for the FNMA (Federal National Mortgage Association) and for the bonds issued by that U.S. agency. See also **Ginnie Mae.**

Far East, the
The concept of the Far East, comprising all the countries of eastern Asia, including China, Japan, Korea, eastern Siberia, the Malay Archipelago and Indo-China, has remained relatively stable, unlike the associated terms *Middle East* and *Near East.* However, there is variation in that *Far East* is sometimes taken to include the Indian subcontinent as well. See also **Middle East, Near East.**

Farm, the
A nickname for Monash University, Melbourne's second university.

Far North, the
A collective term applied to the regions of the world around and beyond the Arctic Circle: northernmost Scandinavia, the frozen Eurasian tundra, Greenland, the maze of islands to the north of Canada, northern Alaska, and the Arctic icecap itself.

Farther India
An archaic name for the region now known as Southeast Asia or Indo-China.

Far West, the
In the United States, an area encompassing those states that are the farthest west, namely, Nevada, California, Oregon, and Washington. Compare **Pacific Northwest, Southwest, West.**

Fashion Avenue
An official nickname, which appears on the street signs along Seventh Avenue between 35th and 40th streets, in New York City's Garment District. See also **Garment District.**

Faubourg St Honoré, Rue du
The fashionable and exclusive shopping street of Paris, which runs parallel to and north of the Champs-Élysées. It is lined with elegant houses and smart shops and is the centre of Parisian haute couture and parfumerie: Lanvin, Yves St Laurent, and Courrèges are all to be found here.

Feast of Lanterns
A name sometimes used by outsiders for the Japanese Buddhist festival
Bon, held 13–16 July, when it is believed that the souls of the dead return
to earth. Graves are cleaned, and lanterns are hung at graves and house-
gates to guide the souls.

Featherbed Lane
A street near Jerome Avenue, in The Bronx, New York, a continuation of
Mt. Eden Avenue. Its name is said to derive from the efforts of house-
wives who supplied General George Washington with featherbeds to en-
able his men to move their cannons silently during the night across the
Harlem River to Washington Heights to surprise the British.

Fens, the
A low-lying area to the south and west of the Wash in eastern England,
including parts of Cambridgeshire, Lincolnshire, and Norfolk. The rivers
Nene, Great Ouse, Witham, and Welland flow through it to the North
Sea, and in former times much of it was desolate marshy land. Then,
from the 17th to the 19th centuries, as drainage techniques improved, the
waters were gradually pushed back, and in the present century the rich
alluvial soil thus reclaimed has proved invaluable for the growing of
vegetables and flowers.

Fertile Crescent, the
A name used to characterize the area from the Persian Gulf, along the
Tigris and Euphrates rivers, to the eastern Mediterranean coast. Its well
watered plains allowed for the growing of relatively abundant crops,
while the Mediterranean allowed access to important trade. It formed the
cradle of many ancient civilizations, including the Sumerian, Babylonian,
Assyrian, Phoenician, and Hebrew. The term was coined by archaeologist
James H. Breasted. See also **Mesopotamia**.

Fifth Avenue
A north-south avenue in New York City, beginning at Washington
Square Park and extending to about 135th Street, in Harlem. It has
always been associated with wealth: for many years before World War II,
much of its length was graced by the mansions of millionaires. Most of
these are now gone, the rise in property values having made it impractical

to retain them and the difficulty of obtaining servants impossible to maintain them. The few that remain have been acquired by professional associations and institutions. They were replaced by high-rise office buildings and, below 59th Street, by department stores and fashionable retail shops. Most of the swanky retail businesses in the world are represented: Saks Fifth Avenue, Bergdorf Goodman, Gucci, Buccellati, Cartier, Tiffany, Dunhill, and others. At 58th Street is the Plaza, a square with a fountain, alongside which is the Plaza Hotel. From 59th Street northward, where Fifth Avenue borders Central Park (to 110th Street), the buildings are mainly expensive high-rise cooperative apartment houses, though here and there can be found the occasional private townhouse. The Temple Emanuel, at 65th Street, is the largest Reform synagogue in the world. There are a number of museums, too, among them the Museum of the City of New York (105th Street), the Guggenheim Museum (89th Street), and, facing Fifth Avenue from the Park at about 81st Street, the Metropolitan Museum of Art. North of 96th Street the neighbourhood begins to deteriorate, especially above 105th Street, near Mt. Sinai Hospital. Above 110th Street, the northern end of Central Park, Fifth Avenue passes into east Harlem, where it assumes the character of that area. From its starting point at Washington Square, for its entire length, Fifth Avenue serves as the demarkation point between the East and West Sides of Manhattan, all buildings being numbered starting there.

Filene's Basement
The basement shopping facility at Filene's, a Boston department store, is associated with sales at which the prices of merchandise are greatly reduced; and it seems probable that the expression *bargain basement* was given currency by Filene's Basement as well as by Macy's and Gimbels basements (in New York City) which offer similar good buys. See also **Gimbels, Macy's.**

Fire Island
A barrier beach (also known as Great South Beach, but never called that), little more than a sand bar, 32 miles long and half a mile across at its widest point, running east and west, parallel to the south shore of Long Island, New York, east of New York City. Robert Moses (formerly Fire Island) State Park is at its western end, Captree State Park is at its eastern end, at Moriches Inlet; its southern shores are on the Atlantic Ocean; between its northern shores and Long Island lie Great South Bay and part

of Moriches Bay. Although two bridges connect its extremities to Long Island, there are no longitudinal roads on the island, and motor vehicles, except for emergency vehicles and certain service trucks, are prohibited. There are some taxis available, but they and most of the other cars use the beach as a roadway. A number of communities are dotted along its length, each with its own character. The oldest and largest is Ocean Beach, which has paved streets, frame houses, mostly traditional in design, and a number of restaurants and other facilities. Farther east is Point o' Woods, an older, elegant community characterized by its large homes and, especially, by its trees and shrubbery, which contrast with the beach plums, stunted pines, blueberry bushes, and generally scrubby plant life seen elsewhere on the island. Cherry Grove, farther east, has many modern houses; it and Fire Island Pines (called "The Pines"), to the east, have had much to do with giving Fire Island its reputation for being a summer focus of homosexual life in the New York area. While it is true that homosexuals have for many years gravitated to these communities, most of the others on the island—Ocean Bay Park, Seaview, Saltaire, Davis Park, etc.—are occupied by families, many with young children who, because of the general absence of cars, can roam about with a freedom not accorded them by any but a few resorts of comparable character. With no cars, residents and visitors get about by bicycle, along the wooden boardwalks in many communities or paved walks in others. Children's wagons, often brightly painted and decorated, are widely used to transport groceries, baggage, and other goods, and scores can be seen, chained and locked against unauthorized appropriation, at the quays where the ferries dock. Many who own houses on the island rent them, at appropriately exorbitant rates, often to a group of beach-lovers who share the expense. These are called "groupers", for obvious reasons, and there may be as many as four occupying each bedroom in a house on alternate weekends from July 4th to Labor Day, in early September. From the point of view of those on Fire Island, Long Island is "the mainland", and access to the various communities is gained by ferry from different towns along its southern shore. The barrier beach itself, on the ocean side, is relatively empty, even on a holiday weekend at the height of the season—that is, although crowds may clump together at the beach near certain hotels or other facilities, one need stroll only a few hundred yards to have an acre of beach entirely to oneself. There are wooden walks and stairs for crossing the high dunes, which afford the only protection against storms and where walking is prohibited. There is also a "Sunken Forest" that lies on a part of the beach below sea level and that is protected by the dunes. A slightly elevated boardwalk meanders through the 73 acres of holly, tupelo, and sassafras trees, permitting bird watching and a view of the abundant ground level growth. The winds and blowing sand shear off the tops of the trees when they reach a height of about 35 feet and are no longer protected by the dunes. Hurricanes have occasionally devastated certain areas of Fire Island, destroying expensive homes and wreaking havoc. Yet, those enamoured of the beauty and the free life on the Island persistently rebuild.

First State, the
The official nickname of Delaware, so called because it was the first to ratify the US Constitution.

Firth of Forth Bridge
A cantilever railway bridge about one mile long, built in 1889 across an inlet (firth) of the North Sea west of Edinburgh, Scotland. Painting it has become a symbol of a never-ending task, for, as soon as painting has been completed, the workers move to the other end and start all over again.

Fisherman's Wharf
A section of the waterfront of San Francisco, famous for its restaurants and especially for the stalls where crabs and other seafood specialities may be purchased, to be eaten with the sourdough bread for which northern California is known. See also **Embarcadero.**

Fitzrovia
The unofficial name for an area of the West End of London, to the north of Oxford Street and the east of Tottenham Court Road, that in the 1940s was a somewhat bohemian quarter, rivalling Chelsea as a haunt of hard-living, hard-drinking artists and littérateurs. Augustus John, Dylan Thomas, and Wyndham Lewis were among its more noted denizens. It probably got its name from the Fitzroy Tavern, a favourite watering-hole in Charlotte Street, just to the south of Fitzroy Square.

Five Points
An intersection on the Lower East Side, in New York City, at the south end of the Bowery. In the 19th century, when the area declined, it became the gathering-place of toughs and criminals, from whom passersby were not safe. Notable was the Five Points Gang, a collection of hoodlums

who caused the police great trouble before they were finally apprehended, at about the turn of the century.

Five Towns, the
Today there is only one town—Stoke-on-Trent—which has reached out and made suburbs of its former neighbours Tunstall, Burslem, Hanley, and Longton; but in former times these were the five autonomous cornerstones of the **Potteries** (*q.v.*), the great china- and earthenware-manufacturing centre of England, in Staffordshire in the northwest Midlands. They and their inhabitants were vividly dissected in the novels of Arnold Bennett, notably *Anna of the Five Towns* (1902), in which they go under the pseudonyms Knype, Turnhill, Bursley, Hanbridge, and Longshaw.

Flanders
An area in northwest Europe which in medieval times was a powerful self-governing principality; its territory is now divided up among Belgium, France, and the Netherlands. Flemish towns such as Ypres and Armentières saw some of the bitterest fighting in World War I, and the area gave its name to the Flanders poppy, used as a symbol of those who died there in both World Wars.

Fleet Street
A busy street in the City of London, which extends from the eastern end of the Strand to Ludgate Circus. In former times it was famous for the large number of booksellers' shops it contained, but since the late 19th century it has become firmly associated, indeed synonymous, with the British newspaper industry. Most of the national newspapers have had their premises on or near the street, and many provincial ones have offices there, too. However, towards the end of the 20th century, with the need to introduce more modern computerized methods of production, the publishers are beginning to move elsewhere, most of them to redeveloped sites in London's Dockland, and it remains to be seen whether the name *Fleet Street* will follow them or fall into disuse. A rather dated nickname for Fleet Street is *the Street of Ink*; more recently, it has been called *the Street of Shame*, apparently in reference to the proliferation of lurid and sensational stories in some sections of the British press.

Flixborough
A village near Scunthorpe in Lincolnshire, in eastern England, which entered modern folklore on the first of June 1974 when a chemical plant

there exploded and burned down, killing 29 people. Its name has been firmly associated ever since with the hazards of large-scale manufacture of flammable chemicals. The plant was actually reopened in 1979 but finally closed down in 1981. Compare **Bhopal.**

Florida Parishes

The collective name for the part of Louisiana lying east of the Mississippi River and north of Lake Pontchartrain, so named because this part of the state was once under Spanish rule. In 1810, the settlers there rebelled against Spain and briefly established an independent republic.

Foggy Bottom

A section of downtown Washington, D.C., where a number of office buildings of the Department of State are situated. The phrase, first used by James Reston in *The New York Times* in 1947, has become a metaphor for the State Department.

Foley Square

A large, open plaza in downtown New York City, behind City Hall, north of the Brooklyn Bridge, with Chinatown to the east. It is the site of a number of municipal and state office buildings, but it is known principally as an area where there are many courthouses—municipal, state, and federal. The name, *Foley Square,* has become a metaphor for these courthouses and for the legal activities associated with them.

Folies Bergère

A theatre-nightclub in Paris, famous throughout the world for its Busby-Berkely-like extravaganzas, lavish costumes, risqué entertainment, and its *tableaux vivants*, which are carefully costumed and posed 'living pictures' that duplicate well-known classic paintings by peopling them with performers. Its star for many years was the Chicago-born emigrée Josephine Baker. In these liberated times, it may be considered anachronistic, but the *tableaux* tradition was begun in days of Victorian prudery, when the (French) law allowed women to appear on stage in the nude as long as they did not move. Still an attraction after so many decades, the *Folies* continues as a symbol of Parisian profligacy, eliciting a sly wink among those who are of a conservative turn of mind. See also **Moulin Rouge.**

Fontainebleau

One of the most famous chateaux in France, located southeast of Paris, Fontainebleau, originally a medieval hunting lodge, is an excellent example of French Mannerism (after Italian Mannerism), having been almost entirely rebuilt and completely redecorated in the 16th century by such artists as Benvenuto Cellini, at the direction of Francis I. It is set in a beautiful wood, about 65 square miles in area; the village of Barbizon, at its edge, has given its name to the school of bucolic painting that originated with depictions of the forest.

Fontainebleau Hotel

A resort hotel in Miami Beach, Florida, regarded as the epitome of garishness and poor taste, visited mainly by sunseekers from the North, especially New York City. Although it is named for **Fontainebleau** (*q.v.*) in France, it bears that lovely edifice no resemblance, even in name, for many refer to the hotel as 'the Fountainblue'.

Forbidden City, the

A name given to a city to which access is restricted, usually for religious reasons. It has two specific applications. First, to Lhasa, the ancient political and religious capital of Tibet; as a strict stronghold of Buddhism, it was virtually closed to foreigners in the 19th century. And second, to the inner sanctum of Peking, China. It is at the centre of the Chinese boxes that constitute the former imperial capital. At the circumference is the Outer City; within, the walled-off Inner City; beyond this again, the Imperial City; and at the heart of it all, behind its purple walls, the Forbidden City, containing the former imperial palace and various temples, halls, and gardens.

Ford's Theatre

A theatre in central Washington, D. C., where President Abraham Lincoln was assassinated (April 14, 1865) by John Wilkes Booth.

Foreigner State, the

A nickname of New Jersey, so called in reference to Joseph Bonaparte, king of Spain, who fled to New Jersey about 1812 and lived in palatial splendour on 1400 acres he bought near Bordentown.

Forest Hills

A shortened form of Forest Hills Tennis Club, in Forest Hills, Queens, New York City, where the U. S. Tennis Association's National Championship, called the U. S. Open, was held annually, until about 1982 when its site was changed to Flushing Meadows, also in Queens.

Forest Lawn

Forest Lawn Memorial Park is a cemetery in the city of Glendale in the Los Angeles metropolitan area. Designed to promote feelings of reverence rather than morbidity in the visitor, its chapels are used for weddings as well as for burials. With its branch parks, Forest Lawn has grown from its original 55 acres to the present 1200. It has gained worldwide fame not only because it is the last resting place of many well-known people, especially Hollywood celebrities, but because its design elements have been widely imitated. It has been the object of perennial interest of writers dealing with American culture and especially with American burial customs, like Aldous Huxley, Jessica Mitford, and Evelyn Waugh.

Formosa

A name given by the Portuguese to an island off the coast of China when they discovered it in 1516; in their language it means 'beautiful'. The island is Taiwan, and it is now so called both officially and generally, but the name *Formosa* remained in quite frequent usage until well into the 1950s and '60s. The state which occupies it is officially known as the Nationalist Republic of China (in contrast with the People's Republic of China on the mainland), which is often abbreviated to Nationalist China.

Fort Dearborn

A U. S. army post that was the first permanent establishment (1803) in the Chicago area. It was named for Henry Dearborn, Secretary of War under President Thomas Jefferson. Around the fort and nearby trading posts, the community grew to the size of a city, despite the hostility of Indians angered by their displacement. On August 15, 1812, at the start of the War of 1812, the Fort Dearborn garrison of soldiers and settlers was ordered to evacuate in order to shrink the military's western perimeter against the British. About two miles south of the fort, the contingent was attacked by a large Indian force; fifty-three men, women, and children were killed and those remaining taken prisoner in what is now known as the Fort Dearborn Massacre. The fort, burned by the Indians the day after the attack, was rebuilt in 1816 and remained functional until 1837.

Today, a landmark plaque commemorates the site, at the bend near the mouth of the Chicago River, just west of where it joins Lake Michigan.

Fort Knox
Although there is a military reservation at this locale, in northern Kentucky, southwest of Louisville, it is known chiefly as the repository of all of the gold owned by the United States government.

Fort McHenry
An old fort, now a monument, in the harbour of Baltimore, Maryland. It is remembered as the site of a bombardment by British naval forces on September 14, 1814, in the War of 1812, during which Francis Scott Key wrote the words to *The Star-Spangled Banner*, later set to the tune of an English melody, popular at the time, *To Anacreon in Heaven*. The song was officially adopted as the national anthem by an act of Congress in 1931.

Fortnum & Mason
A small department store in Piccadilly, London. Although clothing and other general items of merchandise are sold there, it is known chiefly for its elaborate food hall, where virtually anything, no matter how exotic, can be obtained with the help of one of the shop assistants, who are attired in morning dress. Its restaurants are also popular, especially at tea time.

42nd Street
A main cross street in New York City, terminating at the Hudson River on the west and the United Nations complex on the east. The part of it usually referred to is between Sixth Avenue (Avenue of the Americas) on the east and Eighth Avenue on the west. In the early days of the 20th century, when it was still 'uptown', 42nd Street was the site of many legitimate and vaudeville theatres. The Metropolitan Opera stood nearby, at 40th Street between Broadway and Seventh Avenue, before it moved to new quarters (in the mid 1960s) at Lincoln Center. One of the best-known and most popular vaudeville theatres of the time, the New Amsterdam, is on 42nd Street west of Seventh Avenue, though it has long been a cinema. That the street retained its earlier personality into the 1940s is evidenced by a popular musical of the time, *42nd Street*, revived in the 1980s with great success. Gradually, the area deteriorated, especially during World War II, and became what it is known for today—a disreputable street

populated by drunks, pimps, prostitutes, pick-pockets, drug-pushers, conmen, and other of society's dregs; many of the movie houses, which stand, cheek by jowl, along both sides, offer pornographic films, and the shops, where they can be shoehorned in between, cater largely to the same low trade. Nonetheless, it is brilliantly lit by the flashing neon and other signs on store fronts and theatre marquees, and is a mecca for young people who find it exciting, if a bit frightening, especially late at night.

47th Street
A block-long area of West 47th Street, between Fifth and Sixth avenues, in New York City, site of the diamond market, along with 46th Street. See also **Hatton Garden.**

Four Main Centres, the
A name given to Auckland, Wellington, Christchurch, and Dunedin in New Zealand. They are the largest centres of population and the chief business and administration centres in the country.

Fred's
A British upper-class nickname for **Fortnum & Mason** (*q.v.*), the upmarket purveyor of provisions to tourists and the gentry in Piccadilly, London.

Freedom Trail
A marked path, one and a half miles long, which passes many of Boston's most famous historic landmarks along its route from downtown into the North End. It begins and ends at **Faneuil Hall** (*q.v.*), where Bostonians met before the War of Independence to protest against British 'taxation without representation' and unfair trade policies. It passes the site of the Boston Massacre, where British soldiers shot into an angry mob of colonists, killing five of them and wounding scores more; the Old State House which served as the seat of the colonial government; the Old South Meeting House where more fiery speeches inspired the Boston Tea Party; and the Old North Church where the lanterns were hung to warn of the British attack. Among other points of interest along the trail are the site of Benjamin Franklin's birthplace; Paul Revere's home at the time of his midnight ride; the original site of the Boston Latin School, the first public school in the Western Hemisphere, opened in 1635; the Old Granary Burying Grounds, final resting place of Samuel Adams and Paul Revere;

the Park Street Church where gunpowder was stored during the War of 1812; and King's Chapel, America's first Unitarian church.

Free-O
The nickname of Freemantle, a seaport near Perth, in Western Australia.

Free World, the
A name applied by their inhabitants to those parts of the world in which a Communist or other totalitarian government does not hold sway. In practice it usually refers to the West and to a fluctuating list of Third World countries. See also **Third World**.

Fremantle doctor, the
A refreshing sea breeze that blows into Fremantle and Perth on hot afternoons.

French Quarter, the
In the United States, the oldest part of New Orleans, Louisiana, originally founded by Jean Baptiste Le Moyne, Sieur de Bienville, in 1718. It is the area enclosed by Canal and North Rampart streets, Esplanade Avenue, and the Mississippi River. Long a tourist attraction and symbol of the life style of the city, the French Quarter is famous for its Mediterranean architecture, jazz, antique shops, and restaurants, and as a haven for artists and writers. A major landmark is Jackson Square (formerly Place des Armes), adjacent to which are found St Louis Cathedral, the Cabildo, the Presbytre, and the Pontalba buildings.

French Riviera, the
On the Mediterranean coast of France to the east of Marseilles, *the Riviera*, as it is often simply called, officially stretches from Cannes to the Italian border just beyond Menton; between the two, strung out like pearls along the Corniche, the precipitous coast road, are those playgrounds of the beau monde, Nice, Monte Carlo, Antibes, Cap Ferrat, and Juan-les-Pins. The area was developed as a vacation centre by the English aristocracy in the late 19th century (though chiefly not as a summer resort), and ever since the rich and famous have been maintaining its luxurious image. In the postwar years, though, it has come to be viewed by some as staid and 'establishment', and further along the coast to the west, St Raphael and St Tropez began to encroach on its reputation with the then daring display of topless sunbathers. Most people would

now regard this stretch of coastline as part of the Riviera, too. Compare **Italian Riviera**.

Friendly Confines, the
A nickname for Wrigley Field, a baseball park in Chicago.

Frisco
A nickname for San Francisco, usually used by non-residents; San Franciscans are said to dislike the sobriquet.

Frogland
A derogatory nickname for France. French people were originally called *Frogs* or *Froggies* apparently because of their supposed penchant for eating frogs' legs, although in fact in the 17th century these words were applied to the Dutch.

Frogtown
A fairground near Angels Camp, California, the site of an annual frog-jumping contest, the Jumping Frog Jubilee, originally planned to celebrate the paving of the street in downtown Angel Street, supposedly on the spot where Mark Twain's short story, 'The Celebrated Jumping Frog of Calaveras County', took place.

Frozen Wilderness, the
A nickname of Alaska.

Furness
A peninsula in Cumbria, in northwest England, just to the southwest of the Lake District. Its main town is Barrow-in-Furness, famous as a ship-building centre.

G

Gabba, the
A nickname for the Queensland Cricket Association's ground at Woollongabba, a suburb of Brisbane.

Gaiety, the
A burlesque theatre, formerly at 46th Street in Times Square, in New York City. It was closed by Mayor Fiorello H. La Guardia (along with other such places of entertainment) in the mid 1930s, but continued as a cinema. In its heyday, it featured strippers like Ann Corio, Sally Rand, and Gypsy Rose Lee, and, among those who can recall those days, it remains a symbol of the lost opportunities to indulge youthful fantasies.

Gaiety Delicatessen
A large Jewish delicatessen on Seventh Avenue between 53rd and 54th streets, in New York City. Very popular with visitors of every nationality, it offers the typical fare of such restaurants—hot pastrami, corned beef, salami, and other sandwiches on rye bread in which the ingredients are piled so high that it is difficult to see how to bite into them. It has long been a favourite 'noshery' of show-business people, and continues to offer kosher dill pickles as a condiment and 'celery' tonic for washing it all down.

Galloping Gertie
A nickname of the suspension bridge across the Narrows of Puget Sound at Tacoma, Washington, which, during a high gale in 1940 was seen to buckle and sway violently, tossing vehicles into the waters below. It was so called because the roadbed flexed like a ribbon.

Galloway
A region in the extreme southwest of Scotland, which has given its name to a breed of hardy black cattle. At its tip is the Mull of Galloway, a headland which forms the southernmost point of Scotland.

Gamblers Express
Any mode of transportation for carrying passengers to a casino, race-track, etc., as the trains or buses between New York City and Atlantic City, New Jersey.

Game-cock State, the
A nickname of South Carolina, so called in reference to the determined
fighting the state waged against the abolition of slavery, which led to its
being the first state to secede in 1860.

Garden of England, the
A nickname given over the centuries to many of the more picturesquely
fertile counties of England, including Worcestershire, but finally bestowed firmly on Kent, which in early summer billows with apple and
cherry blossoms.

Garden of France, the
A name often applied to the Touraine, an area of northwestern central
France that straddles the Loire River. This is lush agricultural country,
justly famous for the excellence of the vegetables and fruit its farmers
produce.

Garment District
An area in New York City, one of the busiest places in the world,
bounded by Seventh Avenue on the east, Eighth Avenue on the west, and
35th and 40th streets on the south and north. It is a neighbourhood of
high-rise loft buildings where many of the major women's clothing manu-
facturers have their factories and showrooms. Down below, the shops
along the side streets are sources for buttons, decorations, and all kinds
of trimmings used in the garment trade, and the streets are virtually
impassable by cars owing to the double-parked trailer trucks, vans, and
other vehicles delivering piece goods, hangers, and other supplies, and
carting away finished clothing. Seventh Avenue, nicknamed 'Fashion Avenue' (*q.v.*), is a bustle of messengers, workers, salesmen, models, executives, and the ubiquitous wheeled clothes racks used for transporting
merchandise to and fro.

Garryowen
(In rugby ball) an extremely high kick that lofts the ball to keep it in the
air long enough to enable the offensive team to reach the opposition
players to whom the ball was kicked. It is named for the Irish club where
the play was first used tactically.

Gateway Arch

A tall, metal arch on the west side of the Mississippi River, at St Louis, Missouri, designed by Eero Saarinen and symbolizing the city's reputation as the 'Gateway to the West'. It contains a lift that enables visitors to ride to the top, 630 feet above the ground, for a view of the surrounding countryside.

Gateway of the West, the

A nickname of New York that was acquired during the 19th century when the completion of the Erie Canal connected the Hudson River and Lake Erie.

Gatwick Airport

An airport south of London, formerly (before the completion of the M-25 motorway) difficult of access from anywhere but London. It serves many international flights, especially charter flights. See also **Heathrow.**

Gay Nineties, the

A nickname, not conferred till the 1920s, for the last decade of the 19th century, which, in retrospect, seemed so carefree in comparison with the vicissitudes of the first decade of the 20th century, marked by the fall in the stock market in 1905, and of the second decade, marked by the World War. See also **Mauve Decade.**

Gaza Strip, the

A 100-square mile-coastal area at the southeastern corner of the Mediterranean, of disputed ownership. It is almost entirely surrounded by Israel, but was administered by Egypt between 1949 and 1967, when it contained over 200,000 Arab refugees. In the Arab-Israeli war of 1967 it was taken over by Israel. In 1978 an Egyptian-Israeli agreement called for a five-year period of self-government to be followed by a decision about its future status, but to date no arrangement for self-government has been established.

Genesis rock

The nickname for one of the rocks, believed to be more than four billion years old, brought back from the Apollo 15 moonlanding (1971).

gentleman in black velvet, the *or* **little gentleman, the**
A nickname for the mole that made the hillock that tripped William III's
horse, thereby causing the king's death (1702), as used in a Jacobite toast.

Geordieland
A nickname for the Northeast of England. *Geordie* (a diminutive of the
name *George*) used to be a local dialect word for a coalminer, and hence
is now applied to the inhabitants of this coalmining region. See also
Northeast.

George Cross Island
Because Malta was a key British naval base in the Mediterranean in
World War II, it became a constant target for German attacks, particularly by air. The people of the island put up such a heroic (and successful)
resistance to these assaults that in 1942, in a most unusual gesture, Malta
itself was awarded the George Cross, a British medal given for great
bravery in battle. The nickname *George Cross Island* which it thereby
gained is no longer much used, but the Maltese flag still carries a representation of the medal.

George V
A first-class hotel in Paris, always called 'the George Sank' by Americans.
There is more luxurious accommodation available in Paris, but the
George V stands out as the mecca of many tourists who can afford it,
especially Americans.

German Coast
A nickname for a part of Louisiana, consisting of St Charles, St John the
Baptist, and St James parishes, so named because the area was originally
settled on both sides of the Mississippi River by Alsatians and Germans
between 1719 and 1722. John Law, the perpetrator of the **Mississippi
Bubble** (*q.v.*), encouraged this settlement as part of his attempt to colo-
nize Louisiana. The original Côte des Allemands, as it was called in the
days of French governance, was 40 miles in length, on both sides of the
river, extending about 20 miles north of New Orleans. The area is still
marked by some distinctive customs and by the persistence of some German surnames, some of which have been Gallicized.

German Ocean, the
A name used formerly for the North Sea, the sea separating the east coast of Britain from the continent of Europe. It is a direct translation of a term used by the ancient Greek geographer Ptolemy.

Ghan, the
A nickname for the train to Alice Springs, Northern Territory, since 1980 a standard-gauge link with Adelaide but historically especially the narrow-gauge track from Marree. The name is a shortened form of *Afghan*, either because immigrants from Northern India used it or because the original railhead was at Oodnadatta, an Afghan settlement.

Ghirardelli Square
An area in San Francisco around the Ghirardelli Chocolate factory. The factory was restored in the early 1960s, and the entire district bcame a model for urban revitalization, with many restaurants, shopping facilities, etc.

Gib
An informal nickname for Gibraltar, a British colony at the southern tip of Spain which guards the entrance to the Mediterranean. It has always been an important naval base, and *Gib* is used particularly in Royal Navy parlance. See also **Rock**.

Gibraltar in the Pacific
A nickname of Hawaii, so called because of the naval base at Pearl Harbor.

Gibraltar of America, the
A nickname of Vicksburg, Mississippi, so called after a fort built by the Spanish on its high banks at the junction of the Mississippi and Yazoo rivers.

Gibraltar of the North
A nickname for the Sveaborg Fortress, in Finland, now named Suomenlinna. Completed in the 1770s, it was bombarded (unsuccessfully) by an Anglo-French fleet in 1855.

Gimbels
Formerly, a large department store in New York City. Its sole branch in the city was at 32nd Street and Sixth Avenue; in the 1960s, a full-scale store was opened at 87th Street and Lexington Avenue to serve the increasing market on the Upper East Side. A store offering trendy merchandise, in former times it was regarded chiefly as a foil for Macy's, with which it waged price wars. Gimbels Basement became proverbial among New Yorkers as a source of bargains. See also **Filene's Basement, Macy's.**

Ginnie Mae
A nickname for the (United States) Government National Mortgage Association (GNMA) and for the mortgage-backed securities issued by that agency. See also **Fannie Mae.**

Ginza, the
A main shopping district in Tokyo, situated in the eastern part of the city, with Harumi Street at its centre.

Giotto's Tower
A campanile in Florence, designed by Giotto early in the 14th century as the bell-tower for the cathedral, or Duomo, designed by Brunelleschi and dating from 1420. Its exterior is surfaced with green and white ceramic tiles.

Glamorous Glennis
The nickname for the Bell X-1, an experimental plane, in which Chuck Yeager became the first person to fly faster than the speed of sound. The event took place on October 14, 1947, in Burbank, California. The plane was named after Yeager's wife.

Glastonbury
A town in Somerset, in southwest England. It has many mystical associations especially with Glastonbury Tor and as the burial place of King Arthur; the Holy Grail is said to be buried there, brought by Joseph of Arimathea.

Glencoe
A valley in the southwestern Highlands of Scotland, just to the south of Fort William, which occupies a very special place in Scots history. At the end of the 17th century the new English king, William III, demanded that

the Scottish clans swear an oath of allegiance, promising that they would no longer support the dethroned James II. It seems the Macdonalds procrastinated, and the king ordered a terrible retribution; on February 13th, 1692, government troops, accompanied by many Campbell clansmen (traditional enemies of the Macdonalds), cold-bloodedly massacred nearly 40 of the Macdonalds in Glencoe, drove the rest of them into the surrounding mountains, where most died from exposure, and burned down their houses. The incident greatly embittered Scotsmen's feelings towards England, and ever since that day Glencoe has been known as the 'Glen of Weeping'. The stark beauty and grandeur of its scenery are undeniable, but many would also claim that an air of melancholy pervades it.

Glens, the
A collective name for the craggy valleys of the Highlands of Scotland. Perhaps the most impressive of them is the Great Glen, also known as Glen More, a great geological rift which slices Scotland in two between Inverness and Fort William; it contains a series of lochs, including Loch Ness, and above it lowers Ben Nevis, the highest mountain in Britain. Among other well-known glens are Glen Eagles, which gave its name to the Gleneagles Hotel and golf course; Glenfiddich, where a celebrated malt whisky is produced; and Glengarry, after which a particular sort of Scottish hat was named. See also **Glencoe**.

Glitter Gulch
A nickname for downtown Las Vegas, Nevada, so called because of the brightly lit, gaudy canyon formed by the high-rise hotels and other buildings.

Gloucester
A town on Cape Ann, on the coast of Massachusetts, formerly a very important fishing village where many of the boats that fished the Grand Banks were berthed. It was on Norman's Woe, a reef off Cape Ann, that the 'Wreck of the Hesperus', of Longfellow's poem, took place. It has won its established place in fiction, notably in Rudyard Kipling's *Captains Courageous*; its history and the men lost at sea making it are commemorated in a bronze statue of a fisherman, at the helm of his boat, bearing the inscription from Ps. 107.23:

They that go down to the sea in ships. . . .

God's acre
A nickname for a churchyard.

God's Own Country
An Australian's name for Australia or a New Zealander's name for New Zealand.

Golconda
Historically, an ancient city in south central India, to the west of Hyderabad, noted for its fabulous wealth, particularly in diamonds. Conquered in 1687 by the Mogul emperor Aurangzeb, the city and its fortress now lie in ruins; but its name lives on as a synonym for a source of limitless riches.

Gold Coast
A three-block-wide strip of luxury homes and high-rise apartment buildings along **Lake Shore Drive** (*q.v.*) in Chicago, bordering Lake Michigan, on the city's North Side. The area features a number of famous mansions dating from the early 1900s, including the Victorian-style manorhouse on North State Parkway that served for a time as the Playboy Mansion and which is now used for classes and as a dormitory by the School of the Art Institute of Chicago; this four-story, 72-room structure, built between 1903 and 1914, has been renamed Hefner Hall, after Playboy editor/publisher Hugh Hefner. See also **Lake Shore Drive.**

Golden Chersonese, the
A name given in former times to the Malay Peninsula. It arose originally from the line in Milton's *Paradise Lost*: 'Thence to Agra and Lahor of great Mogul, down to the golden Chersonese'. *Chersonese* is the ancient Greek word meaning 'peninsula', and in classical times was often applied specifically to the Thracian peninsula, a finger of land to the west of the Hellespont.

Golden Crescent, the
1. An area around the juncture of the borders of Iran, Afghanistan, and Pakistan, which is a major centre for opium production. Its name is based on that of the Golden Triangle, with a sideglance no doubt at the crescent symbol of Islam.

2. An epithet for the coastal area between the **Golden Triangle** (*q.v.*, def. 3) and Brownsville, Texas, so called because of the rapid and profitable development of the petrochemical industry in the area.

Golden Gate City, the

A nickname of San Francisco, California, so called because both the break in the Coast Range Mountains along which it is located and the strait running through it that connects the Pacific Ocean with San Francisco Bay are called the Golden Gate.

Golden Horn, the

The name given in English to the Bosporus, an inlet of the Sea of Marmara, around which Istanbul, Turkey, is situated and which forms its harbour; in Turkish it is known as *Haliç*. Its name probably comes partly from its shape—in former times, *horn* was a word often used for the curve of a bay—but may also refer to the rich harvest of fish it has always yielded, cornucopia-like.

Golden Mile, the

1. A name given to a section of seafront at the holiday resort of Blackpool, in the Northwest of England. There are seven miles of beach there in all, but the Golden Mile itself starts just to the south of Blackpool Tower and bulges with all manner of amusement arcades, seafood stalls, shops, and bingo halls.
2. The name for the gold-bearing reef that forms the basis of the Kalgoorlie goldfield of Western Australia, a series of rich goldmines between Kalgoorlie and Boulder, five kilometres away. A statue of the discoverer, Paddy Hannan, stands near the Town Hall and Kalgoorlie's main street is named after him, but Hannan did not acquire great wealth as a result of his find.

Golden Triangle, the

1. A name given to the triangle of land in Southeast Asia at whose centre the borders of Burma, Thailand, and Laos meet, and which is notorious as a source of much of the world's (illicit) opium. It is estimated that between 500 and 700 tons of it were produced there in 1984, most of it in northern Burma, where it is refined into heroin and smuggled into Thailand for export. Compare **Golden Crescent**.
2. An epithet for the triangular section of downtown Pittsburgh, formed by a cross street at the north and the confluence of the Allegheny and

Monongahela rivers, where many large companies maintain their executive offices and headquarters.
3. An epithet for a triangular area on the Texas coast, with the cities of Beaumont, Port Arthur, and Orange at the apexes. See also **Golden Crescent, 2.**

Golders Green
An area of northwest London, to the northwest of Hampstead. It is noted for its large proportion of well-to-do middle-class Jewish residents.

Golgotha
1. A nickname for Temple Bar, in the Strand, London, before the 1880s. It was so called because the heads of decapitated traitors and other criminals were once exposed there, impaled on the iron fence spikes or on tall pikestaves.
2. A nickname for the dons' gallery in Great St Mary's, at Cambridge University. It was so called because the heads of the colleges meet there.
[*Golgotha* appears in Latin, Greek, Aramaic, and other languages and goes back to Hebrew *gulgōleth* 'skull'].

Gondwanaland
A name given to the supercontinent believed to have existed in the southern hemisphere over 200 million years ago; it later split up into continents that became Africa, South America, Australia, Antarctica, and India. Compare **Laurasia, Pangaea.**

Gong, the
A nickname for Wollongong, New South Wales.

Gooney Bird
The World War II nickname for the United States twin-engined aircraft, the C-47, known commercially as the DC-3, developed in 1935, so called from its awkward appearance.

Gorbals, the
A district in southeast central Glasgow, Scotland, on the south bank of the Clyde River. In former times it was notorious for its great concentration of slums, which housed the workforce for the city's heavy industry and shipbuilding; but in the latter half of the 20th century the depressing tenements have been gradually cleared away.

Gorkii

A city in the USSR, to the east of Moscow, which was originally called
Nizhnii Novgorod. Its name was changed in 1932 in honour of the Soviet
writer Maxim Gorki (1868–1936).

Gotham

A nickname of New York City, so named by Washington Irving in
Salmagundi (1807), in reference to the village in Nottinghamshire, England, whose inhabitants were known for their humour and canniness.

Grand Central

Called 'Grand Central' or 'Grand Central Station' by many, it is properly
Grand Central Terminal, for, unlike Pennsylvania Station, it is the New
York City *terminus* of the trains that serve it. Before the days of Amtrak
and Conrail, it was the main terminal for New York Central trains from
the west and from the northeast, including those of the New York, New
Haven, and Hartford Railroad, which served commuters from southern
Westchester and western Connecticut. It stands at 42nd Street, where it
straddles Park Avenue, which divides and runs around it on an elevated
roadway before returning to street level to continue north from 46th
Street. A radio programme of the 1930s, 'Grand Central Station [*sic*]',
was introduced by an announcer who intoned a description of a train
approaching the Terminal, ending with the following words:

> . . . dives with a roar into the two-and-a-half-mile tunnel
> that burrows beneath the glitter and swank of Park Avenue
> and then— [grandly] Grand Central Station, crossroad of a
> million private lives, giant stage on which are enacted a
> thousand dramas daily. . . .

Grand Central Terminal is a magnificent example of Roman style; its
main concourse, 120 feet wide and 275 feet long, has a ceiling, 60 to 125
feet above the marble floor, that is painted in pale blue with signs of the
zodiac in silvery white. Once a truly grand edifice, it is now dwarfed by
high-rise office buildings, especially the Pan Am Building, which loom
over it from all directions except the south, where the upper part of its
limestone façade and pediment can be viewed from Park Avenue.

Grand Corniche

The main roadway along the Riviera, in the south of France; it winds
along the Mediterranean coast, often affording spectacular views as it

rises and dips among the Maritime Alps. Its extent is approximately from Cannes, on the west, eastward to Monte Carlo and Menton, at the Italian border.

Grand National, the
A steeplechase horse race run every spring at the Aintree racecourse near Liverpool in northwest England. It is famous for the severity of some of the fences the horses have to jump, particularly one called Beecher's Brook, which regularly claims its share of victims. The race is often familiarly known simply as *the National*.

Grand Strand
A sixty-mile-long stretch of beach between Cherry Grove and Pawleys Island, on the barrier beach of South Carolina. At its centre is Myrtle Beach, a popular resort, said to be named for the creeping myrtle (*Vinca minor*) that grows there. There are two amusement parks, the Myrtle Beach and the Grand Strand, as well as holiday homes and other facilities.

Granite City, the
A nickname given to Aberdeen, a city on the northeast coast of Scotland, because of the somewhat austere and spartan aspect of its streets and public buildings, made of the local granite. In the 1970s and '80s, however, it might with more justice be called the 'Dallas of the North', since it is the centre of Scotland's oil industry.

Granta
The name given locally to the part of the River Cam that flows through Cambridge, England. Compare **Isis**.

Grant's Tomb
A huge mausoleum at Riverside Drive and 122nd Street, in New York City, erected in the 1890s to honour Ulysses S. Grant (1822–85), general of the Union Army in the Civil War and 18th president of the United States (1869–77). His wife is buried there with him. It is the butt of a harmless old joke: for many years, the comedian Groucho Marx, on his television quiz program 'You Bet Your Life', in order to avoid allowing a losing contestant to go away empty-handed, would ask 'Now, for fifty dollars, Who is buried in Grant's Tomb?'

Grauman's Chinese Theater
The name of a movie theatre on Hollywood Boulevard in the Hollywood section of Los Angeles. It was named for the theatre entrepreneur Sid(ney) Grauman (1879–1950), who had earlier opened the Million Dollar, Egyptian, and other theatres. Grauman's Chinese Theater opened on May 18, 1927, with Cecil B. de Mille's 'King of Kings'. In its architectural style, the theatre is a flamboyant version of a Chinese temple. It is especially famous for the hand- and footprints of movie stars in the cement pavement in front of the theatre. It was renamed Mann's Chinese Theater in the 1970s to reflect its membership in the Mann chain of theatres.

Gravesend
A port on the south side of the Thames, some twenty miles east of London, the first landfall encountered in approaching the estuary from the sea.

Graveyard of the Atlantic, the
A nickname of Cape Hatteras, North Carolina.

Great Britain
See **Britain.**

Great Dismal
A nickname of the District of Columbia, attributed to Daniel Webster, probably because when he lived there in the early 19th century the district was poorly lit and paved and was muddy, damp, and unhealthy.

Great Wen, the
A derogatory nickname (a *wen* is a wart or tumour) applied to London, especially in the 19th century, with reference to the unsightly and unhealthy growth of the metropolis into the surrounding country. The phrase was popularized particularly by the radical writer William Cobbett.

Great White Way
A nickname of Broadway, in New York City, especially the part that passes through Times Square, so called because of the brilliant illumination afforded by the lights of the theatre marquees and advertising signs.

Greek Street
A street between Soho Square and Old Compton Street, in London,
known mainly for its restaurants. See also **Soho**.

Green Belt
In England, a buffer zone of parkland required to be included in city
planning, especially around London, to avoid the uncontrolled spread of
residential or commercial building.

Greenham Common
A Royal Air Force station near the village of Greenham in Berkshire, to
the west of London, which achieved an unwanted fame in the early 1980s
as a base for the deployment of nuclear cruise missiles and, consequently,
as the scene of extensive anti-nuclear demonstrations—particularly those
undertaken on a permanent basis by an all-female group who became
known in the press as the 'Greenham Women'.

green pound
A nickname for an accounting system set up in 1975 by the European
Economic Community to calculate British farm prices.

green room
The name given to the room backstage at a theatre (now, also, a television
studio) where performers and others gather to await their cues to go
onstage. The origin of the term, for which evidence has been found dating
to the 17th century, is uncertain, one theory holding it to be a corruption
of 'scene room'.

Green Venice
A name sometimes given to the low-lying area of wetlands on the west
coast of France, to the north of la Rochelle; its official designation is the
Marais Poitevin 'the Marshes of Poitou'. As the nickname suggests, the
whole area is crisscrossed with waterways, many of which are turned into
virtual tunnels by the luxuriant vegetation that overgrows them; the main
means of transport there is flat-bottomed boat.

Greenwich Observatory
An astronomical observatory built in 1675 at Greenwich, on the Thames
east of London, to the design by Sir Christopher Wren. In 1884, by
international agreement, O° longitude was established as passing through

it and as the point of reckoning the world time standard, Greenwich Mean Time. Most of the facilities of the observatory have since been transferred (1948–58) to Herstmonceux, a village in Sussex, near Eastbourne.

Greenwich Village

A section of downtown New York City bounded on the east by Washington Square Park and on the north by 12th Street; its other bounds are somewhat vague and changing, but, in general, may be said to be Hudson Street on the west and Houston Street on the south. It is an older part of the city, with many fine private homes—some hundreds of years old—maintained in good condition by their owners. These stand in carefully preserved streets, where the developers who would construct highrise apartment houses on the valuable property are kept at bay. During the 1920s to '40s, Greenwich Village acquired a reputation as a bohemian neighbourhood populated by artists and writers and some students. The rooms and flats were slightly run-down and the rents were cheap. There were many inexpensive restaurants, notably, in the late 1930s and early '40s, Cholmondley's, where a simple meal could be bought for less than a dollar, and nearby The Blue Mill, where a full dinner, with lamb chops, could be purchased for about $1.15. Nightclubs opened there in the later years, among them Nick's, at 10th Street and Seventh Avenue (Sheridan Square), which featured famous jazz musicians, Café Society Downtown, where jazz was also offered, and, especially, The Village Vanguard, which featured young newcomers like The Weavers (with Adolph Green, Betty Comden, and Judy Holliday) as well as Pete Seeger, Leadbelly, and others who popularized folk song singing. This bohemian atmosphere persisted into the 1950s, when increasing property values forced the less wealthy and the artists and writers to seek shelter elsewhere. Most of them moved several blocks to the **East Village** (*q.v.*) and, to distinguish the almost contiguous areas from one another, Greenwich Village, long nicknamed 'the Village', became known by its alternate nickname, 'the West Village'.

Gretna Green

A village at the very southwest tip of Scotland, just across the border from England, which has achieved legendary status as the place to which young couples can elope to get married without their parents' permission. In the old days, all that such couples needed to do was to declare their willingness to marry; the ceremony could then be performed forthwith by any functionary (like the local blacksmith), without the formalities of a licence or banns. In practice, though, things have been tightened up over the years. Since 1856 it has been necessary for either the man or the woman to have lived in Scotland for 21 days before the ceremony, and since 1940 marriage by simple declaration has been illegal; whatever village blacksmiths may remain must content themselves with more mundane activities.

Grimethorpe
A mining village in South Yorkshire. Quite apart from the peculiar appositeness of its name, which could almost have been invented by a novelist wishing to encapsulate the soot-flecked drabness of the northern coalfields, it has come to epitomize, through the playing of the now world-famous Grimethorpe Colliery Band, the great tradition of brass bands that is central to the life of northern England.

Grosvenor Square
A large square in Mayfair, in London, identified mainly with the American Embassy, which occupies its western side. Nearby are the Connaught and Claridge's hotels, two of the best (and most expensive) in London.

Groves of Academe
See **Academy.**

Grub Street
The mythical abode of those writers who eke out a precarious and slender living by churning out articles for newspapers and magazines at so much the yard. Renamed Milton Street in the 1820s, the real Grub Street, in the City of London, was indeed formerly "much inhabited by writers of small histories, dictionaries, and temporary poems" (Dr. Johnson), but they have since moved on. The first reference to it in English literature appears as long ago as the early 17th century, and in 1891 George Gissing wrote a well-known novel, *New Grub Street*, about the grim life of impecunious authors.

Guernica
A town in the Spanish Basque province of Vizcaya, symbol of Basque unity. It was nearly destroyed in 1937 in a bombing raid carried out by the German Kondor Legion in the service of General Francisco Franco during the Spanish Civil War. The attack, apparently an attempt to demoralize

the Basque civilian population loyal to the Republican government, was immortalized by Pablo Picasso in a large mural painting, a nightmarish depiction of the horrors of war. Also, **Guernika.**

Guiana
A large area of northeastern South America, to the north of Brazil. Most of it was colonized by the British, the French, and the Dutch, as an extension of their Caribbean empires, but a large part of it, including the Guiana Highlands, also extends westward into Venezuela. The former British and Dutch possessions are now independent states, known respectively as Guyana and Surinam.

Guinea
A former name for the coastal regions of equatorial West Africa. The south-facing coast, running parallel with the equator between Cape Verde and Cameroon, was known as *Upper Guinea*; the west-facing coast, from Cameroon south to Angola, was *Lower Guinea*. The term survives in several present-day geographical names: Guinea is a republic and former French colony to the west of the Ivory Coast; to the north of it is Guinea-Bissau, formerly Portuguese Guinea; further to the east, below Cameroon, is Equatorial Guinea, formerly Spanish Guinea; and the great bay of the Atlantic Ocean formed by the elbow of West Africa is known as the Gulf of Guinea. The former British guinea, a coin worth 21 shillings, was so called from its having originally been made with gold from Guinea.

Guinea Pig State, the
A nickname of Arkansas, so called because its farmers were willing to try the agricultural experiments suggested by the federal government during the 1930s.

Gulf, the
A gulf is a vast bay, but as a proper name its usage varies around the English-speaking world. In the U. S. it usually means the Gulf of Mexico, from which the **Gulf Stream** (*q.v.*) gets its name; in British English it refers to the Persian Gulf, a large inlet of the sea to the east of the Arabian peninsula; and in Australia, it is the Gulf of Carpentaria, a huge shallow bay in the north of the continent. Accordingly, the term *Gulf States* can refer either to Florida, Alabama, Mississippi, Louisiana, and Texas, the American states that fringe the Gulf of Mexico; or to the oil-

producing countries around the Persian Gulf: Iran, Iraq, Saudi Arabia, Kuwait, Bahrain, Qatar, Oman, and the United Arab Emirates.

Gulf Stream
The name of a major ocean current that forms the northwest edge of a large, clockwise system of currents in the North Atlantic ocean. Benjamin Franklin named it, thinking it began in the Gulf of Mexico, but in fact it originates in the western Caribbean Sea, flows through the Gulf of Mexico and the Florida Straits, northward along the Florida coast to North Carolina, then northeast at Cape Hatteras where it separates, the main part continuing northeastward until it breaks up into eddies east of the Grand Banks off Newfoundland. Its water is 11-18° warmer than the surrounding water, and as a result, the prevailing westerly winds blowing across it provide Norway and the British Isles with much milder winters than any other regions of the same latitude, as evidenced by palm trees growing along the southwest coast of Ireland.

gully winds
The cool nocturnal breezes that descend from the surrounding hills on Adelaide, South Australia, after hot days.

gun that won the west, the
A nickname for the Winchester rifle, one of the first with a magazine, first used in 1856.

H

Hadrian's Wall
A stone wall, seventy-three miles long, between Carlisle in the west and Wallsend, near Newcastle, in the east, built during the reign of the Roman emperor Hadrian (completed in A.D. 136) at the northern reaches of Roman Britain, to keep the Picts from invading. Large sections of the wall and its stone forts form one of the largest Roman remains in Britain today. Also called **Picts' Wall.**

Haight-Ashbury
A district in downtown San Francisco, in the vicinity of Haight and Ashbury streets. During the 1960s, it was famous as an area populated by hippies and "flower people".

Halles, les
Until 1979 the Paris food market was situated at les Halles—a vibrant place to be in during the hours before dawn. In that year it was moved, much as London's Covent Garden had been, to the outskirts of the city. The famous old market buildings were demolished, but the area surrounding it, on the right bank of the Seine to the northeast of the Louvre, is still known as les Halles. It is being radically redeveloped as a centre of entertainment, shopping, and culture, and to the east of the district is the controversial and exhilarating Pompidou Centre (known to Parisians as Beaubourg), an arts complex housed in a building of challenging modernity.

Hambledon
A village in Hampshire, southern England, famous as the birthplace of cricket. In fact, the game probably originated centuries before among the shepherds on the South Downs in Sussex, but it was in Hambledon, in the late 18th century, that the legendary village cricket club was founded that took on and beat the best that the rest of England could offer and set the pattern the game was to follow thereafter. In more recent years Hambledon has again been a trendsetter, for it was here in 1952 that Sir Guy Salisbury-Jones planted the vineyard that began the revival of English winemaking. See also **Lord's**.

Hammacher-Schlemmer
A small department store on East 57th Street, in New York City. It is known largely through its mail-order catalogue, which offers some of the oddest and most luxurious wares including (from a 1986 catalogue) an automatic vinaigrette mixer ($24.95), an 'arboreal' chair ($3750), a lighted electric tie rack ($36.95), a cat's door that can be opened only by an electronic key worn on your cat's collar ($124.95), an automatic infra-red-controlled tap ($299.50), a cordless electric pot scrubber ($59.95), a two-person hovercraft ($7995), and other esoteric items.

Hampstead
A residential area on high ground to the north of central London. Like many other outlying parts of London, it used to be a village, and it manages to retain the atmosphere of a separate community better than most. It is a fashionable and very expensive part of the capital to live in, and perhaps paradoxically has the reputation of being a socialist stronghold. The socialism is generally of a genteel, Fabian variety, however, rather than red-blooded and revolutionary; 'Hampstead intellectual' is a common term of mild abuse applied to those who speculate abstractly on schemes for the betterment of mankind. To the north of the area is Hampstead Heath, one of London's best-known open spaces, which commands fine views over the centre of the city.

Hamptons, the
The collective nickname for several towns along the South Shore at the eastern end of Long Island, New York, namely, Bridgehampton, Westhampton, Southampton, and Easthampton, all popular, though expensive, summer colonies where the residents (and investors) let out their houses for the season or a part of it. Easthampton, the farthest east, is the most expensive and the most chic. There are many fine beaches along the Atlantic Ocean, access to which is accorded to residents only.

Handsworth
An inner-city area on the north side of Birmingham, in the West Midlands of England, which made the headlines in 1985 when community tensions broke out into serious rioting.

Hanging Gardens of Babylon
One of the Seven Wonders of the Ancient World, the virtually prehistoric hanging gardens are thought to have been built on terraces formed by the setbacks of a large ziggurat, or step-pyramid, in the ages-old capital of Babylonia, on the Euphrates River.

Hanging Rock
The name of a volcanic mass in the Mt Macedon area of Victoria, Australia, scene of Joan Lindsay's novel, *Picnic at Hanging Rock,* in which three schoolgirls and a teacher mysteriously disappear. The book was the basis of a successful film of the same name.

Hanging State, the
An unkind nickname for Victoria before it became the last Australian
State to abolish capital punishment in 1975.

Hants.
The abbreviated name of the county of Hampshire in southern England,
often used in speech as well as writing. The county gets its name from the
city of Southampton, which was at first, in Anglo-Saxon times, called
simply *Hamtun*, hence the county's original name of Hamtonshire. By
the time of the Domesday Book (1086), this had been shortened to Hantshire, from which we get the abbreviation. The full version with a *p*
developed later.

Happy Valley
An area in Hong Kong, surrounded by prominent hills, long the site of a
well-known race course. The Chinese name is Wong Nei Chong Valley.
The name Happy Valley is said to have been borrowed from Samuel
Johnson's novel, *Rasselas* (1759), in which the 'Province of Abissinia [*sic*]
was confined in the Happy Valley, a paradise surrounded by high mountains'. It is a wealthy residential section with many luxury flats in modern,
high-rise buildings.

Hapsburg lip
The nickname given to the prominent jaw and protrusive lower lip that
first appeared with Frederick III, and was later produced ever more
markedly through intermarriage, especially among the last Hapsburg
kings of Spain. It is supposed to have been inherited from his mother, the
Mazovian princess, Cymbarka.

Harlem
Harlem, traditionally the area in New York City where blacks live, has
shifted both geographically and ethnically. Till 50 years ago, its northern
reaches did not breach the barrier of 145th Street; today, it sprawls as far
north as it can, though chiefly east of Broadway (or, between 116th and
122nd streets, east of Morningside Park). Its southern boundary has long
been at 110th Street, the north side of Central Park west of Fifth Avenue;
east of Fifth Avenue, with the exception of a few enclaves (as at Mt Sinai
Hospital), it extends southwards to 96th Street, which is where the railway tracks emerge from beneath the 'glitter and swank' of Park Avenue.
Below that demarcation point, Park Avenue is the boulevard that gave

Park Avenue its meaning; above 96th Street, Park Avenue (and points east of Fifth, generally) could be characterized chiefly as slums, notwithstanding the new high-rise blocks of flats built there in recent years. During the 19th century, the main north-south boulevards of Harlem, like Lenox Avenue, were occupied by imposing residences, the side streets by neat **brownstones** (*q.v.*). Since the turn of the century, however, the entire area has been in decline, though, during the 1920s and '30s a few hardy (well-protected) souls frequently ventured north into the area to visit nightclubs where black musicians improvised jazz in jam sessions—the visitors called it 'slumming.' The high street of Harlem is 125th Street, a wide east-west thoroughfare that runs to the Hudson River in the west and the Harlem River in the east—actually, into the access roads for the Triboro Bridge, which links the boroughs of Manhattan, The Bronx, and Queens. With the exception of a few high-rise, low-rent apartment blocks, the buildings consist mostly of four-storey terraced houses, once individually owned, now broken up into tiny flats and bed-sitters where, it is said, the beds are occupied on a schedule that does not allow them to cool down. In the 1930s, Congressman Vito Marcantonio encouraged Puerto Ricans to move to New York, thus creating **Spanish Harlem** (*q.v.*); since then, various areas within black Harlem have been encroached on by the Hispanic immigrés. Generally, Harlem is regarded by the rest of New Yorkers as an area to avoid, partly because of its high crime rate, partly because whites are made to feel unwelcome there. Like the old **Limehouse** (*q.v.*) district of London and the former **Five Points** (*q.v.*) area of New York City, Harlem is a dangerous place, for residents no less than for visitors.

Harlem River

The narrow, yet navigable river that separates Manhattan Island from The Bronx, New York, between **Hell Gate** (*q.v.*) and Spuyten Duyvil Creek. See also **East River.**

Harley Street

A street in the West End of London, to the south of Regent's Park, largely the abode of distinguished, or at least expensive, medical consultants, specialists, and psychoanalysts whose fees are not covered by the National Health. Anyone who insists on a Harley Street physician or surgeon is likely to be a person who does not worry about the amount charged.

Harringay
A district in north London, the boundaries of which are somewhat unclear. The area just to the north of Finsbury Park is called *Harringay*; its station is called Harringay, and it contains Harringay Stadium, a well-known greyhound racetrack. However, in 1963 a new London borough was created around it, called Haringey, which contains a much larger area than the original Harringay. The new version is a reintroduction of an old spelling, but it has proved hard to remember which name refers to the district and which to the borough.

Harrods
A large department store, in Knightsbridge, London, a renowned mecca for shoppers where, it is claimed, virtually anything in the world can be purchased or ordered, from camels to luxury automobiles.

Harrow
An internationally famous school for boys, founded (1571) at Harrow-on-the-Hill, a suburb west of London. See also **Eton.**

Harry Percy of the Union, the
A nickname of South Carolina, so called to recall the determination of its citizens, in comparison with that of a fiery English soldier who died in a rebellion against Henry IV in the Battle of Shrewsbury (1403).

Harry's American Bar
A bar and restaurant in Paris, frequented for generations by Americans (as well as others) who regard it as a safe haven—a sort of home away from home, especially if they are visiting France for the first time, and where they can be assured of getting the 'perfect' martini. For years its advertisements in the *International Herald Tribune* have advised readers to 'Just ask the taxi driver to take you to Sank Roo Doe Noo' ('5 rue Daunou').

Harvard Yard
The centre of the original Harvard College, in Cambridge, Massachusetts (near Boston). This historic, grassy, tree-shaded area is surrounded by libraries, dormitories, and classroom buildings in a variety of architectural styles; George Washington's troops were housed in Massachusetts Hall during the War of Independence, and the provincial council met in Harvard Hall. The twelve residential houses for students are modelled

after those at Oxford and Cambridge, each with its own dining room, athletic facilities, and library.

Hastings
A town and seaside resort on the coast of Sussex, in southeastern England. It is celebrated as the site of the Battle of Hastings, fought in 1066, when the Norman invaders defeated the Anglo-Saxons; but in fact the battle did not take place at Hastings at all: it was fought 6¾ miles inland, at a place where the village of Battle now stands. Purists often refer to it as the Battle of Senlac, since its actual site was near a stream called Senlac (which means, literally, 'sandy brook').

Hatton Garden
A street in central London that goes from Clerkenwell Road to Holborn Circus, just to the north of Fleet Street. It is lined with jewellers' shops, and has long been celebrated as the centre of the London diamond market. Until the mid 17th century the site had been the garden of Ely Place, London residence of the bishops of Ely, which was famous for its roses and fruit.

Hawkeye State, the
The official nickname of Iowa, so called either after a feared Indian chief of that name or after J. G. Edwards, nicknamed 'Old Hawkeye', editor of the Burlington *Patriot,* later named the *Hawkeye and Patriot.*

Hay, Hell, and Booligal
A trio of hot places in Banjo Paterson's poem, 'Hay and Hell and Booligal'. Hay and Booligal are towns in New South Wales. The expression echoes a traditional English trio *Hull, Hell, and Halifax,* from which vagabonds prayed to be spared, since both Halifax and Hull had severe laws directed against thieves. In neither expression is *Hell* the town in Norway on the railway between Trondheim and Storlien.

Haymarket, the
1. An old food market area north of Faneuil Hall, in Boston.
2. A broad, short thoroughfare in London, leading from Piccadilly Circus to Pall Mall.

Haymarket Square
The site, on the Near West Side of Chicago, of the May 4, 1886, Haymarket Riot, an incident in which seven policemen and four others were killed and about 70 persons injured by a bomb thrown when police sought to disperse a gathering of some 1500 labour protesters and sympathizers said to have been spurred by a small group of anarchists. Public sentiment, fanned by the establishment press, ran high against the anarchists, despite the sizable amount of support they enjoyed among workers. In what is now considerd to have been a gross miscarriage of justice, eight anarchists were convicted; of these, four were hanged and one, facing a like fate, committed suicide. In 1893, Illinois Governor John Peter Altgeld pardoned the surviving three anarchists on the ground that their trial had been unjust, a decision that hurt his political career. The actual bomb-thrower, who has never been conclusively identified, escaped.

Heart of Midlothian, the
The nickname of the old Edinburgh Tolbooth, or prison, demolishd in 1817. Its fame rests on the novel of the same name, by Sir Walter Scott, in which much of the action is centred on the prison. Midlothian is a former county of Scotland, in which Edinburgh was situated; in 1975 it became merged into the new Lothian region.

Heathrow
The main airport serving London, which is about 15 miles to the northeast. One of the busiest in the world, Heathrow Airport is in a continuous state of construction and expansion. See also **Gatwick.**

Hell Gate
A strait between Eastchester Bay, leading into the Long Island Sound to the east, and the East and Harlem rivers in New York City, bordered by the boroughs of Queens on the south and The Bronx on the north. Owing to the strong currents and tides, it is a turbulent, dangerous body of water, which is probably why it was so named. A huge fixed railway bridge rises high above its waters, the western reaches of which are traversed by one branch of the Triboro Bridge between Randall's Island and Queens; over its eastern end are the Bronx Whitestone and Throggs Neck bridges, linking The Bronx with Long Island. See also **East River, Harlem River.**

Hell's Kitchen

Formerly, the nickname given to the area, on the West Side of New York City, bounded by 42nd and 57th streets on the south and north and Eighth and Tenth avenues on the east and west. An elevated railway ran along Tenth Avenue till about 1940, making the street dark and dingy below. This, together with the generally run-down, slum-like nature of the neighbourhood, created an atmosphere where crime was rampant, giving rise to the epithet. The reputation of the area was such that, in 1936, Richard Rodgers wrote the music for a ballet which he named *Slaughter on Tenth Avenue*.

Hell Upon Earth

A description by its inmates of the Confederate prison at Andersonville, Georgia, during the American Civil War. A complete lack of shelter and sanitary facilities, a dearth of food and clothing, and the filth of the 16-acre enclosure into which as many as 30,000 prisoners were crowded caused the death of more than 12,000 men. Similar conditions existed in various Union prisons.

Helvetia

The Latin name for Switzerland, originally a Roman province in central Europe in the area of present-day southern Germany and northern and western Switzerland, in ancient times inhabited by the Celtic Helvetii tribe. *Helvetia* is still used on Swiss stamps, avoiding the need to choose among the French, German, Italian, and Romansh versions of the country's name.

Henley

A town in Oxfordshire, on the River Thames—its full name is Henley-on-Thames. It is synonymous with rowing, for every July the famous Henley Royal Regatta is held here, in which the best crews in Britain and many from around the world compete. The event began in 1839, and as the 19th century wore on attendance became a mandatory part of the fashionable London society season. It retains a powerful aura of Edwardian high summer, with parasoled girls in frilly dresses and young men sporting straw boaters and colourful blazers.

Hennessy Road
The main thoroughfare between the central district eastward to North Point, in Hong Kong. It is an important street in the downtown business area and, at 100 feet in width, is one of the widest in the city.

Herald Square
Today, Herald Square is an unprepossessing area formed by the angular crossing of Broadway and Sixth Avenue, at 34th Street, in New York City. If it is known for anything, it is that Macy's occupies the western side of it, from 34th to 35th streets. Around the turn of the century, however, before the central commercial focus of the city had moved on up towards Times Square, ten blocks to the north, Herald Square was still a part of the Great White Way, as Broadway is known. That fame is preserved in George M. Cohan's song (1904), 'Give My Regards to Broadway', which begins:

> Give my regards to Broadway,
> Remember me to Herald Square.
> Tell all the boys on Forty-Second Street
> That I will soon be there.

Herring Pond, the
A somewhat dated, humorous nickname for the North Atlantic Ocean, often abbreviated to simply *the Pond*. It is first recorded in the late 17th century.

Hibernia
A name given by the Romans to Ireland. It derives ultimately from the same Gaelic source that yielded Erin, the poetic name for Ireland.

High, the
To all habitués of Oxford, the High Street is familiarly known as *the High*. Among the colleges here are Magdalen, Queen's, Brasenose, St Edmund Hall, and University College. See also **Broad**.

Highgate
An area in north London, just to the northeast of Hampstead, and like Hampstead on the top of a hill. In character, too, it somewhat resembles Hampstead: it is a high-class and trendy residential area, the resort perhaps of those whose pockets do not quite stretch to the west side of

Hampstead Heath. It is famous as the spot where in the 14th-century Dick Whittington thought better of his decision to leave London, and for its cemetery, which houses several luminaries, including Karl Marx.

Highlands, the
A mountainous region in the north of Scotland. Its southern limit is not universally agreed upon. Some see it as starting to the north of the central Lowlands, and thus including the Grampian mountains. In this context, the town of Stirling, to the northeast of Edinburgh, is often known as 'the gateway to the Highlands'. Alternatively, some would exclude the Grampians, and say that the Highlands start just to the south of the long valley that includes Loch Ness. This view is probably influenced by the fact that the official Highland region more or less corresponds with this area; it was formed in 1975 from the former counties of Caithness, Sutherland, Nairnshire, and most of Inverness-shire and Ross and Cromarty. This is a remote and spartan land, where scattered crofters eke out a bare living; but it is also famous for the dramatic scenic beauty of its heather-covered hillsides. It remains a bastion of the Scots Gaelic language and culture. Its chief town is Inverness, at the northern end of Loch Ness. See also **Capital of the Highlands.**

Highveld, the
A high flat treeless plateau in the Transvaal, in northeastern South Africa. It is sometimes also known as the *Northern Karoo* (see under **Karoo**).

Hill, the
1. A nickname for Capitol Hill, a small hill in Washington, D. C., on which stands the Capitol Building in which the Congress holds its sessions. Capitol Hill is used metaphorically to refer to the Congress. See also **Capitoline.**
2. The name given to the uncovered area in front of the scoreboard at Sydney (Australia) Cricket Ground and to its patrons, the Hillites, sometimes described as noisy.

Hilton Head Island
A major resort area in South Carolina, the largest sea island between New Jersey and Florida, situated about thirty miles north of Savannah, Georgia.

Hindustan

A name ultimately derived from *Hind*, the Persian word for India, but for obvious reasons so closely linked with the Hindu religion and the Hindi language that in modern usage it is usually applied to those parts of the Indian subcontinent inhabited by Hindus, in contrast to Muslims, and those parts in which Hindi is the main language. In practice, this means the portion to the north of the Deccan, and more particularly the area around the Ganges.

Hog Butcher for the World

A nickname of Chicago, bestowed by Carl Sandburg in his poem, 'Chicago'.

Hokonui

The name of a district in the South Island of New Zealand; it has become a nickname for illicitly distilled whisky, that is, *moonshine*.

Holland

1. A name commonly applied to the Netherlands. Historically it referred to a county of the Holy Roman Empire, which constitutes only a part of the modern Netherlands; now divided into the provinces of North and South Holland, it contains Rotterdam, Amsterdam, and the Hague.
2. In former times, an adminstrative area of Lincolnshire, in eastern England. It was in the southeastern part of the county, based at Boston. Its title in full was the Parts of Holland. Its name is now incorporated into that of a local parliamentary constituency. Compare **Kesteven, Lindsey**.

Hollywood

A section of Los Angeles located between Beverly Hills and downtown Los Angeles. Laid out and named in 1886 by Horace Wilcox, it was incorporated in 1903 and then was annexed by Los Angeles in 1910. The movie business began around 1910, and within a decade the name Hollywood became almost synonymous with American cinema. Since the advent of television, the movie studios have moved elsewhere, and today few actors actually live in Hollywood: but the name still retains its earlier connotations. 'Hollywood' and related forms such as 'hollywoodish' are universally used to describe individuals or places that are showy, glamorous, or flamboyant (or sometimes cheap and tawdry). Its glitter and brashness have earned Hollywood (and, by extension, all of Los Angeles)

the name of 'Tinseltown', said to have originated in a derisive remark
made by Oscar Levant in the 1940s.

Hollywood and Vine
A reference to the intersection of Hollywood Boulevard and Vine Street
in the Hollywood district of Los Angeles. Although it has been called
'The Times Square of the West' (a name also applied to Hollywood
Boulevard), it is only an intersection of normal size and has no unusual
characteristics. There are no significant historical or literary associations,
and the adjacent buildings have never been particularly noteworthy.
Somehow the intersection of Hollywood and Vine acquired the reputation
of being a place where one could see film stars or perhaps a place where
celebrities would congregate. It all might have started with a joking
reference on a radio comedy show and then been perpetuated despite its
falsity. Any sightseers attracted to Hollywood and Vine by this rumour
could only be disappointed.

Holy Land, the
1. A name given to the ancient territory of Palestine or sometimes more
specifically to Judea. It is first recorded, in its Latin form, *terra sancta*, in
the 11th century, and refers to Jesus's birth, life, and death there. It was
further reinforced during the Crusades by the presence of the Holy Sepulchre in Jerusalem.
2. In the 19th century, the parish of St Giles, London, just to the east of
Soho, was familiarly known as the Holy Land, from the large number of
Irish (Roman Catholic) people who lived there.

Holy Mother of the Russians
An epithet for Moscow, chiefly in the 19th century.

Holy Name Cathedral
The Near North Side seat of the Roman Catholic archdiocese of Chicago,
and centre of one of the largest of the city's 449 Catholic parishes. The
cathedral occupies ground given to the Catholic Church by William B.
Ogden and Walter L. Newberry, owners of a large amount of North Side
property and advocates of a city-built bridge over the Chicago River at
Clark Street to provide easier access to their land from the Loop. It is said
that in return for the valuable block along State Street on which Holy
Name stands today, bridge proponents were delivered the sizable Catholic
vote. Constructed in 1874–75, in place of a church that was burned down

in the Great Chicago Fire of 1871, the cathedral has been renovated several times, most recently in 1968–69. Ironically, Holy Name has served as a setting or backdrop for at least two bloody Prohibition-era incidents. Across the street, on November 9, 1924, gangster and flower fancier Dion O'Banion was gunned down—in the flower shop he co-owned—by members of the South Side Al Capone/Johnny Torrio gang. Two years later, the cathedral itself was riddled with machine-gun bullets when O'Banion's successor, Hymie Weiss, and his chauffeur were cut down on the cathedral steps by Capone henchmen.

Home Counties, the

A collective name for counties surrounding and bordering on London; it is not, though, an exact term, and not everyone would agree on which ones are included. By common consent, Surrey is one—indeed, it is perhaps the quintessential home county—and all authorities agree that Essex and Kent can bear the name, as could Middlesex when it existed. Most people would also include the counties to the north and west of London, Hertfordshire, Buckinghamshire, and Berkshire. The Home Counties have a rather unexciting public image; they are inhabited on the whole by 'nice', comfortable, and conformist middle-class people, many of whom commute to London to work, and the area as a whole is more safely buffered against economic stringency than much of the rest of Britain. Compare **Southeast**.

Home of the Cheeseburger, the

A nickname of Denver, Colorado, so called because this sandwich was invented there during the 1930s.

Honkers

A nickname for the British colony of Hong Kong, used especially by British people who live and work there or elsewhere in the Far East.

Hoosier State, the

The official nickname of Indiana, so called either in reference to *hoozer* 'hill dweller' or 'highlander', or to the settlers, who were said to be so inquisitive that they pulled the latchstring of any new house they passed and yelled "Who's here?"

Hornet's Nest, the
A nickname of Charlotte, North Carolina, so called because it was the
centre of opposition to the Union forces during the American Civil War.

Horn of Africa, the
The name given to the vast pointed peninsula of land at the northeastern
extremity of Africa, which projects to the south of Arabia. It contains
Somalia and the southeastern part of Ethiopia.

Horse Latitudes, the
A name given to two belts around the oceans of the world at about 30°
north and south of the equator, characterized by light variable winds and
long periods of flat calm. In the days of sail they were best avoided if one
wished to make a speedy voyage. It is thought that their name may come
from the high death rate of horses carried as cargo in ships that became
becalmed there, but many even more bizarre explanations have been
offered. See also **Doldrums**.

House, the
A name applied familiarly to several institutions, particularly as a short-
ened form. Legislative bodies are often so designated; in the U. S., the
House of Representatives, and in Britain the House of Lords or, more
typically, the House of Commons. If any grave political matter arises in
England, it is sure that 'questions will be asked in the House'. In addi-
tion, the London Stock Exchange is informally called the House, as is
Christ Church, a college of Oxford University.

House of Burgesses
The first representative legislature in America, formed in 1619, in James-
town, Virginia, the first meeting of which was called by Governor George
Yeardley. The House of Burgesses met with the governor and his council
and this combined lawmaking body was called the General Assembly of
Virginia.

House That Ruth Built
A nickname for the Yankee Stadium, a sports arena in the west Bronx, in
New York City. The home of the New York Yankees baseball team, it
was built during the 1930s when Babe Ruth, the Yankee pitcher whose
record for home runs stood for almost forty years, played there and

proved a significant enough attraction to ensure the financial success of the team.

Hub of New York City

Columbus Circle at 59th Street where Broadway and Eighth Avenue intersect is so called because distance on all roads is measured from here. See also **Broadway**.

Hudson River

A river that flows from Lake George, in the Adirondack Mountains, 300 miles south to empty into New York Bay. It was once a great fishery resource, especially for sturgeon and, in the spring, shad; but pollution has destroyed most of the widlife larger than a microbe. It flows along the west side of Manhattan Island, which, a century ago, offered bathing clubs along its shores. At the Tappan Zee, it widens to more than a mile (in the area of the town of Harmon and Bear Mountain State Park), while further south, as it approaches New York City, its western banks rise hundreds of feet in a row of picturesque cliffs, about forty miles in length, called **the Palisades** (*q.v.*).

Hull House

A part of the famous social settlement in Chicago established in 1889 by Jane Addams and Ellen Gates Starr; they, with other reformers, helped pioneer such welfare laws as workmen's compensation and insurance, an eight-hour work law for women, and tenement-house regulations. The spiritual birthplace of the profession of social work, Hull House performed many services for the multi-ethnic Near, or Lower, West Side neighbourhood in which it stood, while emerging as a national focal point and symbol for most of the liberal causes of the day—particularly women's suffrage and pacifism. The two remaining buildings of the original Hull House complex have been restored and are now national landmarks, while remnants of the old 'settlement style' neighbourhood stretch west along Taylor Street.

Huntingdonshire

A former county in the east Midlands of England. In the local government reorganization of 1974 it became part of Cambridgeshire.

Hyde Park Corner

Being almost rectangular, London's Hyde Park has four corners, but it is only the southeastern corner (where the park's main entrance is situated) that has appropriated the name. It is at the confluence of several major roads, including Knightsbridge, Piccadilly, Park Lane, and Constitution Hill, and the junction, officially called Wellington Place, is the busiest traffic centre in London; it has been calculated that well over a hundred vehicles pass there every minute. See also **Speakers' Corner.**

I

Iberia

The name given by the Romans to the southwestern European peninsula now occupied by Spain and Portugal; it derives from *Iberus*, the ancient name for the River Ebro. It remains in fairly common use in the phrase 'Iberian peninsula', a handy means of coupling its two modern states. Confusingly, Iberia was also in former times a region in southwestern Asia, to the south of the Caucasus, which corresponded to modern Georgia in the Soviet Union. See also **Peninsula.**

Icebox of the United States, the

A nickname of International Falls, Minnesota, so called because it is almost always the coldest city in the U.S.

Ice House Street

From the early 19th-century, trading vessels from America that carried Oregon pine to Hong Kong used ice as ballast; when unloaded, it was stored in specially built godowns near the waterfront, hence the name of this street, which is today at the centre of a busy commercial area.

'In' and 'Out', the

The nickname of the Naval and Military Club, in Piccadilly, London, so called after the signs on the columns that flank the driveway before its entrance.

Indian-Appian Way

The nickname of the Maumee and Wabash rivers (in Indiana, USA), so called because the Indians and fur traders made as extensive use of it as people in the Roman Empire made of the Appian Way, which ran from Rome to Capua.

Indian summer

A name for a period of warmer than usual weather in late autumn, usually mid November.

Indies, the

An archaic term that referred to much of the southern and southeastern parts of the Asian continent, including not only India but also Indo-China and the East Indies. The area's fabled wealth was a magnet for 15th- and 16th-century voyagers, but attempts to find a westward route to it got no further than the islands of the Caribbean. Their discoverers were under the misapprehension that they had arrived at their goal, hence the name for the islands that survives to this day: the West Indies.

Indochina

A somewhat ambiguous term, it standardly refers to the mainland of Southeast Asia, a peninsula at the southeast corner of Asia, sandwiched between India and China, that contains Burma, Thailand, Cambodia, Laos, Vietnam, Malaya, and Singapore. However, it also happens to be the collective name the French gave to their colonial possessions in this area: Annam, Cochin China, and Tonkin (now joined together to form Vietnam), as well as Cambodia and Laos. Because of the potential confusion between *Indochina* and *Southeast Asia*—and also perhaps because of the unwelcome taint of colonialism—the term is not heard as much today as formerly. See also **Southeast Asia**.

Inland Empire, the

A roughly rectangular region of plains, centred on Spokane, Washington, in the Pacific Northwest of the United States, bounded on the west by the Cascade Mountains, on the south by the Blue Mountains, on the east by the Rocky Mountains, and on the north by the Selkirk range. About 200 square miles across, irrigated by the Columbia River, it is an economic region, originally established in the 1880s as an agricultural area where wheat and peas were grown; subsequent development of its mineral and timber resources led to its becoming a rail centre. Physically in Washington, Oregon, Idaho, Montana, and Canada (British Columbia), it flourished well into the 20th century. It received its name from a Congregational missionary, George Henry Atkinson, who, in 1848, analysed its soil and foresaw its great potentials.

Inner Mongolia
Although it may sound like an informal epithet or a nickname, Inner Mongolia is the shortened form of the officially named Inner Mongolian Autonomous Region, under the control of China. See also **Outer Mongolia.**

Inns of Court and Chancery
The Inns of Court at London are Gray's Inn, Lincoln's Inn, the Inner Temple, and the Middle Temple. The first two became established in the 13th century literally as inns where students of law resided with their masters and read law; they are named for the men who operated them. The latter two were established later, in the early part of the 15th century, and are named for the seat of the Knights Templars, suppressed in 1312, whose premises they later occupied. All were rented from their owners and bore their names. As it later developed, it was unnecessary for all those engaged in legal work—as in the drawing of wills, the transfer of land, and so forth—to be educated in the refinements of law required of those who practised in the courts, and the inns of chancery, severally attached to the inns of court, emerged. In the 16th century, the division was formalized, resulting in the present division between barristers and solicitors, belonging to inns of court and chancery, respectively. In the early 19th century, the system finally broke down after 200 years of decay and was reestablished in 1854 by order of the common law commissioners, with all four inns functioning as a unified educational body. In Ireland, a body, the King's inns, similar to that of the original inns at London, was instituted, but the separation into barristers and solicitors was not brought about there till 1866. In Scotland, the Faculty of Advocates at Edinburgh functions in a like manner. In the 1980s, there is some move afoot to eliminate the distinction between barristers and solicitors, but the outcome is unlikely to be resolved for some years.

Irish Channel
A neighbourhood of New Orleans, Louisiana, bounded by St Joseph and Constance streets, Louisiana Avenue, and the Mississippi river, that had a

reputation for rowdy and disorderly behaviour, street gangs, and crime, especially in the last quarter of the nineteenth century. Named for the large number of Irish immigrants who settled there beginning in the 1840s, it is still popular with those of Irish extraction.

Irish Free State, the
From 1921 to 1937, the name of the country now known as the Republic of Ireland.

Iron City
A nickname of Pittsburgh, Pennsylvania.

Iron Curtain, the
A name given to the boundary between the communist countries of Eastern Europe and the capitalist countries of the West. It refers in part to the closely guarded physical frontier, which runs along the western edge of East Germany, Czechoslovakia, Hungary, and Yugoslavia; but to a greater extent it suggests the ideological and cultural barrier that impedes the free flow of ideas and people between the two sides and symbolizes the hostility with which the two camps regard each other. States to the east of the dividing line are known as 'Iron Curtain countries'. The name was popularized by Winston Churchill in his speech at Westminster College, Fulton, Missouri, in March 1946, but he was by no means the first to use it. As a general term for a sinister and impenetrable barrier it has been traced back to the Earl of Munster's journal of 1817, and it is first applied to the Soviet Union and its influence in Ethel Snowden's book *Through Bolshevik Russia* (1920). There are several references to it in 1945–46, and Churchill himself used it before his Fulton Address, in a cable to President Truman in June 1945. Compare **Bamboo Curtain**.

Iron Men of May
In New England folklore, the three days around the last full moon in May, traditionally the last potential frost dates, when plants can be set out without likelihood of their freezing.

Isis
In Oxford and further upstream towards its source, the River Thames is known as the *Isis*. The name is a corruption of *Tamesis*, the Latin for 'Thames'.

Island, the

1. A nickname for the Isle of Wight, a largish island in the Channel south of Portsmouth and Southampton, popular among Britons as a holiday site. Its associations are largely Victorian, for Queen Victoria and Prince Albert often sojourned there. It is known to yachtsmen for **Cowes Week** (*q.v.*), a strenuous programme of day-sailing races, and for the Round-the-Isle yacht race, usually an all-day affair but in 1986 won by a trimaran in about four hours. Its main physical feature is **the Needles** (*q.v.*). three tall natural chalk obelisks at the western side of the Island, an easily identified landmark from the sea.

2. A nickname, for New Yorkers and others who are in the region, for Long Island, a hundred-mile-long island east of New York City. South Shore is along the Atlantic Ocean; North Shore forms the southern boundary of the Long Island Sound, with Connecticut on the shore opposite. On its western end are the boroughs of Queens, to the north, and Brooklyn, to the south, both of which are part of New York City. The nickname really refers only to Nassau County, east of New York City, and, east of Nassau, to Suffolk County, which splits, east of Riverhead, around Peconic and Gardiner bays, into the North Fork, which ends at Orient Point, and the South Fork, which ends at Montauk Point. Both of these counties are part of New York State. With the improvement of commuter transportation over the years and the increase in local business and industry, the Island has become a year-round residential region. But its eastern reaches, particularly along the South Shore, were and still are summer resort areas. See also **Fire Island, Hamptons, North Shore, South Shore.**

Isle of Athelney, the

A low hill to the northeast of Taunton, Somerset in the Southwest of England. Its classification as an isle comes from the fact that until comparatively recently the region around it was wetland and marsh, and the hill was the only piece of solid ground for some distance. It owes its fame to King Alfred's taking refuge there from Viking attack in 878.

Isle of Dogs, the

Not an island at all, but a sort of peninsula formed by a loop of the Thames in the East End of London, opposite Greenwich. It is at the heart of London's Dockland, and contains the East and West India Docks and the Millwall Docks. These were finally closed to commercial traffic in 1980, and the area was subsequently developed for light industry and as a centre for leisure activities. Its curious name has never been satisfactorily explained, but it probably derived either from a royal kennels in the area in former times or from the fact that dead dogs floating down the Thames used to be washed up on its left bank.

Isle of Ely, the
An enclave of the county of Cambridgeshire in eastern England, in the heart of the Fens. In former times it was a county in its own right, but in 1965 it was merged into Cambridgeshire. Its identity survives as the name for the local parliamentary constituency. Before modern techniques of drainage transformed the landscape, the area around the city of Ely was very much an island surrounded by watery wastes, and the great gothic cathedral still dominates the Fenland skyline.

Isle of Thanet, the
An area at the northeastern corner of Kent, in southeastern England, which contains the seaside vacation resorts of Margate, Ramsgate, and Broadstairs. It is no longer an island at all, but in former times it was completely separated from the mainland by the rivers Stour and Want-sum. Tradition has it that Thanet is where the Saxons first landed in England.

Islington
A residential district in northeast London, to the north of King's Cross. Within living memory it was a rather seedy working-class area, but as West End rents rose, its 18th- and early 19th-century squares and terraces began to seem more desirable to London's up-and-coming young bourgeois, and in the 1970s it became perhaps the archetypal gentrified inner-city suburb.

Italian Riviera, the
The northwest coast of Italy, from the French border to La Spezia. Chief among its holiday resorts is San Remo. See also **French Riviera**.

J

Jack Dempsey's

A former restaurant on Broadway, at the northern end of Times Square, in New York City. Owned and operated by 'Jack' (William Harrison) Dempsey, world heavyweight boxing champion from 1919 to 1926, it was for many years a popular meeting-place for sports figures, celebrities, and various Broadway types.

Jackson Road

The title of a daily political cartoon in the *South China Morning Post*. The author is anonymous, but the copyright is shown in the name of Hung Mo Gwai, which means 'red-haired devil' to the locals.

Jackson's of Piccadilly

A speciality shop, formerly in Piccadilly, London, near Fortnum & Mason. Long a traditional place to shop for exotic foods, condiments, soaps, perfumes, and colognes, Jackson's gave up its retail business in the early 1980s when it failed to come to terms on a new lease with the owners of its building, leaving its former clientele with little more than an occasional pang of nostalgia.

Jacob's Pillow

A summer school of dance founded by modern dance pioneer Ted Shawn in the mid 1930s, situated in the Berkshire mountains of western Massachusetts, and named after a rock formation that suggested the biblical story. Reflecting the eclectic tastes of its founder, the summer school continues to offer instruction in ethnic dance, modern dance, and ballet and a wide variety of concert dance performances to the public.

Jamdung

A Jamaican nickname for the island of Jamaica. *Dung* represents the local pronunciation of *down*, and the word combines Jamaica with the notion of ordinary Jamaicans being oppressed, or 'jammed down', by their political masters.

Japan
The name used in English (and, with variations, in other European languages) for the country known by its inhabitants as Nippon. The immediate source of the word is Malay *Japung*, which in turn comes from Chinese *Jih-pun* 'sunrise, orient'. This seems to be a direct translation of Japanese *Ni-pon*: *ni* 'sun' and *pon* 'origin'. *Nihon* is an alternative version, with the same meaning. See also **Land of the Rising Sun.**

Jardine Matheson
The leading *hong* of China, known as 'the Princely Hong', which owns some forty percent of the land of Hong Kong, including many prime sites in the Central District. Jardine's is almost entirely Scottish in its 'taipanry', and its head traditionally moves on to the chairmanship of Matheson's in London, thence to that of the Royal Bank of Scotland.

Jarrow
A town on the south bank of the River Tyne, in the Northeast of England; in the latter part of the 20th century it forms virtually a suburb of Newcastle-upon-Tyne. Its name is intimately linked with the famous Jarrow march of the early 1930s; the Great Depression had caused crippling unemployment in the town's shipyards, and many of the workers marched en masse to London to bring their plight to the attention of Parliament. To the present day, Jarrow is synonymous with such so-called 'hunger marches'.

Jeep
A nickname for a small, usually open, four-wheel drive vehicle, capable of carrying five people. It was so named by soldiers in World War II as a shortened form of GP (for 'General Purpose') vehicle.

Jericho
A district in the northwest corner of Oxford, through the middle of which runs Jericho Street. Very much on the other side of the tracks from the gothic and classical splendour of academic Oxford, it is a jumble of small residential streets clustering round the large premises of Oxford University Press.

Jermyn Street
A street in St James's, in the West End of London, linking St James's Street with Regent Street. It is famous for its small but fashionable shops

where many of the accoutrements of gentlemanly living may be purchased, notably shirts: Jermyn Street is synonymous with fine shirtmaking.

Jewel of the Adriatic, the
A nickname of Venice, Italy.

Joburg
An abbreviated name often used for Johannesburg, South Africa's largest city. It is in the northeast, in the Transvaal, and is the country's goldmining centre. See also **Rand.**

Jockey Club
Of the four most powerful elements in Hong Kong, the Jockey Club is said to be at the top of the list; the others are, descending in order, Jardine Matheson, the Hong Kong and Shanghai Bank, and the Governor.

John Bull
A rather dated personification of the English nation, used in former times to symbolize particularly its stalwartness or its insularity. In pictorial representations he usually appeard as a stout jovial gentleman in early 19th-century costume, embellished with a Union Jack waistcoat. His first recorded appearance is in the satire *The History of John Bull* (1712) by the Scottish writer John Arbuthnot. The Irish dramatist George Bernard Shaw wrote a play dealing with Ireland, entitled *John Bull's Other Island.*

Johnstown
A city in Pennsylvania that has been associated since its founding (1793) with three devastating floods. One, in 1889, killed more than 2000 people; another, in 1936, killed 25 and did $40 million in damage; and in 1977, a third killed 85, with property damage of more than $300 million.

Jolly Roger, the
A nickname for the pirates' black flag with white skull and crossed bones, from *roger,* an obsolete word meaning 'rogue'.

Jumbo State, the
A nickname of Texas, acquired before the admittance of Alaska to the Union (1959) made Texas the second largest state.

Jutland
The mainland part of Denmark (in Danish, *Jylland*), which protrudes northward between the North Sea and the Baltic. Its name preserves that of the Jutes, a Germanic tribe of the European Dark Ages. (The Jutes who invaded England in the 6th century A.D. probably came from a little further west, near the mouth of the Rhine.)

K

Kangaroo Valley
A name conferred in the 1960s on the Earl's Court area of West London because of the large number of more or less temporary Australian immigrants who live there.

Kansas Bibles
The nickname given to rifles bought with money collected in churches by abolitionists in the northern and eastern states and used to ensure that Kansas would remain without slaves. Also called **Beecher's Bibles**, thought to be named for Henry Ward Beecher, a violently abolitionist preacher.

Karelia
A region of northeastern Europe, to the southwest of the White Sea. It used to belong to Finland, and although it was annexed by the Soviet Union following the Winter War of 1939–40, its Finnish associations are strongly maintained by Sibelius's *Karelia Suite*.

Karoo, the
A name given to various dry tableland areas in South Africa, particularly the *Great Karoo* and further south the *Little Karoo*, both in the southern part of Cape Province. In addition, the Highveld is also sometimes called the *Northern Karoo*. The term is probably derived from Hottentot *garo* 'a desert'.

Kasbah, the
The name for the old native quarter of Algiers, Morocco, fabled as a
warren of narrow streets and mysterious passageways that have long
provided fiction writers with a setting for eastern intrigue. Also spelled
Casbah.

Kelly Country
The country around Euroa, Jerilderie, and Glenrowan, in northeastern
Victoria, where the outlawed Kelly Gang defied police for nearly two
years. They robbed banks at Euroa and Jerilderie, and their leader, Ned
Kelly, wrote a vindication of their conduct, known as 'the Jerilderie
letter'. The climax to the gang's stand came in June 1880 when Ned and
his brother with Steve Hart and Joe Byrne defended themselves in the
Glenrowan Hotel. Only Ned survived; he was later hanged, on 11 November 1880. The Kelly legend has nourished Australian anti-authoritari-
anism and has inspired numerous literary works. Ned's armour,
fashioned out of a ploughshare, is prominent in Sidney Nolan's paintings
of the Kelly history.

Kemp Town
A district of east Brighton, on the south coast of England, named after a
local MP, Thomas Kemp, who designed and built it in the 1820s.

Kensington
An area of west London, to the west of Belgravia. It is a fashionable and
expensive residential district, similar to but more staid and respectable
than its livelier neighbour to the south, Chelsea. The area known as South
Kensington, familiarly known as *South Ken*, around the Cromwell and
Old Brompton roads, is famous for its museums, including the Natural
History and the Victoria and Albert; the site on which they are built was
bought with some of the proceeds of the Great Exhibition of 1851, at the
instigation of Prince Albert. Further north the area includes the Royal
Albert Hall and Kensington Gardens, the latter long famous as a venue
where nursemaids of wealthy families take their young charges. See also
Royal Borough.

Kesteven
In former times, an administrative area of Lincolnshire, in eastern England. It was in the southern part of the county, based at Sleaford. Its title
in full was the Parts of Kesteven. Compare **Holland, 2; Lindsey**.

Kew Gardens
The informal name for the Royal Botanic Gardens at Kew, in Richmond upon Thames, a borough west of London. Its origins date back to the 17th century. Today it has an important library, extensive museums and greenhouses, and is noted for the pagoda, a Chinese-style building constructed in the 18th century to a design by Sir William Chambers.

Key City, the
A nickname of Vicksburg, Mississippi, so called because of its strategic location, which made it an important base during the American Civil War.

Keystone State, the
The official nickname of Pennsylvania, so called either because its initials were carved into the keystone of the arch of the new Pennsylvania Avenue Bridge when the federal government moved to Washington, D. C., or because Pennsylvania cast the last vote, making unanimous the colonies' decision to issue the Declaration of Independence.

Khyber Pass, the
A pass in the mountains of the Hindu Kush that connects Afghanistan with Pakistan. As one of the few points of entry to the Indian subcontinent it is of key strategic importance and has been the scene of many fiercely contested invasion threats over the centuries. Less nobly, it has passed into the English language, via rhyming slang, as a synonym for 'arse'. See also **Northwest Frontier.**

Kilburn
A district of northwest London, to the southwest of Hampstead. In former times it was a rather down-at-heel working-class area, with a large Irish population, but as with so many inner London suburbs, the latter part of the 20th century is seeing a rise in its status.

King Country, the
A large tract of land in the western central North Island of New Zealand, named after the Maori 'king' Tawhiao. Its Maori name is *Rohe Potae,* meaning 'brim of the hat'; it is said that Tawhiao threw his hat on a map to indicate the country he claimed.

King's City, the
An epithet for Copenhagen (*Kongens By*).

King's Cross
1. A district in north London, to the east of Regent's Park. The term is now virtually synonymous with King's Cross Station (built in 1852), the large terminus from which trains go to northeast England and eastern Scotland, although it has also achieved a certain notoriety as a red-light district. The area originally got its name from a statue of King George IV which once stood at a nearby crossroads. Before the 1830s it was known as Battlebridge.
2. The name of a small district in the Sydney suburb of Darlinghurst, two kilometres east of the city centre, famous for its cosmopolitan character and high living, where the city's prostitutes and ecdysiasts ply their trade. It is sometimes simply referred to as 'the Cross' and was officially called 'Queen's Cross' from 1897 to 1905.

Kingsford Smith
The name of Sydney's airport at Mascot, south of the city, Australia's busiest airport.

King's Road
A lengthy London thoroughfare that starts in Belgravia, passes through Sloane Square, and continues southwest through Chelsea to finish in Fulham. Its heyday was probably in the 1960s and early '70s, when it rivalled Carnaby Street as a vital artery of 'swinging London'. It was the proverbial resort of hippies, and later of punks, and inevitably developed from a mecca of genuine youth culture to a mere tourist attraction. In the 1980s it still abounds in boutiques and smart little bistros, but it has something of the air of a museum exhibit of the '60s, whose outlandishly dressed denizens are liable to ask tourists for money if they wish to photograph them. Compare **Carnaby Street**.

Knightsbridge
An area in the West End of London, to the south of Hyde Park and the west of Belgravia. It takes its name from Knightsbridge, a road that is a westward continuation of Piccadilly. Residentially it is a very exclusive and expensive district, but its fame rests on its stores; highly-priced shops and boutiques abound here, but all are overshadowed by Harrods, the

largest department store in Europe, which seems to exert a magnetic attraction on visitors to London.

Kocourkov

A mythical village in Bohemia, the mayor, aldermen, and citizens of which are typified by their foolish behaviour. Its proverbial character has been preserved in the idiom, '. . . as in Kocourkov', and variants thereof. See also **Chelm, Gotham, Mistelbach.**

Kodak City

A nickname of Rochester, New York, so called because it is the home of the headquarters of Eastman Kodak.

Kowloon City

A major slum on a peninsula opposite Hong Kong island, Kowloon City is a crime-ridden section known as a centre of the drug traffic in the Far East.

Kremlin, the

A citadel in Moscow which since the 12th century has been the seat of power and influence in Russia, and latterly in the Soviet Union. In addition to several government offices, it contains the former Imperial palace and three cathedrals, with their familiar bulbous onion domes. The name has come to be synonymous with the Soviet government, and indeed those who study Soviet policy are known as 'Kremlin watchers', and their discipline as 'Kremlinology'. The word itself came into English via German; a transliteration of the actual Russian name would be *Kreml*.

Kurfürstendamm, the

A street running through the centre of West Berlin. Now that Unter den Linden has been appropriated by the eastern sector, it is the city's main social artery, combining the roles of New York's Broadway and Fifth Avenue.

L

L.A.
A nickname for Los Angeles.

La Brea Tar Pits
Pits in Los Angeles, discovered in 1769, where fossilized remains of prehistoric animals have been found, together with evidence of human habitation some 15,000 years ago.

Ladder Street
A colorful, cluttered street in Hong Kong and a main tourist attraction. Only about 200 feet long, it lies between Hollywood Road and Caine Road.

Lake District, the
An area in Cumbria, in the Northwest of England, renowned for its scenic beauty. As its name suggests, it abounds in lakes, most of which are suffixed -*water* or -*mere*: Derwentwater, Ullswater, Wastwater, and Coniston Water, for example, and Windermere, Thirlmere, and Buttermere. They nestle between hills and mountains that are favourites with walkers and climbers; amongst the peaks is Scafell Pike, the highest mountain in England at 3210 feet. Designated a national park in 1951, it is the largest in England and Wales, covering nearly 900 square miles. Its vogue as a popular holiday destination started as early as the late 18th century, when the sort of wild romantic scenery it offers was fashionable, and its reputation was perhaps established by the poets who came to live in and write about the area in the early 19th century—particularly Wordsworth, Coleridge, and Southey, the so-called 'Lake poets'. In those days it was often known as Lakeland (a name which survives today mainly as an adjective—as in 'Lakeland scenery'), or sometimes as the *Lake Country*, but *Lake District* has gradually established itself as the usual term. An alternative shorthand name in current usage is **the Lakes**.

Lake Shore Drive
A Chicago thoroughfare bordered on the east by Lake Michigan and on the west by a wide variety of luxurious hotels, private mansions, and high-rise apartment houses, as well as a number of such public facilities as museums, hospitals, and parks. A portion of the Drive forms the eastern

border of the Near North Side's **'Gold Coast'** (*q.v.*) area, while its generally faster-than-average traffic flow provides easy access to many lakeside landmarks. See also **McCormick Place, Museum of Science and Industry, Navy Pier.**

Lambeth
An area of central London, on the south bank of the Thames opposite Westminster. It is a working-class residential district, renowned for its Cockney joviality. Its most famous road is perhaps Lambeth Walk, which used to house a well-known street market but is now remembered mainly for a popular song and dance, called the Lambeth Walk, which was all the rage in the 1930s. Lambeth also has close associations with the Church of England: Lambeth Palace is the official London residence of the Archbishop of Canterbury, who can confer honorary 'Lambeth degrees' on servants of the Church. The conference of bishops of the Anglican Communion, held every ten years, is called the Lambeth Conference; and the name 'Lambeth' is used metaphorically to refer to the Anglican Church in England. In 1965 the new London borough of Lambeth was created, which includes Brixton and Streatham, taking in a far larger area than the original Lambeth.

Landes, the
A region on the southwest coast of France, to the south of Bordeaux, covering about 5400 square miles. Today it is mostly covered by scrubby pine forest, but in former times it was a marshy area, and the local shepherds' habit of walking about on stilts surprisingly survived its draining. It is one of the main parts of France in which small wild birds, especially ortolans, are shot (or trapped) for the table.

Land of a Million Elephants, the
A translation of Lanxang, an epithet used formerly for Laos, a state in southeast Asia. Elephants were, and indeed still are important to the economy of Laos as work animals, and three of them appear on the national flag.

Land of Cakes
A nickname of Scotland.

Land of Flowers, the
A nickname of Florida (which means 'flowered' in Spanish).

Land of Little Rain
A nickname for the region of California lying 'between the high Sierras south from Yosemite—east and south . . . beyond Death Valley and on illimitably into the Mojave Desert', as described by Mary Austin in a series of fourteen sketches (1903).

Land of Milk and Honey, the
A nickname of Israel.

Land of Promise
A nickname of Canaan.

Land of the Midnight Sun, the
North of the Arctic Circle, the sun never sets in summer; for more than two months there is continuous daylight. The magic and mystery of this time are reflected in the paradoxical name *Land of the Midnight Sun*, which has been applied to the northern parts of Norway, Sweden, Finland, and the northwest U. S. S. R.; in particular it is often used as an informal epithet for Lapland. In the U. S. it is sometimes used in reference to Alaska.

Land of the Rising Sun, the
Since Japan is regarded as being about as far east as you can go without arriving at the west, it is reasonable that it should be known as the Land of the Rising Sun. The Japanese concur, and their former national flag showed a red sphere, with rays projecting, on a white field.

Land of the Saints, the
A nickname of Utah, so called because the Mormons refer to themselves as Latter-Day Saints.

Land's End to John o' Groat's House
A phrase indicating the length of Great Britain: Land's End being the granite promontory in Cornwall at the southwestern tip of England, and John o' Groat's house, an octagonal structure owned by a Dutchman, Johan de Groot, which formerly occupied the site in Caithness-shire, Scotland, near the northern extremity of Great Britain.

Lanes, the
An area of narrow winding alleyways in central Brighton, on the south
coast of England. They are all that remain of the original 17th-century
fishing village that became Brighton, and in the late 20th century are full
of antique shops, boutiques, and similar enticements for tourists.

Languedoc
A mainly mountainous area of southern France, between the River Rhone
and the foothills of the Pyrenees. It used to be a province in its own right,
but is now merged into the region of Languedoc-Roussillon. Its name
comes from the language spoken in southern France in the Middle Ages,
which used *oc* as the word for 'yes', in contrast to the northerly French
dialect, where *oïl* was used.

Lantern of England
A nickname for the abbey church of Bath, in southwestern England, so
called because of the number and size of its traceried windows.

Lapland
The area in northern Scandinavia occupied by the Lapps. It takes in parts
of Finland, Sweden, and Norway, and also includes the Kola Peninsula at
the very northwest tip of the Soviet Union. It is mostly above the Arctic
Circle. See also **Land of the Midnight Sun.**

Lasseter's Reef
An alleged reef of gold near the Western Australian-Northern Territory
border. Reports of the discovery by Henry Lewis Bell Lasseter led to
various attempts to locate the reef, including a quest by Lasseter himself
which led to his death in 1931. The mystery was the basis of a book,
Lasseter's Last Ride, by Ion L. Idriess and a more factual account,
Dream Millions, by Fred Blakely, the leader of one of the expeditions
seeking the reef.

Latin Quarter (Quartier Latin)
1. An area on the Left Bank of the Paris River Seine, to the south of the
Île de la Cité and immediately to the west of the Boulevard St-Michel. It is
renowned as the hub of Paris's intellectual life, housing as it does Sorbonne University and several other colleges, whose students no doubt do
much to perpetuate the area's reputation for bohemian unorthodoxy. It
gets its name from the fact that in the Middle Ages the scholars at the

educational institutions spoke Latin, the international language of learning at that time. See also **Left Bank**.
2. A part of Old Quebec, so named because it is the site of Laval University.

Laurasia
A name given to the supercontinent believed to have existed in the northern hemisphere over 200 million years ago; it later split up into continents that became Eurasia and North America. Compare **Gondwanaland, Pangaea**.

Law Courts, the
The name commonly used for what are officially called the Royal Courts of Justice, a set of imposing Victorian buildings on the Strand in central London, housing the Supreme Court of Judicature, the main civil court of England and Wales.

LAX
The code used by airlines to designate the city of Los Angeles and the Los Angeles International Airport. The airport now covers an area of 3500 acres and is one of the busiest in the world. The name LAX has grown in popularity worldwide in recent decades, partly because of the growing importance of the airport and perhaps partly because it is one of the few three-letter codes that is an actual word (which might be applied in a derisive manner to Los Angeles). The airport is seen frequently by millions of television and movie viewers all over the world.

Leaping Lena
A nickname for the train running from Birdum to Darwin. Its official name is 'The Sentinel'. Soldiers in World War II called it 'The Spirit of Protest' after 'The Spirit of Progress' which used to run between Melbourne and Albury.

Left Bank, the
The southern bank of the River Seine in Paris. The term *Left Bank* is used for more than just the riverside, however: it covers a largish hinterland, including Montparnasse, St-Germain-des-Prés, and St-Michel. It is the artistic, intellectual district of Paris, with the Latin Quarter at its heart; over the past century most of France's great cultural lions have patronized its famous cafés, such as *les Deux Magots* and *le Dôme*, and despite

recent commercialization the area is still the centre of Paris's bohemian life. See also **Latin Quarter**.

Leghorn

An antiquated Anglicized name for Livorno, a town in Tuscany on the west coast of Italy. It derives from *Legorno*, the local name in the 16th and 17th centuries, which was replaced by *Livorno* as being closer to the original Latin *Liburnus*. Any continued currency it may have in English is probably owing to its associations with a breed of domestic fowl and with a sort of plaited straw from which hats were once made.

Leicester Square

A square in the West End of London, immediately to the east of Piccadilly Circus. It is regarded as the heart of London's theatreland, and is itself surrounded by large cinemas. It bustles with life by day and far into the night. In the 18th century it was a favourite venue for duels.

Leningrad

A city in the USSR which, like so many others in that country, has undergone several changes of name in line with changes in the political system. Originally called St Petersburg, it was renamed Petrograd in 1914, and following the Revolution was given its present name in 1924 in honour of the Revolutionary leader, V. I. Lenin. See also **Gorkii, Volgograd**.

Leon & Eddie's

A popular nightclub during the 1930s and '40s, on 52nd Street, in New York City. It featured many of the swing and jazz singers and musicians of the time and was a favourite oasis of the gossip columnists.

Levant, the

An archaic term for the lands bordering the eastern Mediterranean, what is now Lebanon, Israel, and Syria. *The Levant* originally meant 'the land where the sun rises' (from the French *lever* 'to rise'), and indeed, in the 16th and 17th centuries, the High Levant was used in reference to the Far East. Compare **Orient**.

Liberty Hall
Not a specific place at all but any place where one can do as one pleases.
It is usually used in reference to free-wheeling hospitality. [So used by
Squire Hardcastle in Oliver Goldsmith's play, *She Stoops to Conquer*]

Limehouse
A district in the Dockland area of the East End of London. In former
times it was a fairly tough and violent neighbourhood, and in the 19th
century London's Chinatown was situated there, but in the latter part of
the 20th century, with the closing down of the docks and the development
of the area for light industry and leisure, it is acquiring a better image. A
particular present-day association of Limehouse is with the evolution of
the Social Democratic Party in the early 1980s; one of its founding fathers
lived there, and its formative caucus, of Roy Jenkins, David Owen,
Shirley Williams, and William Rodgers, was known as the 'Limehouse
Four'. In the early twentieth century the verb *to limehouse* meant 'to
make fiery political speeches'; the usage arose out of a speech given by
Lloyd George at a turbulent rally at Limehouse in 1909.

Lindsey
In former times, an administrative area of Lincolnshire, in eastern England. It was in the central and northern parts of the county, based at the
city of Lincoln. Its title in full was the Parts of Lindsey. Compare **Holland, 2; Kesteven.**

Lindy's
A restaurant at Broadway and 50th Street, in New York City, frequented
by the famous of the world of sports and entertainment, who attracted
many Broadway 'types' as well as newspaper columnists and feature
writers during its heyday, from the 1920s to the 1950s. (Its famous cheese-
cake is still shipped around the world to those who can't get to the
restaurant.) It was immortalized as 'Mindy's' in the short stories of
Damon Runyon, a journalist who often wrote about the 'Broadway
Scene' and whose short stories formed the basis for several films and the
musical, *Guys and Dolls*.

Little Britain
A small street in the City of London, to the north of St Paul's Cathedral,
which contained the offices of the lawyer Mr Jaggers in Dickens's *Great
Expectations*. It apparently gets its name from the fact that the Duke of

Brittany had a house there. In medieval times Brittany (in northern France) was often known as Little Britain, to distinguish it from Great Britain (England, Scotland, and Wales), the spelling of Britain and Brittany in those days being frequently identical. From the 17th to the 19th centuries it was, along with the nearby Paternoster Row and St Paul's Churchyard, a major centre of the book-publishing business in London.

Little Cuba
A nickname of Miami, Florida, so called in reference to the number of Cuban immigrants living there after the establishment of the Castro regime in Cuba.

Little Dipper
An American name for the constellation Ursa Minor, so called from the outline formed by its stars.

Littlehampton
A seaside resort near Brighton, on the English Channel. It is not particularly noteworthy, but British comedians occasionally refer to it archly as 'Little Hampton', 'Hampton' being short for 'Hampton Wick', which is riming slang for *dick*, a vulgar word for penis.

Little Italy
A nickname for a neighbourhood, in a large American city, occupied mainly by Italians and those of Italian descent. In New York City it is situated on the East Side, north of Canal Street, between the Bowery on the east and Centre Street on the west. Its main street is Mulberry Street where, once a year, at the Feast of San Gennaro, the patron saint of many who settled there, a gala festival is held, with the carts of peddlers of Italian foods and other native goods lining the crowded ways. Many New Yorkers make an annual visit there to join in the festivities.

Little Siberia
A nickname, translated from the French *La Petite Sibérie*, for the Belgian headquarters of NATO, so called because the personnel from sixteen countries do not mix well and because of its isolated site.

Little Venice
Just to the north of Paddington station in west London, the Regent's Canal branches off the Grand Union Canal. The attractive canal basin at

their junction is always crowded with moored pleasure craft, and the feeling of a watery environment in the heart of a city gives the surrounding desirable residential area its name.

Little Vietnam
A nickname for Tondo Foreshore, in the Philippines, once notorious as the largest slum in southeast Asia, so called because of its violence.

Lizard, the
The southernmost point in Britain, a promontory near the western tip of Cornwall in the Southwest of England. Its name has no connection with reptiles; it comes from the Cornish *lis* 'place' and *ard* 'high'.

Llanfairpwllgwyngillgogerychwyrndrobwllllantysiliogogogoch
A village on the island of Anglesey, off the northwest coast of Wales. Its celebrity rests on its name, which at 58 letters is the longest place-name in Britain. It is in fact a somewhat bogus name, and not surprisingly it is very seldom used in practice. It was revived in 1973, when the railway station reopened, so as to make something of a tourist attraction of the station signs, but in ordinary everyday use the place is known as Llanfairpwllgwyngill. The full name means 'St Mary's church by the pool of the white hazel trees, near the rapid whirlpool, by the red cave of the church of St Tysilio'.

L. L. Bean
A large, old mail-order company, situated in Freeport, Maine, offering mainly sports clothing and camping equipment of quality construction and fairly priced. Although it originally catered to country-dwellers and sportsmen, its popularity spread during the early 1970s, and its catalogue expanded to include informal wear for men and, later on, women. In that period it acquired a status of its own, and in the 1980s its identifying labels began to appear prominently on the outsides, instead of the insides of its clothing.

Lloyd's
An institution, headquartered in the City of London, whose business is to provide insurance, particularly marine insurance. It consists of about 14,000 members, known as underwriters, who jointly or severally accept liability for the sums insured. In the U. S., where it is usually referred to as Lloyd's of London, the connotation is nearly always of insurance of an

unusual nature, as the insuring of a dancer's legs against injury and loss of income. Since its beginnings in the late 17th century, Lloyd's has always gathered and disseminated accurate information relating to the world's shipping, and one of its classifications, *A-1*, meaning that a vessel is in first-class condition, has passed into everyday English, meaning 'excellent'. See also **Lutine bell.**

Loamshire

An imaginary southern English county sometimes used by writers of fiction when they wish to avoid naming a real place. Its associations are distinctly rural and agricultural. Compare **Mummerset.**

Lombard Street

A street in the City of London, leading up to the Bank of England, in which the headquarters of many banks and other financial institutions are situated. It derives its name from the bankers from Lombardy, Italy who set up business in the street from the 13th century onward. In the 16th and 17th centuries, banks and money lender's shops were often known as *lombards*, and indeed *Lombard Street* itself used to be used figuratively to refer to London's banking industry, although the expression now has a rather dated air. Another somewhat outmoded phrase that once enjoyed a considerable vogue is *all Lombard Street to a China orange*, used when making an assertion in the form of a wager, staking something of great monetary value against something worthless (a China orange being just an ordinary orange, originally brought from China); it is first recorded in 1819, but an alternative version, of greater antiquity, is *all Lombard Street to an egg shell.*

London

The amorphous British metropolis spreads ever wider, and spawns new names to keep pace with its expanding size and status. At its heart is the original City of London, now the nation's financial centre. But even in medieval times, London was seeping out of its city walls; the districts that were to become known as the East End and the West End began to grow up. By the middle of the 19th century it became clear that though only the City was London in name, a much larger area was London in fact. To recognize this, the County of London was formed in 1888, by taking chunks of the counties of Middlesex, Surrey, and Kent and adding them officially on to the City. Often known by the nickname *the Youngest*

County, it was governed by the London County Council. London continued to elbow its way through the suburbs in the 20th century, however, gobbling up most intervening patches of green, so it was not long before a new accommodation had to be made. In 1965, *Greater London* was called into being, which added fresh bits of Surrey and Kent to London County, plus part of Hertfordshire, and totally engulfed Middlesex, which disappeared off the map altogether. The whole vast area covers 620 square miles, and is divided into Inner London (twelve boroughs nearest the centre) and Outer London (the rest). British people's concept of what *London* actually means has not really kept in step with official nomenclature. Certainly London is no longer thought of simply as the City, but equally many people find it difficult to think of some of the more outlying boroughs, such as Croydon or Bexley, as being really part of the metropolis. For those who live on its fringes, London is most often known familiarly as *town*, as in 'I'm going up to town for the day to do some shopping'. See also **Great Wen, Smoke.**

London Bridge

Any of several bridges spanning the River Thames between Borough High Street in Southwark and King William Street in the City of London. The Old London Bridge of nursery-rhyme fame was built between 1176 and 1209 and was the only crossing of the river at London until the 1740s, when Westminster Bridge was built. In the 1820s the Old Bridge was demolished and replaced by New London Bridge. This in turn was replaced in 1960, but the masonry facing was shipped to the U. S. and it has been re-erected at Lake Havasu City, Arizona, where it is a very popular tourist attraction. It is thought that when the promoters of the project in Arizona bought London Bridge, they were under the impression that they were buying Tower Bridge, which still functions in London.

London Underground

London's underground railway system. It has nine different lines, most of which do indeed run at varying depths below ground in central London (the Circle line surfaces here and there). Several of the lines extend out into the commuterland of the suburbs, where for the most part they run above ground. Londoners call the system the 'Underground' or the 'Tube'. See also **Drain.**

Lone Star of Civilization, the

A nickname of Santa Fe, New Mexico, so called because for a century
after its founding (1609) it was the only town in a million square miles of
desert and mountains.

Lone Star State, the

The official nickname of Texas.

Loop, the

Specifically, the structure for the elevated railway, dating from 1897, that
forms a loop around two square miles of downtown Chicago, the historic
heart of the city; generally, the term refers to this area and its immediate
environs. The generally run-down South Loop area has been showing
signs of rebirth in recent years, thanks to the development of such areas
as 'Printer's Row' on South Dearborn Street between Congress Parkway
and Polk Street, with its many sturdy old commercial buildings ideal for
refurbishing into loft apartments, art galleries, and related business establishments. On South Wabash Avenue, Big Jim Colosimo's Café, now an
empty lot, served during Prohibition days as informal headquarters for
practitioners of organized crime, whose widespread bootlegging and other
illicit activities reaped fortunes for such underworld leaders as Al
Capone, Johnny Torrio, and Bugs Moran. Nearby were the notorious
Lexington and Metropole hotels much frequented by Capone and his
cronies.

Lord's

A cricket ground in St John's Wood, in northwest central London, to the
west of Regent's Park. It was opened by Thomas Lord in 1814 and has
since become both the spiritual home and the administrative centre of
English, and indeed world cricket. It is the headquarters of the International Cricket Conference (cricket's governing body), of the venerable
Marylebone Cricket Club, and of Middlesex County Cricket Club. International matches and many important domestic matches are played here
each summer. See also **Oval**.

Los Angeles

A large city in southern California, founded by the Spanish in 1781. The
original name of the settlement, according to some, was La Reina de los
Angeles 'The Queen of the Angels'; according to some modern writers it

was Nuestra Señora la Reina de los Angeles de Porciúncula; in the American period (beginning in 1846) the name was shortened to Pueblo de los Angeles (or the 'City of the Angels') and then simply to Los Angeles. The citizens have long resisted the abbreviation 'L. A.', just as San Franciscans have rejected 'Frisco', but the abbreviation no longer has the opprobrium that it once had and is now commonly used by a large part of the citizenry. It is thought that the abbreviation might have been used by people who were unsure of the pronunciation of the name. For years people debated whether the letter 'g' in Los Angeles should be pronounced like the 'g' in 'angle' or in 'angel'; Mayor Fletcher Bowron finally decided in favour of the latter when he appointed a jury of citizens to debate the issue in 1952. Los Angeles is thought by people in other cities to have an unusual character. Residents of San Francisco and New York, in particular, like to contrast the idiosyncrasies of Los Angeles with the virtues of their own cities. Known throughout the world for the stereotypical descriptions of the city, its inhabitants, and the 'L. A. lifestyle', 'laid-back' and 'flaky' are two of the adjectives most commonly used by outsiders to describe Angelenos. In 1976, Jack Smith, a popular columnist for the *Los Angeles Times*, called Los Angeles 'The Big Orange' by analogy with 'The Big Apple' (New York), but the name has not stuck.

Lost Colony, the

The nickname for the second of the first two American colonies settled by the British (1585 and 1587) on Roanoke Island off the North Carolina coast, thirty-three years before the Pilgrims landed at Plymouth Rock. The first group returned to England, but crewmen of a supply ship which arrived there three years later found no trace of the second group, only the word 'Croatoan' carved on a tree. Virginia Dare, the first child born to English parents in America, was among those who vanished. What became of them has remained a mystery to this day.

Low Countries, the

A somewhat dated collective term applied to the countries occupying the low-lying shoulder of land that projects into the North Sea at the northwest corner of Europe. It now comprises Belgium, the Netherlands (a translation of Dutch *Nederland*, which itself means 'low country') and sometimes Luxembourg; but the origin of the name goes back beyond the formation of these modern states, and it used to include such regions as Brabant, Flanders, and Zeeland. See also **Benelux**.

Lower East Side, the

An area of New York City, somewhat vaguely delineated on the north by 14th Street, on the west by Lafayette Street, on the south by Canal Street, and on the east by the East River (South Street). It is one of the oldest parts of the city but is best known for its settlement by Jewish immigrants from the 1870s onward for about fifty years. It was always a poor neighbourhood, but many of those who spent their childhood there became famous: Al Jolson, Fanny Brice, George and Ira Gershwin, Irving Berlin, as well as others who went on to become well-known writers, judges, teachers, businessmen, etc. On Second Avenue flourished the Yiddish theatre, under the direction of Maurice Schwartz, which starred Molly Picon, among others. Because the sabbath is observed on Saturdays, the area around Delancey Street is open for business as usual on Sundays, and New Yorkers looking for bargains and for ethnic Jewish food often shop then. The Essex Street Market, where one can see block-long rows of kosher salamis hanging above the counters, is also popular. Generally, the Lower East Side is associated with both poverty, reflecting the condition of the immigrants who lived there, and success, exemplified by those who had the talent and resourcefulness to emerge, frequently at the top of their profession. See also **East Side.**

Lowlands, the

A roughly fifty-mile-wide corridor of relatively low ground running east and west across central Scotland between the Southern Uplands and the Highlands. It contains Scotland's major cities of Edinburgh and Glasgow and the valleys of the Forth and Clyde. Culturally distinct from the Highlands, it is where the Scots version of the English language, known as Lallands (Lowlands), is spoken, as contrasted to the Gaelic that still survives further north. See also **Highlands.**

Lucky Country, the

A nickname for Australia, not always quoted with awareness of the ironical flavour of its original use as the title of a book by Donald Horne in 1964. Horne presented Australians as provincial, second-rate, and derivative, prosperous only through luck, but innocently happy.

Luna Park

The name of a Sydney fun parlour opened in 1935 near the Harbour Bridge. Once considerd a classic example of fairground art, it was partly dismantled and rebuilt after a fire in the early 1980s.

Lutine bell
The ship's bell salvaged from the *Lutine* (rhymes with *routine*), a British warship wrecked at sea. It hangs at the offices of **Lloyd's** (*q.v.*) of London and is tolled before announcements of ships lost or long overdue.

M

M & S
A frequent abbreviation for Marks and Spencer, one of Britain's largest chain stores. Almost as often heard, but more colloquial, is the rhyming *Marks and Sparks*.

Macao *or* **Macáu**
A Portuguese port and overseas territory across the bay from Hong Kong, Macao, founded in 1557, is an important trading centre in the Far East and has served as a funnel through which European goods and culture have been introduced to China. The languages and cultures of Portugal, China, and England blend here to the apparent advantage of all.

MacDowell Colony
A composers' and writers' summer residence, established in Peterborough, New Hampshire, by the widow of Edward Alexander MacDowell (1861-1908), the U. S. composer, as a memorial.

Macy's
Formally, R. H. Macy & Company, a department store at Herald Square (34th Street and Broadway) in New York City. It is the largest such store in the world. During the late 1930s and early '40s, Macy's 'feuded' with Gimbels, a nearby store nearly as large, which had the motto, 'We will not be undersold', and occasional price wars kept customers racing back and forth between the two to find the best bargains. As a result of competitive advertising and strategic merchandising planning, New

Yorkers (at least) added to their speech the query 'Does Macy's tell Gimbels?' to identify some piece of information better kept confidential.

Madison Avenue

A north-south avenue in New York City, extending from Madison Square, at the southern end, up into Harlem at the northern. Its blocks between 40th and 57th streets are identified mainly with advertising agencies, many of which have—or once had—their offices there. But the avenue has many high-rise office buildings along it, and there are many other businesses there. The association of Madison Avenue with advertising extended to publicity and other kinds of promotion which, in the minds of the public, in turn became associated with spurious claims made for what often turn out to be specious products and services. Hence, 'Madison Avenue' has a pejorative connotation, carrying the idea of insincerity and phoniness. In its application to some of the wilder representations, it is shortened to 'Mad Avenue'.

Madison Square Garden

The name of three different structures in the recent history of New York City, all arenas for sporting events, circuses, and other such happenings. The original, a converted station, was, aptly enough, at Madison Square; its main claim to fame was its roof garden restaurant, where Harry K. Thaw, in 1906, shot and killed Stanford White, a noted architect and partner in the firm of McKim, Mead, and White, when he found him dining with his showgirl wife, Evelyn Nesbit, a beautiful redhead who was billed in a contemporary extravaganza as 'The Girl in the Red Velvet Swing'. In 1925, that building was demolished and a new Madison Square Garden, usually called 'The Garden' among sports aficionados, was built on Eighth Avenue, at 50th Street. That was torn down and Madison Square Garden moved on to a structure built (1968) over the Pennsylvania Station (at 33rd Street and Seventh Avenue), the former station building having been demolished. In the mid 1980s it was rumoured that this venue, too, would soon be vacated in favour of a new site, a few blocks away. Any New Yorkers who may retain any nostalgia for the old 'Garden' probably think of the one at 50th Street, where boxing matches and other sports were presented but more likely where one attended the rodeo and, especially, the Ringling Brothers, Barnum & Bailey Circus—'The Greatest Show on Earth'.

Maelstrom, the
A powerful current in the Arctic Ocean, to the northwest of Norway. Its
tidal race funnels through a restricted channel in the Lofoten Islands, and
mariners' tales built its reputation into that of a huge and violent whirlpool that sucked ships into it from miles around. Its name, which comes
from a Dutch word meaning 'grinding or whirling stream', has come to
be applied to any threatening whirlpool, or more generally to a confusing
and dangerous situation. Edgar Allan Poe wrote a short story about it, 'A
Descent into the Maelstrom'.

Mae West
1. A World War II nickname coined by the Royal Air Force for an
inflatable life vest, so called because the wearer resembled the well-en-
dowed actress.
2. A nickname used in fast-food restaurants for a sweet cake in the shape
of a figure eight.

Mafeking
A town and important rail junction in South Africa which sprang to fame
during the Boer War when the garrison of British troops which had been
besieged there was relieved on 17 May 1900. The so-called 'Relief of
Mafeking' led to such uproarious rejoicing in Britain that the newspapers
of the time coined a new verb, *to maffick* 'to indulge in exultant national
celebrations'. The town's subsequent history was uneventful, until in
1980 it was ceded to the newly 'independent' bantustan (black enclave) of
Bophutatswana; in the process its name reverted to its original form,
Mafikeng, which in the Tswana language means 'place of stones'.

Maghreb
An all-embracing term for the northwestern part of Africa, including
Algeria, Morocco, Tunisia, and sometimes also Libya. In Arabic it means
literally 'the West'.

Magic Valley
A nickname of the Rio Grande Valley, in reference to its abundant
production of vegetables and citrus fruits.

Magnificent Mile, the
A Chamber of Commerce phrase for that segment of Michigan Avenue in
Chicago on the Near North Side, stretching north from the Loop to Oak

Street and featuring generally finer shops, department stores, restaurants, and hotels. Landmarks include the Wrigley Building; Tribune Tower; the old **Water Tower** (*q.v.*); the Water Tower Place shopping complex (the world's tallest reinforced-concrete building); the 100-story John Hancock Center; the **Playboy Building** (*q.v.*); the Drake Hotel; and One Magnificent Mile, a 58-story combination of shops, offices, and condominiums.

magpie houses
A nickname for the half-timbered Tudor period houses whose black-painted wood and white plaster resemble the coloration of the bird.

Maida Vale
A district in northwest London, to the north of Paddington Station, which takes its name from Maida Vale, a large thoroughfare which runs through it. This in turn commemorates the battle of Maida in Italy (1806) during the Napoleonic Wars. In the late 20th century Maida Vale is an upwardly mobile area, not quite as fashionable as Little Venice to the south, but certainly a better place to live than Kilburn to the north. A suburb of Perth, Western Australia, is also called Maida Vale. See also **Little Venice**.

Mainland, the
1. The Australian mainland from the point of view of Tasmania.
2. In New Zealand, a title jocularly claimed for the North Island by its inhabitants and similarly for the South Island by its inhabitants.
3. The term used in Hawaii to refer to the continental (contiguous) United States.

Main Line
The suburbs of Philadelphia, associated with wealth and upper-class toniness, served by the *Paoli Local* commuter train, namely, Merion, Narberth, Wynnewood, Ardmore, Haverford, Bryn Mawr, Rosemont, Villanova, Radnor, St Davids, Wayne, Devon, Berwyn, and Paoli.

Main Street
The central or chief thoroughfare of an American village or town, corresponding, in Britain, to the High Street, though the terms are not used interchangeably. In the United States, Main Street connotes the more important activities going on in a town; it also carries with it the notion of small-town life in general and the pervasive stolidity associated with it.

This sense is best reflected in Sinclair Lewis's novel *Main Street* (1920). To some, the term connotes salt-of-the-earth solidity and home-town friendliness. These connotations are absent in the British use of High Street, which is associated chiefly with the street as the focus of commerce: the term *High Street shops* denotes those that are economically important, whose volume of business, attitudes towards economic factors, etc., are reported in the financial news.

Main Street of America, the
A nickname of US 66, the federal highway formerly the most direct route from Chicago to Los Angeles, which passes through some of the most outstanding agricultural and scenic sections of Illinois, Missouri, Oklahoma, New Mexico, Arizona, and California.

Main Trunk, the
The name *main trunk* is used for the chief north-south railway in New Zealand, especially the 426 miles connecting Auckland and Wellington in the North Island, passing through mountainous terrain in the **King Country** (*q.v.*). Its construction required more than forty years and was officially declared completed on 6 November 1908.

Malabar Coast, the
The southwest coast of India, from Cape Comorin, the southern tip of India, northward to the former Portuguese colony of Goa. Compare **Coromandel Coast.**

Malibu
An unincorporated coastal area in Los Angeles County. Its limits are rather indefinite, but it is commonly considered to be the stretch of beach from the Pacific Palisades section of Los Angeles west for about 26 miles along the coast of the Pacific Ocean as far as the Ventura County line. Malibu is an Indian name, and the present spelling first appeared in the name of the Topanga Malibu Sequit land grant in 1805. Malibu has become famous for surfing and for the residences of film stars and other celebrities. The name is thought to have a certain cachet and has been used for a model in the Chevrolet line of automobiles. Malibu includes the Malibu Beach Colony, often known simply as 'The Colony', a mile of beach houses belonging mostly to rich people associated with the entertainment world.

Mallee, the
A name given to a region in northwest Victoria after *mallee,* scrub consisting of short many-stemmed varieties of eucalyptus. *Mallee root* is rhyming slang for *prostitute.*

Malvinas, Islas
See **Falkland Islands.**

Manhattan
An island, about thirteen miles long and, at its broadest, two and a half miles wide, constituting the main part of one of the five boroughs of New York City, which includes also Brooklyn (technically, Kings County), The Bronx, Queens, and Staten Island (until 1975 named Richmond). It is the focal point of theatre—many say for the entire western hemisphere—the financial world (in the Stock Exchange and Wall Street), of the garment industry, the advertising business, of those who run the large radio and television networks, of music and book publishing, and, probably, of many other businesses in the United States. Geologically consisting of solid rock, it has afforded the opportunity to build tall buildings, called skyscrapers, for which the city is known, and these, crowding along the north-south avenues and side streets, create canyons through which New Yorkers walk and where they sit in cars, taxis, and buses, waiting for the perpetual traffic jams to move. Manhattan has been the inspiration for songwriters and bartenders, one of whom named a cocktail after it. Millions of people work in Manhattan, commuting there via train, subway, bus, car, helicopter, boat, and Hovercraft from a radius as great as one hundred miles. Relatively few of these, however, live there, for, although tradition has it that Peter Minuit purchased the island from the Indians in 1626 for $24-worth of beads and trinkets, it today includes some of the most valuable real estate in the world, and there are not many who can afford either the high rents or the huge prices demanded for cooperative apartments. Yet, it remains one of the most populous cities in the world. It is also one of the busiest and, in many ways, the cultural centre of the United States. Its libraries, museums, art galleries, ballet and opera companies, orchestras, and other facilities are so numerous that a person could spend his entire life going from one to another without attending the same performance or exhibition twice. It is host to millions of American and foreign tourists yearly, and many national associations include it among the cities where they hold conventions. Its commercial exhibition centres draw enormous crowds, not only from the

outlying areas, but from among New Yorkers, who are not always as cynical as they seem. Bordered on the east by the East and Harlem rivers and on the west by the Hudson (or North) River, Manhattan is filled with and emptied of people through various railway and four vehicular tunnels, ferries, more than a dozen bridges (only one across the Hudson), and an aerial tramway (to Roosevelt, formerly Welfare, Island). Its virtual centre is occupied by Central Park, almost half a mile wide and about two and a half miles long, which is used for concerts, informal sports and games, strolling, horse riding, ice- or roller-skating, rowing (on its pond), model sailboat racing (on another pond), and, at night, for mugging those foolish enough to enter its precincts. It also has a zoo with a special children's zoo, where adults are forbidden unless accompanied by a child. Street vendors can be found—indeed, cannot easily be avoided—on many corners throughout the downtown (commercial) areas, selling fruits, nuts, roasted chestnuts, ice cream, gelati, cold drinks and every other conceivable kind of food, as well as all kinds of merchandise. It is, in short, one of the most provocative, exciting places on earth, and it evokes a complex of myriad associations for all those who live and work there, who visit it, and even for those whose only experience with it is vicarious.

Mansion House, the
The official home of the Lord Mayor of London. An imposing classical building erected between 1739 and 1753, it stands to the southwest of the Bank in the City of London, opposite the Bank of England. The word *mansion-house* originally meant any dwelling house, and only gradually came to be applied specifically to official residences—particularly, in early days, to those of high-ranking ecclesiastics.

Maoriland
An older or poetic name for New Zealand. Its use seems to be confined to the late 19th and early 20th centuries. Edward E. Morris, in his dictionary, *Austral English* (1898), called it a 'modern name' and in 1884 *Maoriland* was the main title of an illustrated handbook of New Zealand. The *Maoriland Worker,* a weekly workers' newspaper was begun in 1910. The *OED Supplement* has no record of the use of *Maoriland* later than 1915. See also **Pig Island**.

Marais, the
An area of eastern central Paris, on the right bank of the Seine to the
north of the Île de la Cité. It is the oldest part of the city, and retains a
powerful flavour of the past, with its narrow winding streets, its elegant
17th-century mansions, and its many museums.

Marches, the
1. A *march* is a boundary, particularly a disputed one—it is connected
with the word *mark*. In a British historical context, the Marches are the
border areas between England and Wales (or occasionally England and
Scotland). In the Middle Ages, the Welsh Marches were a particular
security risk for England, and the king appointed 'Marcher lords', powerful vassals based in Hereford, Shrewsbury, and Chester, whose duty was
to guard the frontier against Welsh incursion.
2. A region of Italy, on the Adriatic coast to the east of Florence, is also
known as *the Marches* or, in Italian, *le Marche*.

Mare Nostrum
The name used by the ancient Romans for the Mediterranean Sea. As its
literal translation, 'our sea', suggests, they viewed the whole of the Mediterranean as merely Roman territorial waters, and few were able to chal-
lenge that view for long.

Marseillaise of the Unemotional Yankee
A nickname of *The Battle Hymn of the Republic*, written by Julia Ward
Howe in 1861, a reference to its use by Yankee soldiers as a camp song
during the Civil War.

Marshall Field's
A Chicago department store, more commonly known as Fields. Long
considered a local institution, it was established in 1902 at its present site
in the city's Loop, after having done business at several other locations.
The 12-story edifice occupies an entire block and features 71 acres of floor
space, a Tiffany-domed ceiling and a brass-encased, nearly eight-ton clock
above the sidewalk at State and Washington that has become a famous
Loop landmark. The store's reputation and success have been built on a
stringent policy of guaranteeing customer satisfaction, in keeping with
Marshall Field's famous admonition to an apparently unhelpful floor
manager: 'Give the lady what she wants!'

Marylebone
An area of central London to the west of Regent's Park. In the early
Middle Ages it was known as Tyburn, for a stream of that name flowed
there; but Tyburn's increasing association with the gallows, on the site of
what is now Marble Arch, led to its name being changed in the 15th
century to Maryburn, after the church of St Mary which stood nearby
and *burn* 'stream, brook'. In the 17th century the name evolved to Marylebone, with the extraneous *le* perhaps being introduced by analogy with
St Mary-le-Bow, a church in the City of London, perhaps influenced by
the French *Marie la Bonne.* Since that time the area has been known
variously as St Marylebone or just plain Marylebone: the former London
borough, for example, that existed until 1965, was called St Marylebone,
but the local station, which is a terminus for certain Western Region
services, is Marylebone. See also **Tyburnia.**

Mason-Dixon Line
Properly called Mason and Dixon's Line, it is the line determined
(1763–67) by two English astronomers, Charles Mason and Jeremiah
Dixon, who were hired to survey the border and thus end the dispute
between Pennsylvania and Maryland. It is the east-west boundary dividing Pennsylvania from Maryland and part of West Virginia, and the
north-south boundary between Maryland and Delaware. Prior to the
Civil War, the southern boundary of Pennsylvania was considered the
dividing line between slave and non-slave states, thus giving rise to the
common belief that the line divides the North and the South. See also
Dixie.

Mauve Decade, the
A nickname for the 1890s, bestowed by Thomas Beer (1889–1940) in his
book of the same title (1926), in which the decade is viewed as a peaceful,
prosperous, and complacent period in Europe and America. See also **Gay
Nineties.**

Maxim's
A well-known restaurant in Paris, on the Boulevard de la Madeleine. It
has been famous for almost a century as the gathering-place of the
wealthy and elegant, and its rich red and gold rococo decor has been
widely imitated. It is the Maxim's of Sigmund Romberg's operetta *The
Student Prince,* in which it figures in a song which begins:

I go off to Maxim's,
Where all the girls are dreams.

Maxwell Street

A colourful Near Southwest Side market area in Chicago that derives its
name from the street that forms its core. Crowded streets, aggressive
sidewalk vendors, and the pungent aromas of food all are elements of its
zesty—but increasingly seedy—ambiance. At its busiest (especially Sundays) the multi-ethnic area is filled with buyers, sellers, and sightseers
making their way among shops, stands, stalls, and pushcarts that offer a
wide variety of merchandise, old and new, and almost all at negotiable
prices.

Mayfair

A fashionable area of the West End of London, bounded on the west by
Park Lane, on the east by Bond Street, on the north by Oxford Street,
and on the south by Piccadilly. It was originally known as Brookfield, but
it came to fame because of the fair held there every May in the 17th and
18th centuries, and the new name gradually evolved. In the 18th century it
was a rather disreputable quarter which saw a good deal of gambling and
drunken debauchery—so much so that the fair was eventually officially
suppressed. But as early as 1704 building had begun there, and in the 19th
century imposing squares and boulevards began to be laid out, providing
town residences for the English aristocracy. Among them are Grosvenor
Square, Berkeley Square, South Audley Street, and Curzon Street. A
Mayfair address continued throughout the early 20th century to provide
the ultimate in cachet, but spiralling costs since World War II have
reduced Mayfair's residential importance, and today, while its name retains a very special aura, it is mainly a commercial area, with a sprinkling
of luxury hotels.

Mayflower

The name of the ship that brought the first group of Pilgrims from
England to America, in 1620, landing them in Massachusetts, traditionally at Plymouth Rock. All American schoolchildren are familiar with the
story; it is not till later that they are made aware that there are a number
of extant families that trace their forebears to those who sailed on the
Mayflower. Although some of these are indubitably genuine, it has been
said that if all such claims were valid, the *Mayflower* would have to have
been as large as the *Queen Elizabeth II*.

Maze, the
An internment camp near Lisburn, Northern Ireland, in which gunmen and bombers who have blighted the Province are put to cool their heels. It is noted particularly for the 'H-blocks', prison buildings so named from their H-shaped ground plan, intended to facilitate security. The Maze was formerly known as Long Kesh.

McAdoo Tubes
A former nickname for the Hudson and Manhattan Railroad Company tunnels, completed in 1912, connecting New Jersey with Manhattan, so called because it was mainly through the efforts of William Gibbs McAdoo that the financing was secured to build them.

McCormick Place
The world's largest exhibition centre, on Lake Shore Drive, in Chicago south of the Loop. Destroyed by fire in 1967, it was rebuilt twice its original size and reopened in January 1971, and has since been still further expanded.

Med, the
An informal nickname for the Mediterranean Sea.

Megalopolis
A nickname that has been bestowed on the chain of cities from Boston, Massachusetts, to Washington, D. C., as their suburbs have continued to spread outward till they meet in one long continuum. The name is made up of the Greek elements *megalo-* 'great, large' and *-polis* 'city', and has been bestowed on very large cities that have grown extensively, like Los Angeles and Tokyo.

Melanesia
A collective term for the islands off the northeast coast of Australia, to the south of Micronesia. Its main constituents are Papua New Guinea, Fiji, New Hebrides, New Caledonia, the Solomon Islands, and the Bismarck Archipelago. The name literally means 'black islands', and was originally coined because of the dark skins of the inhabitants. See also **Micronesia, Oceania, Polynesia.**

Melting Pot, the

A nickname of New York City, so called because most immigrants to the U. S. entered through this port, many remaining and blending their cultures.

Melton Mowbray

A town in Leicestershire, in the Midlands of England, that has powerful associations with food and with foxhunting. It is the headquarters of the manufacture of Stilton cheese (the village of Stilton itself, where the cheese was first sold, is away to the southeast in Cambridgeshire), and it is famous, too, for its pork pies. But it is also at the heart of the Shires, and the noted Quorn hunt operates in the area. Its most bizarre contribution to the terminology of field sports must be the *Melton pad*, a sort of hernia truss specially made to be worn on horseback. In former times Melton Mowbray was a clothmaking centre, and *melton* is a heavy woollen fabric named after it.

Mercia

A kingdom which occupied large parts of the Midlands of England in Anglo-Saxon times. Its most powerful king was Offa (757–96). In modern times the name has been revived and applied to various administrative areas in the region; the West Mercian police, for example, are responsible for the western Midlands, based at Worcester. See also **Offa's Dyke**.

Merseyside

A metropolitan county above the Mersey River in the Northwest of England, comprising the city of Liverpool and surrounding districts. Its name is associated in the public imagination particularly with the Mersey sound, pop music of the sort played by Gerry and the Pacemakers and similar Liverpool groups in the 1960s; but sadly, in the 1980s, it is coming to be linked increasingly with inner-city decline and social tension, as the once busy docks have fallen silent and unemployment has grown.

Mesopotamia

The name for a land in ancient times that lay between the Tigris and Euphrates rivers; much of this is now in modern Iraq. This fertile area was the centre of the Sumerian, Akkadian, Babylonian, and Assyrian civilizations. The term, in Greek, means '(land) between the rivers'. See also **Fertile Crescent**.

Metroland

A name given to a large area of land fanning out from northwest London into the Home Counties. In the early 20th century it was served by the Metropolitan Railway, and the name was coined to publicize the scheme by which the railway company bought up large tracts of countryside on both sides of the line and built houses on them; to their remote rural quietness London office workers could return gratefully each evening. The railway, now the Metropolitan Line of the London Underground, starts at Baker Street Station, passes through what was once Middlesex, and continues into the depths of Hertfordshire and Buckingham-shire—'beechy Bucks', in the words of John Betjeman, the poet who captured the essence of Metroland so evocatively. The name came still further into prominence with Margot Metroland, a character in several of Evelyn Waugh's novels. It has subsequently been applied more generally to any residential belt surrounding a metropolis.

Mezzogiorno, the

The southern part of Italy. In area it corresponds roughly to the ancient Kingdom of Naples; its northern limit is usually taken to be the River Garigliano, just to the north of Naples, and it extends down into the toe of Italy. Superficially a land of sun and wine (*mezzogiorno* is Italian for 'noonday'), the reality has not always been so idyllic; problems of back-wardness, poverty, poor soil (not to mention the Mafia) have led to depopulation as people move to the north of Italy in search of work and prosperity.

Micronesia

A collective term for the islands that comprise the northwestern section of Oceania, to the north of Melanesia, in the South Pacific Ocean. Its main constituents are the Caroline Islands, the Marianas (of which Guam is one), the Marshall Islands, Kiribati (formerly the Gilbert Islands), and Nauru. The name literally means 'small islands'. See also **Melanesia, Oceania, Polynesia**.

Middle Border, the

A name for an area in the Upper Midwest of the United States, including North and South Dakota and parts of Minnesota, Iowa, Wyoming, and Montana.

Middle East, the

The Middle East, or *Mideast* as it is also called, especially in American English, is a vaguely defined area that has moved considerably westward over the years. When it first came into existence as a concept, it was situated, quite neatly and logically, between the Near East and the Far East, and comprised Iran, Iraq, Afghanistan, India, and Burma. Since then, however, its occidental shift has eaten up most of what was formerly the Near East, and left much of its own former territory without a distinguishing epithet. In the 1980s it covers northeast Africa and much of southwest Asia, and by convention includes Egypt, Saudi Arabia, Syria, Iraq, Israel, Lebanon, Jordan, Yemen, the Gulf States and probably Libya and Iran; many would also include Turkey. With the notable exception of Israel, therefore, the Middle East is made up exclusively of Arab, or at least Islamic states, and is often thought of in a shorthand way as corresponding with the Arab World, excepting, of course, Israel. See also **Far East**, Gulf States under **Gulf, Near East**.

Middle Kingdom, the

The name by which China was known in the West in Renaissance times. It is a translation of a term the Chinese themselves used to describe their empire, believing it to be at the centre of the world. See also **Cathay**.

Middle Passage, the

A name given in the days of slavery to the middle section of the Atlantic Ocean. It was the route taken by the slave ships from West Africa to North America and the Caribbean, and was probably originally so called because the voyage formed the central part of the slaves' journey from their homes to the estates and plantations where they were being taken.

Middlesex

A former county in southeast England, to the west of London. It became absorbed into London in 1965, but although it no longer officially exists its ghost has certainly not been laid. Teams known as 'Middlesex' continue to play in the English county cricket and rugby competitions, for example, and it is probably true to say that most local residents still regard themselves as living in Middlesex. During its official existence it was one of the Home Counties, and in the early 19th century its beauties inspired the poet Keats; but long before its change of status its little

villages and hamlets, such as Harrow-on-the-Hill, Twickenham, Isleworth, and Ruislip, had become merged into the general subtopia of
London.

Midgetman
A small, mobile, ground-based, intercontinental ballistic missile, the
SICBM, scheduled in 1986 for development by the United States.

Midi, le
The French term for what in English is more usually referred to as the
South of France. There is a distinction in usage, however; for while *South
of France* conjures up mainly the Riviera, *Midi* embraces the hinterland
of Mediterranean France. It has no precise boundaries, but the 45th
parallel—45° north—is a traditional northern extremity; to the south of
this is a land of warmth and sunshine, a land where the classic ingredients
of Midi cuisine reign supreme: olive oil, garlic, and tomatoes. Its range
west to east extends from the Spanish border to the Italian, although
there is some tendency to favour the term *Midi* for the section to the west
of the River Rhone, in contrast to Provence to the east.

Midlands, the
A name applied, somewhat by default, to those areas of England that are
not the North, the South, the West, or East Anglia. Since the application
of these terms is a little vague, the boundaries of the Midlands themselves
are rather loosely drawn; but on the whole it may be said with confidence
that the Midlands include Leicestershire, Lincolnshire, Northamptonshire, Oxfordshire, Staffordshire, and Warwickshire. Most people would
also include at least the southern parts of Cheshire, Derbyshire, and
Nottinghamshire, the northern parts of Buckinghamshire and Bedfordshire, and the western part of Cambridgeshire. Although Shropshire and
particularly Hereford and Worcester are often regarded as being in the
West, they too are not infrequently counted as being in the Midlands. In
addition to this general application, a more specific but now somewhat
dated usage links the Midlands with the foxhunting counties of the eastern Midlands, particularly in Leicestershire and Northamptonshire—the
Shires, as they are often known. See also **East Midlands, West Midlands**.

Midwest, the
In the United States, an area encompassing those states in the central and
somewhat eastern part of the country, namely, Ohio, Indiana, Illinois,

Wisconsin, Minnesota, Iowa, Missouri, Arkansas, and Kentucky. The area has no specific definition and its boundaries depend on the point of view of the speaker. Compare **East, South, West.**

Mile High City, the
A nickname of Denver, Colorado.

Milton Keynes
A town in Buckinghamshire, in southern England. Until the 1960s it was a small village, but in 1967 it was officially designated a "new town", and it has since been radically transformed: modern buildings have sprouted enthusiastically, commerce and light industry have moved in, the Open University (which operates via broadcasting) was established there in 1971, and it has become a thriving population centre. Many feel, though, that like most man-made towns, it suffers from not having grown organically, and it has become something of a byword for artificiality—typified perhaps by a notorious set of plastic cows placed in a field there to foster an air of rural tranquillity.

Mincing Lane
A street in the City of London that is traditionally the centre of the capital's tea and wine trades. Its name has nothing to do with chopping things up small; it comes from a convent of *minchins* (an old word for 'nuns') that used to hold property there.

Minsky's
The shortened name of Minsky Brothers' National Winter Garden, a burlesque theatre in lower Manhattan, operated by four brothers, Billy, Herbert, Morton, and Abe Minsky. From its early development in the 1870s, burlesque had provided entertainment—'fun for all the family'—which, while not entirely wholesome fare, was characterized more by vulgarity than by lewdness or lasciviousness, even in the eyes of the New York Society for the Suppression of Vice, an organization founded in 1873 by J. P. Morgan to monitor the art, literature, and theatre presented to the people of the city. Burlesque in those days was the humour of dialect comedians, of the raucous slapstick of the comics who beat one another with inflated bladders, of leather-lunged 'coon-shouters' and other singers, and of the line of costumed dancers, from which the modern musical-comedy chorus line developed. It was where the *haut monde* and hoi polloi rubbed elbows with the likes of Robert Benchley,

Reginald Marsh, e. e. cummings, and Edmund Wilson. Minsky's head-lined shimmy dancers like Mademoiselle Fifi, a twenty-year-old, well-constructed blonde billed as 'Mlle Fifi from Paris, France, former Prima Ballerina Assoluta, Imperial Opera House, St Petersburg, Russia'. She was actually Betty Buzby, daughter of George Buzby, a police officer in Philadelphia's Vice Squad. On the night of April 20, 1925, Mlle Fifi for the first time removed her clothes on stage and, at the direction of John Sumner, Secretary of the Society for the Suppression of Vice, police swarmed through the theatre, arresting dancers, comics, and all the other performers they could lay hands on. Seven weeks later the verdict was returned: the case was dismissed. Yet, partly because of the notoriety of the trial and partly because of subsequent developments in the promotion and staging of burlesque, the form deteriorated into a sordid bump-and-grind striptease exhibition, offering little entertainment and appealing only to the prurient. It suffered a revival during the Depression, when Minsky opened theatres on 42nd Street, but then closed in 1937, when Mayor Fiorello H. La Guardia directed the revocation of licenses and forbade even the use of the name, *burlesque*.

Miracle Mile

A stretch of Wilshire Boulevard in Los Angeles, extending approximately one mile from La Brea Avenue to Fairfax Avenue. The name was applied in the 1930s by a real estate developer, A. W. Ross, in order to promote the commercial possibilities of the Boulevard. The decentralization of Los Angeles' central business district began in the 1920s and development was directed westward along major arteries, Wilshire Boulevard in particular. The Miracle Mile became a great commercial success with the establishment of a number of fashionable stores on the boulevard and the motorization of the shopping public.

Mississippi Bubble

The nickname given to a failed scheme, devised and executed in Paris (1716) by the Scottish economist, John Law, in which a monopoly of trade with Canada and the Mississippi Territory, both then under control of France, was funded by paper currency. After prospering initially, the overissuing of paper money, together with a failure of the promoters to further the development brought about its collapse, in 1720, placing the government of France and thousands of its prominent families in or close to bankruptcy. See also **German Coast.**

Mistelbach
A town in Austria, about 20 miles north of Vienna, which has long been the target of jokes about the silly speech and behaviour of its inhabitants. See also **Chelm, Gotham, Kocourkov.**

Mistress of the Seas
A nickname of Great Britain.

Mitchell Library
The major source of documentary material relating to Australia, named after its founder, David Scott Mitchell, who bequeathed his private library in 1901 to what was then the Public Library of New South Wales. It now forms part of the New South Wales State Library.

moaning Minnie
A World War II soldiers' nickname for a German mortar shell *Minnenwerfer*, later transposed to the air-raid warning sirens.

Mo Bay
A nickname in frequent local use for Montego Bay, a luxurious vacation resort on the north coast of the island of Jamaica, which attracts large numbers of American tourists.

Mohawk Trail
A road between North Adams and Pittsfield, in northwestern Massachusetts, named for the Mohawk Indians, who once dwelt in the area. Parts of it were undoubtedly used as a 'trail' by the early inhabitants, but it is not said to follow a particular historic route as is, say, the **Appalachian Trail** (*q.v.*). Now a scenic highway that winds through the northern parts of the Berkshire Mountains, just south of the Vermont border, the Mohawk Trail is a popular drive for tourists, especially in the autumn, when the variegated foliage of the great variety of trees in the surrounding forests can be appreciated to its best advantage.

Mongolia
The region of central Asia inhabited by the Mongols. In the Middle Ages, when it was known as Tartary, the Mongols' sphere of influence, particularly under Genghis Khan, extended over a vast area, from eastern Europe to the Pacific. But today Mongolia is somewhat more circumscribed. It is divided up between three nations: Inner Mongolia, which is a region

of China; Tuva, a republic of the Soviet Union; and the Mongolian People's Republic. The last was a Chinese province, known as Outer Mongolia, from 1691 to 1924; since then it has been an independent state. In the West, Outer Mongolia has long been suggestive of the ultimate in remoteness. See also **Tartary**.

Monitor and *Merrimack*

The first ironclad warships whose battle at Hampton Roads, Virginia in 1862 marked a turning point in naval warfare by focusing attention on the importance of armour-plated ships. The *Monitor* was built of iron as well as being ironclad. The *Merrimack* was originally wood and had been scuttled by Federal troops when they evacuated the Navy yard at Portsmouth, Virginia. The Confederates raised it, covered it with iron plates, and renamed it the *Virginian*, though it is usually known by its original name.

Monkey State, the

A nickname of Tennesse, so called in reference to the bill passed in its House of Representatives (1925) that prohibited the teaching of the theory of evolution in any of its schools supported in whole or in part by public funds.

Montmartre

A district in northern central Paris famed as an artists' quarter. It is built on a hill—Parisians' nickname for it is *la Botte* 'the hillock'—and the white domes of the Sacré Coeur cathedral on its summit are a well-known Paris landmark. Its bohemian reputation owes more to history than to present-day fact. Most of the artists moved over to the Left Bank before World War I, and the artistic efforts on display today in the Place du Tertre are laid on purely for the benefit of tourists. But despite commercialization Montmartre manages to retain much of its quaint village atmosphere. Nightlife is still a local specialty, too, as it was in the days of Toulouse-Lautrec; Pigalle is here, and the girls continue to can-can in the Moulin Rouge.

Moor, the

A familiar abbreviation for Dartmoor, bleak granite uplands in Devon, southwest England. It is used particularly with reference to Dartmoor prison, at Princetown in the heart of the moor, whose isolated position makes it an ideal place to house long-term or dangerous prisoners.

Morgue Motorway
A nickname given to a four-lane highway near Marbella, Spain, notorious
for its high death toll. Formerly a mere goat track, it is now patrolled by
fleets of speeding Rolls Royces, belonging in many cases to the more
dubious denizens of the **Costa del Crime** (*q.v.*), which offer a constant
threat to life and limb.

Morningside
A well-to-do southern suburb of Edinburgh, Scotland, that is celebrated
for the supposedly ultra-refined accent of its inhabitants. There is a theory that it was first introduced by the Irish elocutionist Thomas Sheridan,
father of the more famous Richard Brinsley Sheridan, the playwright.

mortgage belt
A nickname for the outer suburbs of new houses in any Australian city,
likely to contain voters concerned about home-loan interest rates.

mosquito armada
The nickname for the courageous fleet of private boats, from rowboats to
pleasure cruisers, that joined the Royal Navy in rescuing British troops
from across the English Channel on the beaches at Dunkirk in 1940.
Because of their extraordinary bravery, they were later honoured by being
allowed to fly the cross of St George.

Mosquito Coast
An epithet of the coasts of Nicaragua and Honduras, along the Gulf of
Mexico.

Moss Bros
A familiar name (pronounced 'Moss Bross') for Moss Brothers, a well-
known British firm of gentlemen's outfitters that is particularly associated
with the hire of formal wear. A classy wedding, with many morning coats
and toppers in evidence, is most certainly a Moss Bros affair.

Mother-in-Law of the Navy
A nickname of Norfolk, Virginia, so called because the Norfolk Navy
Yard, one of the oldest and most important, is directly opposite it on the
Portsmouth side of the Elizabeth River.

Mother of Parliaments, the
A name often applied to the British Parliament at Westminster, as being the assembly on which many other such institutions around the world are based. However, the source of the expression, John Bright's 'England is the mother of parliaments' (1865), shows its original application to have been slightly different.

Mother of Presidents
A nickname of Virginia, so called because eight of her native sons became presidents of the United States: George Washington, Thomas Jefferson, James Madison, James Monroe, William Henry Harrison, John Tyler, Zachary Taylor, and Woodrow Wilson. However, Ohio also claims the title, for her seven sons: Ulysses S. Grant; Rutherford B. Hayes, James A. Garfield, Benjamin Harrison, William McKinley, William Howard Taft, and Warren G. Harding. William Henry Harrison was living in Ohio when he became president.

Mother of States
A nickname for Virginia, so called because all or part of eight other states were formed from western territory originally claimed by her: Illinois, Indiana, Kentucky, Michigan, Minnesota, Ohio, West Virginia, and Wisconsin.

Motown
A nickname of Detroit, Michigan, from 'motor town' because it is the centre of the automobile industry in the United States. The name came into prominence also because it was used as a trade name for a company (in California) that has published popular musical records and tapes.

Moulin Rouge
Literally, the 'Red Mill', though why it was so named is shrouded in the mysteries of the 19th century. A theatre-nightclub in Paris that, historically, at least, gained its reputation as a place of wild abandon, frequented by the *trottoises* of Pigalle but, especially, by Henri de Toulouse-Lautrec, the painter who made it famous through his posters advertising the establishment and, notoriously, the dancer Jane Avril. It is said to be the place where the can-can was first danced, but there are those who would credit the **Folies Bergère** (*q.v.*) with that accomplishment.

Mrs O'Leary's barn

The structure in which Mrs O'Leary's cow is said to have kicked over a
lantern to start the Great Chicago Fire of October 8–10, 1871. The fire
killed more than 250 people, destroyed some $200 million worth of prop-
erty and left about 100,000—a third of the population—homeless. A long
period of dry weather and subsequent tinderbox conditions helped the fire
to spread rapidly. Most historians agree that the blaze did, in fact, begin
in the O'Leary barn on DeKoven Street, about a mile south and just west
of the present Loop area, but whether it was caused by the family cow is
not certain, and several other possible causes have been given. (Mrs
O'Leary blamed a careless neighbour known to have entered the barn just
before the fire began.) The site is today occupied by the Chicago Fire
Academy.

Mummerset

An imaginary southwestern English county usually invoked to express
spurious rusticity; a country yokel portrayed in a play or book as speaking in an exaggerated West Country fashion, with many outlandish but
probably obsolete dialectal expressions, is said to have a 'Mummerset
accent'. The name is a blend of *mummer*, an itinerant entertainer in
former times, and *Somerset*, a West Country county. Compare **Loamshire**.

Muscle Shoals Area

This area includes the cities of Florence, Muscle Shoals, Sheffield, and
Tuscumbia in northwest Alabama, as well as the nearby surrounding
areas. The name came from the Muscle Shoals of the Tennessee river, a
former navigational hazard that was eliminated by the building of Wilson
Dam. One theory of the origin of the name holds that it comes from the
Cherokee word *dagunahi*, meaning 'mussel place'—'muscle' being a vari-
ant spelling of *mussel*. A second, but less probable explanation in the
local area attributes the name to the fact that negotiating the original
shoals required considerable 'muscle'.

Muscovy

A name applied in former ties to Russia. In strict terms Muscovy was a
Russian principality, whose capital was Moscow (from which it derived its
name) and which existed between the 13th and the 16th centuries; but
with the vagueness of early geography, the name soon spread to the rest
of the country.

Museum of Science and Industry
The oldest, largest, and most popular museum of its kind in the United States, located in Jackson Park, on the South Side of Chicago. The museum houses a wide range of technological—often nostalgic—exhibits in a spacious edifice that was erected as the Palace of Fine Arts for the World's Columbian Exposition of 1893. Many of the displays are constructed so as to enable visitors to interact by means of knobs, buttons, and other controls. Attractions include a visitable coal mine, an extensive model-railway layout, and a German U-boat (U-505) captured intact on June 4, 1944, the first enemy warship captured by the U. S. Navy after the War of 1812. See also **White City, 1.**

Namibia
A territory of disputed nomenclature (and ownership) in southwestern Africa, to the north of South Africa. Until 1919 it was a German colony, known as German Southwest Africa. Following World War I it was confiscated, and in 1920 was assigned by the League of Nations as a trust territory to South Africa, since when it has officially been called South-West Africa. The mandate was cancelled by the United Nations in 1966, but South Africa refused to give up the territory. In affirmation of its *de jure* independent status, the UN in 1968 declared its name to be Namibia (the Namib is a desert that occupies its coastal region). However, the situation remains fluid, and, whether as a compromise or for clarity, it is often referred to as South-West Africa-Namibia and is shown on maps as Namibia (South-West Africa).

Naples
A city of proverbial beauty on the west coast of Italy. The saying 'See Naples and die' implies that anywhere else in the world would be a visual anticlimax, and indeed Naples' setting, built on hills surrounding the wide Bay of Naples, with Mount Vesuvius nearby, is most striking. There is a

possible irony in the aphorism, however, for Naples used to be notorious for its rampant cholera and typhoid.

Narrows, the
A strait, about one mile wide, joining Upper and Lower New York Bays, that separates Staten Island from Brooklyn.

Natchez Trace
The name of a trail between Nashville, Tennessee, and Natchez, Mississippi, important in the early development of those areas.

National, the
See **Grand National.**

Nation's Most Corrupt State
A nickname for Rhode Island at the turn of the century, in reference to the graft and corruption there.

Native States, the
A collective term used for those states that were more or less self-governing during the time when Britain ruled India. Also known as the *Indian States and Agencies*, there were no fewer than 562 of them, the largest being Hyderabad, Gwalior, Baroda, Mysore, Cochin, Jammu and Kashmir, Travancor, Sikkim, and Indore. They were ruled by their own rajahs and maharajahas, but a British resident or adviser was always present to provide a guiding hand. After independence in 1947 they were gradually merged into India and Pakistan.

Navel of the Nation, the
A nickname of Kansas, because it lies almost at the geographical centre of the 48 contiguous states.

Navy Pier
A Lake Michigan facility, located just north of the Loop in Chicago. Originally known as Municipal Pier, the 3,000-foot-long facility has been eclipsed in recent years by the major port developed at Lake Calumet on the city's Far South Side, some thirteen miles south of the Loop. Nowadays, the city-owned pier is the site of many ethnic and cultural events.

Naze, the

A headland on the north Essex coast, just to the east of Colchester in East Anglia, England. The name, which may be connected with the word *nose*, is also applied to Lindesnes, a promontory at the southern tip of Norway.

Near East, the

A term with a dated air to it, which has generally fallen out of use since World War II. In its earliest use it referred more or less to the western lands of area now known as the Middle East: Libya, Egypt, Arabia, Palestine, Syria, and Turkey. But confusingly, *Near East* also once referred to Turkey, the Levant, and large parts of the Balkans, in southeast Europe: in other words, the Ottoman Empire. However, the Ottoman Empire no longer exists, and *Middle East*, though not as specific, is in far wider use as a geographic reference; if it is used at all today, *Near East* most often refers to Turkey. See also **Asia Minor, Far East, Middle East.**

Near North Side

A diverse, trendy, generally upscale section of Chicago where much of its cultural and professional life is centred. Stretching north and a short way west from the Loop and the Magnificent Mile, the Near North Side includes the often overlapping Old Town, New Town, Lincoln Park, Lakeview, and Wrigleyville areas. Particularly rich in theatres, specialty shops, and ethnic restaurants, the atmosphere of the area bears a distant but growing likeness to that of Greenwich Village in New York City. See also **Billy Goat Tavern, Biograph Theater, Bughouse Square, Cabrini-Green Public Housing Project, Gold Coast, Holy Name Cathedral, the Magnificent Mile, Navy Pier, New Town, Old Town, Rush Street, Water Tower, Wrigleyville.**

Neasden

A district in northwest London immortalized in the 1960s by the satirical magazine *Private Eye*. Innocent of any fine architecture, historical sites, or literary associations, it is of such resounding dullness that it inspired the *Eye* to adopt it as the archetype of grey suburbia, where even monotony would be exciting. Neasden, **Clapham** (*q.v.*), and **Wigan** (*q.v.*) epitomize what in other times and other cultures appear in the folk literature as **Gotham** (*q.v.*) (with its 'Wise Men'), **Kocourkov** (*q.v.*), **Mistelbach** (*q.v.*), and, for eastern Europe, **Chelm** (*q.v.*).

Needles, the
A line of three tall sharp chalk pillars that form the western extremity of the Isle of Wight, off the south coast of England. They protrude from the sea like gleaming teeth, and a lighthouse is situated at their tip to warn shipping. See also **Island, 1.**

Neogaea
In the scientific study of the distribution of animal species around the world, the name given to South and Central America. Compare **Arctogaea, Notogaea.**

Nevada Proving Grounds
The site, in southeast Nevada, of the U. S. Atomic Energy Commission's nuclear tests conducted at Yucca Flat and Frenchman Flat in 1951.

Never Never
A name for remote inland areas of northern Australia, especially northwest Queensland and the Northern Territory. The name was popularized by a well-known book, *We of the Never-Never* (1908), by Mrs Aeneas Gunn, a record of her life with her husband on a cattle station on the Roper River, some 500 kilometres south of Darwin.

New England
The area in the northeastern part of the United States encompassing the states that were the places of early settlement by colonists from England, namely, Maine, New Hampshire, Vermont, Rhode Island, Massachusetts, and Connecticut. See also **East.**

New Forest
An area of woodland, with some heath, in southern Hampshire, near Southampton, in England. It has been so called for about 900 years.

Newgate Prison
A prison, built in 1769 in London, that figures occasionally in English literature. It was demolished in 1902, and the **Old Bailey** (*q.v.*) now occupies the site.

New Holland
An early name for Australia, especially the western side of the continent.

Newmarket

A town in Suffolk, just to the northeast of Cambridge, that is synonymous with horseracing in England. The first race took place on Newmarket Heath in 1619, watched enthusiastically by King James I, and the place has gone from strength to strength ever since. Today it is home to the Jockey Club, the governing body of English racing, has many training stables for racehorses, holds a famous annual bloodstock sale which realizes many millions of pounds, and hosts several celebrated races, including the 1000 and 2000 Guineas and the Cesarewich.

News of the Screws, the

A facetious nickname for the *News of the World*, a popular British Sunday newspaper that specializes in lurid stories of sexual shenanigans.

New Sweden

A nickname of Delaware, so called because in 1638 a fort at what is now Wilmington was manned by Swedes and Finns, and for many years thereafter, the peninsula was under Swedish rule.

New Town

A richly diverse area of the Near North Side of Chicago, noted for its nightlife and shopping and as the heart of the city's sizable gay community. It is one of several Near North areas currently undergoing so-called 'gentrification', the process in which the well-to-do move in, rehabilitate charming old houses, increase property values, rents, and taxes, and attract new businesses—meanwhile forcing away the poor, who can no longer afford to live there.

New Town, the

In the 18th century, increasing prosperity in Edinburgh, Scotland's capital, provided the impetus to expand and break out of the crowded old city huddled around the castle and to build anew and splendidly. The result was the New Town, an area of magnificent Georgian terraces, squares, and crescents, designed mostly by James Craig, fully befitting the dignity of the Athens of the North. Its southern boundary, and most famous thoroughfare, is Princes Street, which has shops along its northern side but to the south is open to a splendid vista of the Castle Rock.

New World, the

A term applied to the Americas by their European discoverers. It was still a sufficiently live general epithet in the late 19th century for Anton Dvořák to name his Ninth Symphony 'From the New World'. In the present day, though, its main use is probably in zoological and botanical contexts, with reference to the Western Hemisphere as a whole. Compare **Old World**.

NIDA

A familiar name (pronounced NY-da) for the National Institute of Dramatic Art, founded in 1958 under the joint sponsorship of the University of New South Wales, the Australian Theatre Trust, and the Australian Broadcasting Commission.

Nine Elms

An area in southwest London, on the south bank of the Thames, just to the north of Battersea. It contains Battersea Power Station, a famous London landmark with its towering chimneys and monolithic cathedral-like nave; and in 1974 it became the home of London's principal fruit and vegetable market, when the New Covent Garden Market was opened.

NoHo

A nickname given to a neighbourhood in mid Manhattan, west of Lafayette Street, east of Sixth Avenue, and, as the name suggests, *no*rth of *Ho*uston (pronounced HOWstin) Street. It is a later development than SoHo (so named because it is *so*uth of *Ho*uston), in somewhat jocular imitation of it. It consists largely of commercial loft buildings in which former office and factory areas have been modernized and fitted out as dwelling places and, occasionally, as studios for the artists who occupy them. Also, **No-Ho**. See also **SoHo**.

no man's land

A piece of disputed territory between opposing armies. The expression gained currency during World War I, when it referred to the areas in France across which German and Allied armies seesawed for many months. As these were totally laid waste in the process, the term acquired the additional notion of 'wasteland', which it sometimes retains today. According to citations in the *Oxford English Dictionary*, the phrase goes back to the early 14th century, when it referred to a section of barren land, north of London Wall, where executions sometimes took place.

Nore, the
A sandbank in the mouth of the River Thames, off Sheerness. It is best known for the naval mutiny that occurred there in 1797.

North, the
1. In the broadest terms, the North in Britain is anywhere north of London; for example, the route indicated to 'The North' on a road sign takes one up to Scotland. More specifically, the North is northern England, but its southern limit is purely a relative matter; to someone from the South, the North quite possibly includes places like Derby and Nottingham, whereas for a Tynesider Sheffield (which is north of Derby and Nottingham) is distinctly in the Midlands. Traditionally, the River Humber is said to mark the boundary between the North and Midlands, but this has the disadvantage of excluding, for example, Manchester and Liverpool, which most Britons would assign to the North. In practice, two factors are probably decisive. First, accent: anyone who speaks a dialect roughly similar to that of Yorkshire or Lancashire is likely to be regarded as a Northerner. And second, industrialization: the stereotyped view of the North is of a continuous vista of factory chimneys, cooling towers, coal mines, and slag heaps (although, in fact, it contains areas of great natural beauty). A general rule of thumb based on these factors would be to say that, starting from the west, the North includes northern Cheshire, probably dips down to take in Derbyshire and Nottinghamshire, and then shades off northeast towards the Humber estuary; anywhere between there and the Scottish border is the North. Culturally and sociologically it is quite distinct from the southern part of the country, which is on the whole wealthier and has a preponderance of middle-class inhabitants. Compare **Midlands, Northeast, Northwest, South.** See also **Tyneside, Watford.**
2. In the United States, those states in the northeastern and north central parts of the country north of the Mason-Dixon line, especially those that sided against the Confederates in the Civil War. See also **South.**
3. In geopolitical terms, *the North* has taken on new connotations in the latter part of the 20th century. As contrasted with the South, it refers basically to the economically advantaged and industrially developed nations of the northern hemisphere—the world's 'haves'. But since, like East and West, it is not a strictly geographical term, southern-hemisphere countries like Australia are included in the North as well. It was popularized as a concept by the publication in 1980 of the so-called *Brandt*

Report, in full *North-South, a programme for survival; report of the Independent Commission on International Development*.

North Africa
A term used for Africa north of the Tropic of Cancer. It includes Morocco, Algeria, Tunisia, Libya, and Egypt.

North Britain
A circumlocution for Scotland which enjoyed some popularity from the 17th to the 19th centuries. It first came into regular use after 1707, when Scotland and England united to form Great Britain; according to the *Oxford English Dictionary*, it was still current in the 1880s, albeit 'chiefly in postal use'. It never succeeded in ousting *Scotland* as the standard name for the country, but its memory is preserved particularly in the famous North British Hotel, on Princes Street in Edinburgh.

North Country, the
Geographically, the North Country in Britain corresponds more or less to the North, but its connotations are markedly different. Whereas *the North* suggests a grimy industrialized landscape, *the North Country* stresses its prelapsarian state, before the Industrial Revolution. It conjures up visions of windblown moors and fells, ruddy-cheeked countrymen and women, good ale and beef, and laconic humour. Compare **Broad Acres**.

Northeast, the
1. The northeastern corner of England, including the counties of Northumberland, Durham, Tyne and Wear, and probably also Cleveland. Although often sweepingly included under the broad category, *the North*, the Northeast is proudly distinct from its southerly neighbour, Yorkshire, which Northeasterners often dismiss, only half in jest, as belonging to the Midlands. The heart of the region is probably Newcastle-upon-Tyne and the surrounding Tyneside, whose inhabitants, the Geordies, have given the Northeast its nickname, Geordieland. Geordie is the name of the dialect they speak, too, a lilting speech which in its pure form can often be impenetrable to outsiders. See also **Geordieland, Jarrow**.
2. In the United States, the District of Columbia and those states generally running northwards along the Atlantic coast to New England, namely, Delaware, Maryland, Pennsylvania, New Jersey, New York, and the New England states.

Northeast Corridor

A general term, encountered chiefly in railway jargon, referring to the rights of way between New York City and Boston, though, technically, it goes beyond into Maine. With the spread of the northeastern **Megalopolis** (*q.v.*), it has lately been extended southward in concept to include Washington, D. C.

Northeast Kingdom

A nickname for a rural part of northeastern Vermont, comprising Caledonia, Orleans, and Essex counties, thought to have been coined in 1949 by George D. Aiken, former governor and U. S. senator. It has become a useful term to designate the area for socio-political, economic, and planning purposes.

North End

The informal name given to that part of Boston bounded by the **Haymarket** (*q.v.*), the Northeast Expressway, and, on the east, the Atlantic Ocean. Primarily a section settled by Italians that retains its ethnic reputation in its restaurants and food markets, the North End has in recent years become gentrified and its population in the mid 1980s would be said to be homogeneous.

Northland, the

A term applied to the northernmost outposts of many countries and continents. In the past it was used for the top third of Scotland, to the north of Inverness, and in present-day usage it covers both the peninsula that contains Norway and Sweden and the northern fastnesses of Canada. Severnaya Zemlya, a Soviet archipelago in the Arctic ocean, means literally 'North Land'.

North Pole

The northern end of the earth's axis of rotation which, owing to libration, changes slightly; the geographic north pole. It is not the same as the north magnetic pole, which varies as much as one degree in a year and may be 12° away from the geographic pole. The surrounding area is composed entirely of ice floes, which float atop the Arctic Ocean. In fancy, it is a cold, remote place inhabited only by polar bears (who actually live farther south) and by Santa Claus. See also **South Pole.**

North Shore

1. An informal name for the east-west shore of Long Island (see **Island**) that borders on the Long Island Sound, between Sands Point and Orient Point, at the tip of the North Fork. It has many old, picturesque, and wealthy communities, notably Sands Point and Oyster Bay, where millionaires long ago established large estates with impressive mansions. Its shores are configured by many deep-water harbours, as at Oyster Bay, Northport (Lloyds Harbor), and Port Jefferson, which are densely occupied by yacht clubs and marinas. The further east one travels, the sparser the concentration of such facilities, and east of Port Jefferson, the shoreline, with only a few inlets for boats, has remained quite rural. See also **South Shore.**
2. A section north of Boston beginning north of Lynn and extending as far as Portsmouth, New Hampshire, along the Atlantic coast. It is associated in the main with affluent horse-owners of inherited wealth, who pursue sports like fox-hunting and polo. It was settled early and its shore is dotted with shipyards, as those at Marblehead, once known for the building of whalers, in recent years for the design and construction of yachts.

North Side

Multi-ethnic, economically diverse area of Chicago stretching north from the downtown, Loop area to the northern city limits and reaching roughly two miles west from the bordering Lake Michigan; on the west is the city's Northwest Side, which includes some of the oldest middle-class enclaves of Polish, Czechoslovakian, and other European immigrants; on the north, along the lake, is the town of Evanston, home of the main campus of Northwestern University, the Chicago area's first university, founded in 1850. Distinctive North Side areas include the generally upscale Near North Side, the Andersonville section, settled by Swedish immigrants, and the relatively poor, often troubled Uptown area, in the latter part of the 20th century the home of many subsistence-level residents, including sizable numbers of Appalachians, American Indians, and Latinos. Also on the North Side, bordering the lake, is Lincoln Park, with its zoo, beaches, jogging paths, and other facilities, and Graceland Cemetery, the spacious, park-like burial place of such figures as George Pullman, builder of the railway sleeping-car and of the company town of **Pullman** (*q.v.*), now a section of the city's South Side; Cyrus McCormick, inventor of the harvesting machine; architects Louis Sullivan and Daniel Burnham; meat magnate Philip Armour; merchant Marshall

Field; real-estate developer Potter Palmer; and former Illinois governor John Peter Altgeld. On the Far North Side, in the northwest reaches of the city, is O'Hare International Airport, the world's busiest. See also **Aragon Ballrom, Haymarket Square, Near North Side, O'Hare International Airport.**

Northumbria

In Anglo-Saxon times, an extensive independent kingdom that stretched all the way from the River Humber to the south of modern Yorkshire, to the Firth of Forth in Scotland. In modern usage it is sometimes employed as an alternative name for the county of Northumberland, a much more circumscribed area.

Northwest, the

1. The western half of the North of England, which is comprised of Cumbria and Lancashire, including Manchester and Liverpool.
2. In the United States, those western states that lie towards the north, namely, Montana, Wyoming, Washington, and Oregon. Compare **Pacific Northwest, Southwest, West.**

Northwest Frontier, the

The name given to the boundary between Afghanistan and Kashmir. The region is of considerable strategic importance to India, as it controls the Khyber Pass, and in 1901 it became part of British India; it was subsequently the scene of many tribal incursions, and the British army was called into action there on many occasions. Post-independence, Northwest Frontier Province is now the northernmost region of Pakistan.

Northwest Passage, the

From the late 15th century, a route from the Atlantic to the Pacific was sought around the north of the American continent. This was the fabled Northwest Passage, which baffled and killed so many explorers, from Sebastian Cabot in 1497-98, through Sir Martin Frobisher, Henry Hudson, William Baffin, and George Vancouver, to Sir Robert McClure, who finally discovered it in 1850. Roald Amundsen was actually the first to navigate it, in 1903-05.

Notogaea

In the scientific study of the distribution of animal species around the world, the name given to Australasia. Compare **Arctogaea, Neogaea.**

Notting Hill

An area in northwest central London, to the north of Holland Park. The prominent West Indian community in the western part of the district is responsible for the annual Notting Hill Carnival, which draws large crowds of participants and onlookers from all parts of London. The eastern part, Notting Hill Gate, a wealthier residential area, gets its name from a turnpike gate which once stood there.

Nullabor Plain

The name of an arid, virtually unpopulated plain extending behind the Great Australian Bight some 300 kilometres west and 250 kilometres east of the border between Western Australia and South Australia. Its maximum width from the coast is about 250 kilometres. Its only settlement of any size is Eucla, with some 200 inhabitants. It is crossed by the Eyre Highway and the Trans-Australian railway. The *Nullabor nymph,* a semi-naked woman reported near Eucla in 1972, was apparently a fiction. The name *Nullabor* is said to be formed from Latin *nullus arbor,* 'no tree'.

Number One, London

The former sobriquet of Apsley House, the London residence of the Duke of Wellington, which is now the Wellington Museum. It is situated at Hyde Park Corner, to the northwest of Buckingham Palace, and was once the westmost house in Piccadilly before the open spaces of Hyde Park and Kensington Gardens.

Number 10

Or, more fully, *Number 10 Downing Street*, the official London residence of the British prime minister. Since the late 19th century the name has become virtually synonymous with the office of prime minister, or indeed with the British government itself—as in 'A Number 10 spokesman said today. . .'. As such, it is often contrasted with 'Whitehall', which tends to stress more the administrative, civil-service aspect of government. The house itself is a rather drab, unremarkable affair in a side street off Whitehall, to the south of Trafalgar Square. It was assigned to Britain's first prime minister, Sir Robert Walpole, in 1732 in his official capacity as First Lord of the Treasury, and has been used by holders of that post ever since. (Although in practice this means that it has been the prime minister's house, that term did not become usual before the middle of the 19th century.) Next door, Number 11 is the official home of the Chancellor of the Exchequer.

Nuremberg eggs
The nickname for the egg-shaped silver watches made there since the 16th century.

Nutmeg State, the
A nickname of Connecticut, so called because the settlers were said to be so canny that they could sell wooden nutmegs.

O-bahn
The name of a system of rapid transport by means of buses running on a specially constructed concrete track to connect central Adelaide, South Australia, with its northeastern suburbs. When completed, the Adelaide O-bahn will be the world's longest guided busway. The name is from German and means a 'track, road' (*Bahn*) 'above ground' (*ober*).

Oberammergau
A village high (elev. 3000 ft.) in the Bavarian Alps where the passion play is performed every ten years (in years evenly divisible by ten). It all began in 1634, when the townspeople put on the passion play in hopes of stopping an epidemic of the Plague, which had killed almost a hundred people in the valley during the Thirty Years' War. The decadal event draws tourists from all parts of the world.

Oceania
A collective term for all the territories of the South Pacific Ocean. It is standardly taken as comprising the island groups of Micronesia, Melanesia, and Polynesia, but very often Australia and New Zealand are included as well, and sometimes also the Malay Archipelago. See also **Australasia**.

Odeon

The proper name of many theatres in the western world. It comes originally from Greek ōideîon 'place of song; music hall' via Latin odeum,
with the same meaning. Thus, it can be seen to be related to ode, but,
likewise, the ignoring of the Latin form, because of its similarity to odium
'hatred', can easily be understood. Its popularity as a name transcends
language barriers: there is an Odéon in Paris, for example; in the United
States it appeared possibly only slightly less frequently as a cinema name
than Bijou, which means 'jewel' in French.

Oder-Neisse Line, the

A line that marks the boundary between Poland and East Germany. It
more or less follows the course of the Oder River from Stettin, on the
Baltic coast, to the south of Frankfurt, where the Neisse River branches
off and continues south to the Czech border at Zittau. Before World War
II, large areas to the east of these rivers belonged to Germany, and the
line was originally set up in 1945 to separate those parts of Germany that
would be under direct Soviet control from those that were to become part
of Poland.

Offa's Dyke

A barrier, in the form of an earthwork, built under the direction of Offa,
king of Mercia (q.v.), England, in the 8th century. Its purpose was to
create a boundary between the English and the Welsh settlements, from
the mouth of the Dee to that of the Wye.

Off Broadway, Off-Off Broadway

'Broadway' in these expressions is taken to refer to the mainstream of
American theatre, not necessarily to the name of the street (q.v.). In fact,
few (in 1986, only one—the Palace) of the legitimate theatres in New
York City are actually situated on Broadway: all are in the side streets in
the 40s. At the end of World War II, with the revival of the theatre, the
costs of staging productions became so great that it was impossible to
raise the money to produce any but those that could successfully capture
the imaginations of wealthy 'angels'. Theatre rents were high, too, so
small theatre groups took to staging their productions in more modest
settings—often just a hired hall—far from the expensive theatre district.
During the late 1940s, such theatrical productions, which, because of the
quality of the original plays and that of the performers were gaining the

attention of reviewers for major periodicals, acquired the generic nickname 'off Broadway'. In the ensuing years, some of these groups became
well established (some as repertory companies), and the theatres where
they performed began to acquire a stability which their owners exploited
by increasing the rents. In time, a new generation of theatrical hopefuls
found the Off-Broadway theatres beyond their reach; undaunted ('The
show must go on'?), they found, in the late 1960s, even more modest
accommodation and settled into abandoned cinemas and other such facilities, even if they were available for only a few nights a week. As New
Yorkers have proved themselves indefatigable theatre buffs, these often
primitive venues—sometimes nothing more than a large restaurant closed
for business that evening—attracted audiences. This manifestation of
thespian perseverance, at two removes from the glitter and gold of Broadway, was dubbed 'Off-Off Broadway'. It is not to be disparaged, for a
number of the plays that began Off-Off Broadway—the term is also used
adverbially—became popular enough to be staked to Broadway-scale in-
vestments (*Oh! Calcutta!*, for example); and some of the players who
were first observed strutting their stuff on dime-sized stages in downtown
Manhattan neighbourhoods so deserted at night that even the rats went
uptown, hit the 'big time', as, for example, did Bernadette Peters, who
starred in *Dames at Sea* in just such a pint-sized palace.

Ogaden, the
A high arid plateau in southeastern Ethiopia, bordering on Somalia. Over
the years it has seen fierce fighting between government troops and local
separatist forces, backed by Somalia, who wish to break away and form
their own state.

O'Hare International Airport
Covering 60,000 acres (almost 94 square miles) in the northwest reaches
of Chicago and handling some 120,000 travellers a day and the arrival or
departure of, on the average, four aircraft every three minutes, Chicago-
O'Hare ranks as the world's busiest airport.

Ohio's Jewels
The nickname for a group of seven statues on the grounds of the capitol
at Columbus, namely, Ulysses S. Grant, William Tecumseh Sherman,
Edwin McMasters Stanton, James A. Garfield, and Rutherford B. Hayes,
all native sons, and Philip Henry Sheridan and Salmon Portland Chase,
who lived in the state for a time.

Oil Dorado
A nickname of the vicinity around Titusville in the northwestern part of Pennsylvania where oil was first discovered (1859) in the United States.

Ol' Man River
A nickname for the Mississippi River, from the song written by Jerome Kern and Oscar Hammerstein II in 1927 for the musical *Showboat*.

Old Bailey
Officially, Old Bailey is a street in the City of London—a turning to the left going up Ludgate Hill to St Paul's. But its name has been transferred to its most famous building, the Central Criminal Court—*the Bailey*, as it is known, affectionately to those who work there, perhaps not so affectionately to those who stand trial there. The street has always had associations with the administration of justice, because the grim Newgate Prison once stood there, and until 1868 it was the scene of public hangings. At the end of the 19th century the prison was demolished and on its site the courthouse was built, with its dome surmounted by the familiar figure of Justice. Here have been conducted most of the celebrated English murder trials of this century, including those of Dr Crippen, George 'Brides in the Bath' Smith, and John Christie.

Old Colony State
A nickname of Massachusetts, so called in reference to the area of the state that was part of the original Plymouth Colony and older than the Massachusetts Bay Colony.

Old Dart, the
A dated Australian nickname for England. Its origin is unknown, but it may well be a scornful reference to the broad arrow, a symbol of British government property familiar to those who were transported to Australia as criminals.

Old Dominion
The official nickname of Virginia, so called because the Colony's acceptance of Charles II of England as their king in 1660 so pleased him that he elevated them to the position of a dominion. In 1663 he quartered the Arms of Virginia on his royal shield, thus ranking them with his four other dominions: England, France, Ireland, and Scotland. The name was

adopted in remembrance of Virginia's being the oldest and most faithful of the Stuart settlements in America.

Old Glory

A popular name for the (officially named) Flag of the United States, reputed to have first been used by William Driver, skipper of the brig *Charles Doggert* in 1837. See also **Stars and Bars, Stars and Stripes.**

Old Ironsides

The affectionate nickname for the famous frigate of the United States Navy, *Constitution*, now docked on the Charles River in Boston. She is still in commission and is the oldest warship afloat in any of the world's navies. Built at a Boston shipyard between 1794 and 1797, she is 204 feet long, could carry provisions for 475 crewmen, and has a hull of oak with masts of white pine. She was launched in 1797 but won her nickname during the War of 1812 in a battle against the English warship *Guerrière*, during which a seaman is said to have seen British shot bouncing off her sides and to have exclaimed she had sides of iron. She was ordered destroyed as unseaworthy in 1830 but Oliver Wendell Holmes's poem of the same name, which declaims, 'Oh, better that her shattered hulk/Should sink beneath the waves', aroused the public and she was rebuilt and restored to service in 1833. After another rebuilding in 1877 she was finally drydocked in 1897 to be preserved as a memorial. In 1927, American schoolchildren raised money for her reconditioning for a tour of U. S. ports; and in 1931, with the help of additional funds appropriated by Congress, she was once again commissioned. After sailing 22,000 miles, she was at last returned to the Boston Naval Shipyard in 1934, where tourists visit her every year.

Old Kent Road, the

A road in the south London borough of Southwark which holds a key place in the working-class mythology of London. Celebrated particularly in the famous old song 'Wot Cher', or 'Knocked 'em in the Old Kent Road', it is the main thoroughfare of Bermondsey, Walworth, and Camberwell. In the past it was a noted haunt of Cockney costermongers, street traders who sold fruit and vegetables from barrows. The road is at the beginning of the traditional route from London (starting at the Borough) to Dover, and thence to the Continent. See also **Borough.**

Old Lady of Threadneedle Street, the
A nickname since the late 18th century for the **Bank of England** (*q.v.*), the main entrance of which is in Threadneedle Street in the City of London. It gets its name from the female sculpture above this entrance, although no doubt there is some passing reference, too, to the Bank's staid and respectable status amongst financial institutions. In the early 19th century the English radical William Cobbett denounced the directors of the Bank as 'old ladies of Threadneedle Street' for their reactionary policies.

Old Line State, the
The official nickname of Maryland, so called both because in early colonial days the state was the dividing line between the Crown land grants of Lord Baltimore and those of William Penn and because it was the only state with regular troops 'of the line'.

Old North Church
The popular name for Christ Church, the oldest public building in downtown Boston. From this steeple were hung the lanterns warning of a British attack (the 15th of April, 1775) during the Revolutionary War. The tower contains the first set of church bells in the American colonies, cast in 1744. The spire has been rebuilt three times, most recently in 1955 to its original height of 190 feet.

Old Quebec (Vieux-Québec)
The name of an area of Quebec, Canada, including Place Royale, the Old Port, and the Latin Quarter, noted for its historical landmarks.

Old Sarum
A site in Wiltshire, in southern England, which was occupied as long ago as the early Iron Age, and in Norman times boasted a castle and a cathedral. However, following a dispute between the military and the ecclesiastical authorities, the latter moved out and in 1220 began to build a new cathedral a few miles further south. The city which grew up around this is now known as Salisbury, and a few ruined walls are all that remain of Old Sarum. It is, however, remembered as being one of the notorious 'rotten boroughs', parliamentary constituencies with only a handful of electors, that were swept away by the Reform Act of 1832, and for the so-called 'Use of Sarum', the order of divine service used in England, Wales, and Ireland before the Reformation.

Old Town
A once-bustling and still surviving business and residential area on the
Near North Side of Chicago, just east of Lincoln Park and Lake Michigan. Old Town, centred on a short stretch of North Wells Street, was a
precursor of the nearby, diversely upscale 'New Town' area. A boom area
in the sixties, replete with quaint buildings, offbeat shops and lively bistros, Old Town in the 1980's is undergoing something of a revival after a
spell of seediness. Its many culturally vital attractions include the **Second
City** (*q.v.*) cabaret theatre and The Old Town School of Folk Music.

Old Vic, the
Originally an affectionate nickname, but now the standard name by which
London's Royal Victoria Theatre is known. Situated in the Waterloo area
south of the Thames, it achieved its considerable reputation under the
guiding hand of Lilian Baylis, who instituted a celebrated series of Shakespeare there in the first part of the 20th century. It was the first home of
the National Theatre Company when it got under way in 1963.

Old World, the
According to a Eurocentric world view, the Old World included those
parts of the globe known to exist before the discovery of the Americas.
By extension, it has come to mean the whole of the Eastern Hemisphere,
and is used particularly in zoological and botanical contexts: Old World
monkeys, for example, are different in certain crucial respects from those
found in the Americas. Compare **New World**.

Opéra, l'
The sombrely imposing Paris Opera House was built in the 1860s, and the
quarter surrounding it has since become known as *l'Opéra*. It is the centre
of the city, to the north of the Louvre, and was largely laid out by the
renowned town-planner of Paris, Baron Georges Eugène Haussmann. Its
wide boulevards are lined with impressive examples of 19th-century architectural *gravitas*, many of them housing smart and expensive stores.

Oregon Trail
The longest of the overland routes used in the westward expansion of the
U. S., it wound 2000 miles from Independence, Missouri, to Fort Van-
couver and the Willamette Valley of Oregon, through prairies and deserts
and, most important, across the Rocky Mountains through the South
Pass. Explorers and fur traders first traced the Trail; Benjamin Bonneville

is credited with taking the first wagon train through the South Pass in the 1830s. Sections of the deeply rutted road cut by wagon wheels can still be seen today.

Orient, the
A concept that has dimension in time as well as space, and perhaps exists more in the mind than on the ground. Certainly the Orient is now more—and less—than the East. Originally it referred to any lands east of the Mediterranean or of Southern Europe, that is to say, 'the East' from a Roman point of view, including what we would now call the Near and Middle East. The famous luxury train, the **Orient-Express** (*q.v.*), went no further east than Istanbul, then Constantinople. In the present day, however, the geographical focus of the Orient has moved further east, to the Far East and Southeast Asia, perhaps shading westward to include India. But it is for its connotations and associations, rather than its exact denotative value, that the term is mainly used now. The term conjures up the mysterious lands on the far edge of the earth that Marco Polo visited, with their unsettlingly inscrutable inhabitants, their fabled wealth in jewels, silks, and spices, and their mystical religions and philosophies. The word *Orient* derives ultimately from the Latin verb *oriri* 'to rise', with reference to the rising of the sun in the east. In the late 19th century, before usage fixed it firmly on the Far East, it was occasionally used in American English to refer to the whole of the Eastern Hemisphere, or even specifically to Europe. Compare **Far East, Levant, Middle East, Near East.**

Orient-Express
1. A luxurious train that plied between Paris and Giurgin on the Danube, about 45 miles from Bucharest. The service opened on October 4, 1883; at that time passengers bound for Constantinople had to suffer the discomfort of disembarking to take a ferry across the Danube, travel by train to Varna, Bulgaria, on the Black Sea, thence to Constantinople via ship. Subsequently, the Orient-Express underwent many changes of routing and accommodation, and there were the obvious lacunae in service during the 1914–18 and the 1939–45 wars. Its heyday, perhaps, came in the 1920s, when its magnificent carriages could cover the Paris-Constantinople run in 56 hours. (Constantinople was not renamed Istanbul till 1930.) It gained a reputation as a conveyance for spies and other agents involved in eastern European intrigue during this period, though the owners wrily point out that the company would soon have gone out of

business had they relied solely on such passengers. However, Kings' Messengers and Royal Couriers did travel by it, as well as businessmen, holiday-makers, theatrical touring companies, government officials, and others who could afford it or whose way was paid. In the early days of air travel, the Orient-Express travelled to Athens and Turkey in less time than aircraft, because they then had to make night stopovers. The romance of the train and the many associations evoked by references to the intrigues of its passengers are reflected in the half dozen films and nineteen books that are at least partially set aboard it, though it must be pointed out that Agatha Christie's book, *Murder on the Orient-Express*, originally bore the title *Murder in the Calais Coach* and was not changed till after several editions. There was even a foxtrot, 'Orient-Express', published as sheet music in 1933. Officially the Venice Simplon Orient-Express, the train today enjoys a return to its earlier glory in the completely refurbished lavish carriages that cover a complex of routes offering day trips within England and between a number of continental cities. It is possible today to take the train from Victoria Station, London, to Folkestone, transfer to the ferry to Boulogne, and resume the journey (albeit on different carriages) all the way to Venice, leaving before noon and arriving early the following evening. As in the past, the tourists are more likely to outnumber the secret agents—if one can distinguish them among the gentlemen in dinner jackets and ladies in silks and jewels.

2. A proposed supersonic (called 'hypersonic') U. S. aircraft, capable of suborbital flight and of flying between Washington, D. C., and Tokyo, a distance of 6769 miles, in two hours.

Orly

The name of one of the airports serving Paris, the other being Charles de Gaulle.

Outer Banks

The name of a chain of barrier islands and beaches, almost 500 miles in length, between Bogue Inlet to the south and the North Carolina-Virginia border to the north. It includes Cape Hatteras and Roanoke Island, the site of the first English colony in the New World. The actual shoreline measures 6250 miles, almost twice that of California.

Outer Mongolia
Sometimes used jocularly to identify a place of great remoteness, Outer Mongolia was the former name of a republic officially named the Mongolian People's Republic. See also **Inner Mongolia.**

Outlaw Country
The brush country in the hills along the Big Sioux River in northwest Iowa and the hills along the Big Sioux River in eastern South Dakota. If the law was after a man on the Iowa side, he would cross the river, over the rapids, into South Dakota; and if the law was after a man on the South Dakota side, he would cross the river into Iowa.

Oval, the
A cricket ground in Lambeth, London, headquarters of the Surrey County Cricket Club. See also **Lord's.**

Oval Office
An oval room in the wing of the White House where the President of the United States has his office, often used metonymically for the office of the presidency. See also **1600 Pennsylvania Avenue.**

Over South
An old nickname for the Bay View section of San Francisco.

Oxbridge
A portmanteau word coined for the convenience of referring simultane-ously to England's two most ancient and prestigious institutions of higher education, Oxford University and Cambridge University. It can be a neutral term: 'Amanda's hoping to get into Oxbridge' (i.e., one or the other); but it can also be somewhat censorious, evoking the privileged status these universities enjoy in Britain, which some feel is not always commensurate with their academic excellence.

Oxford Street
A street in the West End of London, that runs between St Giles Circus to the east and Marble Arch to the west. It is London's chief shopping street—not as expensive as Bond Street and the rest of Mayfair on its southwestern flanks, but more like an ordinary town's main street, with an accent on clothing stores. Probably its flagship is Selfridges, a huge department store famous around the world; but there are many other

large emporiums there, including big branches of Marks and Spencer, C & A, and John Lewis.

Oxon.
An abbreviated name for the English county of Oxfordshire, from its Latin name *Oxonia*. *Oxon.*, from Latin *Oxoniensis* 'of or from Oxford', is also used for the town and university of Oxford; a graduate would be designated "B.A. *or* B.Sc. Oxon.", for example, and the Bishop of Oxford signs himself "Oxon.". The Cambridge equivalent is *Cantab.*, for *Cantabrigiensis,* used for such designations but not as an abbreviated name for the county of Cambridgeshire.

Oz
A humorous nickname used by Australians for Australia. It is basically an affectionate term and redolent of the open, unstuffy nature of Australian society. It is short for *Aussie*, which is itself sometimes used for *Australia*, although it more usually means 'an Australian'. Its reference is to the magical place in L. Frank Baum's books, notably, *The Wizard of Oz*. See also **TOTO**.

P

Pacific Northwest, the
In the United States, an area encompassing those western states that border on the Pacific Ocean, namely, Washington and Oregon. In some people's minds, the northernmost parts of California would be included but not Alaska, which is too remote. Compare **Northwest, West.**

Paddington
An area in west London, to the north of Hyde Park and the east of Bayswater. It contains some elegant streets, but much less so as it comes within the orbit of Paddington Station, the main London terminus for rail services to the West and Wales. In the very southeast corner of the area is Paddington Green, the original village green of Paddington,

remembered particularly in the old ballad about 'pretty little Polly Perkins of Paddington Green'. A more modern association is with the fictional Paddington Bear, who was discovered at the station having been
sent as a parcel from Peru.

Paddo
An Australian nickname for Paddington, an inner suburb of Sydney,
Australia. A hilly area of Victorian terraced houses, it is one of Sydney's
trendiest residential districts.

Pak Pai
In Hong Kong, the term for taxis not officially licenced as such by the
government. They are called *pirate taxis* in Hong Kong, *gypsy cabs* in
New York City. *Pak pai* means 'white licence' in reference to the white
registration plates bearing black numerals, like those on private cars.

Pakistan
An Islamic state in the northwest of the Indian subcontinent. When it was
formed in 1947, following the independence and partition of British
India, its name was concocted from those of constituent or contiguous
areas whose people had long been Muslims, including the Punjab, Afghanistan, and Kashmir. Originally it was a two-part state, with West
Pakistan being separated by the width of India from East Pakistan (formerly East Bengal), but in 1971 the eastern part broke away to form the
autonomous state of Bangladesh.

Palace, the
British journalistic shorthand for Buckingham Palace, frequently used as
a synonym for the sovereign or the royal household (as in 'A Palace
spokesman today denied that . . .'). See also **Buck House.**

Palatinate, the
Either of two regions in Germany that in medieval times were ruled by the
Count Palatine, a nobleman of the Holy Roman Empire who exercised
virtually imperial power within his own domain. Both were subsequently
absorbed into Bavaria, but in 1946 the Lower Palatinate became part of
the new state of Rhineland-Palatinate (in German, *Rheinland-Pfalz*) in
southwest Germany. The Upper Palatinate is on the Czech border.

Palatine, the
One of the Seven Hills of ancient Rome. According to legend it was the site of the first human settlement in Rome; Romulus reputedly ploughed his first furrow at its foot, marking the foundation of the city. In historical times, the Roman emperors had their palace there, and indeed from the hill's original Latin name, *Palatium*, we get the English word *palace*.

Palestine
A region in the Middle East with a fluctuating history that stretches back to Biblical times. It occupies the territory between the Dead Sea and the shores of the Mediterranean and first appeared as a separate entity under the name *Canaan*. It underwent innumerable changes of rule in pre-Christian times, and its role as the scene of most of the events in the Bible led to its being known in later centuries as the Holy Land. It was ruled by Rome from 63 B.C. onward, passed in due course into the Byzantine Empire, and from 638 to 1918 was under Muslim rule; from 1920 it was controlled by Britain as a mandated territory. It finally became an independent Jewish state in 1948, changing its name in the process from Palestine to Israel. Its former name is however kept vigorously alive by the Arabic inhabitants of the area; part of it was actually retaken into Arab hands in 1949—land west of the River Jordan that was captured back by Israel in 1967—and the establishment of an independent Arab state there is the ongoing aim of the Palestine Liberation Organization.

Palisades, the
The name of the basaltic precipices along the west bank of the Hudson River, extending from Jersey City, New Jersey, to near Piermont, New York.

Pall Mall
A street in the West End of London, between Trafalgar Square and St James's Palace. It is one of the main thoroughfares of London's **Clubland** (*q.v.*), and contains the premises of several distinguished gentlemen's clubs, including the Athenaeum, the Reform, the Army and Navy, and the Travellers'. Its curious name comes from *paille-maille*, a game similar to croquet, which was played on a course constructed there in the late 17th century.

Palm Springs

A desert resort city in Riverside County, California. Earlier names were Palmetto Spring, Big Palm Spring, and Agua Caliente; but the name Palm Springs was applied to the post office created in 1890. The community has attracted a wealthy clientele since the 1930s because of its desert climate and its proximity to the Los Angeles metropolitan area to the west. Palm Springs attracts sunseekers in winter, but it also has a fair-sized resident population (1980 population 32,171). It is a mecca for golfers and tennis players. A place of great wealth (but not of flamboyance), it is known worldwide for the affluence of its residents and visitors, particularly celebrities connected with the entertainment industry, and, latterly, retired politicians.

Pamplona

A city in the northeastern Spanish region of Navarre, famous for its annual festival, *Fiesta de San Fermín*, during which bulls are stampeded through the narrow streets and the young men of the city try to outrun them. The picturesque, bacchanalian fiesta figures prominently in Ernest Hemingway's novel, *The Sun Also Rises*.

Pangaea

A name given to the earth's supposed primordial supercontinent that split up over 200 million years ago into Gondwanaland and Laurasia. See **Gondwanaland, Laurasia.**

Panhandle, the

Any area of one of the United States that is somewhat longer and narrower than the rest of the state and is shaped like the handle of a pan, as the western extensions of Florida, Texas, and Oklahoma.

Pantiles, the

A street in the spa town of Tunbridge Wells, Kent, in southeast England. Its elegant Regency arcades were built as a promenade for those who came to take the waters in the 18th and 19th centuries; they now house shops. Its name comes from the flat tiles with which it was originally paved (although a pantile is strictly speaking a curved roofing tile).

Papal States, the

A collective name for the area of central Italy that for a long time was under direct papal rule. It was given to the popes by King Pepin III of the

Franks in 754, and remained in their control for more than 1100 years. Most of it was absorbed into the newly united kingdom of Italy in the mid 19th century, although the papacy clung on to Rome itself until 1870 and did not recognize the new state of affairs officially until 1929. The Papal States were also known as the *States of the Church*.

Paper Mill Playhouse

A theatre in Millburn, New Jersey, owned and operated for many years by Frank Carrington, who was also the director. Popular among New Yorkers as well as the residents of northern New Jersey, the Paper Mill Playhouse was famous for staging the musicals of Sigmund Romberg, Jerome Kern, Rudolf Friml, Noël Coward, and others—productions like *The Chocolate Soldier, Showboat, The Desert Song, Bittersweet*—many of which were made into movies after successful Broadway runs. The Paper Mill burned down, was rebuilt, then burned down again; last rebuilt in 1982, it is now housed in a modern, fireproof structure where the audience lounges in seats that would have impressed earlier patrons as the height of luxury.

Park Avenue

A major north-south street on the East Side, in New York City. It begins officially at 34th Street at the south and runs up into east Harlem at the north. Although it extends southward below 34th Street to 8th Street, that interval is named Park Avenue South, a relatively recent change from Fourth Avenue, its name before some time in the late 1940s. Until the 1950s, for most of its length as far as 96th Street, Park Avenue was characterized by its expensive, luxurious apartment houses and hotels. A broad, double roadway divided by a mall (inaccessible except for viewing at a distance), which is maintained with seasonal floral displays by the Park Avenue Association, it has retained much of its former character except for the area between 40th and 57th streets, which has succumbed for the most part to the encroachments of high-rise office buildings. Yet, even in that interval, the Waldorf-Astoria Hotel, the New York Racquet Club, St Bartholomew's church, and a few other buildings have resisted the commercial invasion. For many years associated with great wealth, Park Avenue has remained a place as well as a symbol of luxurious residences. The trains serving Grand Central Terminal, which blocks the entire roadway between 42nd and 43rd streets, run beneath Park Avenue to emerge north of 96th Street onto elevated tracks. Here the neighbourhood changes, gradually, at first, because of high-rise (low-

rent) housing bordering the roadway, then drastically, as the slums of
Harlem are approached and the elevated tracks cross over the Harlem
River (at about 135th Street) to go on through the Mott Haven train yard,
in The Bronx.

Parkdale

The name of a district in Toronto, Canada, that evokes images of its once
tough reputation, despite the increase, in recent years, of middle-class
residents.

Parker House, the

A long-established, first-class hotel in Boston, famous mainly for the
Parker House roll, a circular roll baked from a round piece of white
bread dough folded almost in half.

Parklands

A name given in Adelaide, South Australia, to the green belt surrounding
the inner city. Colonel Light, the surveyor who planned Adelaide, laid
out exactly a square mile (259 hectares) for the inner city and the surrounding parklands were to be sacrosanct. There have been inroads,
always leading to a public outcry, but there are still 700 hectares (7000
square kilometres) devoted to gardens, golf courses, and other areas for
sports, picnics, and recreation.

Park Lane

A road in the West End of London, leading from Marble Arch in the
north to Hyde Park Corner in the south. It forms the western boundary
of Mayfair and has always been the haunt of the extremely wealthy. In
former times it was lined with aristocratic mansions, which commanded a
fine view over Hyde Park. The stately homes have since been replaced by
stately hotels, such as the Dorchester, the Hilton, and the Grosvenor
House, and the once unspoilt view is now marred by a very busy multi-
lane roadway.

Patagonia

In broadest terms, the southernmost part of the South American continent, extending below about 40° and containing the southern parts of
Chile and Argentina. In more specific use, the name is applied to the most
southerly region of Argentina, to the south of the Colorado River, a

rugged desolate plateau that sweeps from the lower slopes of the Andes eastward to the Atlantic.

Paternoster Row
A street in the City of London, just to the north of St Paul's Cathedral. It gets its name from the makers of paternosters, or rosaries, who in pre-Reformation times traded there. Subsequently, in the 18th and 19th centuries, it became a major centre of the publishing business in London, along with the nearby Little Britain and St Paul's Churchyard. However, much of it was destroyed by incendiary bombs in 1940, and the publishing firms had to move on.

Path of Gold
A nickname of Market Street in San Francisco, so called because it is one of the greatest commercial thoroughfares in the city and is elaborately lit at night.

Peacehaven
A village on the Sussex coast of England, to the east of Brighton. An invented name for an invented place, it was built just after World War I as a piece of speculative development by a local businessman, and has since become synonymous with the sort of bland development, with uniform rows of uninspired bungalows, which covered much of the south coast of England during the interwar years. During World War I, Australian and New Zealand troops were stationed nearby, and hence the area was for a time nicknamed *Anzac-on-Sea*.

peacemaker, the
1. A nickname used during the frontier days of Texas and other western states for a gun, especially the Colt .45 revolver, the use of which settled all difficulties.
2. A nickname bestowed in 1984 by President Ronald Reagan on the M-X missile.

Peak District, the
A hilly area of outstanding scenic beauty in Derbyshire and Staffordshire at the southern tip of the Pennines, the mountain chain that bisects northern England. The whole district now forms a national park, 540 square miles in extent. The northern part, known as the High Peak, or Dark Peak, from the dark millstone grit rock of which it is formed, is an

area of stark windblown moorland. Southward it merges into the Low
Peak or White Peak, a limestone landscape riddled with caverns and
potholes. Until comparatively recently the whole area was known simply
as the Peak.

Pearl Harbor

A large U. S. naval base on the island of Oahu, Hawaii. It is notable
mainly as the target of the Japanese surprise air attack of December 7,
1941, which drew the United States into World War II. Thousands of
naval and military personnel were killed in the attack, both on the naval
base and at the nearby Army Air Force base, Hickham Field. The projecting parts of the *USS Arizona*, one of the battleships sunk, now serve as a
memorial to those who died aboard her and to the others who perished.

Pearl of the Orient

A nickname of Manila, the Philippines.

Peloponnese, the

The southern part of Greece, a rocky peninsula joined onto the northern
mainland by the narrow Isthmus of Corinth. In ancient times it contained
the cities of Sparta and Corinth.

Peninsula, the

In general terms, a peninsula is a piece of land almost but not completely
surrounded by water, but until the late 19th century the word was also
used more specifically to refer to the Iberian Peninsula, which contains
Spain and Portugal. Today the usage survives only in the *Peninsular War*,
the name given to the war fought there from 1808 to 1814 by Spain and
Portugal, aided by the British under Wellington, against the French under
Napoleon.

Pentagon, the

A huge (3.7-million-square-foot) office building, a hollow pentagon in
plan, in Alexandria, Virginia, across the Potomac River from Washington, D. C. It serves as the headquarters for the Departments of Defense,
Army, Navy, Air Force, and Coast Guard, and its name is used metaphorically to refer to the United States military establishment.

Pentonville
A down-at-heel area of north London, just to the east of King's Cross. It is bounded on the south by Pentonville Road. Its most famous association is with Pentonville Prison, which is in fact over half a mile to the north of the area, in the Caledonian Road. The prison's name is often familiarly abbreviated to 'the Ville'.

Père Lachaise
A celebrated cemetery in Paris. It was opened in 1804, and its incumbents include Honoré de Balzac, Frédéric Chopin, Gioacchino Rossini, Colette, Édith Piaf, and Oscar Wilde. The site was formerly occupied by a Jesuit religious foundation, which was enlarged by Père Lachaise, confessor of Louis XIV.

Persia
A name associated with southwestern Asia since the 6th century B.C., when the great Persian Empire was founded by Cyrus the Great. It lasted two centuries before it was overthrown by Alexander the Great. In modern times its inhabitants have always known their country as Iran, and this was made official in 1935, but in 1949 the government sanctioned the use of *Persia* as an alternative. Nevertheless, in modern usage *Persia* has a rather dated air, and *Iran* is now the standard term.

petro-dollars
The nickname coined in 1974 for Arab profits from the increased prices demanded by OPEC.

Petticoat Lane
A famous London street market selling clothes and various sorts of household goods. The road it takes place in has since the 1830s been officially called Middlesex Street (just to the east of Liverpool Street Station in the City); but it is still popularly known as Petticoat Lane. In former times, Huguenot silk weavers settled there, and its associations with the clothing trade have continued ever since; from the 17th century onward it was London's chief second-hand clothing market. In the 20th century its range of merchandise has widened, and it has become a popular tourist attraction offering broad slices of Cockney life. It is open on Sunday mornings only.

Phoenix City
A nickname of Chicago, bestowed by Henry Ward Beecher after the recovery from the fire (1871).

Piccadilly
1. A fashionable shopping street in the West End of London, running from Piccadilly Circus in the east to Hyde Park Corner in the west. In addition to emporia such as Fortnum and Mason and the shops of Burlington Arcade, it contains Burlington House, the home of the Royal Academy, and the Ritz Hotel. See also **Jackson's of Piccadilly.**
2. The central area of Manchester, in the northwest of England. It forms the focus of the city, and has attractive gardens and a splendid plaza with shops, offices, etc. It gives its name to one of the city's main railway stations.

Piccadilly Circus
A roundabout in London, where Piccadilly, Upper and Lower Regent streets, and Shaftesbury Avenue meet, similar in tawdriness and character to Times Square in New York City. At its centre is an aluminium statue called 'Eros', though it is actually of 'Christian Charity', erected to honour the Earl of Shaftesbury who was originally responsible for much of the property development of the area.

Pigalle
An area of Montmartre, northern central Paris, centred on the Place Pigalle. It has a risqué reputation for its titillating cabarets and as a place of assignation with ladies of the night, and, in the 1980s, is known for the sex-shops and strip-joints that line its streets.

Pig Island
A nickname for New Zealand, referring to the pigs left by Captain Cook, which went wild. The term is jocular and seems to have become current about the time of World War I. Perhaps its replacement of the term **Maoriland** (*q.v.*) indicates a general shift from the romantic to the ironical in outlook and language.

Pillars of Hercules, the
A name given in ancient times to two rocks that guard the Straits of Gibraltar, at the entrance to the Mediterranean. They were then called Calpe and Abyla and are now known as Gibraltar (Spain) and Jebel Musa

(Morocco). According to legend they were once joined together, but Hercules tore them asunder in order to pass through. They represented to the ancients the western boundary of the known world.

Pilsen

A vital Near Southwest Side neighbourhood of Chicago, first U. S. home to successive waves of immigrants—Germans, Irish, Czechoslovakians, Poles, and Latinos. Named in commemoration of one of the principal cities of their homeland by the Bohemian immigrants who played a major role in settling the neighbourhood, Pilsen still contains many characteristically sturdy brick cottages dating from the 1860s.

Piltdown man

Named for the village of Piltdown, in southeast England, a collection of fossil bone fragments presented, in 1912, as the authentic remains of a prehistoric hominid. Although the find was somewhat suspect, it was not conclusively proved a hoax till the 1950s, when radiocarbon dating and other evidence showed it to be utterly without merit and, in fact, a deliberate fraud.

Pimlico

An area in central London, on the north bank of the Thames to the south of Victoria. It is quite a fashionble first step on the residential ladder for those whose means cannot yet afford Belgravia. It probably gets its name from a tavern run there many centuries ago by a certain Ben Pimlico. In the mid 19th century it was still mainly open fields, but these gradually became filled in with a maze of streets, and public consciousness of it as an area with a separate identity was probably sealed by the 1948 film *Passport to Pimlico*, a fiction in which the local residents set up their own state, declaring unilateral independence from the United Kingdom.

Pine Gap

The common name of a classified Australian and United States joint defence space research facility nineteen kilometres southwest of Alice Springs. It became operational in 1969 and, though surrounded by secrecy, is known to contain seven large radomes and an expanding computer complex. It is formally administered by the U. S. National Reconnaissance Office (NRO) but is operationally controlled by the CIA. It is able to intercept Soviet and Chinese military communications and radar transmissions important in monitoring agreements on disarmament. Like other U. S. installations in Australia, Pine Gap has led to vigorous controversy.

Piovro
A nickname in Italy for organized crime; *piovro* means 'octopus' in Italian.

Pitt Street
A major thoroughfare in Sydney, Australia. It is the city's financial centre, but in former times was famous for its brothels. A 'Pitt Street farmer' is an Australian slang expression for an absentee farm landlord.

Place Royale
A part of Old Quebec known as the 'cradle of French civilization in North America', so named because of the statue of Louis XIV erected there.

Playboy Building
An office building, formerly the Palmolive Building, near the John Hancock centre in Chicago at the northern end of the Magnificent Mile, on the city's Near North Side. The two-billion-candlepower Lindbergh Beacon atop the building, though unused today, once served as a powerful navigational aid to vessels on Lake Michigan. The building now houses the *Playboy* magazine editorial offices, as well as other business and professional offices.

Plaza, the
A small, open square in New York bounded by Fifth Avenue on the east, Central Park South (59th Street) on the north, 58th Street on the south, and a service road on the west. It is dominated by the Plaza Hotel, on the west side, and by Bergdorf Goodman, a department store, on the south, which combine to give the area a swanky, dignified air. There is a small fountain at its centre which feeds into a circular pond.

Plymouth of the West, the
A nickname of San Diego, California, so called because it was one of the first settlements on the West Coast, founded in 1769 by Father Junípero Serra.

poison pill
A nickname for any measure taken by a company to make it unattractive for takeover by another company.

Polish Corridor, the
A name given to the territory granted to Poland under the terms of the Treaty of Versailles in 1919, in order to give it access to the Baltic Sea just to the west of Gdańsk. It more or less followed the line of the Vistula River and in so doing cut a great swath through what had been German territory, isolating East Prussia from the rest of Germany. This arrangement was naturally not popular with the Germans, and the Polish Corridor was one of Hitler's prime territorial targets. It came firmly back under Polish control after World War II, while East Prussia was divided between Poland and the Soviet Union.

Polynesia
A collective term for the islands that comprise the eastern section of Oceania, in the South Pacific Ocean. Its main constituents are Samoa, Tahiti, Tuvalu (formerly the Ellice Islands), the Marquesas, the Cook Islands, Pitcairn Island, and Easter Island. Hawaii is very often included too. When the name, which means 'many islands', was coined in the 18th century, it had a very general application to the islands of the South Pacific, including those we now know as Melanesia and Micronesia, and today it is still often used in this looser meaning. Many ethnologists, moreover, would regard New Zealand as part of Polynesia, since its Maori inhabitants are descended from successive waves of Polynesian immigrants. See also **Melanesia, Micronesia, Oceania**.

Pompey
A nickname for Portsmouth, a city on the south coast of England. It is Britain's main naval dockyard, and the name is chiefly used in naval contexts; but it has also come to be applied to the city's soccer team. The first record of its use comes from the late 19th century, but its origin is obscure; certainly it has no discernible connection with the Roman general of the same name. Natives of the city are sometimes referred to as *Pomponians*.

Pool, the
1. A local nickname for Liverpool, a large city and port in northwest England.

2. See **Pool of London**.

Pool of London, the
Or, more simply, the Pool, a name given since at least the 17th century to
the two-mile stretch of the Thames between London Bridge and Cuckold's Point, beyond which the river bends abruptly south to enter Limehouse reach. The upstream section is known as the Upper Pool, the
downstream as the Lower Pool. It is the farthest upriver that large ships
can find sufficient depth, and in the days when central London was a
major port, myriad vessels would be berthed alongside the wharves and in
the docks on both sides of the river, amid forests of cranes. Working-
class areas extend beyond the waterfront warehouses: Wapping and
Shadwell to the north, Bermondsey and Rotherhithe to the south. In the
1980s, with the docks no longer active, the Pool has lost the air of
bustling activity it had when so much of Britain's imports and exports
flowed through it.

Poor Man's Paradise, the
A nickname of San Francisco, so called in reference to its year-round
moderate climate and to the abundance of cheap fruits and vegetables.

Porte, the
See **Sublime Porte**.

Portland Place
A wide street in the West End of London, just to the south of Regent's
Park. At its southern end is Broadcasting House, headquarters of the
British Broadcasting Corporation (BBC). *Portland Place* itself is some-
times used as a synonym for the BBC, particularly those parts of it
connected with administration and higher management.

Portobello Road
A street in the Notting Hill area of west London which houses a famous
flea market. The days have perhaps gone when genuine bargain antiques
could be spotted there among the bric-à-brac, but the market remains a
lively place to visit. It is there only on Saturdays; during the rest of the
week a general market takes over, with a West Indian flavour appropriate
to the immigrant community in the area.

Port o' Missing Men, the
A nickname of San Francisco, so called because a man could easily hide amid the cosmopolitan citizenry or escape aboard one of the many ships in the port.

Porton Down
A name which makes British people feel uneasy, for it belongs to the place where research into chemical and bacteriological warfare is carried out in Britain. Situated in Wiltshire, in southern England, it is officially called the Chemical Defence Establishment (CED), and is run by the Ministry of Defence, although much peaceful and medically important work is done on the same site by the Centre for Applied Bacteriology and Research.

Potteries, the
An area around and including Stoke-on-Trent, in Staffordshire, in the northwest Midlands of England, which is the major centre of the china and earthenware industry. Clay has been worked and fired for centuries in the *potbanks* (the local word for *pottery*), although the name *Potteries* is not recorded until 1825. See also **Five Towns**.

Prado, the
A large art museum in Madrid, Spain, built between 1787 and 1819. It is known particularly for its fine collection of Spanish masters such as Goya, Velásquez, El Greco, Murillo, Zurbarán, and others. It takes its name from the meadow, or *prado*, that once surrounded it.

prairie oyster
A nickname for the testis of a calf, used as food.

Prairie Provinces, the
A name for Alberta, Saskatchewan, and Manitoba, which together comprise about one-fifth of Canada's land area.

prairie schooner
The nickname for a huge canvas-covered wagon, requiring ten mules to pull it, that was used during the second half of the 19th century to carry supplies, merchandise, and food across the western plains to the frontier settlers.

Premier State, the
A nickname of New South Wales, appearing on motor registration plates. The name recalls that New South Wales was the first state, perhaps with a hint of supremacy as in the Australian use of the term *premiership* for the winning of an organized competition among sporting clubs. Outside its borders New South Wales has sometimes irreverently been called the *Ma State*.

Principality, the
A principality is a state ruled by a price or a territory from which a prince takes his title—Monaco, for example. In Britain, however, *the Principality* is always Wales. The Welsh rulers of Wales had been known as princes since the eleventh century; but it was in the 14th century, after Wales had been conquered by England, that Edward III conferred the title of Prince of Wales on his young son Edward, the Black Prince, and the eldest sons of British monarchs have held that title ever since.

Printing House Square
A former square in Blackfriars in the City of London, now disappeared but long famous as the site of the headquarters of *The Times* newspaper. The name is very much still associated with the paper, and when it moved its premises to Grays Inn Road in 1974, its new offices were named New Printing House Square. However, it does not seem to have followed *The Times* in its further move to a site in London's **Dockland** (*q.v.*); there, such was the stringency of the security measures adopted to counter feared incursions by disaffected members of the printers' union that the paper's headquarters were nicknamed 'Fortress Wapping'.

Promised Land, the
A name used in the Bible for Canaan, an area in the Middle East that corresponds roughly to later Palestine. It refers to the promise given by God to Abraham (Genesis 12:7) that he and his descendents would own the land in perpetuity. It has not worked out quite as straightforwardly as that, and in modern usage the term refers, generally, to any future condition in which one's hopes and aspirations will finally be fulfilled.

Provence
An area of southeastern France, formerly a province in its own right but now a part of the administrative region of Côte d'Azur. It is very much an area with its own separate cultural identity; it has its own language

(Provençal) and literary tradition and belongs to the Mediterranean world. In ancient times it came under Roman rule considerably earlier than other parts of France, and was known simply as *(nostra) Provincia* 'our (*or* the) Province'; hence the name Provence.

Province, the

A name sometimes applied to Northern Ireland. It refers back to the territory's origins as part of the ancient Irish province of Ulster, which was partitioned when the Republic of Ireland became independent in 1921. (The other provinces of Ireland are Connacht, Leinster, and Munster.) The use of the designation *province* as an actual name is by no means unprecedented: it gave rise to modern Provence.

Prussia

A former state in northern and central Germany; its German name is *Preussen*. In the 19th century it was the leading and most belligerent power among the German states, with a reputation for truculent militarism fostered by its landowning aristocracy, the Junkers. After World War II, it was divided up between East and West Germany, Poland, and the Soviet Union.

puffing billies

A nickname for the steam engines used on the first railways in the early 19th century.

Puke State, the

A nickname of Missouri, possibly from a corruption of *Pikes*, a word used in California to refer to white migratory workers believed to have come from Pike County, Missouri; or because so many Missourians showed up at the Galena, Illinois, lead mines in 1827 that those already there stated 'the state of Missouri has taken a "puke" '.

Pullman

A recently refurbished Far Southeast Side area in Chicago that started life as a 'company town' in 1881, known also as Pullman Community or Pullman Village. Sleeping-car inventor and manufacturer George Pullman's belief that the town should turn a 6 percent profit led to the Pullman strike of 1894, after worker-residents suffered cuts in wages but not in rents. The strike ended only after President Grover Cleveland

ordered in federal troops. Surviving Pullman landmarks include the or-
nate, Victorian-style Florence Hotel, Greenstone Church, and the administrative clock tower.

Q

Quai d'Orsay, the
A street along the Left Bank of the River Seine in Paris, between the Pont
de l'Alma and the Pont de la Concorde. It houses the French Foreign
Ministry, and also the National Assembly, and consequently is often used
as a name for the Foreign Office.

Quaker State, the
A nickname of Pennsylvania, so called in reference to William Penn, a
Quaker who originally owned the land and encouraged Quaker settlers.

Queen of the Antilles
A former nickname for Cuba.

Queen of the North
A nickname for Edinburgh.

Queen of the Sea
A former nickname for Tyre.

Queens
A borough of New York City on Long Island, north of Brooklyn. It has
some industrial activity, especially at its western end (Long Island City),
but is for the most part residential, being divided, more or less, into
neighbourhoods named Astoria, Jackson Heights, Forest Hills, Rego
Park, Whitestone, Flushing, etc., each with its own character. The residents all agree, though, that they live in Queens, not on 'the Island'. Its
two main east-west thoroughfares are Queens Boulevard and Northern

Boulevard. Essentially a dormitory community, many of its residents work in Manhattan. La Guardia Airport is situated in its northwest.

Queen State, the
A nickname of Maryland, so called in honour of Henrietta Maria, Queen of Charles I of England.

Queen Street West
The name for a bohemian area of Toronto, associated with avant-garde artists and their work.

Quincy Market
An alternative name for **Faneuil Hall** (*q.v.*), a public market in Boston, U. S. A.

Quirinal, the
One of the Seven Hills of ancient Rome, now known as Monte Cavallo. On it is a palace, *il Quirinale*, formerly occupied by the kings of Italy, and in the early 20th century 'the Quirinal' was used as a metaphor for the Italian monarchy and government, especially as contrasted with the Papal authority of the Vatican.

R

R & A, the
A familiar abbreviation for the Royal and Ancient Golf Club, the governing body of golf in Britain, which is based in St Andrews, Scotland. It was founded in 1764 as the Society of St Andrews Golfers, and the royal prefix was added in 1834, with the approval of William IV.

RADA
A familiar name (pronounced RAHda) for the Royal Academy of Dramatic Art, London's most famous drama school which has produced

many of the country's most famous actors and actresses since its foundation, in 1904, by Beerbohm Tree.

Radio City Music Hall

A world-famous motion-picture theatre at Rockefeller Center, in New York City, known for its family-style entertainment and its spectacular stage shows. Opened in 1932, the theatre featured a troupe of thirty-two precision dancers called The Roxyettes: their name was changed to The Rockettes in 1934. Originally a sixteen-member troupe from St Louis, called the Missouri Rockets, their name was changed to The Rockets; then, when they appeared at the Roxy Theatre in New York City, to the Roxyettes. Renowned for their high kicks, the dancers have performed the 'Parade of the Wooden Soldiers' routine at the annual Christmas show since 1934.

raj, the

The name given to the British rule of India, derived from Hindi *rāj*, which comes from Sanskrit *rājya*, from *rājati* 'he rules'.

Rand, the

A nickname for Witwatersrand, the goldmining centre of South Africa. Situated in the Transvaal, in the northeast of the country, its great metropolis is Johannesburg, which sits on top of the richest gold deposits in the world. Although applied to the area in general, in strict terms the Rand refers to the range of rocky hills that dominates the landscape; it is also known as *the Reef*. The full name is best known in association with the local university, founded in 1921.

Rann of Kutch, the

A great salt flat, about 9000 square miles in extent, in the Indian subcontinent, on the border of India and Pakistan, which alters seasonally from marsh to desert and back. Possession of the area was long a matter of contention between the two countries, but in 1968 international arbitration awarded about ten per cent of it to Pakistan.

Rapes

In former times, English counties were subdivided for administrative purposes into what were usually called *hundreds* (see **Chiltern Hundreds**), or in some counties *wapentakes*. A few had an additional, higher tier of local government: in Kent, for example, a group of hundreds was called a *lathe*, while in Sussex they were *rapes*, six in all (the Rape of Hastings, the Rape of Arundel, etc.) The word is not connected with *rape* 'ravage'.

Rebel Capital
A nickname of Philadelphia, used by the British when it became the capital of the thirteen colonies in 1776.

redbrick
A nickname, coined by professor Edgar Allison Peers in 1943, for universities other than Oxford and Cambridge, and especially those built after World War II, which used brick, and later concrete, glass, and steel, rather than the stone of the older universities.

Red China
A nickname for the People's Republic of China, coined with reference to its Communist government. A term commonly encountered in the 1950s and '60s, it subsequently went out of use as relations between the West and China improved and as China seemed to abandon Communism as its official ideology.

Rednaxela Terrace
The official name on a street sign in Hong Kong, apparently made by a Chinese reading *Alexander* from right to left.

Red Planet, the
A name given to the planet Mars, which shines redly in the reflected light of the sun. The redness of its surface is caused by dust and oxidation of rocks.

Red Spot, the
The name given to a vast elliptical mark on the surface of the planet Jupiter, which over the centuries has appeared in various shades of red. It is now thought to be a gigantic swirling hurricane, which could swallow up the Earth three times over, but the reason for its colour remains obscure.

Red Square
A great open area in the centre of Moscow which serves as the venue for Soviet state ceremonies. It is through Red Square that the tanks and

missiles rumble in the May Day and October Revolution parades. Situated below the eastern walls of the Kremlin, it also contains the Lenin Mausoleum (from atop which high officials observe the parades), the state department store, GUM, and the celebrated Cathedral of St Basil (built 1554–60), an architectural phantasmagoria surmounted by ten onion domes of different colours.

Reeperbahn, the
The main thoroughfare of the red-light district of Hamburg, a city in northern West Germany. It has achieved worldwide renown for the lavishness and explicitness of the sexual goods on display there.

Reform Club, the
A gentlemen's club in Pall Mall, in the West End of London, founded in 1836. It takes its name from the great Reform Act passed in 1832, which radically extended voting rights in England, and its membership from the Liberal Party. Among its claims to fame are Lamb Cutlets Reform, a recipe of the legendary Alexis Soyer, who was chef to the club for a time in the 19th century, and the fact that Phileas Fogg, in Jules Verne's novel *Around the World in Eighty Days* (1873), began and ended his epic journey at the club.

Ren Cen
A nickname for the Renaissance Center, a large area of downtown Detroit that was renovated in the 1970s. It includes hotels, a sports arena, office buildings, and a convention centre.

Repulsive Bay
A nickname for Repulse Bay, in Hong Kong.

Rhineland, the
The name given to the territory along the banks of the River Rhine as it flows through Germany, from the Dutch border southward through the industrial areas around Düsseldorf, past the cities of Cologne and Bonn, and on into the quintessential Rhineland of beetling wooded crags with fairytale castles on their summits and steep vineyards where some of the world's great white wines are produced.

Rhine of America, the

A nickname of the Hudson River, in New York, a reference to the high, rocky hills and beautiful scenery along its length.

Rialto

A market area in Venice that has become generic for such exchanges and shopping marts in other cities around the world. The familiar expression, 'What's new on the Rialto', which New Yorkers use in inquiring about happenings on Broadway, echoes the words of Shylock in *The Merchant of Venice*.

Ridings, the

Yorkshire is the largest county in England, and for administrative purposes it has always been divided into three parts. Since the reorganization of English local government in 1974 these have been known, rather prosaically, as North Yorkshire, West Yorkshire, and South Yorkshire. Before then, however, they were the Ridings. The North Riding covered the area of the Yorkshire Moors and Dales, from Middlesbrough in the north down as far as Harrogate and York. The West Riding was the great industrial heartland, including the manufacturing towns and cities of Leeds, Bradford, Huddersfield, Doncaster, and Sheffield; it is now divided between West and South Yorkshire. The East Riding, always a rather separate and isolated area, with the fishing port of Hull as its main city, was divided up; part went to North Yorkshire, and part is now Humberside, and no longer officially part of Yorkshire at all, although most true Yorkshiremen would dispute this. There never was a South Riding, incidentally, despite the novel of that name by the Yorkshire writer Winifred Holtby. The word *riding* has nothing to do with *to ride*; it comes from an old Viking word *thrithjungr*, or *thirding* as it might be in modern English, meaning 'a third part'. And although it has gone out of use in Britain, it has been exported. As early as 1675, reference was made to the north and west ridings of Long Island, New York, and it is still applied to administrative and electoral districts in Canada.

Rio Grande Valley

A low-lying, flat region north of the Rio Grande in southeastern Texas, often (locally) shortened to 'the Valley'.

Riverina, the
The country in southern New South Wales between the Lachlan and the Murray rivers and west of Wagga Wagga.

Riverland, the
The area round Renmark, South Australia, in the Murray Valley, noted for fruit production and vineyards.

Roaring Forties
A region in the southern oceans between 40° and 50° south, where gale-force westerly winds are the rule rather than the exception. The term is sometimes also used for the part of the North Atlantic that is at a similar latitude to the north of the equator.

Roaring Twenties, the
A nickname given to the 1920s, especially in the United States, where the decade was characterized by the fashions associated with the 'flappers', young women who wore short skirts, long necklaces, and bobbed hair and who submitted to every dance craze, especially the Charleston; by Prohibition, which bred bootleg whisky, speakeasies, and gangsters; and by a financial boom that continued till October 1929, when the stock market crashed, bringing about the Great Depression.

Rock, the
An abbreviated name commonly used for the Rock of Gibraltar, a 1300-foot-high limestone outcrop on a peninsula at the southern tip of Spain. Gibraltar is a British colony, and the language spoken by the inhabitants, which is a mixture of Spanish and English, is known as 'Rock English'. See also **Gib**.

Rockefeller Center
A complex of high-rise office buildings between 48th and 51st streets, on the south and north, and Fifth and Sixth avenues, on the east and west, funded by John D. Rockefeller and built in the 1930s on a site leased from Columbia University. The first such complex in the world, it reflected the concern that skyscrapers were creating dark, cavern-like streets, so on its three-block site were built a 66-story skyscraper and 13 smaller buildings with ample space and a plaza between. The use of landscaping, fine-quality materials and artwork, together with the consideration of light, air, and space produced a project that influenced such

construction in the rest of the world. Originally, several of the buildings were occupied by large corporations after which the buildings were named, though they did not use the buildings exclusively. Thus, the RCA Building, the tallest, (called 'Radio City') was occupied partly by the Radio Corporation of America, the Time-Life Building by the publishers, Time, Incorporated, and so on. (The latter have since moved to another building, across Sixth Avenue, which is not a part of the original complex.) A large area, sunk below street level between 49th and 50th streets, west of Fifth Avenue, contains an ice-skating rink, dominated by a large golden sculpture, called *Prometheus,* by Paul Manship. The complex has a vast underground network, with shops and services, that connects with all of the buildings. Rockefeller Center, limestone-faced in Art Deco style moderne, is a favourite among visitors and natives alike, who enjoy strolling along its flower-bedecked Mall and visiting **Radio City Music Hall** (*q.v.*).

Rockies, the
The nickname for the Rocky Mountains, the largest mountain system in North America, extending more than 3000 miles from the Yukon Territory in Canada, to north central New Mexico. The highest peaks are in Colorado: Mt. Ebert is the tallest at 14,443 feet, but there are 46 others in the state higher than 14,000 feet. Included in the system are the Sangre de Cristo Range, the Middle, Northern, and Canadian Rockies, and the Mackenzie Range. For most of their length they include the Continental Divide. With the lowest pass through them exceeding 10,000 feet in height, they were a formidable barrier to the westward migration of the 1800s, which made the **Oregon Trail** (*q.v.*) so valuable. Also called the **Backbone of North America, the Backbone of the Continent, Roof of the Continent.**

Rodeo Drive
A street in Beverly Hills, California, Rodeo Drive is largely residential, but the short stretch between Wilshire and Santa Monica boulevards is one of the richest shopping streets in the world, comparing with such places as Fifth and Madison avenues in New York, the Via Condotti in Rome, and the rue de Faubourg Saint-Honoré in Paris. Some of the same high-priced luxury goods would be offered on each of these streets. Rodeo Drive differs from the others in its relative newness: its reputation has been forged largely since 1970. It does not carry much heavy traffic, and so one hears jokes about people double-parking their Rolls-Royces there

in order to run into one of the shops to purchase a diamond tiara. *Rodeo* is pronounced 'ro-DAY-o'.

Roedean

A private secondary school for girls just to the east of Brighton, on the south coast of England. It is the most famous establishment of its type in the country; it was founded in 1885, and has since become virtually synonymous with girls' 'public schools'. The image it conjures up is perhaps not altogether positive; the strain of haughtiness and upper-class exclusivity which it suggests is captured in this quote from F. Branston (1977): 'a Roedean accent which could have flayed the skin off a waiter'.

Ronan Point

A block of flats in London's Dockland the celebrated demise of which became a powerful focus of feeling against high-rise building in Britain. In May 1968, after it had been occupied for only two months, a gas explosion in one of its flats set off a domino-effect chain reaction which led to the collapse of one whole corner of the block, killing three people. Widespread unease about the construction methods and the poor quality of the workmanship and materials used for such buildings (as revealed by later investigation) necessitated considerable rethinking among architects and planners, and the name, Ronan Point, continues to exert a powerful grip on the public imagination as a negative symbol of modern building practices.

Roof of the World, the

A name applied to various lofty locations in central Asia, including Tibet and Mount Everest itself. Its principal application, however, is to the Pamirs, a mountainous plateau 30,000 square miles in area at a basic height of 12–13,000 feet above sea level, situated largely in the Soviet Union at the border with China, Pakistan, and Afghanistan. The term is a direct translation of the local name, *Bam-i-Dunya*.

Roost, the

The name given to a violently powerful current that flows to the north of Scotland, around the Orkney and Shetland Islands, where the Atlantic Ocean and the North Sea meet. The word is of Scandinavian origin.

Rosedale
The name of a suburb of Toronto that is associated with affluence and power.

Rotten Row
A road along the south side of Hyde Park, parallel to the Knightsbridge Barracks, from Kensington Gardens to Apsley Gate, in London, long known as a bridle path where people rode and promenaded their horses, especially on Sundays. The origin of its name is unknown, but it might have been a sarcastic reference to the wealthy who frequented the area.

round pound
A nickname for the one-pound coin that was issued by the British government in 1984 and, by 1986, had replaced all paper currency of that denomination.

Round Table at the Algonquin
A group of writers who met more or less regularly at the dining room of the Algonquin Hotel, on West 44th Street, in New York City, for 'liquid lunches' during the 1920s and '30s. In later years, especially after its disbandment about the beginning of World War II, the group became known for its clever quips and somewhat acid commentary on the contemporary scene. Although the cast changed from time to time, the central figures consisted of Harold Ross, Alexander Woolcott, Robert Benchley, Franklin P. Adams, Deems Taylor, George S. Kaufman, Heywood Broun, Edna Ferber, Oscar Levant, and Dorothy Parker.

Route 128
A broad highway designed to allow traffic to bypass Boston on the south and west. Since the 1970s, a number of computer and high-technology companies have built offices and plants along it (and along the Massachusetts Turnpike, towards the west), which has occasioned the nickname, 'Silicon Valley of the East'. Local residents are somewhat offended by the pretentious naming of the road to 'America's Tech Highway'.

Roxbury
A section of Boston occupied predominantly by blacks.

Royal Borough, the
A name sometimes applied to Kensington and Chelsea, a borough in west central London, although in fact three other boroughs in England and Wales are officially royal boroughs as well: Kingston-upon-Thames (London), Windsor (Berkshire), and Caernarvon (North Wales). Royal status was granted to Kensington in 1901 by King Edward VII in honour of Queen Victoria, who was born at Kensington Palace. The boroughs of Kensington and Chelsea were merged in 1965, and they now jointly enjoy the honorific title.

Royal Mile, the
A name given to the road which runs from Edinburgh Castle down to the royal palace of Holyroodhouse, in Edinburgh, Scotland. The official names of the streets of which it is comprised are successively Castle Hill, the Lawnmarket, the High Street, and Canongate.

Rugby
A school for boys in Rugby, a town in Warwickshire, England. It is probably best known for having developed the game of rugby football (nicknamed *rugger*), on which American football is modelled, and as the setting for perennially popular books, starting with *Tom Brown's Schooldays*, (1857) by Thomas Hughes. Its headmaster for many years was Thomas Arnold (1795–1842), father of the author Matthew Arnold and noted educational reformer.

Ruhr, the
A region around the valley of the River Ruhr, a tributary of the Rhine in northwestern West Germany. The centre of the country's coalmining and heavy industry, it was the target for severe Allied bombing in World War II.

Rumelia
A name given to the part of the Balkans, in southeastern Europe, that used to belong to the Ottoman Empire. It covered parts of what are now Greece, Yugoslavia, Albania, and Bulgaria. Its inhabitants were known as Rumeliotes.

Runnymede
A meadow on the south bank of the River Thames, about three miles from Windsor, to the west of London. It was there in 1215 that the

rebellious English barons finally forced King John to put pen to paper and agree to their demands. The resulting document, the famous Magna Carta, has subsequently been interpreted as being a crucial step in the establishment of certain constitutional liberties for English subjects.

Ruritania
An imaginary central European kingdom invented by the 20th-century English writer Anthony Hope for his novel *The Prisoner of Zenda*. It has since come to symbolize swashbuckling adventure, cloak-and-dagger intrigue, and perhaps chiefly the incongruity of royal pomp and circumstance in the matter-of-fact world of the 20th century.

Rush Street
A Near North Side section of Chicago that takes its name from its main thoroughfare. Long known for its often raucous nightlife, Rush Street still draws tourists, conventioneers, and suburbanites in great numbers, especially on weekend nights.

Russia
In ordinary usage, the name *Russia* is frequently used as a synonym for the Soviet Union, but technically it is only one, albeit the most important, of the constituent republics of the Union of Soviet Socialist Republics. Russia, or in full the *Russian Soviet Federated Socialist Republic*, occupies more than three quarters of the total territory of the Soviet Union, extending from the Baltic in the west to the Pacific in the east, an area of more than 6.5 million square miles. Moscow serves as the capital of both Russia and the Soviet Union. Until the Revolution of 1917 Russia was a vast empire, ruled by the Czar of all the Russias. See also **Soviet Union**.

Rutland
In the East Midlands of England, a former county which was swallowed up by the neighbouring Leicestershire in the local government reorganization of 1974. It was the smallest English county.

S

Sahel, the

A region west of Chad, in north Africa, to the coast, bordering the southern part of the Sahara desert and comprising eight countries and about 35 million people.

St Andrews

A town on the east coast of Scotland, to the north of Edinburgh, that is virtually synonymous with golf. Records of the game there go back to the 15th century, and it is still the headquarters of the 'R & A', the Royal and Ancient Golf Club, which is the governing body of golf in Britain. There are no fewer than four courses there, including the famous Old Course, on which members of the public may play fora relatively small charge. St Andrews also houses a venerable university, founded in 1411.

St James's

A fashionable area of the West End of London, bounded on the north by Piccadilly and on the south by the Mall. St James's keynote is restrained and discreet elegance, as befits a former residential area inhabited by the aristocracy, rather than the sometimes rather flashy opulence of its near neighbour Mayfair. At its heart is St James's Street, one of the centres of London's Clubland: scattered anonymously up and down the street are many of the most venerable and exclusive gentlemen's clubs, while nearby all the accoutrements necessary to a gentleman are deferentially purveyed by hatters, bootmakers, wine merchants, gun makers, and cigar merchants. At the foot of St James's Street is the Tudor St James's Palace; it was for many years the sovereign's official home in London, until Queen Victoria moved to Buckingham Palace. See also **Clubland, Mayfair**.

St John's Wood

An area in northwest central London, to the west of Regent's Park. Its wide boulevards, elegant villas, and luxurious blocks of flats bespeak a wealthy and respectable population, but in the early years of the 20th century it had the reputation as a quarter where gentlemen might obtain clandestine pleasures.

St Luke's summer
The English name for a period of warmer than usual weather in October, so called because the feast of St Luke falls on October 18th.

St Paul's
An inner-city area of Bristol, western England, which achieved an unwanted notoriety in April 1980 when severe riots broke out on its streets. One of the poorest districts of the city (and also a red-light area), a large percentage of its population is black, and racial tensions were held largely responsible for the disturbances.

Salem
A name used in the Old Testament for Jerusalem. In Genesis 14:18 we read 'And Melchizedek king of Salem was brought forth bread and wine'; and in Psalm 76:2 'In Salem also is his tabernacle, and his dwelling place is Zion'. See also **City of David.**

Sally Army, the
A jocular British nickname for the Salvation Army, a Christian organization founded in 1865 to evangelize and improve the social conditions of the poor.

Salop
In the West Midlands of England, an alternative name for the county of Shropshire. It has always had a certain currency as a sort of abbreviation (compare **Hants., Oxon.**), but it received apparently final sanction in 1974, when it was declared to be the official name of the county. However, the local people did not take kindly to being told what to call their county, so they campaigned—successfully—to get the old name back: since 1980 Shropshire has again been Shropshire. The alternative continues in unofficial use, however; many locals refer to the county town of Shrewsbury as 'Salop', and former pupils of the local public school are called 'Old Salopians'.

Sandhurst
A village in Berkshire, to the southwest of London, the name of which has been virtually taken over by the nearby Royal Military College, an army training college for officer cadets that was built in the early 19th century by prisoners-of-war captured during the Napoleonic Wars.

Sandlapper State, the

A nickname of South Carolina, so called because the poorer settlers, who lived on almost barren sand ridges, were said to have been compelled to eat sand in order to survive.

Sandringham

Officially, Sandringham House, a royal residence in Norfolk, England. It is said to have been the favourite of George VI.

San Fernando Valley

A large, flat-floored valley between the Santa Monica and Santa Susana mountains of southern California. It is usually referred to simply as 'The Valley'. It differs significantly from the rest of Los Angeles—or so the other Angelenos would have it believed. They make particular reference to the Valley's summer heat, comparative lack of industry, low-density residential areas, and especially to the character of the Valley residents. Jokes about 'Valley girls' are legion, with particular reference to their hair and clothing styles, their taste in music, and their unusual (limited) vocabularies.

Santa Fe Trail

A trade route from Fort Leavenworth, Kansas, to Santa Fe, New Mexico, begun in 1821, before transcontinental railways, by William Becknell, who first brought goods to Santa Fe from Missouri. In 1849 a stagecoach service starting from Independence, Missouri, used the same trail.

Sardi's

A restaurant on 44th Street, west of Broadway, in New York City. It is popular with actors and others connected with the theatre and by those who hope to catch a glimpse of a favourite celebrity—as well as by those aspiring to be noticed by a casting director. It is also frequented by newspaper people: the offices of *The New York Times* are around the corner, on 43rd Street. The walls are covered with photographs of show-business celebrities, many inscribed 'To Vincent Sardi', the former owner.

Sargasso Sea, the
A two-million-square-mile area of the western Atlantic Ocean, on the Tropic of Cancer and to the east of Florida, characterized by huge floating masses of gulfweed and similar brown seaweeds, which quickly entangle any ship that ventures into them. It harbours many forms of marine life, and is famous as the breeding ground of eels; adult eels from American and European rivers congregate there in the autumn to lay their eggs, and the young hatch out and eventually find their way back to their parental rivers. The name comes from *sargasso*, an alternative name for the weed derived from Portuguese *sargaço*.

Sarsaparilla
A fictional, ugly, materialistic outer Sydney suburb in some of Patrick White's novels, plays, and stories.

Sauchiehall Street
A major thoroughfare in northwest central Glasgow, Scotland, and perhaps the city's most famous street. It is noted for its shops, theatres, and cinemas, and is a favourite promenade for the Glaswegian citizenry.

Savile Row
A street in Mayfair, in the West End of London, that runs between and parallel to Bond Street and Regent Street. Its name is virtually synonymous with fine tailoring for gentlemen; any well-dressed man about town will proverbially wear a 'Savile Row suit'.

Savoy, the
A name still occasionally used for an area of central London between the Strand and the Thames, which in the Middle Ages was the site of the Savoy Palace. From housing princes and nobles it went downhill until in the late 17th century it was a notorious haunt of thieves and ruffians; but in the 20th century it is once again frequented by the rich and fashionable, for the Savoy Hotel is situated there. The hotel, known as 'the Savoy', is a luxurious caravanserai built to accommodate quests who attended the Savoy Theatre, venue of the Doyly Carte productions of the operettas of Gilbert and Sullivan.

Scandinavia
A collective term for the countries of northwestern Europe: Denmark, Norway, and Sweden, and usually also Finland and Iceland. The name

seems to be related ultimately to *Skåne*, the very southern part of Sweden. In more restricted usage it refers to the long narrow peninsula containing Norway and Sweden.

Scandinavian Shield, the

A name for the northernmost parts of Norway, Sweden, and Finland along with the Kola Peninsula (including Murmansk). It is called *Nordkalotten* 'the northern skull-cap' in Norway, Sweden, and Denmark; the Finnish name is *Pohjoiskalotti*.

Scarsdale syndrome

A feeling of guilt observed by psychologists among upper middle-class people who have moved to expensive suburbs, named for Scarsdale, such a suburb of New York City, in Westchester County.

Schrafft's

A tradename of G. Shattuck Company for its chain of restaurants, in the Northeast, especially in New York City, and its products, chiefly chocolates and ice cream. Formerly, there were many restaurants, which were known for their light meals of superior quality, their soda fountains, and their excellent ice cream and chocolates. Except for a Men's Grill, in the multi-storied restaurant at 45th Street and Fifth Avenue, the atmosphere of the others was rather tea-roomy, giving rise to their identification with 'little old ladies', many of whom did, indeed, frequent Schrafft's. The restaurants have disappeared, replaced by the ubiquitous 'fast-food' restaurants where lingering over tea with a ham sandwich on toasted cheese bread, were it available, would be strictly discouraged.

Scollay Square

A former square in downtown Boston, replaced entirely by Government Center, with its formal, formidable high-rise office buildings. Till the 1960s, Scollay Square was widely known as the honky-tonk centre of eastern New England; dance halls, striptease shows, prostitutes, and those who associate themselves with such activities were well established. Those establishments, their personnel, and their clientele were displaced by the construction of the formal, proper, somewhat sterile Government Center and must now be sought in the **Combat Zone** (*q.v.*).

Scotland Yard
The name popularly applied to the Metropolitan Police (the police force that covers the whole of Greater London except the City), or more particularly to its criminal investigation branch. 'Scotland Yard baffled' means that its detectives have so far failed to find any clues, a situation often rectified after someone, detained, has been kind enough to 'help the police in their enquiries'. More officially, *New Scotland Yard* is a building, in the Victoria area of London, that houses the headquarters of the Met. It takes its name from the street, on the north bank of the Thames near Westminster Bridge, in which the previous headquarters were situated until 1967. Before this again, the police had premises in Great Scotland Yard, a small street off Whitehall, from their foundation in 1829 until 1890. See also **Yard.**

Scylla and Charybdis
Respectively, a rock and a whirlpool which jointly constitute a hazard to shipping in the narrow strait of Messina, which separates Sicily from Italy. In classical mythology they were depicted as sea monsters which devoured ships and drowned sailors. In modern usage, to be 'between Scylla and Charybdis' means to be faced with two equally unpleasant situations, of which avoiding one will necessitate facing up to the other; the same notion is often rendered in a less literary manner by 'between a rock and a hard place'.

Sears Tower
The world's tallest building, at 1454 feet, situated at the southwest corner of the Loop in Chicago. The city's next two tallest buildings—the Standard Oil Building (1136 feet) and the John Hancock Center (1127 feet)—are also among the world's five tallest. See also **Chrysler Building, Empire State Building.**

Second City, the
1. A nickname for Chicago from the 1890s onward (a comparison with New York City; Chicago is now actually third in U. S. population), 'Second City' is also the name of the popular Old Town cabaret theatre. Founded in 1959 in a former Chinese laundry, it is known for such alumni as Mike Nichols, Elaine May, Ed Asner, and John Belushi. A sister club, also to be called 'Second City', is planned for Los Angeles—the city that recently overtook Chicago as America's second most populous.

2. A nickname for Birmingham, in the West Midlands of England. At 1,062,000, its population is second only to that of London.

Senegambia

An area in West Africa bounded to the north by the River Senegal (the northern frontier of the State of Senegal) and to the south by the River Gambia (the main artery of the state of the Gambia, which forms a long narrow enclave in Senegal).

Seven Dials

The junction of several rather run-down roads in the West End of London, just to the east of Soho. In former times the Seven Dials area was a notorious warren of thieves and other disreputable characters, but in the late 20th century it is merely rather seedy (although an increasing number of upmarket boutiques are now infiltrating the area). It gets its name from a column with seven clock faces on it which used to stand there.

Seven Hills, the

The hills on which the walls of ancient Rome were built. Their names were the Aventine, Caelian, Capitoline, Esquiline, Palatine, Quirinal, and Viminal.

Seven Seas, the

A collective name, variously explained as being either all the major oceans of the world: North and South Atlantic, North and South Pacific, Indian, Arctic, and Antarctic, or principal seas of navigation and trade: Arabian Sea, Atlantic Ocean, Bay of Bengal, Mediterranean Sea, Persian Gulf, Red Sea, and South China Sea. It is a romantic rather than a strictly geographical term, associated with the days of sail, with pirates and explorers, galleons and windjammers.

Seven Sisters

An epithet applied originally to the Pleiades, a group of stars, and over the years to various groups of seven people or things. In modern usage it is the name of three places in Britain: an area of Tottenham, in northeast London, which gets its name from the Seven Sisters Road running through it (this in turn was probably named for a group of seven elm trees nearby); a dramatic range of seven chalk cliffs on the south coast of England, to the east of Brighton, which culminates in the 500-feet-high

Beachy Head; and a village in West Glamorgan, Wales, the name of
which derives from a nearby coal mine that was called 'Seven Sisters
Colliery' after the seven daughters of its first owner.

Shaftesbury Avenue

A street running northeast from Piccadilly Circus to Charing Cross Road,
the focus of the theatre district of London. See also **Piccadilly Circus.**

Shambles, the

An area in the city of York, in northern England, which used to be the
butchers' quarter, housing slaughterhouses and butchers' shops. Today
its narrow street, near the Minster (cathedral), is a major tourist attraction, lined on each side by boutiques and antique shops. The word *shambles* originally meant 'a stool'; then 'a table for displaying goods', later
specifically 'meat'; then 'a meat market'; then 'an abattoir'; then 'a scene
of great carnage, such as a battlefield'; and finally today 'a ruination or
mess'.

Shangri-La

1. An imaginary land of endless and unblemished happiness, whose fame
has spread far beyond the confines of the novel in which it originally
appeared. It was thought up by the English writer James Hilton, who set
his *Lost Horizon* (1933) in a lamasery in the (totally fictitious) Tibetan
valley of Shangri-La, the inhabitants of which never grew old.
2. Because of the imaginary (if not the romantic) nature of the fictional
place, its name was adopted in 1942 by President Franklin D. Roosevelt
as a code name for the aircraft carrier *Hornet*, from which the bombers
were launched on April 18th, under the direction of General James P.
Doolittle, for the first World War II air raid on Japanese soil—on Tokyo
itself as well as Nagoya and other cities.
3. Because of its remote, possibly utopian attributes, *Shangri-La* was later
(1945) applied by President Franklin D. Roosevelt to Camp David, Maryland, to avoid identifying its location, which had been secretly established
as a presidential retreat, away from the immediate pressures of Washington and the Oval Office.

Shankill Road

A main thoroughfare of Belfast, Northern Ireland, that runs west from
the city centre. The area around it is a major Protestant stronghold from

which the Ulster loyalists derive a lot of their support. The road runs parallel to the Catholic **Falls Road** (*q.v.*) to the north.

Sheba

The biblical name of the ancient kingdom of Saba, situated in the area of modern Yemen, in the southwestern part of the Arabian peninsula. In the years between about 930 and 115 B.C. it was a powerful and wealthy nation, having secured a monopoly of the spice trade in its area. Its most famous denizen was its queen, who visited King Solomon with a most impressive display of riches and pomp—'with a very great train', as the Bible puts it. According to the Koran her actual name was Balkis.

Sheffield of Germany

A former epithet of Solingen, in (modern West) Germany, so called originally because of the high quality of the swords and foils made there and, more recently, its cutlery. The original Sheffield, in England, has long enjoyed a reputation for sword-making, cutlery, and silver plate.

Shepheard's Hotel

Formerly, an important hotel in Cairo, frequented by western visitors, especially the British, during the occupation (1880-1922) and afterwards, till it was destroyed by fire in the 1950s. Romantic tales were woven about it as a focus of Middle-East intrigue, but it was probably best known for its bartender, Joe, who served concoctions, in tall glasses, called the Dying Bastard and the Dead Bastard, the latter with slices of cucumber floating in it.

Shepherd Market

A little maze of streets and alleyways in the southwestern corner of Mayfair, just off Piccadilly in the West End of London. It was laid out in 1735 by a certain Edward Shepherd, on part of the site of the original May fair which gave its name to the area as a whole. It is a noted haunt of prostitutes. See also **Mayfair.**

Shepherd's Bush

A residential area of west London, to the west of Kensington. In former times it was a decidedly downmarket district, but with the arrival of the BBC Television Centre in 1960 it went up in the world to a certain extent. The origin of its name is uncertain.

Shires, the
In medieval times in England, a *shire* was synonymous with a *county*, but gradually its use became limited mainly to a combining form for counties (e.g., Hertfordshire, Lancashire, Devonshire). However, the term *the Shires* has had some specialized uses: in the 18th and 19th centuries it seems to have been applied by inhabitants of southeast England to any parts of the country other than their own, as being foreign and outlandish regions; then, from the second half of the 19th century onwards, *the Shires* was the foxhunting area of the English east Midlands, particularly Northamptonshire and Leicestershire, which in the season became the private playground of the aristocratic members of the Quorn and the Pytchely, the Fernie, the Cottesmore, and the Belvoir (the names of various hunts); finally, in more recent times *the Shires* or Shire Counties has taken on political connotations: the term *knights of the shires* used to denote landed gentry who represented their counties in Parliament, and from that usage 'Shires' has come to mean the rural areas of England, which can be relied on to return Conservative members to Parliament.

Shop, the
A nickname for Melbourne University established late in the 19th century.

Show Me State, the
The official nickname of Missouri, so called after an expression attributed to one of its former U. S. Representatives, Willard D. Vandiver.

Siam
The former name of Thailand, a kingdom in southeast Asia. It was called Siam until 1939, when its name was officially changed to Thailand; then in 1945 it reverted to Siam, but in 1949 it was changed back again to Thailand, which it has remained ever since.

Siberia
A huge region in north central and northeast Asia, which includes most of the Soviet Union to the east of the Urals. Much of it is desolate and sparsely populated, but the Trans-Siberian railway, built between 1891 and 1916 to link Moscow with Vladivostok on the Pacific coast, has gradually made some economic progress possible. Much of Siberia is north of the Arctic Circle, and it has become almost proverbial for cold desolation; any prolonged period of snow and ice is liable to be dubbed 'a

Siberian winter'. More sinisterly, it has gained a reputation as an area to which Soviet dissidents and traitors are sent to moulder in the oblivion of the labour camps and the infamous 'salt mines'.

Sick Man of Europe
A former nickname for the Turkish empire, bestowed by Kaiser Wilhelm (William II), emperor of Germany (1888–1918). See also **Sick Man of the East.**

Sick Man of the East
A former nickname for the Turkish empire, bestowed by Nicholas II, Czar of Russia (1894– 1917). See also **Sick Man of Europe.**

Silent Service
A nickname for the submarine service in the British, American, and (possibly) certain other navies.

Silicon Glen
A nickname for the central lowland belt of Scotland, roughly between Glasgow and Edinburgh, in which a flourishing microelectronics industry has developed during the 1970s and '80s. American and British computer companies have set up many factories in towns such as Livingston, Cumbernauld, and Glenrothes to produce silicon chips, microcircuits, semiconductors, and so forth. The name is modelled on Silicon Valley, California's microelectronics centre, *glen* being the Scots word for 'valley'. See also **Silicon Prairie, Silicon Valley.**

Silicon Prairie
A nickname for an area near Dallas, Texas, so called because of the large number of high-technology and computer companies situated there. See also **Silicon Glen, Silicon Valley.**

Silicon Valley
An area south of San Francisco where companies manufacturing microcomputers built plants during the 1970s, so named after the silicon micro-chip which is at the heart of those devices. Companies engaged in ancillary activities, such as the design of software, soon moved there, too, and Silicon Valley became known for its modern buildings, in a park-like setting, occupied by phenomenally successful firms employing some of the highest-paid computer specialists in the world, 'boy wonders', many

of whom were under thirty. With the decline of popularity of microcomputers, owing partly to saturation of the market, partly to their loss of novelty, and, to a greater extent, to the entrance into the market of huge companies like IBM, the successes of many of the companies were turned to failures. See also **Silicon Glen, Silicon Prairie.**

Silver City
A nickname for Broken Hill, a mining town in the far west of New South Wales. See also **Big Australian.**

Simpson's (in the Strand)
A very old restaurant in the Strand, in London, known for its beef, especially its roast beef, which is carved at the table from a huge joint on an elaborate trolley.

Simpson's of Piccadilly
A department store in Piccadilly, in London, specializing mainly in conservative men's clothing, shirts, and other accoutrements of attire. The rear of the store faces **Jermyn Street** (*q.v.*).

Sind
A region in southeast Pakistan, centred on the lower reaches of the Indus River. Its greatest claim to fame is that it gave rise to perhaps the most celebrated pun ever made on a place-name: in 1843 British forces under Sir Charles Napier conquered the area; his message back to London was the single word *peccavi*, which is Latin for 'I have sinned'.

Sioux State, the
A nickname of North Dakota, so called because it was the home of the Sioux Indians who called themselves *Dakotas*, meaning 'allies'.

Six Counties, the
A name sometimes given to Northern Ireland, which is made up of the counties of Armagh, Antrim, Down, Derry, Fermanagh, and Tyrone.

1600 Pennsylvania Avenue
The street address of the White House, official residence of the President of the United States, often used metonymically for the office of the presidency. See also **Oval Office.**

Skevington's daughter

An instrument of torture invented by Sir W. Skevington, Lieutenant of the Tower of London in the reign of Henry VIII (1509–47). It consisted of a broad hoop of iron which so compressed the body that blood was forced from the nose and ears and sometimes from the hands and feet. Also called **scavenger's daughter.**

skid row

The name for an area in a city where vagrants gather. It is also used metaphorically and, converted to a verb, appears as *hit the skids*, in reference to someone who is down-and-out. The origin of *skid row* is uncertain, one popular theory proposing it was named for a street that (in the 1850s) ran up and down a steep hill in Seattle, Washington, that had a timbermill at the bottom. Logs delivered at the top of the street were skidded down to the mill. As the street along which this was done scarcely allowed for a high grade of businesses or residences, it was characterized by the presence of run-down saloons, shabby hotels, and cheap restaurants, which today characterize the areas frequented by those on their uppers.

Slave Coast, the

A term sometimes used in the 18th and 19th centuries for the coast of West Africa between eastern Ghana and eastern Nigeria. Names of this type, referring to a major local product, are quite common in this area—Ghana was known as the Gold Coast in colonial days, and next door to it is a state still called the Ivory Coast. In former times slaves, destined for the Americas, were West Africa's leading export.

slider

A nickname for the hamburgers sold by the U. S. chain, White Tower, a two-ounce square patty of minced meat cooked by steam, in its bun, in a bed of onions. Also called **belly buster, gut bomb.**

Sloane Square

An unremarkable-looking square in the heart of London's Belgravia, but one that is the spiritual home of a curious breed of young person first noted by amateur anthropologists in the late 1970s—'Sloane Ranger' (or 'Sloane', for short). These sons and daughters of wealthy establishment families introduced reactionary chic, which made it fashionable to wear sensible tweedy clothes that in the 1960s and '70s would have seemed very stuffy. Their usual haunts are Belgravia, Chelsea, and Knightsbridge, although they often decamp to country houses at the weekends.

Slough
A town in Buckinghamshire, to the west of London. Partly no doubt because of its unprepossessing name, with its suggestions of mire and despondency, Slough has an unenviable and not altogether deserved reputation as being the epitome of drab and brain-numbing subtopia, full of uniform streets and occupied by people with uniform tastes and attitudes. It is forever associated with these lines of John Betjeman:

> Come, friendly bombs, and fall on Slough
> It isn't fit for humans now,
> There isn't grass to graze a cow
> Swarm over, Death!

Smithfield
An open area (named for *Smith's field*) in what, at the time, was north of the City of London. There, on every Friday, unless it happened to be a solemn festival, was held 'a great market for horses, whither earls, barons, knights, and citizens repaired, to see and to purchase'. William Fitz-Stephen, a Canterbury monk, in *Descriptio Nobilissimae Civitatis Londini* (1174), wrote 'merchants brought their wares from every nation under Heaven. The Arabian sent his gold; the Sabaeans, spice and frankincense; the Scythians, armour; Babylon, its oil; Egypt, precious stones; India, purple vestments; Norway and Russia, furs, sables, and ambergris; and Gaul, its wines'.

Smith Square
A square in Westminster, scarcely five minutes' walk from the Houses of Parliament. It has always been popular as a place of residence for those Members who can afford it, but its best-known occupant is the headquarters of the Conservative Party, with whose organization and party machine it has almost become synonymous. It also contains **Transport House** (*q.v.*), the former headquarters of the Labour Party. Compare **Walworth Road.**

Smoke, the
In the days before clean-air legislation, when soot was a major component of the urban atmosphere, large metropolises came to be known,

particularly to those in the provinces, as *the Smoke,* or *the Big Smoke.* More specifically, London is *the Smoke* to Britishers, while Australia, where the nickname was first recorded as an Australian Aboriginal term for a city, it is usually applied to Melbourne or Sydney.

Snake, the

A nickname for the European Monetary System (founded 1979), under which the exchange rates of the currencies of member nations fluctuate within certain fixed limits. All EEC countries except Britain and Greece belong. The name derives from the original descriptive epithet of 'the snake in the tunnel', whose wriggling was supposed to be suggestive of the currencies' (limited) movements.

Snake Gully

A name best known as the locale of a radio serial 'Dad and Dave', a rustic comedy. But there is a real Snake Gully, and it is, in the words of a well-known folksong 'five miles from Gundagai', in New South Wales. It is the site of tourist shops and the statue of a dog sitting on a tuckerbox, a reference to the same folksong.

Snowdonia

A mountainous area of northwest Wales which takes its name from Mount Snowdon, at 3560 feet the highest mountain in Britain south of Scotland. Five mountain ranges and the many lakes make this a region of spectacular scenic beauty, and most of it—about 850 square miles—is a national park. In extent it coincides fairly closely with the ancient realm and modern county of Gwynedd.

Sodom and Gomorrah

1. The names of cities in Canaan destroyed because of their depravity and wickedness. [Gen. 19:24 ff]
2. A nickname for Stockholm, used among the people in Gothenburg, who consider that city a wicked place.

Sodom of India

A former nickname of Hyderabad, so called because of the beauty of the country and the depravity of its inhabitants. [Brewer's *Reader's Handbook*]

SoHo

A nickname for a neighbourhood in mid Manhattan, west of Lafayette Street, east of Sixth Avenue, north of Canal Street, and, as the name suggests, *so*uth of *Ho*uston (pronounced HOWstin) Street. It was developed beginning in the 1960s by artists and others who were attracted by the large former manufacturing lofts, which had fallen into disuse. Several of the more enterprising (and somewhat wealthier) among them bought the smaller buildings and with ingenuity and paint, converted the lofts into studios and living space. Gradually a community sprang up that included galleries exhibiting the paintings and sculpture of SoHo inhabitants and of others. With the passing years, though SoHo has gained in its reputation for panache, its cachet has diminished as the properties increased in value and attracted more and more yuppies (Young Upwardly-mobile Professionals). Also, **So-Ho.** See also **NoHo.**

Soho

A district in the West End of London, to the east of Mayfair and to the north of Trafalgar Square. It has had a rather checkered history. As its small and congested streets, clustered around Soho Square, suggest, it has never been the most fashionable part of the West End. Since the 17th century it has attracted large numbers of immigrants—from France, Italy, Greece, and elsewhere. The cosmopolitan atmosphere that this fostered survives to this day, as is evident from the diversity of foreign restaurants and food shops. Soho's reputation has always remained rather *louche*. In the immediate postwar years it was the haunt of the avant-garde arty set. It had always, too, been a noted centre for prostitution, and in the 1960s and '70s the strip clubs, sex cinemas and shops, peep shows, and any other lucrative form of sleazy entertainment grew apace. In the 1980s, a concerted effort has been made to discourage such establishments, and the area acquired, through the increased property values, an 'establishment' tone. The area is now rejuvenated as a place for nightlife, with its wine bars, bistros, and exotic restaurants—notably Chinese, for there is now a considerable Chinese community in Soho. Compare **SoHo.**

Soke of Peterborough, the

A former administrative area of the county of Northamptonshire in the East Midlands of England, which lost its separate identity in 1965. In medieval times a *soke* was a district under the jurisdiction of a local court.

Solent, the
The name given to the strait that separates the Isle of Wight from the southern coast of England, familiar, at least in former times, to passengers in the great transatlantic liners that passed along it on their way to or from the port of Southampton. At its widest it is about four miles across.

Somerset House
A building in the Strand, in London, formerly housing the National Records Office, more recently occupied by the Courtauld Institute of Art. It was built in 1776 on the site of an unfinished 16th-century palace.

Somers Town
An area of north London just to the west of King's Cross Station. In former times it had the reputation of being a very poor district, and in the early years of its existence many penniless refugees from the French Revolution came to live there.

Sooner State, the
The official nickname of Oklahoma, so called in reference to those who sneaked in ahead of the gun fired to signal that the territory was opened for settlement.

Sound, the
The English name for the busy strait that separates Zealand, the main island of Denmark, from Sweden and joins the Kattegat with the Baltic. At its narrowest point, where Sweden's Helsingborg faces Denmark's Helsingör (the Elsinore of *Hamlet*), it is only three miles across. Further south on opposite coasts are Copenhagen and Malmö. The waterway's Danish name is Öresund.

South, the
1. In the United States, generally an area comprising those states south of the Mason-Dixon Line, namely, Virginia, Kentucky, Arkansas, North and South Carolina, Tennessee, Georgia, Alabama, Mississippi, and Louisiana. Although Florida is, physically, in *the South*, only its northern part is usually considered as being a part of the cultural, social, and economic community associated with the other states mentioned. Compare **Deep South.**
2. In broadest terms, the South of England includes any parts of the country that are not the North, the Midlands, or East Anglia. In practice,

however, the Southwest is often excluded too (the phrase 'the South and Southwest' is often used), and in this narrower sense the South comprises the core of London and the Southeast, plus Hampshire, the eastern parts of Dorset and Wiltshire, all of Berkshire, and the southerly parts of Oxfordshire. Its reputation is as the Southeast's: economically, as well as climatically, it is the most favoured part of Britain, and it is often looked at askance by Northerners, who regard the stereotypical Southerner as effete and aloof.

3. Geopolitically, *the South*, in Britain, has taken on new connotations in the latter part of the 20th century. As contrasted with the North, it refers basically to the economically underprivileged and industrially underdeveloped nations of the southern hemisphere—the world's 'have-nots'. It was popularized as a concept by the publication in 1980 of the so-called *Brandt Report*, in full *North-South, a programme for survival; report of the Independent Commission on International Development*.

South American Alps
A nickname for that part of the Andes Mountains between Chile and Argentina, so called because members of the jet set go to ski resorts such as Portillo after the end of the European season.

South Bank, the
A stretch of the Thames embankment in London just across the river from the Houses of Parliament, from the northern end of County Hall to Waterloo Bridge. The large site was used for the Festival of Britain in 1951, and subsequently has been developed as a national centre for the arts. The Royal Festival Hall led the way in 1951, and this has been followed successively by a cinema, further concert halls, the Hayward Art Gallery, and the National Theatre. From a strict geographical point of view, the South Bank is for the most part the east bank of the Thames.

Southeast, the
The southeastern corner of England, centred on London. In extent it is similar to the Home Counties, plus the capital, but as well as Surrey, Kent, and Essex, it includes Sussex, and usually excludes the western half of Berkshire and the most northerly parts of Hertfordshire and Buckinghamshire. The large concentration of middle-class professional people who live there, many of them close to places of work in London, makes the Southeast the wealthiest and most economically privileged part of

Britain; levels of unemployment, for example, are usually significantly lower here than in other areas of the country. Compare **South, 2**.

Southeast Asia
A region consisting of a large bulge of land at the southeastern corner of Asia and of the islands to the south and east of it (the Malay Archipelago). It contains the states of Burma, Thailand, Cambodia, Laos, Vietnam, Malaysia, Singapore, Indonesia, Brunei, and the Philippines. See also **Indochina**.

Southern Uplands, the
A hilly region, including the Lowther, Moorfoot, and Lammermuir hills, that covers much of the southern part of Scotland, between the Borders and the Lowlands. See also **Highlands**.

Southie
An area of the south side of Boston, occupied predominantly by people of Irish descent and associated with South Boston High School. Its residents retain strong ties with Northern Ireland and express their sympathies with the militant pro-Catholic factions there, which are bent on separating the country from British rule, by supporting the Sinn Fein and the Irish Republican Army (I.R.A.), both financially and politically, especially by thwarting legislation in the United States directed at the extradition of those who are wanted by the police for their alleged involvement in bombings, shootings, and other acts of violence against British personnel and property.

South of France, the
A term applied to the Mediterranean area of France—it embraces the southern coast stretching westward from the Riviera past Marseilles to the Spanish border, and the hinterland of Provence and Languedoc. It is a land of sun and wine, garlic and olive oil, and a popular vacation area for Europeans. Indeed for most English-speakers the South of France means above all the Côte d'Azur (in contrast to the Midi, the French term it usually translates, which embraces the inland areas to a far greater degree). The name retains the whiff of glamour and wealth that first attached itself to it in the 19th century when the titled English disported themselves on their yachts at Monte Carlo and Nice, occasionally venturing ashore for a turn at the casino tables. Latterly, resorts such as Cannes

and St Tropez have outstripped them in chic, adding still further to the sybaritic image of the South of France. Compare **Midi**.

South Pole
The southern end of the earth's axis of rotation which, owing to libration, changes slightly; the geographic south pole. It is situated on the continent of Antarctica, a large land mass, explored only superficially, where several nations maintain bases for research. Unlike the North Pole, it is inhabited, along its shores, by penguins and other birds and by a variety of other sea life. See also **North Pole**.

South Seas, the
A term that can broadly refer to any of the oceans south of the equator, but in practice is usually used today for the South Pacific. In the wider context, 'the southern oceans' is the usual term nowadays. In former times, *South Seas* was the standard, neutral name for the area—the famous financial crash of 1720, for example, known as the *South Sea Bubble*, involved a company that traded with the Southern Hemisphere—but in modern usage it has more romantic connotations. The 'South Sea Islands', in particular, evoke images of snow-white beaches, grass-skirted maidens, and carefree living in an ideal climate, largely as a result of the novels of Charles Nordoff and James Norman Hall and of idyllic motion pictures made in the 1930s.

South Shore, the
A local designation for the southern shores of Long Island, east of New York City.

South Side
A large area south of the Loop in Chicago and reaching roughly two miles west from bordering Lake Michigan. The major part of the South Side, lying due south of the Loop and reaching east along the southeastern curve of the lake, is the home of most of the city's large black population, with many industrial and poor residential areas, punctuated by such enclaves as the Hyde Park area, in which the University of Chicago is situated. Lake Calumet—some thirteen miles south of the Loop, on the city's Far South Side—is an important port for commercial shipping. On the Far Southeast Side is the historic **Pullman** (*q.v.*) area. The South Side also includes Jackson Park, Washington Park, and the

Midway Plaisance (commonly known as, simply, 'the Midway') connecting the two. Among its attractions are the **Museum of Science and Industry** (*q.v.*), Chinatown, Comiskey Park (home of the Chicago White Sox baseball club) and such well-known bastions of blues and soul music as the Checkerboard Lounge. A former South Side landmark, the Union Stockyards, was the famous—and, to some observers, infamous—nexus of the nation's meatpacking business. Nearby are the multi-ethnic, historically important Bridgeport and Back of the Yards neighbourhoods; Bridgeport, a favoured area of Irish immigrants, is especially noted as the home of four successive Chicago mayors, spanning forty-six years (1933–79): Ed Kelly, Martin Kennelly, Richard J. Daley, and Michael Bilandic. See also **McCormick Place, Pilsen, Stagg Field, Union Stockyards, West Side, 2.**

Southwest, the
1. In the United States, an area encompassing the western states of Colorado, Utah, Nevada, Arizona, New Mexico, and Texas. Compare **West.**
2. The southwestern extremity of England, including the counties of Cornwall, Devon, and Somerset, and usually also western Dorset. It forms the southern and western section of the West Country. Compare **West, 2.**

Soviet Russia
A (post-Czarist) synonym for Russia, and used similarly to mean either the Soviet Union or, more strictly, the Russian Soviet Federated Socialist Republic. See also **Russia, Soviet Union.**

Soviet Union, the
A useful shorthand term usually used in preference to the officially correct but long-winded Union of Soviet Socialist Republics, or U. S. S. R. It is, in area, the largest country in the world, extending from the Polish and Romanian border in the west across most of northern Asia to the Pacific in the east, and covering one seventh of the world's total land surface, more than 8.5 million square miles. It is a federal state consisting of fifteen individual republics, the largest of which is Russia. *Soviet* is the Russian word for a governing council, a system of which, from the local level up to the Supreme Soviet, was put in place throughout the land following the Revolution of 1917. See also **Russia.**

Spaghetti Junction

A nickname given to any major road interchange of bewildering complexity, especially that at Gravelly Hill in north Birmingham, in the West Midlands of England.

Spanish Harlem

A general name given to those sections of Harlem, in New York City, where poorer Puerto Rican families settled upon moving to the mainland of the United States. An enormous influx of Puerto Ricans began to move to New York City, beginning in the late 1930s and early 1940s, largely at the instigation of Vito Marcantonio, a United States Congressman who invited them to move into the district he represented. As Puerto Rico is a commonwealth associated with the United States, its citizens may travel and settle freely anywhere in the U. S. As most of those who settled in New York City were indigent, they readily qualified for welfare (then called relief), the meagre support of which left them still better off than if they had remained in Puerto Rico. Ironically, the district represented by Marcantonio included not only these poorest sections of the city but the upper reaches of Fifth and Park avenues, as well; but these were relatively sparsely settled, especially in contrast to the overcrowded conditions of the Harlem slums, and, with the residents of Spanish Harlem to vote him into office, term after term, the wealthier residents found themselves vastly outnumbered in their attempts to vote him out of office. It was in those days that there originated the term 'Silk Stocking District' in reference to the area occupied by Marcantonio's wealthy constituents. By the 1970s, as these Puerto Ricans began to assimilate and to move out of their confining ghetto, the term "Spanish Harlem" began to refer more to the Spanish-speaking population of Harlem than to any well-defined area. See also **East Side, Fifth Avenue, Harlem, Park Avenue, Upper East Side.**

Spanish Main, the

Originally, the Spanish Mainland—that is to say, the Spanish colonies on the northern coast of South America from the 16th century onward. In later use, however, the Spanish Main came to mean the stretch of sea offshore: the southern Caribbean, through which Spanish treasure galleons sailed for Europe with their freight of gold. Such seas were the natural habitat of predatory buccaneers and freebooters in the 17th and 18th centuries; ever since, the Spanish Main has been used as the setting of adventure yarns about pirates.

Speakers' Corner
The northeast corner of Hyde Park, London, near Marble Arch, which was moved to its present location from its former site as an entrance to the Palace Gardens and Buckingham Palace. Speakers' Corner is where those who wish to regale listeners on any of a variety of subjects are seen and heard, holding forth from soapboxes or other makeshift platforms. See also **Hyde Park Corner.**

Speck, the
A nickname for Tasmania (from its size).

Spice Islands, the
A term used since at least the 17th century for islands in the East from which spice was imported, but usually applied more specifically in past times to a group of islands between Sulawesi (Celebes) and Papua New Guinea, in the East Indies. In the 16th and 17th centuries they were at the focus of a fierce contest for the monopoly of the spice trade between Portugal, Spain, and Holland, in which the Dutch prevailed. In later years they were known as the Moluccas, and since 1949 they have been part of the republic of Indonesia, of which they form the Maluku province.

Square Mile, the
A nickname given to the City of London, particularly with reference to its status as a financial centre. Its precise area is in fact 675 acres, just over one square mile.

Squatter State, the
A nickname of Kansas, so called in reference to the many settlers rushed into the territory by both pro- and antislavery groups just before the Civil War.

Stagg Field
An athletic facility, birthplace of the Atomic Age, which began in Chicago on December 2, 1942, when Enrico Fermi and University of Chicago scientists, working on the 'Manhattan Project', achieved the first self-sustaining nuclear chain reaction. The research was conducted in a converted old squash court under a stadium grandstand; the site is now marked by a sculpture by Henry Moore.

Stamboul

An archaic form of the Turkish name for the city previously known by its Greek name, Constantinople, and in more modern times as Istanbul. It is perhaps best remembered from the title of Graham Greene's novel, *Stamboul Train*, which concerns events on the Orient-Express to the then Turkish capital.

Stannaries, the

In the Middle Ages, tin was mined and smelted extensively on Dartmoor, in western Devon and eastern Cornwall, southwestern England. The mining area became known as *the Stannaries* (from Latin *stannum*, 'tin'), and in its heyday was virtually a self-governing enclave; the tinners had their own courts ('stannary courts') with very wide jurisdiction, and their own parliament, which met in the open air on Crockern Tor from 1304 to 1749. The whole legal apparatus was abolished in 1896, but tin continues to be mined in Cornwall when prices on the world market warrant.

Star Chamber

The name of an apartment in the Palace of Westminster, in London, where the King's Council dispensed justice in medieval times. It was named for the stars that decorated its blue ceiling. During the reign of the Stuarts, the Court of Star Chamber, its successor, dispensed such arbitrary and ruthless justice that 'star-chamber proceedings' came to be associated with injustice. The Court was abolished in 1641.

Star Hotel

An Australianism for the open, outside: to sleep in the *Star Hotel* is to sleep with the canopy of stars as a roof.

Stars and Bars

A nickname for the flag of the Confederate states of America during the Civil War, consisting of two horizontal red bars on white, and a circle of eleven white stars on a field of blue. See also **Old Glory, Stars and Stripes.**

Stars and Stripes

A nickname for the (officially named) Flag of the United States, first used in 1897 by John Philip Sousa for his march, 'Stars and Stripes Forever'. It was next used for a U. S. army newspaper published in France during World War I, then again during World War II when an army publication for soldiers was so named.

Star Wars
The nickname for the Strategic Defence Initiative, a United States plan of the 1980s for placing into fixed orbit in space over the earth weapons capable of detecting and destroying missiles launched against the U. S.

State of Excitement, the
A nickname adopted by Western Australia and used on its motor registration plates from 1979 to 1983, when it was (temporarily) replaced by the slogan 'Home of the America's Cup'.

Stealth
A nickname for the Advanced Technology Bomber, a United States military aircraft, the existence of which is denied by officials, designed to make its presence difficult to detect by ordinary means such as radar and other sensory devices.

Steel City
1. A nickname for Newcastle, New South Wales, the site of a steelworks established by the Broken Hill Proprietary Company Ltd.
2. A nickname for Wollongong, New South Wales, where a steelworks was established at Port Kembla in 1928.

Stoke Mandeville
A village to the southeast of Aylesbury, in Buckinghamshire, northwest of London. Its name has become virtually synonymous with that of its world-famous hospital for paraplegics, whose regime of active therapy culminates in the Stoke Mandeville Games, a sort of mini-Olympics.

Stork Club
For almost three decades, till his death in the 1960s, Sherman Billingsley operated the Stork Club, on 53rd Street between Fifth and Madison avenues, in New York City. During those years it became a focal point of the night life of the city, catering to celebrities and café society alike, while the goings-on and gossip were reported by the columnists Walter Winchell, 'Cholly Knickerbocker', Leonard Lyons, Ed Sullivan, Dorothy Kilgallen, and others.

Storyville

Attempts to limit the spread of prostitution in New Orleans, Louisiana, were culminated in 1897 when the City Council passed a municipal ordinance establishing a red-light district where those practices would be tolerated. The limits of this district, called Storyville after Alderman Sidney Story, the sponsor of the ordinance, were the blocks of the city contained within Customhouse (later renamed Iberville), Robertson, St Louis, and Basin streets. In its heyday a flourish of about 2000 strumpets in about 230 houses plied their profession there, the brothels ranging from sparsely furnished cribs to opulent parlour houses. New Orleans jazz had many of its roots in Storyville, and the neighbourhood served as a tawdry tourist attraction. It was already in considerable decline when it was closed in 1917 under pressure from the Navy Department.

Strawberry Fields

A Salvation Army orphanage in Liverpool, in the Northwest of England, immortalized in the Beatles song of the same name, which they first recorded in 1967.

Strawberry Hill

A fine home in Twickenham, near Richmond-upon-Thames, west of London, once the seat of Horace Walpole.

Street, the

1. A nickname for Wall Street.
2. A nickname for any area or circumstance where news may be exchanged, rumours heard, etc. 'What do you hear on the Street?' usually means 'What rumours are about? What's the latest news?' It usually refers to goings-on in a particular trade, profession, or industry.

Strip, the

1. The section of highway in Las Vegas, Nevada, that is lined with hotels, gambling casinos, and other places of entertainment.
2. The name of the downtown area of Toronto, that is the focus of amusement and entertainment, somewhat parallel in connotation to Times Square in New York City or the Sunset Strip in Los Angeles.
3. See **Sunset Boulevard.**

Subcontinent, the

In modern usage, a word used for the vast triangular peninsula at the south of the Asian landmass, containing the states of India, Pakistan, Bangladesh, Sri Lanka, Nepal, and Bhutan. In more general terms, a subcontinent is any large subdivision of a continent, with some sort of separate character of its own, and indeed up until the beginning of the 20th century the word was used specifically to refer not to India but to South Africa.

Sublime Porte, the

The name given to the government and court of the former Ottoman Empire. A French term, it is a direct translation of the Turkish *Baba Ali* 'imperial [*literally* high] gate'; this probably refers ultimately to the entrance to the sultan's tent, where in ancient times audiences were held. The term was often abbreviated to simply *the Porte*, and in the 17th and 18th centuries was commonly mistaken as a reference to Constantinople as a seaport.

subtopia

A word coined by British architect journalist Ian Nairn in the 1950s for suburban housing estates, the owners of which devote many hours each day to making the best of their small plots.

Sucker State, the

A nickname of Illinois, so called either because the local miners went to the mines in the spring and returned in the fall, as the suckers (fish) did in the rivers, or because, in the early days of settlement, the prairie water was usually to be found only in crawfish holes and had to be sucked up by means of hollow reeds, which the people called 'suckers'.

Sudan, the

A name given to the vast sweep of the African continent that lies south of the Sahara desert and north of the tropical rain forests. From the 4th century onward it was the seat of the powerful and vigorous Sudanic civilization, a Negro culture the leading states of which were Ghana, Hausa, Kanem, and Songhai. It declined as Islam began to filter southward in the Middle Ages, and had disappeared by the 19th century; but the memory of its name is preserved in the modern state at its eastern extremity, which is the largest country in Africa.

Sudetenland, the
An area along the northwestern border of Czechoslovakia, occupied by
two mountain ranges: the Erzgebirge on the frontier with East Germany,
and the Sudeten Mountains on the frontier with Poland. It achieved an
unwanted celebrity in 1938 when Adolf Hitler's annexation of the area to
Germany, using as a pretext its having, historically, been inhabited by
German-speaking people, became one of the factors leading up to World
War II. In 1945 it was returned to Czechoslovakia, and most of the
German-speaking population was expelled.

Sugar Hill
A vaguely circumscribed neighbourhood in north Harlem, in New York
City. On a high promontory, at about 135th Street and St Nicholas
Avenue, overlooking the areas to the east—the Harlem River and The
Bronx beyond—it was a residential section where the wealthier blacks
lived. It was so named because those who resided there had the 'sugar' to
afford it.

Sunbelt
A geographical area of the southern United States that includes those
states, particularly Florida, Arizona, and New Mexico, that have relatively milder weather than the rest of the country all year round and tend
to attract retired people and those who prefer subtropical to temperate
climates.

Sunraysia
The area round Mildura on the River Murray, in southeastern Australia,
a centre of the dried fruits industry.

Sunset Boulevard
An east-west road, approximately thirty miles long, running from downtown Los Angeles to the Pacific Ocean. Commercial structures dominate
the eastern half of Sunset Boulevard (east of Beverly Hills), residential
structures the western half (Beverly Hills, Bel Air, Westwood, Brentwood, and Pacific Palisades). The images of Sunset Boulevard held by
outsiders are those provoked by the commercial stretches, especially the
Sunset Strip, often known simply as 'The Strip', the section of the
Boulevard between Beverly Hills and Fairfax Avenue. The Strip is an area
of restaurants, nightclubs, boutiques, and garish billboards. Schwab's
Drugstore still exists, but the Garden of Allah Hotel (1927–59) is no

more. Those who know the area mostly through its fictional representations will think of Billy Wilder's movie, *Sunset Boulevard,* (1950), when the name is mentioned.

Sunshine State
A nickname arrogated by Florida, New Mexico, and South Dakota in their efforts to merchandise their climates.

Surrey
A county in southern England, immediately to the south and southwest of London. It is one of the Home Counties, and is often regarded slightingly as possessing quintessential Home County characteristics: a comfortable plasticized commuterland with respectable villas and neatly mown lawns interspersed with patches of mild scenery that have been allowed to remain undeveloped.

Swiss Cottage
A small, fairly trendy area of northwest London, to the north of St John's Wood. Its curious name comes from a pub there, built in the style of a Swiss chalet. Originally called the Swiss Tavern, it was put up in 1803–4, and its name was subsequently changed to the Swiss Cottage. When a London Underground station was opened there in the late 19th century it was called Swiss Cottage, and the name spread thence to the district. The pub is still there, although it has passed through several metamorphoses since its original construction.

Swone-one
British Sloane Ranger slang (pronounced SWUN-WUN) for the Battersea area of London, whose designation as a postal district is SW11. See also **Sloane Square.**

T

T, the
The local nickname for the train system serving urban and suburban Boston; Boston Transport.

Table Mountain
The name of a flat-topped mountain, more than 3600 feet high, that dominates the area of Cape Town, South Africa. Its *table cloth* appears occasionally—a flat-topped white cloud that seems to hang halfway down over its sheer face.

Taranaki
A province of New Zealand popularly associated with rather primitive dairy farming. It gives its name to the *Taranaki gate,* a detachable piece of a wire fence tied with a wire loop. In Australia the same device might be called a *Mallee gate.*

Tarheel State, the
The official nickname of North Carolina, originally a derisive nickname given by Mississippians to a brigade of North Carolinians who failed to hold their position during a battle in the Civil War.

Tartary
A vast sweep of central Asia occupied in the Middle Ages by the Tartars, a fierce Mongoloid people. Under Genghis Khan the Tartar empire extended from eastern Europe as far eastward as the shores of the Pacific; in 1552, it was conquered and subdued by the Russians. See also **Mongolia**.

Tassie
A colloquial abbreviation of *Tasmania* or *Tasmanian.*

Taumatawhakatangihangakoauauotamateapokaiwhenuakitanatahu
The name of a small hill near Porangahau, in Hawke's Bay, New Zealand. It is the longest place-name in New Zealand and means 'the hill where Tamatea-Pokai-Whenua played his flute'. The longest names Australia can muster are both names for lakes, Lake Cadibarrawirracanna in South Australia, and Lake Mirranpongapongunna in the Simpson Desert.

Tea and Sugar
The name of a non-passenger supply train that runs from Port Augusta to Kalgoorlie, bringing fresh supplies for isolated settlements along the Trans-Australian railway.

Telford
A new town in Shropshire, England. It was so designated in 1963 for development purposes, but it is associated with the industrial revolution and is the site of the famed Iron Bridge.

Temple, the
An area of central London between Fleet Street and the Thames. In early medieval times it was occupied by the buildings of the Knights Templars, but their order was suppressed in 1312, and since the mid 14th century the site has been given over to the law. In modern usage, *the Temple* refers first and foremost to the buildings of the two Inns of Court (societies of lawyers) known as the Inner and Middle Temples. As a term for the area in general, it was reinforced by the naming of the local London Underground station as 'Temple'.

Terra Australis
An early name for an undiscovered southern land mass, later sometimes applied to Australia, especially eastern Australia.

Territories, The
The collective name for the Yukon Territory and the Northwest Territories, which together cover about one third of Canada's land area. They consist chiefly of forest-covered mountains, with the rest of the region being frozen most of the year, and are very rich in mineral deposits.

Territory, the
A colloquial abbreviation by which the Northern Territory is known in Australia. It is an administrative area (rather than a fully fledged state) in northern central Australia which, apart from its tropical coastal strip, is a semiarid wilderness. See also **Centre**.

Texas Tea
A nickname for oil and natural gas.

Thames Valley, the
The low-lying country in southern England through which the River
Thames flows, particularly the upper reaches of it, to the west of London,
in the counties of Berkshire and Oxfordshire. It is a gentle and peaceful
landscape, with still many unspoiled stretches of river, and several charming towns and villages, such as Henley and Marlow. Its chief centres of
population are Maidenhead, Reading, and Oxford. Its name is used in
certain official designations: the local police force, for example, is known
as the Thames Valley police.

Third Avenue
In the late 19th and early 20th centuries, when elevated 'subways' were
being built along various north-south thoroughfares in New York City to
improve transportation for those who were beginning to populate the
outlying sections of the city, little heed was paid to the effects these
continuous steel bridges would have on the avenues below. One of the
typical results was to create a dark and dingy atmosphere beneath them
through which sunlight barely penetrated; another was to create a maze
of steel pilings that proved a hazard to traffic. Because of the noise and
dirt of the steam locomotives, not replaced by electric trains (which made
almost as much noise) till many years later, the once-broad boulevards on
which the elevated train systems (called 'els') were set lost much of their
property value and became, above the inevitable retail establishments
below, slums. In general, this situation was not relieved till the 1950s,
when the last of those in downtown Manhattan was demolished. Third
Avenue was one of the first to be burdened by an 'el', and it came, over
the ensuing years, to epitomize the worst sort of neighbourhood along its
entire length, with disreputable bars, seedy hotels, flophouses, and lunch
counters; the only area that fared worse was Tenth Avenue (see **Hell's
Kitchen**). Finally, upon the removal of the elevated structure in the 1950s,
Third Avenue began gradually to recover: retail shops moved in, new
apartment houses were built above 60th and below 40th streets, and, in
between, posh modern office buildings rose above the din of the street
traffic below.

Third World, the
On the view that the capitalist and communist blocs represent the two
major ideological Establishments, the countries outside these two political
camps have taken to themselves—or been given—the label *Third World*,

at once an affirmation of separate (and nonaligned) status and an admission of the pecking order. In general it is taken to include most of the countries of Africa, Asia, and South America, but there are, of course, crucial exceptions to this broad classification, such as Japan and South Africa. *Third World* is increasingly a synonym for 'economically undeveloped; poor'.

Thirteen Original Colonies

The earliest areas in North America settled by English colonists during the seventeenth and eighteenth centuries, called colonies till 1776, after which they became states of the United States of America, namely, New Hampshire, Massachusetts, Rhode Island, Connecticut, New York, New Jersey, Pennsylvania, Delaware, Maryland, Virginia, North Carolina, South Carolina, and Georgia.

Thorney Island

An unpromising dreary tract of silt that was the germ in the Dark Ages of the area of London now known as Westminster. According to tradition a church was first built on this island in the Thames in 616, and the original Westminster Abbey was founded in 750. Since then the abbey has gone through several metamorphoses into the magnificent Gothic structure of today, and Thorney Island has long since merged into the mainland of the north bank of the Thames.

Throgmorton Street

A street in the financial heart of the City of London. Often abbreviated familiarly to Throg Street, it has come to be used as a shorthand term for London's stockmarket dealings; the Stock Exchange is at the corner of Throgmorton and Threadneedle streets.

Thule

A name given in ancient times to an island or piece of land six days' sailing to the north of Britain. It is not clear precisely what it refers to—Shetland and a part of Norway have been put forward—but its general signification was the northern limit of the known world, as its frequent epithet, *ultima Thule*, suggests. In modern usage, Thule is a U. S. airforce base in northwest Greenland.

Thunderer, the
A nickname of *The Times*, coined in the 19th century when its editorial
columns inveighed powerfully against the misdeeds of governments and
scourged errant ministers. It is in allusion to a passage in an article by
Captain Edward Sterling, its editor, who wrote, 'We thundered forth the
other day an article on the subject of social and political reform'. In
many people's eyes the right to the sobriquet was forfeited in the 20th
century, when the newspaper became much more the organ of the Establishment. See also **Turnabout.**

Tidal Basin
A large pond, in Washington, D. C., an inlet of the Potomac River, in
front of the Jefferson Memorial. During late March—early April each
year, it is an attraction to visitors who come to view the blooming of
hundreds of cherry trees, a gift of the Japanese government in 1912.

Tidewater Virginia
The name given to one of the five main land regions of the state of
Virginia. The other four are Appalachian Plateau; Appalachian Ridge
and Valley Region; Blue Ridge; and Piedmont. Each has its own distinctive dialect. Also called the Atlantic Coastal Plain, the term is applied to
the lowland coastal section extending as far west from the Atlantic Ocean
and Chesapeake Bay as its rivers are affected by the tides. It is divided
into three peninsulas by the James, Potomac, and Rappahannock rivers,
and includes the Virginia portion of the Delmarva peninsula. It was the
first part settled by colonists.

Tierra del Fuego
The name of an archipelago at the southern tip of South America, separated from the continent by the Strait of Magellan. It is composed of the
main island, also called Tierra del Fuego, and smaller ones, which include
Desolation, Clarence, Dawson, and others. Divided politically between
Argentina and Chile, it was discovered by Magellan in 1520. The name,
which means 'Land of Fire' in Spanish, does not refer to the climate,
which is raw, cold, windy, and snowy for much of the year, but rather to
the scores of Indian camp fires the explorers could see at night.

Tiffany's
Properly, 'Tiffany and Company', this New York City landmark, at 57th
Street and Fifth Avenue, long ago entered the language as a symbol of the

wealth and elegance associated with diamond necklaces and tiaras, brace-
lets, and brooches. On an international scale, it vies for prominence with
Van Cleef and Arpels, across Fifth Avenue, and with Cartier, farther
down Fifth Avenue, at 54th Street. But to New Yorkers, Tiffany's epito-
mizes the finest in precious gems, an image that was contributed to by
Truman Capote's short story, 'Breakfast at Tiffany's', later made into a
film.

Timbuktu

A town in the republic of Mali, West Africa, near the Niger River. Its
name evidently has a bizarre sound to Western ears, since in the past it
has often been used to suggest any imprecisely located town or city that
seems improbably remote or exotic. This comic verse attributed to Bishop
Wilberforce (1805-73) betrays a lack of exact geographical knowledge:

> If I were a cassowary
> On the plains of Timbuctoo,
> I would eat a missionary,
> Cassock, band, and hymn-book too.

tin Lizzie

The affectionate nickname for the first mass-produced car, the 'model T',
15 million of which were produced by Henry Ford between 1908 and
1927.

Tin Pan Alley

A term used both in Britain and the U. S. for the haunt of popular song
writers and music publishers. In New York City, where the term was
coined in the early 1900s, referring specifically to an area at Broadway
and West 28th Street, then the centre of the popular music industry. In
Britain the nickname has traditionally been applied to Denmark Street, a
small alleyway just off the Charing Cross Road in London, but in recent
years Old Compton Street, a couple of hundred yards to the southwest in
Soho proper, has taken over the mantle. In New York City, as businesses
moved uptown, so did Tin Pan Alley, and for several decades its focus
has been at 1650 Broadway (at 50th Street) and in the Brill Building.

Tintagel
Properly, Tintagel Head, a promontory on the west coast of Cornwall, England, site of Tintagel Castle, now a ruin, the legendary birthplace of King Arthur.

Tivoli Gardens
A large park, in central Copenhagen, containing restaurants, amusement areas, horticultural gardens, and, at night, attractive lighting.

Toddling Town, That
A nickname of Chicago derived from the lyrics of the song, 'Chicago' (1922), by Fred Fisher.

Todd River
This river, which runs through Alice Springs, sometimes has water in it, but not during the famous Todd River Regatta; the boats are carried by runners along the dry bed of the river.

Tolpuddle
A village in Dorset, in southern England, famous for the so-called 'Tolpuddle Martyrs', a group of farm workers sentenced to be transported to Tasmania in 1834 for setting up an early form of trade union to resist wage cuts. The name is actually something of a bowdlerization: it is derived from the local river, the Piddle, and other villages in the area, such as Piddletrenthide and Piddlehinton, retain the original form.

Tommy (Atkins)
A nickname for British soldiers, equivalent to G. I. Joe in the U. S., used by Rudyard Kipling in his 'Barrack Room Ballads' (1892):

> O it's Tommy this, an' Tommy that, an' 'Tommy go away';
> But it's 'Thank you, Mr Atkins', when the band begins to play.

Tommy gun
A World War II nickname for the Thompson sub-machine gun.

Toothpick State, the
A nickname of Arkansas, so called because it was held that the early settlers used their bowie knives as toothpicks. See also **Bowie State.**

Top End, the
An informal Australian name for the extreme north of Australia, which lies well inside the tropics.

Torquay
A seaside resort in Devonshire, England, on the English Channel. It is considered comparatively expensive and is frequented mainly by upper middle-class visitors, especially the elderly. As a sardonic jingle has it, 'Dover for the continent, Torquay for the incontinent'. See also **Bournemouth.**

TOTO
The nickname for the Totable Tornado Observatory, at the National Severe Storms Laboratory, Norman, Oklahoma, so called both as an acronym and after Dorothy's dog in *The Wizard of Oz*, by L. Frank Baum. See also **Oz.**

Tower, the
Any reference to 'the Tower' in Britain will be instantly recognized as signifying the Tower of London, the famous fortress on the north bank of the Thames. In modern usage, of course, a tower is a relatively lofty structure, not, like the Tower of London, a castle spread over a wide site; but it seems that the Tower as a whole took its name from the White Tower, the tall Norman keep which formed its original nucleus. Aside from its reputation as a prison through the centuries, the Tower also serves as the repository for the royal treasure or *regalia*, closely guarded by the Yeomen Warders, and still dominates the Thamesside scene.

Tower Bridge
A lift bridge across the Thames near the Tower of London. It has a lofty tower at each end, but derives its name from **the Tower** (*q.v.*). Much to the amusement of Londoners (and others in the know), it is thought that the Americans who bought and transported to Arizona what was designated as **London Bridge** (*q.v.*), a rather ordinary structure, thought that they were buying the Tower Bridge, which is much more picturesque and figures often as a symbol of London and of England.

Tower Hamlets
A new London borough formed in 1965 by combining the former East End boroughs of Bethnal Green, Poplar, and Stepney. In feudal times

these three boroughs, or *hamlets* as they then were, belonged to the Tower of London.

Town That Moved Overnight, the
A nickname of Hibbing, Minnesota, so called because after it had grown to considerable size, it was moved to provide access to the huge beds of iron ore beneath it.

Toxteth
An underprivileged area of Liverpool that achieved an unwelcome notoriety in the early 1980s as the scene of inner-city unrest and rioting. In an attempt to defuse the negative connotations of the name, many locals tend to refer to the area by its postal designation, Liverpool 8.

Track, the
1. A nickname, especially in the Northern Territory, for the Stuart Highway, joining Darwin to the south. The laconic understatement in this description of a north-south link now paved for all of its more than three thousand kilometres is not untypical of Australians.
2. The name of the red-light district in Toronto.

Trail of Tears
The name given, figuratively, to those wilderness roads over which the members of the Five Civilized Tribes (Choctaw, Chickasaw, Cherokee, Creek, and Seminole) travelled to Indian Territory (later Oklahoma) under terms of the Indian Removal Act (1830).

Trans-Australian Railway
The railway was originally conceived as a link between Western Australia and the rail systems of the other States, and the promise of such a railway was an inducement to Western Australia to join the eastern states in forming the Australian Commonwealth. The line in standard gauge between Kalgoorlie and Port Augusta was completed in 1917. Upgrading and extension of the railway have continued since. Passenger services are provided by the Trans-Australian between Perth and Port Pirie each day and (since 1970) by the Indian-Pacific, linking the two oceans, from Sydney to Perth, three times a week. Both trains have sleeping, dining, and lounge cars and are air-conditioned.

Trans-Jordan
A name (literally 'across the (river) Jordan') given to the territory now occupied by the kingdom of Jordan, when it was administered by the British under a League of Nations mandate between World Wars I and II.

Transport House
The headquarters of the Transport and General Workers' Union, Britain's largest trade union. It is situated in **Smith Square** (*q.v.*), London, just to the southeast of the Houses of Parliament, and until 1980 also housed the headquarters of the Labour Party, with whose organization and party machine it became almost synonymous. In 1980 the party moved its headquarters to **Walworth Road** (*q.v.*).

Transylvania
A region in northern Romania, bounded to the south and east by the Carpathian Mountains. Until 1918 it belonged to Hungary. Its remote forests and valleys provide a fitting setting for chilling stories of vampires, and its reputation for eeriness has become fixed in the public imagination since the publication of Bram Stoker's *Dracula* (1897).

Tribeca
A relatively new section at the West Side of New York City, an acronym from 'the *tri*angle *be*low *Ca*nal Street'. It is one of several areas reclaimed for residential use by the renovation of dilapidated commercial loft buildings. (See also **NoHo, SoHo.**) Most of its residents are energetic younger people, particularly writers and artists.

Triple-headed Monster
A disparaging name for the Constitution of the United States, used by those states that opposed its ratification. It refers to the three branches of government: the legislative, judicial, and executive.

Trossachs, the
An area of great natural beauty to the north of Glasgow, in western Scotland. Its lochs and wooded valleys inspired the pen of Sir Walter Scott, and his loving descriptions in *Lady of the Lake* and *Rob Roy* made it a tourist attraction in the early 19th century—a status it has retained ever since.

Trucial States, the
A collective name formerly used for seven emirates on the Arabian coast
of the Persian Gulf in the days when together they formed a British
protectorate. Also known as Trucial Oman or the Trucial Coast, they
became fully independent in 1971, since when they have been called the
United Arab Emirates; they are Abu Dhabi, Dubai, Sharjah, Ajman,
Umm al Quaiwain, Ras el Khaimah, and Fujairah. In former times piracy
and sea warfare were rife in this part of the Gulf (the area used to be
known as the *Pirate Coast*), but in 1835 the truculent local sheikhs, at the
inducement of the British government, signed a truce promising to end
their maritime hostilities; the name Trucial States derived from this truce.

Tullamarine
The name of the international airport serving Melbourne.

Tunbridge Wells
A town in Kent, southeast England, the full name of which is Royal
Tunbridge Wells. It is one of only two towns in England (the other is
Royal Leamington Spa) allowed to use this prefix, granted in honour of
visits by Queen Victoria. It is a staid middle-class residential town, populated in the public imgination by reactionaries and stuffed shirts; anyone
composing a parody of an angry letter to the newspapers complaining
about the moral degeneracy of modern times will standardly sign it 'Dis-
gusted, Tunbridge Wells'.

Turl, the
A small street in Oxford that links the **Broad** (*q.v.*) with the **High** (*q.v.*).
Officially called Turl Street, its name may derive from a 'twirling gate', or
turnstile that restricted access to it in former times.

Turnabout, the
A former nickname of *The Times*, in allusion to the changes towards the
political attitudes it espoused; it was not consistently either Whig or Tory.
See also **Thunderer.**

Tussaud's Waxworks, Madame
An attraction housed in a building in Marylebone Road, London, that
consists mainly of waxen figures, both historical and contemporary, executed with amazing skill. Most are merely on exhibition, but some are
placed in appropriate and vividly reconstructed historical settings. The

figures are so life-like that visitors are sometimes deceived into believing
that one of the guards, purposely remaining immobile for some minutes,
is one of the exhibits. Madame Tussaud was a Frenchwoman who, it is
said, created waxen images as memento mori of royalty from death masks
obtained after they had visited the guillotine during the French Revolution. She took her collection to London, where she established the museum; today, greatly expanded, it proves one of the most interesting and
popular drawing-cards in London, for residents and tourists alike.

'21' Club

Formally, 'Jack and Charlie's 21 Club', this hangout of the rich and
famous on 52nd Street, west of Fifth Avenue, started as a speakeasy,
during Prohibition. With Repeal, it opened its doors legitimately and has,
ever since, been a more or less exclusive luncheon and dining place for
executives of the publishing and entertainment worlds where the occasional member of 'high society' can still be seen. As in the cast of that
erstwhile cafe society mecca, the Stork Club, the comings and goings of
those who came and went in 'stretch' limousines, whose chauffeurs chat-
ted outside the wrought-iron railings, were reported by the gossip columnists of the New York newspapers and syndicated press services. Its
brownstone staircase, with wrought-iron banister, is decorated with
'jockey hitching-post' figures which are painted in the stable colours of
the 21 Club's patrons.

Twickenham

A part of Richmond-upon-Thames, in greater London. It is associated
with rugby football, and the headquarters of the English Rugby Football
Union are situated there.

twopenny tube

A former nickname of Central London Railway (underground).

Tyburnia

A nickname given in the 19th century to a residential area in the West End
of London, to the north of Hyde Park. The gallows humour of its
derivation may account for its going out of use: until 1783, Tyburn
(where Marble Arch now stands) was the site of public executions in
London.

Tyneside
A name given to the industrialized conurbation that sprawls on both sides of the River Tyne, in the Northeast of England, from South Shields and Tynemouth on the coast inland to Newcastle-upon-Tyne. Geographically it is the focus of the metropolitan county of Tyne and Wear; culturally it is the heart of Geordieland.

U

Uluru
The Aboriginal name for Ayers Rock.

Uncle Sam
A cartoon figure recognized in 1961 by Congress as the national symbol of the United States, but in use since the 1830s, when Seba Smith, a humorous political essayist, was cartooned as Uncle Sam, and Dan Rice, a clown during the 1800s, popularized the costume decorated with stars and stripes. The name was first used as an unfriendly nickname for the United States government during the War of 1812, and first appeared in print in a newspaper in Troy, New York, in 1813; by 1816 it had become so popular that a book was written about *The Adventures of Uncle Sam*. It is thought to have derived from the initials *U.S.* stamped on barrels of salt meat by Samuel Wilson, an army meat inspector and provisioner. See also **Brother Jonathan.**

Uncle Sam's Crib
A nickname of the U. S. Treasury.

underground railway
The nickname for any secret system used to help people escape to safe territory. It originated during the Civil War in the U. S. when abolitionists set up 'stations, junctions', and 'conductors' to help fugitive slaves get to the North or Canada. During World War II allied servicemen caught or shot down behind enemy lines were aided by Europeans in this

manner, and during the 1980s groups have used the same sort of system to bring those seeking political asylum into the U. S. from Central America, with the name being applied in each case.

Union Jack, the
A nickname for the national flag of the United Kingdom of Great Britain and Ireland, properly used only when the small form, the 'jack', is flown, as at the tip of a vessel's bowsprit. The reference is to the union of the cross of St George with the diagonal crosses of St Andrew and St Patrick, patron saints of England, Scotland, and Ireland.

Union Station
One of the last major railway stations in Chicago, completed in 1925, and today the centre of all Amtrak travel into and out of the city. A recent renovation has restored some of the station's former splendour, but it is still only a ghost of its former glamorous self, when movie stars all seemed to make a point of arriving there on Santa Fe's 'Super Chief', from Los Angeles, New York Central's 'Twentieth-Century Limited' or Pennsylvania's 'Broadway Limited', the latter two providing overnight runs between Chicago and New York.

Union Stockyards
A former complex of slaughterhouses and meatpackers in Chicago, now the site, on the city's South Side, of a range of light industries. Once the heart of America's meatpacking industry, the Union Stockyards were opened in 1865 and thrived for nearly 100 years before being made obsolete by the rise of a system of regional slaughterhouses. In its heyday, the odoriferous, often unsanitary complex, the employees of which were cruelly exploited, was the target of reform-minded writers like Upton Sinclair, whose novel, *The Jungle* (1906), aroused public indignation and led to improved conditions.

United Kingdom, the
In full, the United Kingdom of Great Britain and Northern Ireland, the official name of the British state since 1922, when the rest of Ireland became independent. The term had been used long before that, however: in the 18th century it referred to the union of Scotland with England and Wales in 1707; and in 1801 its scope was enlarged to include Ireland, which in that year entered into the union. See also **Britain, England**.

Unter den Linden
A street in East Berlin. In the days when a united Berlin was the capital of all Germany, this was its main social artery, leading from the Tiergarten to the Royal Palace and lined with department stores, luxurious hotels, foreign embassies—and, of course, the lime trees that gave it its name.

Upper East Side, the
Generally, the area in New York City bounded by Fifth Avenue on the west, the East River on the east, and 59th and 96th streets on the south and north. It is, especially at its eastern and western extremes, characterized by luxurious town houses and expensive cooperative apartments and by the people who can afford such accommodation. See also **East Side, Lower East Side.**

uptown
In some cities of the United States, the residential areas and neighbourhoods, away from the downtown, commercial areas. See also **downtown.**

U. S. S. R., the
The Union of Soviet Socialist Republics. See **Soviet Union..**

V & A
The colloquial name for the Victoria and Albert, a museum in South Kensington in West London which houses Britain's national collection of the applied and decorative arts.

Valentine State, the
A nickname of Arizona, so called in reference to 14 February 1912, the date of its entry into the Union.

Valleys, the

In South Wales a series of parallel rivers drain southward from the foothills of the Brecon Beacons towards the Bristol Channel. On their way the Taff, the Rhymney, the Ebbw, and others flow through slate-gray hills dotted with small mining villages. These are the Valleys, which are central to the modern mythology of Wales. In the 19th and early 20th centuries they were at the heart of Britain's industrial might, pouring out coal from the mines and steel from the foundries, and they were cradles of Methodism and Radicalism. Today, with the steelworks closed and the mines in decline, their former glories have passed, but names like Merthry Tydfil, Ebbw Vale, Rhondda, Treorchy, and Tredegar still retain their powerful associations.

Van Diemen's Land

The original name of Tasmania, an island off the southeast corner of Australia. It was bestowed by the island's Dutch discoverer Abel Tasman in 1642 in honour of his patron. It became a British settlement in 1803, and many of Britain's less desirable criminals were transported there; as a result, when this form of punishment was abolished in the mid-19th century, its name was changed to *Tasmania*, since its old name had such unfortunate associations.

Vauxhall

An area (pronounced 'VOXhall') of south central London, on the south bank of the Thames opposite Westminster. It is a largely working-class residential district, but is famous for the Vauxhall Gardens, a public park and pleasure ground that flourished there from 1661 to 1859.

Venice of the East

An epithet for Bangkok, Thailand.

Venice of the North

A title often conferred on Amsterdam, in the Netherlands, because of its extensive system of canals and 290 bridges, but also claimed by Stockholm, Sweden, another watery city.

Venice of the West

An epithet for Glasgow.

Vichy
A town in central France associated with water and collaboration. A place of natural alkaline springs, its vogue as a spa was started in 1861 by Napoleon III, who was much addicted to taking the waters; since then Vichy has spread around the world in bottled form. Less congenial are the memories evoked by the French government set up there under Marshal Henri Pétain in 1940 as a virtual puppet of the German occupiers; the words *Vichy France* leave an unpleasant taste in the mouths of the French who lived through those less than glorious years in their nation's history.

Victoria
An area in southwest central London, to the north of Pimlico and the east of Belgravia. It takes its name from the large rail terminus there that serves the south of England and boat trains to the Continent; it was opened in 1860 and named in honour of Queen Victoria.

Ville, the
See **Pentonville.**

Vinland
The name given to the coastal region of eastern North America visited by Leif Ericson and other Vikings around the year 1000. It was brought to wider fame in 1957 with the discovery of the so-called Vinland Map, an apparently early-15th-century representation of the area which was later shown to be a forgery.

Violet-Crowned City
A name conferred on Athens, traditionally by the ancient Greek poet Pindar and the dramatist Aristophanes in *Equites* and *Acharnians,* because of its association with the Muses, the Graces, and the goddess Aphrodite. It derives from Ion, a legendary founding king of the city (*ion* is Greek for 'violet').

Volgograd
A city in the USSR which until after the Revolution was called Tsaritsyn. In 1925 it was renamed Stalingrad in honour of the Revolutionary leader Joseph Stalin, but in 1961, with Stalin posthumously in official disgrace, the name was changed again, to Volgograd (it is on the river Volga, northwest of the Caspian Sea).

W

Wailing Wall, the

A length of high stone wall in Jerusalem which is said to have been part of the ancient temple of Herod, reputedly on the site of, and containing some of the stones of the original temple of Solomon. It is greatly venerated in Judaism and has become a shrine and centre of pilgrimage. In former times Jews would gather there to lament the diaspora (hence its name), but since Jerusalem was fully absorbed into Israel in 1967 such lamentation has not been so appropriate, and one is now officially encouraged to refer to the wall as the Western Wall.

Waitangi

The North Auckland site of the signing of the Treaty of Waitangi in 1840, which established British sovereignty over New Zealand. The anniversary, February 6th, is a national holiday (Waitangi Day) in New Zealand.

Walden Pond

A pond at Concord, Massachusetts, made famous through the philosophical writings of Henry David Thoreau (1817–62), especially *Walden, or Life in the Woods* (1854). Although Thoreau lived at Walden Pond for only about two years, its associations remain fixed in the minds of modern readers with peace, solitude, and the love of nature.

Wall Street

A short, narrow street in downtown Manhattan. It is the site of the New York Stock Exchange; at its north end stands the United States Subtreasury Building. The surrounding multistory office buildings are occupied largely by brokers' and bankers' offices. The financial centre of the United States and for much of the rest of the world—notwithstanding similar centres in London and elsewhere—*Wall Street* has become the worldwide metaphor for finance and big business.

Wallaby Track

A nickname for the Australian outback: to be *on the wallaby track* or *on the wallaby,* is to tramp the outback in search of work.

Walworth Road
An undistinguished urban thoroughfare to the south of the **Elephant and Castle** (*q.v.*) in Southwark, South London which has become much more widely known since 1980, when the Labour Party moved its headquarters there from **Transport House** (*q.v.*). Compare **Smith Square.**

Wanchai
The Times Square or Piccadilly Circus of Hong Kong, site of numerous restaurants, night clubs (many topless), and other places of entertainment.

Wanchai Burberry
An umbrella with an oiled paper covering, made in Wanchai.

Wardour Street
A street in Soho, in the West End of London, which has come to be synonymous with the British movie industry from the large number of film companies that have had their offices there over the years. In the 19th century, however, it abounded in fake antique furniture shops, and in 1888 the designer and poet William Morris coined the term 'Wardour Street English' for the sort of pseudo-medieval poetic diction that was enjoying a certain vogue among versifiers at that time.

Warren Street
A street west of Tottenham Court Road, near Euston Road, in the West End of London, known for its dealers in second-hand cars.

Wash, the
A large shallow rectangular inlet of the North Sea on the east coast of England, at the point where the bulge of East Anglia meets the coast of Lincolnshire. The Fenland rivers Nene, Great Ouse, and Welland drain into it. Originally, and up until the 18th century, the Wash was known as *the Washes*; this referred to sandbars which were repeatedly washed by the ebbing and flowing tide, and at low tide formed paths that could be used to ford the inlet.

Waterloo
An area in central London, on the southern bank of the Thames just to the rear of the South Bank arts complex. The name celebrates the Duke of Wellington's victory over Napoleon at Waterloo, Belgium, in 1815,

and was originally used for Waterloo Bridge; this was opened in 1817, replacing the old Strand Bridge. It was then adopted for the new rail terminus opened at the southern end of the bridge in 1848, and since has come to be used for the surrounding district. As the capital's main station serving the southern and southwestern suburbs and Surrey, Waterloo is perhaps more closely associated than any other with the commuter treadmill. See also **Bakerloo**.

Water Tower

A distinctive Chicago landmark, on the city's Near North Side, along the Magnificent Mile. Along with its nearby pumping station, the gothic, castle-like tower survived the Great Chicago Fire of 1871, the only two structures in the area to do so. Today the tower serves as a public information centre, and the pumping station houses a free, multimedia promotional view of the city.

Watford

A town in Hertfordshire, just to the northwest of London. As a place it is unremarkable, although it cannot be said quite to rival Slough as the epitome of dull suburbia. It is of considerable geographical importance in modern British folklore, however, for it is often viewed by Southerners as marking the northern limit of civilized life; anywhere 'north of Watford' being deemed provincial and boorish. Those who take this view are unlikely to make any clear distinction between the **Midlands** (*q.v.*) and the actual **North** (*q.v.*).

Watts

A residential area in south-central Los Angeles known especially for the riots that occurred there in a six-day period in August 1965. Occupying an area of about 2½ square miles, Watts was not considered a particularly depressed area or potential trouble spot until the riots, which started with a minor incident but which accelerated rapidly and resulted in 34 deaths and 1032 injuries, as well as great property damage. Watts gained instant national recognition, and its name is invoked whenever troubles arise in black ghettos, not just in Los Angeles but in the United States generally.

Weald, the

A band of hilly sandstone country across the centre of Sussex and Kent in southeastern England, separating the chalky North and South Downs. The word *weald*, cognate with German *Wald*, meant 'forest' in Anglo-

Saxon times, and today sufficient wooded areas survive to give one an idea of the former extent of the woodlands here. In the Middle Ages an iron-smelting and forging industry throve in the Weald, and in the days of wooden ships much of the timber to build the British navy came from Wealden oaks.

Weimar
A city in the southwestern part of (modern East) Germany. In the late 18th and early 19th centuries, during the reign of the Grand Duke Charles Augustus, it was perhaps Germany's leading cultural centre. Goethe, Germany's chief literary and intellectual lion, held court there, and it was also home to Schiller, Herder, and Wieland. In 1919, the constitution under which Germany was to be governed after World War I was drawn up and adopted there, and the political system that held sway until Hitler took over in 1933 was known as the *Weimar Republic*.

Wembley Stadium
A sports arena west of London, in the borough of Brent; it is the British national soccer stadium, accommodating more than 80,000 spectators.

Wessex
A region in the southern part of England that has varied widely in size, status, and character over the centuries. Its origins go back to the late 5th century, when the West Saxons settled and founded their kingdom in the upper Thames Valley. It gradually extended its territory to the south and west, and in the 9th century, under Alfred the Great, it was the dominant English kingdom. It disappeared with the Norman Conquest, but its name was revived in the late 19th century by the English novelist Thomas Hardy for the area in which many of his stories were set; it refers principally to Dorset, but also includes parts of the surrounding counties of Hampshire and Wiltshire. To such an extent has the name caught on that it has returned to official use for certain administrative purposes: the local area of the National Health Service, for example, is known as the *Wessex Region*.

West, the
1. The world divides itself into East and West along a wavering boundary. Where it is drawn is a purely relative matter. In geographical terms the Western Hemisphere is North and South America, and the Eastern Hemisphere takes all the rest; but the situation is not so straightforward. In

ancient and medieval times, *the West* referred to the Western Roman, or later the Holy Roman Empire, as contrasted with the Eastern, or Byzantine Empire and areas further east. This sowed the seeds of our modern view of the West, which from a cultural point of view may be taken as anywhere north of the Mediterranean and west of the Black Sea—in other words, all of Europe (with the exception of the eastern parts of European Russia) and North America. To the south is Africa, which does not enter the East/West equation, but, like the East, lies outside the Christian tradition that is the historical and cultural hallmark of the West. However, the geographical logic of this has been destroyed by the ideological wrangling of the late 20th century. Now, *the East* or Eastern bloc are those nations, including much of Europe, under Soviet influence, while *the West* includes territories of the Eastern Hemisphere such as Japan and Australia, which share the capitalist ethos of much of Europe and North America.

2. In Britain, *the West* is not as established a concept as, say, the **North** (*q.v.*). When it is used, usually in such contexts as 'Wales and the West', it generally includes not just the **West Country** (*q.v.*), but also rather more northerly western counties such as Herefordshire, Worcestershire, and Shropshire. As far as any official distinction is made, for example on road signs, 'the West' refers to the area focused on Bristol, including particularly Avon and Gloucestershire, as contrasted with the Southwest.

3. In the United States, the part of the country called *the West* depends on the point of view of the individual and where he resides. Saul Steinberg, a well-known artist, once produced a cover illustration (for *The New Yorker* magazine) that depicted a 'New Yorker's view of the United States', in which the world stopped, essentially, at the Hudson River, with the rest of the country shown as wasteland except for a small collection of buildings in the middle distance (Chicago) and some glitter on the west coast (Hollywood), accurately reflecting the view of chauvinistic residents of New York City, especially of Manhattan. More generally, though, people in America consider *the West* as including the states west of the Missouri River as far as Kansas City (North and South Dakota and Nebraska), then southward to include Kansas, Oklahoma, and Texas. See also **Deep South, East, Far West, Midwest, Northwest, Pacific Northwest, South, 1.**

West Bank, the
The name given to the territory to the west of the Jordan River and the
Dead Sea which until 1967 belonged to Jordan, but in that year was
annexed by Israel.

West Country, the
The southwestern part of England, which includes the counties of Cornwall, Devon, Somerset, Avon, Gloucestershire, and the western parts of
Dorset and Wiltshire. It covers territory otherwise known as the West and
the Southwest, but the term *West Country* is used particularly if one
wishes to stress the rural aspects of the area: it is redolent of the gentle
rolling hills and sheltered valleys of Devon and Somerset, of ruddy countrymen and -women, with their characteristic West Country burr, and of
the agricultural products of the region: West Country cider, cheeses,
butter, and cream.

West End, the
The western part of central London, north of the Thames. It is almost
more of a concept than a district that can be accurately delimited on a
map. If the City stands for the earnest accumulation of money and the
East End is London's working-class area, the West End is the place to
come for a good time—or to live, if one can afford it. The heart of the
West End, a rectangle bounded by Oxford Street, Regent Street, the
Strand, and Kingsway, is London's theatreland; Londoners going 'up
West' for a show or a meal will make for this area. Its northwest corner
contains the more risqué entertainments of **Soho** (*q.v.*). Beyond this
spreads the commercial quarter of the West End, from the large department stores of **Oxford Street** (*q.v.*) and Regent Street to, further south,
the more exclusive retail establishments and posh hotels of **Mayfair** (*q.v.*),
Piccadilly (*q.v.*), and **St James's** (*q.v.*). And finally come the fashionable
residential areas at the western extremity of the West End: **Belgravia**
(*q.v.*).

Western Desert, the
A portion of the Libyan desert that lies in western and central Egypt. It is
associated particularly with the extensive fighting there between the Allies
and the Axis powers in World War II. Its name contrasts it with the
Eastern Desert, which lies between the River Nile and the Red Sea. It
should not be confused with the Western Sahara, which is in southern
Morocco and northwest Mauretania.

Western Isles, the
A name given to the Hebrides, a collection of over 500 islands off the west coast of Scotland. They fall into two groups. Those nearer the mainland, including Skye, Jura, and Islay, are the Inner Hebrides. Further west, beyond a channel known as the Minch, are the Outer Hebrides, including Harris and Lewis, North and South Uist, and Benbecula. The latter were formally reconstituted in 1975 into a region of Scotland, officially known as the *Western Isles*.

Western Ocean, the
A name used in former times for the Atlantic Ocean, reflecting a Eurocentric geography in which the ocean was indeed to the west of the then known civilized world.

West Midlands, the
A metropolitan county in the middle of England, created in 1974. It is centred on and largely made up of Birmingham, England's second largest city, but also includes the Black Country to the northwest and Coventry to the southeast. It is one of the great industrial heartlands of England, specializing particularly in engineering and the manufacture of motor vehicles. Less specifically, the term *West Midlands* is also used to refer to the western part of the Midlands, including also Shropshire, Herefordshire, Worcestershire, Warwickshire, and western Staffordshire, but because of possible confusion with the new county name this is not officially encouraged. See also **Midlands**.

Westminster
An area of central London immediately to the west of the City of London. In 1900 it was made a city in its own right, and in 1965 large areas of St Marylebone and Paddington in the north and west were joined on to it to make the new borough of the City of Westminster. However, its nucleus, and the part which most people think of as Westminster, remains the area to the west and south of St James's Park, centred on Parliament Square, Westminster Abbey, and the Palace of Westminster. The Palace contains the House of Commons and the House of Lords, and over the years Westminster has become synonymous with the British parliament.

Westmorland
In the Northwest of England, a former county between Cumberland to
the north and Lancashire to the south. In the local government reorganization of 1974 it became part of Cumbria. The name survives in the town
of *Appleby-in-Westmorland.*

West Point
A town in New York on the bluffs overlooking the Hudson River about
fifty miles north of New York City. It is the site of the U. S. Military
Academy, established by Congress in 1802.

West Side
1. To New Yorkers, the West Side represents something of a comedown
when considered in contrast to the East Side. In fact, although the rents
are lower on the West Side and the cooperative apartments, with some
exceptions, are less expensive than those on the East Side, much of the
area, especially along Central Park West (between 59th and 90th streets)
and Riverside Drive (from 72nd Street northwards), is far more attractive
than most of the East Side: the views of Central Park from Central Park
West are comparable to those from Fifth Avenue, and the extended vistas
of the Hudson River from the apartments along Riverside Drive are in
every way more scenic than those of the East River, with its views of the
factory buildings in Queens. Yet, despite the presence of well-known
luxury apartments houses, like the Century, Majestic, and **Dakota** (*q.v.*)
on Central Park West and the Chatsworth at 72nd Street west of Riverside Drive, of Lincoln Center for the Performing Arts, at Lincoln Square
(65th Street and Broadway), and of the fine old private brownstone and
limestone private houses along the side streets, the West Side seems una-
ble to rid itself of the stigma of being somewhat déclassé. Its population is
more homogeneous than that of the East Side, with more younger people
able to afford to live there, but, as in all areas in New York City, there are
some neighbourhoods it is wiser to avoid for the sake of safety, especially
at night. Above 90th Street, along Central Park West, the section begins
to deteriorate slightly, then markedly beyond the end of Central Park, at
Cathedral Parkway (110th Street). But to the west, along Morningside
Drive, Amsterdam Avenue, Broadway, and Riverside Drive, this narrow
corridor improves till one goes north of Columbia University, which owns
much of the property in its neighbourhood and makes a valiant effort to
keep up its standards. There are some fine old apartment houses along
Riverside Drive and Claremont Avenue (which extends from 116th to

124th streets, between Riverside Drive and Broadway), and local landmarks in the neighbourhood are **Grant's Tomb** (*q.v.*), International House (occupied by foreign students), and Riverside Church. This section and points north are commonly referred to as the 'Upper West Side', especially north of 135th Street to Washington Heights, the name for the area between about 155th (site of the Museum of the American Indian) and 168th streets (site of the Columbia Presbyterian Medical Center, usually called just 'The Medical Center'). From 155th Street north, to the tip of Manhattan, the area is dominated by the George Washington Bridge, at 178th Street, a double-decker suspension bridge, opened in the mid 1930s, that spans the Hudson River to New Jersey. When the bridge was first opened, there was a restaurant atop its east tower, reached by a lift, and for many years, north of the bridge on the New Jersey side, was a swanky nightclub, Bill Marden's (later Bill Miller's) Riviera. North of the bridge, in Manhattan, is the Fort Tryon section, named for Fort Tryon Park, which is the site of the Cloisters, a museum, officially part of the Metropolitan Museum of Art (at 83rd Street and Fifth Avenue), that houses one of the finest collections of medieval art in the world. It was endowed by John D. Rockefeller, Jr., who went so far as to buy all the land along the Palisades on the opposite New Jersey shore just to preserve the view. At the foot of the east tower of the bridge stands a small lighthouse, once a navigational beacon to warn ships of the projecting rocky prominence there. No longer needed and long disused, it was to be demolished, but, owing to public outcry, it has survived because it commemorates a popular children's story, 'The Little Red Lighthouse'. See also **Broadway, East Side.**

2. A vast area of Chicago, made up of many culturally distinct neighbourhoods, with large industrial areas and including Columbus, Douglas, Garfield, Humboldt, and Marquette Parks. For more than 100 years, various poor or middle-class West Side neighbourhoods have served as the new home for successive waves of Poles, Germans, Irish, Italians, Greeks, Scandinavians, Czechs, Lithuanians, Ukrainians, blacks, and Latinos, who occasionally blended in but more often retained their ethnic (and a measure of linguistic) independence. Milwaukee Avenue, running diagonally from the city's downtown Loop area to well beyond the northwestern city limits, is one of the West Side's most important, and most colourful thoroughfares, with many small shops, offices, and restaurants; it constitutes, for much of its length, a vital nexus for the city's large Polish and other Eastern European immigrant communities. On the Near Northwest Side are the Wicker Park and Noble Square neighbourhoods,

originally settled by Germans, Poles, and other Europeans, and now predominantly Puerto Rican. Bordering the Loop on the west and southwest is the Near, or Lower West Side, including historic **Haymarket Square** (*q.v.*) and, along a short stretch of Halsted Street, the Greek Town enclave, which once served as home for Greek immigrants, many of whom have since moved to New Greek Town, on the city's Northwest Side. Nearby, to the south, are **Hull House** (*q.v.*) and the adjoining Taylor Street area, heart of one of the oldest Italian settlements (much of which was recently razed to make room for the Chicago Circle campus of the University of Illinois. Also in this vicinity is the site of **Mrs O'Leary's barn** (*q.v.*) where the Great Chicago Fire is believed to have started. Further south are the colourful **Maxwell Street** (*q.v.*) market area and the **Pilsen** (*q.v.*) neighbourhood. Among Southwest Side features are Marquette Park; the upscale Beverly Hills-Morgan Park area; and Midway Airport. The hard-core West Side, reaching west some four miles from the Loop and including the gang-plagued Humboldt Park area, is a gritty mixture of industrial plants and retail outlets, interspersed with various residential subsections. See also **O'Hare International Airport.**

Whitechapel
A district of the **East End** (*q.v.*) of London, immediately to the east of the Tower of London. In the 19th century it had a bad name as an area of slums to be avoided. The more sinister aspects of its reputation were fuelled by the lurid and notorious 'Whitechapel murders' of 1888, in which Jack the Ripper killed and mutilated five local prostitutes. Until well into the 20th century it was to a considerable extent a Jewish quarter, many having settled there after fleeing persecution in Russia in the 1880s. In the latter part of the 20th century they have been largely replaced by immigrants from the Indian subcontinent.

White City
1. The lakefront city-within-a-city, on the South Side of Chicago, that served as the site of the World's Columbian Exposition of 1893, held to celebrate the 400th anniversary of Christopher Columbus' discovery of the Americas. Among the attractions were the first Ferris wheel—the 260-foot tall, steel-and-iron invention of George Washington Gale Ferris—and a cluster of classical palaces, each containing exhibits denoting man's progress in industry and art. Although most of White City is mere memory now, some prized legacies remain, namely the Palace of Fine

Arts (now the **Museum of Science and Industry** (*q.v.*)), Jackson Park and the University of Chicago's Midway Plaisance.
2. An epithet for Helsinki. [A translation of *Den vita staden*.]

White Cliffs, the

The rolling hills of the North Downs of Kent are cut off abruptly by the English Channel. At the point where they meet, ranks of high chalk cliffs stretch out to both sides of Dover, a harbour town at the southeast tip of England. Their distant shimmer of white ascending the horizon is the first glimpse many a traveller from the Continent gets of England, and the 'White Cliffs of Dover' have become a potent symbol of hoped-for homecoming for English people abroad.

Whitefriars

Another name for the **Alsatia** (*q.v.*) area of London in medieval and early modern times, a district near the Thames inhabited by criminals and the like. It got its name from the Carmelite monastery in Fleet Street, founded in 1241; Carmelites were known as white friars, from the colour of their habits.

Whitehall

A street in Westminster, in central London, linking Parliament Square with Trafalgar Square. As well as the Horse Guards, with its mounted troopers of the Household Cavalry outside, and the Banqueting Hall—virtually all that remain of Henry VIII's royal palace of Whitehall—it contains numerous government buildings, including the Treasury, the Foreign Office, and the Ministry of Defence. Downing Street leads off it, on the right-hand side going south. Its name has become synonymous with the British government, particularly the executive side of government—ministers and civil servants—as contrasted with the legislators who inhabit Westminster.

white man's burden

An epithet for Britain's responsibility for her empire, probably coined in the late 19th century.

White Man's Grave, the

A nickname for West Africa in the days of European colonial expansion. The tropical forests of Nigeria and the Guinea coast harbour diseases and noxious insects to which European settlers frequently fell victim.

White Otter Castle
A large edifice with a four-story tower, built single-handedly of logs by Jimmy McOuat in 1914. Situated on remote White Otter Lake, in Canada, it is a symbol of pioneer days on the northwestern Ontario frontier.

Wigan
A town near Manchester, England. Situated in a coal-mining area, Wigan is associated in the minds of the British with the ordinary man-in-the-street, a typically unthinking person representative of the unthinking masses. Music-hall comedians are wont to refer to performances at 'Wigan Pier', and that apocryphal place is retained in the title of a book, *The Road to Wigan Pier,* by George Orwell.

Wilderness City
A nickname of the District of Columbia, attributed to Mrs John Adams who lived there from 1797–1801, when it was still sparsely settled and surrounded by woods.

Wild West, the
The western frontier of the United States before the areas and territories gained statehood. It is an indefinite concept that shifted with the westward expansion during the last two thirds of the nineteenth century and is associated with the legends and traditions of pioneers, outlaws, cowboys, gunslingers, dancehall queens, gambling casinos, and other fixtures of the "untamed" frontier, chiefly as depicted in novels, films, and other fictional media.

Wilhelmstrasse, the
A street in central Berlin in which many German government offices were situated until the end of World War II. The most notable and formidable of these was the Foreign Ministry, and it eventually took unofficial possession of the street's name, in much the same way as the French Foreign Ministry has come to be known as the **Quai d'Orsay** (*q.v.*).

Wimbledon
A middle-class residential suburb to the southwest of London that has become famous around the world for the lawn tennis championships held there every summer at the All-England Club.

Wimpole Street

A road in the West End of London, just to the west of Harley Street. Its fame rests on the mid-19th-century occupants of No. 50, the Barrett family. A daughter of the house, Elizabeth, had fallen in love with the famous poet Robert Browning, but her tyrannical father had forbidden the match; their subsequent elopement is perhaps the most celebrated in English literary history.

Windmill Theatre, the

A theatre in Great Windmill Street, near Piccadilly Circus, in London, built as a cinema in 1910, and later converted into a small—326-seat—theatre in 1931. During the 1930s it became famous for striptease, particularly for the Windmill Girls who posed in the nude (entirely legal provided that they did not move), and later for comedians like Harry Secombe and Tony Hancock, who got their starts there. During World War II, and, especially, the Blitz, the *Windmill* gained fame for continuing its shows through everything, and Londoners felt affection for it because it stuck to its motto, 'We Never Close'. From 1964 till 1981, it changed roles several times, first to become a cinema, then again as a theatre showing risqué comedy and, later, a nude review. It finally did close.

Windscale

A nuclear reprocessing plant on the coast of Cumbria in the Northwest of England which since 1952 has been producing plutonium. Both for its role in the manufacture of nuclear weapons, and because it was the first atomic plant in Britain to suffer an accidental leak, its name has become powerfully linked with the negative aspects of nuclear energy. In 1981 its owners, British Nuclear Fuels, changed its name to Sellafield, after two nearby hamlets, High and Low Sellafield. But if they thought this move would magically transform the plant's public image, they were to be disappointed; it continues to be widely known, particularly by its detractors, by its old name.

Windy City

A famous nickname for Chicago, now taken as literal (though several other large cities are windier), but originally referring to its blustering self-confidence. Credit for the name is generally given to *New York Sun* newspaper editor Charles A. Dana, who used it to characterize Chicago as an upstart for presuming to contend with New York and other cities for the honour of hosting the World's Columbian Exposition of 1893. In an editorial designed to nurture the egos of his readers, Dana advised them to ignore the 'nonsensical claims of that windy city. Its people could not hold a world's fair even if they won it'. Windy or not, Chicago managed to convince Congress that it was the place for the fair, and held it successfully.

Wirral, the

A large oblong peninsula that separates the estuaries of the rivers Mersey and Dee in northwestern England. Its northeastern shore, across the river from Liverpool, is largely given over to the port and shipbuilding facilities of places like Birkenhead and Ellesmere Port, but the sandy beaches have encouraged some vacation resorts to spring up, too, such as New Brighton.

Wolds, the

A line of rolling chalk hills in Humberside (formerly Yorkshire), northern England, which in places rise to 800 feet above sea level. Stone Age and Bronze Age burial mounds are a characteristic feature of the area. The hills continue further south, where they are known as the *Lincolnshire Wolds*, but the name *Wolds* on its own is generally taken as referring to the more northerly section. The word *wold* meant 'forest' in Anglo-Saxon times (the *Weald* comes from it), but interestingly, as Britain's forests began to be cut down in medieval times, particularly in upland areas, it gradually came to mean 'open hilly ground'. Today it only survives in proper names, such as *Cotswolds*, and the *Wolds*.

woolsack, the

A nickname, also used metonymically, for the seat of the Lord Chancellor when presiding over the House of Lords, a reference to the original seat in the 1300s during the reign of Edward III being made of four bound sacks of wool which symbolized its importance in the English economy.

Woolwich

A suburb of London on the south bank of the Thames, east of Greenwich. Perhaps its greatest claim to fame was the Royal Arsenal, the government munitions factory situated there from 1716 until the early 1960s, which produced much of the British Army's ordnance; but it was also the site of the former Royal Dockyard (closed 1869) in which many famous ships were built, such as Henry VIII's *Great Harry*. It is also the south-bank terminus for a cross-Thames ferry.

Wormwood Scrubs
A large open space in west London, to the north of Shepherd's Bush. Its fame rests on the prison of the same name, situated at its southwestern corner, which is often known familiarly as *the Scrubs*.

Wrigleyville
A Near North Side neighbourhood in Chicago, immediately surrounding Wrigley Field, home of the Chicago Cubs baseball team, the only major-league park without lights for night games. The planned installation of lights at Wrigley Field by the Cubs' parent Tribune Company has spurred controversy in the area, with influential groups like C.U.B.S. (Citizens United for Baseball in Sunshine) contesting the issue with those who contend that lights are the only way to keep the team from seeking a new home elsewhere.

Y

Yard, the
A common abbreviation of Scotland Yard, the London Police or its headquarters. It is used particularly in newspapers: 'Yard called in to help local force', a headline might read. In the days of heroic detectives, both real and fictional, particularly successful sleuths were often granted the epithet 'of the Yard': 'Fabian of the Yard', for example, had a vogue in crime fiction for a while. See also **Scotland Yard**.

Yellowhammer State, the
A nickname of Alabama, so called because of the yellowish tinge of the home-dyed grey uniforms worn by the Confederate soldiers.

yellow peril, the
An old name, formerly used by those who feared the domination or destruction of western civilization by Asiatics, owing to their great numbers.

Yerevan
The capital of the Armenian Soviet Socialist Republic. Its radio station is the butt of jokes behind the Iron Curtain, which take the form of Queries and Answers. For example:

> Q: Comrades, the other day I was walking in a
> forest and saw that the entire ground was covered
> with ants. How do you explain this?
> A: Comrade, under the leadership of the
> Party, Soviet industry has achieved numerous
> momentous successes; however, prophylactics and
> contraceptive pills for ants are not scheduled for
> development till the next Five-Year Plan.

You Beaut Country
A name given to the Australian landscape by the artist John Olsen in a series of paintings begun in 1961. The phrase is sometimes used as a general nickname for Australia.

Ypres
A Flemish town in western Belgium, near the French border. It has been trampled in the mud and blood of several military campaigns down the centuries, and in World War I three battles were fought over it at terrible cost. Its name was all too familiar to Allied soldiers, but the English-speaking ones could never quite manage its pronunciation, and it became known to that generation as 'Wipers'.

Yun Yuen Sek
A large outdoor shrine of stone on a hill high over Hong Kong. Here the distressed, the bereft, the unhappy, the unmarried, and others seeking a change of fortune pray and leave tribute, which may be as elaborate as a whole roast pig. Although the name means 'lovers' stone', pleas may be made for grants not necessarily connected with affairs of the heart.

Z

Zululand

An area on the east coast of South Africa that is the homeland of the Zulu people. At just over 10,000 square miles, it is much reduced from the huge territory, covering the present-day Transvaal and Natal, which they controlled at the height of their power in the 19th century. It corresponds in area more or less to the official Zulu bantustan, Kwazulu.

Index

AIDS-Induced Panic Syndrome: AIPS
Aiken, George D.: Northeast Kingdom
Aintree: Grand National, the
AIPS
aircraft carrier: Shangri-La, 2
Aire: Broad Acres, the
Airedale: Dales, the
Ajman: Trucial States, the
Akeman Street: Acemannes burh
Akkadia: Mesopotamia
Alabama: Appalachian Mountains; City of
  Five Flags; Deep South, the; Gulf, the;
  Muscle Shoals Area; South, the, 1; Yel-
  lowhammer State
Alamo, the
Alamo City
Alaska: Far North, the; Frozen Wilderness;
  Jumbo State; Land of the Midnight
  Sun, the
Albania: Balkans, the; Rumelia
Albany: Albany doctor, the
Albany doctor, the
Albany Regency
Albert, Prince: Balmoral Castle; Island,
  The, 1; Kensington
Alberta: Prairie Provinces, the
Albert Embankment: Embankment, the
Albion
Al Borak
Albury: Leaping Lena
Alcan Highway
Alcatraz
Aldebaran
Aldermaston
'Aldermaston marches': Aldermaston
Aldershot
Aldwych: Bush House; Drury Lane
Alexander the Great: Persia
Alexandra Palace: Ally Pally
Alexandria, Virginia: Pentagon, the
Alexiad, The
Alexius I: Alexiad, the
Alfred, King: Isle of Athelney, the
Alfred the Great: Wessex
Algeria: Barbary Coast, the; Maghreb;
  North Africa
Algiers: Kasbah, the

Algonquin Hotel: Round Table at the Al-
  gonquin
Alhambra, The: Alhambra
Alhambra
Alicante: Costa Blanca
Alice, the: Alice Springs
Alice Springs: Ayers Rock; Centre, the;
  Ghan, the; Pine Gap; Todd River
Allegheny Mountains: Appalachian Moun-
  tains
Allegheny River: Golden Triangle, the, 2
All-England Club: Wimbledon
Alligator Alley
all Lombard Street to a China orange: Lom-
  bard Street
all Lombard Street to an egg shell: Lombard
  Street
Ally Pally
Alonzo, Mateo: Christ of the Andes
alpha Tauri: Aldebaran
Alps, the: Brenner Pass
Alps: Bernese Oberland, the
Alsace: Alsatia
Alsatia: Whitefriars
Altgeld, John Peter: Haymarket Square;
  North Side
Amazon basin: Amazonia
Amazonia
Amazon River: Amazonia
Amen Corner
America: America's Cup; Mauve Decade,
  the; *Mayflower*
American Embassy: Eisenhower Platz; Gros-
  venor Square
American Indian, Museum of: West Side, 1
American Nile, the
Americans: Brother Jonathan
American Stock Exchange: Big Board, the
American Workhouse, the
Americas: New World, the
America's Cup
'America's Tech Highway': Route 128
Ames, Ohio: Coonskin Library
Amsterdam: Diamond City; Holland, 1;
  Venice of the North
Amsterdam Avenue: Broadway, 1; West
  Side, 1
Amtrak: Grand Central; Union Station

Amundsen, Roald: Northwest Passage, the
Anatolia: Asia Minor
anatomist's snuffbox
Andersonstown: Falls Road
Andersonville, Georgia: Hell Upon Earth
Andersonville: North Side
Andes Mountains: South American Alps
Angel, the
Angels Camp, California: Frogtown
Anglesey: Llanfairpwllgwyngillgogerychwyrn-
  drobllllantysiliogogogoch
Anglican Church: Lambeth
Anglo-Saxons: Hastings
Angola: Guinea
Angora
Angostura
Angostura bitters: Angostura
Ankara: Angora
Annam: Indochina
Anna of the Five Towns: Five Towns, the
Anne, Queen: Ascot
Antarctica: dinosaur of darkness;
  Gondwanaland; South Pole
Antarctic Ocean: Seven Seas, the
Antibes: French Riviera, the
Antipodes, the
Antrim: Six Counties, the
Anzac-on-Sea: Peacehaven
Aotearoa
Aphrodite: violet-crowned city, the
Apollo: City of the Sun
Apollo 15 moonlanding: Genesis rock
Appalachia
Appalachian Mountains: Appalachia; Blue
  Ridge Mountains, the; Cumberland Gap
Appalachian Plateau: Tidewater Virginia
Appalachian Ridge and Valley Region: Tide-
  water Virginia
Appalachian Trail, the
Appalachian Trail: Mohawk Trail
Appian Way: Indian-Appian Way
Apple Isle, the
Applied Bacteriology and Research, Centre
  for: Porton Down
Apsley Gate: Rotten Row
Apsley House: Number One, London
Arabia: Horn of Africa, the; Near East, the
Arabia Deserta: Arabia

Arabian peninsula: Empty Quarter, the;
  Gulf, the; Sheba
Arabian Sea: Seven Seas, the
Arab-Israeli war: Gaza Strip, the
Arab states: Middle East, the
Arab World: Middle East, the
Araby: Arabia
Aragon Ballroom
Arbuthnot, John: John Bull
Arcadia: Arcadia
Arcady: Arcadia
Arc de Triomphe: Champs-Élysées, the
Archbishop of Canterbury: Lambeth
Archway
Archway Road: Archway
Arctic Circle: Far North, the; Land of the
  Midnight Sun, the; Lapland; Siberia
Arctic icecap: Far North, the
Arctic Ocean: Maelstrom, the; North Pole;
  Seven Seas, the
Arctogaea
Arden
Arden Shakespeare: Arden
Ardmore: Main Line
Argentina: Christ of the Andes; Falkland Is-
  lands, the; Patagonia; South American
  Alps; Tierra del Fuego
Aristophanes: violet-crowned city, the
Arizona, USS: Pearl Harbor
Arizona: Baby State; London Bridge; South-
  west, the, 1; Sunbelt; Tower Bridge;
  Valentine State
Arkansas: Bible Belt; Bowie State; Guinea
  Pig State; Midwest, the; South, the, 1;
  Toothpick State
Armagh: Six Counties, the
Armenian Soviet Socialist Republic: Yerevan
Armentières: Flanders
Armour, Philip: North Side
Army and Navy Club: Pall Mall
Army & Navy Stores
Arnold, Matthew: City of Dreaming Spires;
  Rugby
Arnold, Thomas: Rugby
Aroostook County: Garden of Maine
Around the World in Eighty Days: Reform
  Club, the
arsenal: Woolwich

Gap; Pitt Street; Premier State, the;
Riverina, the; Riverland, the; Sar-
saparilla; Shop, the; Silver City; Smoke,
the; Snake Gully; Speck, the; Star Ho-
tel; Steel City, 1; Steel City, 2; Sunray-
sia; Taranaki;
Taumatawhakatangihangakoauauota-
mateapokaiwhenuakitanatahu; Tea and
Sugar; Terra Australis; Territory, the;
Todd River; Top End, the; Track, the;
Trans-Australian Railway; Tullamarine;
Uluru; Van Diemen's Land; Wallaby
Track; West, the, 1; wire marvel, the;
You Beaut Country
Australia II: America's Cup
Australian Broadcasting Commission: NIDA
Australian Commonwealth: Trans-Australian
Railway
Australian Theatre Trust: NIDA
Austria: Brenner Pass; Mistelbach
Austro-Hungarian empire: Balkans, the
Avalon: Camelot, 1
Avebury
Aventine: Seven Hills, the
Avenue B: East Village, the
Avenue of the Americas: 42nd Street
Avon: West, the, 2; West Country, the
Avril, Jane: Moulin Rouge
Ayers Rock: Uluru
Aylesbury: Stoke Mandeville
Azania
Aztec State, the
B, the
Baalbec: City of the Sun, the
Babylon: Fertile Crescent, the; Mesopotamia
Babylonia: Hanging Gardens of Babylon
Baby State, the
Back Bay
Backbone of England, the
Backbone of the Confederacy
back of Bourke: Bourke
Back of the Yards: South Side
Backs, the
Bad Lands, the
Baffin, William: Northwest Passage, the
Bagshot
Bahrein: Arabia; Gulf, the
Bailey, the: Old Bailey

Baker, Josephine: Folies Bergère
Bakerloo
Baker Street: Bakerloo
'Baker Street irregulars': Baker Street
Baker Street Station: Metroland
Balkan peninsula: Balkans, the
'Balkan problem': Balkans, the
Balkans, the
Balkans: Near East, the; Rumelia
Balkis: Sheba
Ballarat gold-fields: Eureka Stockade
ballet: Covent Garden
Balliol College: Broad, the
Balmoral Castle
baloney dollar
Baltic Sea: Baltic States; Jutland; Oder-
Neisse Line, the; Polish Corridor, the;
Russia; Sound, the
Baltic States
Baltimore, Lord: Old Line State
Baltimore: Fort McHenry
Balzac, Honoré de: Père Lachaise
Bamboo Curtain, the
Banana-bender: Bananaland
banana benders: Bananaland
Banana Curtain: Bananaland
Bananaland
Bananalander: Bananaland
banana republic
Banbury Cross
Bangkok: Venice of the East
Bangladesh: Pakistan; Subcontinent, the
Bank, the
Bank: Bank of England, the; Mansion
House, the
Bank of England, the
Bank of England: Bank, the; City, the;
Lombard Street; Mansion House, the;
Old Lady of Threadneedle Street, the
Bankside
Bank station: Drain, the
Banqueting Hall: Whitehall
Bantam work: Coromandel Coast, the
Banzai Pipeline
barbarian: Barbary Coast, the
Barbary Coast, the
Barbary States: Barbary Coast, the
barber, the

Barbican, the
Barbican Centre: Barbican, the
Barbizon: Fontainebleau
Barcelona: Costa Brava, the
Barchester: Barset
Barefoot Cantonese
bargain basement: Filene's Basement
Baroda: Native States, the
Barrett, Elizabeth: Wimpole Street
Barrett, Richard: Wimpole Street
Barrie, Sir James: Adelphi, the
Barrio, the
Barrow-in-Furness: Furness
Barset
Barsetshire: Barset
Bart's
Baseball Hall of Fame: Birthplace of Baseball
Basin Street: Storyville
Basque: Guernica
Bath: Acemannes burh; Lantern of England
Batman: Capricornia
Battersea: Nine Elms; Swone-one
Battersea Dogs' Home: Battersea
Battersea Power Station: Battersea; Nine Elms
Battle: Hastings
Battle above
Battlebridge: King's Cross, 1
Battle Bridge Road: Battlebridge
Battleground of Freedom, the
Battle Hymn of the Republic, The: Marseillaise of the Unemotional Yankee
Baum, L. Frank: TOTO
Bavaria: Bayreuth; Palatinate, the
Bavarian Alps: Oberammergau
Bay, the
Baylis, Lilian: Old Vic, the
Bay of Bengal: Seven Seas, the
Bay of Naples: Naples
Bayreuth
Bay Street
Bayswater: Paddington
Bay View: Over South
BBC: Ally Pally; Auntie; Beeb, the; Bush House; Portland Place
BBC Television Centre: Shepherd's Bush
Beachy Head: Seven Sisters

Beacon Hill
Beale, Miss: Cheltenham
Bean, L. L.
Beantown
Bear Gardens: Bankside
Bear Mountain State Park: Hudson River
Bearsden
Bearsden and Milngavie District: Bearsden
Beatles, the: Abbey Road; Strawberry Fields
Beaubourg: Halles, les
Beaumont: Golden Triangle, the, 3
Becknell, William: Santa Fe Trail
Bedfordshire: Midlands, the
Bedlam
Bedloe, Isaac: Bedloe's Island
Bedloe's Island
Bedowrie shower: Bourke
'bed-sitter-land': Bayswater
Beeb, the
Beecher, Henry Ward: Kansas Bibles; Phoenix City
Beecher's Brook: Grand National, the
Beehive State, the
Beekman Street: Tribeca
Beer, Thomas: Mauve Decade, the
beer: Burton upon Trent
Begin, Menachem: Camp David
Bel Air: Sunset Boulevard
Belbenoit, René: Devil's Island
Belfast: Andersonstown; Falls Road; Shankill Road
Belgium: accidental war, the; Benelux; Cockpit of Europe, the; European Economic Community, the; Flanders; Little Siberia; Low Countries, the; Waterloo; Ypres
Belgrave: Belgravia
Belgravia: Kensington; King's Road; Knightsbridge; Pimlico; Sloane Square; Victoria; West End, the
Belisha beacon
Bell, Vanessa: Bloomsbury
Bellevue
Bell X-1: Glamorous Glennis
belly-dancers: Chelsea, 2
Belushi, John: Billy Goat Tavern; Second City
Belvoir: Shires, the

Benbecula: Western Isles, the
Benchley, Robert: Minsky's; Round Table at
   the Algonquin
Benelux
Benidorm: Costa Blanca
Bennet, Arnold: Five Towns, the
Ben Nevis: Glens, the
Benton, Thomas Hart: Bullion State
Bergdorf Goodman: Plaza, the
Berkeley Square: Mayfair
Berkshire: Aldermaston; Ascot; Bray; Eton;
   Greenham Common; Home Counties,
   the; Royal Borough, the; Sandhurst;
   South, the, 2; Southeast, the; Thames
   Valley, the
Berkshire Mountains: Jacob's Pillow; Mo-
   hawk Trail
Berlin, Irving: Lower East Side
Berlin: Checkpoint Charlie; Unter den Lin-
   den; Wilhelmstrasse, the
Berlin Wall, the
Bermondsey: Old Kent Road, the; Pool of
   London, the
Bermondsey and New Caledonian Market:
   Bermondsey Market
Bermondsey Market
Bermondsey Street: Bermondsey Market;
   Caledonian Market
Bermuda Triangle, the
Bern: Bernese Oberland, the
Bernese Oberland, the
Berwick: Border, the
Berwyn: Main Line
Bessarabia
Bethnal Green: Bethnal Green in the Sun;
   Tower Hamlets
Bethnal Green in the Sun
Betjeman, John: Metroland; Slough
'between a rock and a hard place': Scylla
   and Charybdis
'between Scylla and Charybdis': Scylla and
   Charybdis
Beverly Hills, California: Beverly Hills Hotel
Beverly Hills: Hollywood; Rodeo Drive;
   Sunset Boulevard
Beverly Hills Hotel
Beverly Hills-Morgan Park: West Side, 2
Bexley: London

Bhopal
Bhutan: Subcontinent, the
Bible Belt, the
Bienville, Sieur de: French Quarter, the
Big Apple, the
Big Australian, the
'Big Bands': Broadway, 1
Big Bang, the
Big Ben
Big Bend
big Bertha
Big Board, the
Big D
Big Dipper
Big Hole, the
Big Inch
Big Jim Colosimo's Café: Loop, the
Big Mac, the
'Big Orange, The': Los Angeles
Big Palm Spring: Palm Springs
Big Run, the
Big Sioux River: Outlaw Country
Big Smoke, the: Smoke, the
Big Tex
Big Town
Bijou: Odeon
Billingsgate
Billingsley, Sherman: Stork Club
Billy Goat Tavern
Biltmore Hotel: Clock at the Astor, Biltmore
bilyatï: Blighty
Biograph Theater
Birdland
Birdum: Leaping Lena
Birkenhead: Wirral, the
Birmingham, Alabama: Appalachian Moun-
   tains
Birmingham: Black Country, the;
   Bourneville; Brum; Bullring, the;
   Edgbaston; Handsworth; Second City;
   Spaghetti Junction; West Midlands, the
Birmingham of America, the
Birmingham University: Edgbaston
Birthplace of American Liberty, the
Birthplace of Aviation, the
Birthplace of Baseball
Bishopsgate: Bedlam
Bismarck Archipelago: Melanesia

Bunker Hill; City of Kind Hearts; Combat Zone; Coonskin Library; Cradle of Liberty; Durgin Park; Faneuil Hall; Filene's Basement; Freedom Trail; Haymarket, the, 1; Holland, 2; Megalopolis; Northeast Corridor; North End; North Shore, 2; Old North Church; Parker House, the; Route 128; Roxbury; Scollay Square; Southie; T, the

Boston Common

Boston Latin School: Freedom Trail

Boston Massacre: Freedom Trail

Boston Post Road

Boston Public Library: Back Bay

Boston Red Sox: Back Bay

Boston Tea Party: Freedom Trail

Boston Transport: T, the

Boswell, James: Athens of the North, the

Botany Bay

Boulder: Golden Mile, the, 2

Boulevard St Germain: Deux Magots, les

Bourget, le

Bourke

Bourke shower: Bourke

Bournemouth

Bourneville

'Bouwerie': Bowery, the

Bow: East End

Bow Bells: Bow

Bow Church: Bow

Bowery, the: Five Points; Little Italy

Bowery bums: Bowery, the

Bowie, James: Alamo, the

Bowie State

Bowling Green: Broadway, 1

Bowron, Fletcher: Los Angeles

Bow Street

Bow Street Magistrates' Court: Bow Street

'Bow Street Runners': Bow Street

Boylston Street: Combat Zone

Boystown

Bozeman, John M.: Bozeman Trail

Bozeman Trail

Brabant: Low Countries, the

Bradford: Broad Acres, the; Ridings, the

Brahmins: Back Bay

Brandt Report: North, the, 3; South, the, 3

Branston, F.: Roedean

Brasenose College: High, the

Bray

Brazil: Amazonia; Copacabana, 1; Guiana

'Breakfast at Tiffany's': Tiffany's

Breasted, James H.: Fertile Crescent, the

Brecon Beacons: Valleys, the

Breed's Hill: Bunker Hill

Brenner Pass

Brentwood: Sunset Boulevard

brewing: Burton upon Trent

Brice, Fanny: Lower East Side

Brickfielder

Brickfield Hill: Brickfielder

Bride of the Sea

Bridewell: B, the

Bridgehampton: Hamptons, the

Bridge of Sighs

Bridgeport: South Side

Brigalow, the

Bright, John: Mother of Parliaments, the

Brighton: Bognor Regis; Costa del Sol; Costa Geriatrica, the; Dr. Brighton; Kemp Town; Lanes, the; Littlehampton; Peacehaven; Roedean; Seven Sisters

Brighton Albion: Albion

Brill Building: Tin Pan Alley

Brisbane: Brizzie; Gabba, the; wire marvel, the

Bristol: St Paul's; West, the, 2

Bristol Channel: Valleys, the

Britain, Battle of: Coventry

Britain, Festival of: Battersea

Britain: Blighty; Border, the; Brum; Dales, the; East Indies, the; England; German Ocean, the; Hadrian's Wall; Henley; House, the; Lizard, the; M & S; North, the, 1; Number 10; Snowdonia; Thule; Tin Pan Alley; Valleys, the

British Broadcasting Corporation: See *BBC* in Index.

British Caledonian: Caledonia

British Columbia: Inland Empire, the

British criminal fraternity: Bethnal Green in the Sun

British criminals: Costa del Crime

British India: Northwest Frontier, the

British Isles: Channel, the; Continent; Gulf Stream
British Museum: Bloomsbury
Brittany, Duke of: Little Britain
Brittany: Little Britain
Brixton: Lambeth
Brixton Prison: Brixton
Brizzie
Broad, the
Broad: Turl, the
Broad Acres, the
broad arrow: Old Dart, the
Broadcasting House: Portland Place
Broads, the
Broadstairs: Isle of Thanet, the
Broad Street: Broad, the
Broadway: Birdland; Columbus Circle; Great White Way; Harlem; Herald Square; Hub of New York City; Jack Dempsey's; Lindy's; Sardi's; West Side, 1
'Broadway Limited': Union Station
Brocken
Brocken spectre: Brocken
Brody, Steve: Brooklyn Bridge
Broken Hill: Silver City
Broken Hill Proprietary Company Ltd: Big Australian, the; Steel City, 1
Bronx, The: Broadway, 1; Brooklyn; Featherbed Lane; Harlem River; Hell Gate; House that Ruth Built; Manhattan; Park Avenue; Sugar Hill
Bronx Whitestone Bridge: Hell Gate
Bronze Age: Wolds, the
Brookfield: Mayfair
Brookline: Back Bay
Brooklyn: Brooklyn Bridge; City of Churches, the; Cobble Hill; Dormitory of New York; East River; Island, the, 2; Manhattan; Narrows, the; Queens
Brooklyn Bridge: Brooklyn; Foley Square; Lower East Side
Brooklyn Dodgers: Brooklyn
Brooklyn Heights: Brooklyn; Cobble Hill
Brooklyn-Queens Expressway: Cobble Hill
Brooks Brothers
Brother Jonathan

Broun, Heywood: Round Table at the Algonquin
Brown Bess
Browning, Robert: Wimpole Street
brownstone
Brownsville, Texas: Golden Crescent, the, 2
Brum
Brummagem: Brum
Brummies: Brum
Brunei: Southeast Asia
Brunelleschi: Giotto's Tower
Bryn Mawr: Main Line
Bubbling Well
Bubbling Well Road: Bubbling Well
bubonic plague: Black Death, the
Buccellati: Fifth Avenue
Bucharest: Orient-Express
Buckeye State, the
Buck House
Buckingham and Chandos, Duke of: Buck House
Buckingham House: Buck House
Buckingham Palace: Buck House; Number One, London; Palace, the; Speakers' Corner; St James's
Buckinghamshire: Chiltern Hundreds, the; Home Counties, the; Metroland; Midlands, the; Milton Keynes; Slough; Southeast, the; Stoke Mandeville
Buddhism: Forbidden City, the
Buffalo: Bison City; City of Flour; Queen City of the Lakes
'Bugger Bognor!': Bognor Regis
Bughouse Square
Bulgaria: Balkans, the; Rumelia
Bull Durham: Bull City
Bulli
Bullion State, the
Bullring, the
Bunker Hill
buns: Chelsea, 1
Burbank
burlesque: Minsky's
Burlington Arcade: Burlington House; Piccadilly, 1
Burlington Gardens: Burlington House
Burlington House: Piccadilly, 1

Burma: Burma Road, the; Golden Triangle, the, 1; Indochina; Middle East, the; Southeast Asia
Burma Road, the
Burnham, Daniel: North Side
Burnham: Chiltern Hundreds, the
Burslem: Five Towns, the
Bursley: Five Towns, the
Burton-upon-Trent
Bush, Irving T: Bush House
Bush House
business, big: Wall Street
Buttermere: Lake District, the
Buzby, Betty: Minsky's
Byrne, Joe: Kelly Country
Byron, George, Lord: Bridge of Sighs, 1
Byron, Lord: Albany
Byzantine Empire: West, the, 1
Cabbage Patch, the
Cabildo, the: French Quarter, the
Cabot, Sebastian: Northwest Passage, the
'Cabrini-Green': Cabrini-Green Public Housing Project
Cabrini-Green Public Housing Project
Cadbury's: Bourneville
Cadibarrawirracanna Lake: Taumatawhakatangihangakoauauotamateapokaiwhenuakitanatahu
Caelian: Seven Hills, the
Caerleon: Camelot, 1
Caernarvon: Royal Borough, the
Café Society Downtown: Greenwich Village
Caine Road: Ladder Street
Cairo, Illinois: Egypt
Cairo: Shepheard's Hotel
Caithness: Highlands, the
Caithness-shire: Land's End to John o' Groat's House
Calais: Chunnel, the
Calcutta: Black Hole (of Calcutta); City of Palaces, the
Caledonia
Caledonia County: Northeast Kingdom
Caledonian Canal: Caledonia
Caledonian Market: Bermondsey Market
Caledonian Road: Caledonian Market; Pentonville
calf's testis: prairie oyster

California: Beverly Hills; Boystown; Burbank; Disneyland; Donner Pass; Far West, the; Golden Gate City; Land of Little Rain; Pacific Northwest, the; Palm Springs; Plymouth of the West; Poor Man's Paradise; Port o' Missing Men; Rodeo Drive; San Fernando Valley; Silicon Glen; Watts
Calpe: Pillars of Hercules, the
Calumet, Lake: South Side
Camargue, the
Camberley: Bagshot
Camberwell: Old Kent Road, the
Cambodia: Indochina; Southeast Asia
Cambria
Cambrian Mountains: Cambria
Cambrian Period: Cambria
Cambridge: Backs, the; Granta; Newmarket
Cambridgeshire: East Anglia; Fens, the; Huntingdonshire; Isle of Ely, the; Melton Mowbray; Midlands, the; Oxon
Cambridge Town: Camberley
Cambridge University: Bridge of Sighs, 3; Golgotha, 2; Oxbridge
C & A: Oxford Street
Camden: Camden Town
Camden Lock: Camden Town
Camden Passage: Camden Town
Camden Town
Camelford: Camelot, 1
Camelot
Cameroon: Guinea
Camino Real, el
Campagna, the
Campbell: Glencoe
Camp David: Shangri-La, 3
Camp David Accords: Camp David
Cam River: Backs, the; Granta
Canaan: Land of Promise; Palestine; Promised Land, the
Canada: Acadia; Atlantic Provinces, the; Bay Street; City of Saints, the; D.S.N.C.O.; dust bowl, the; Far North, the; Inland Empire, the; Mississippi Bubble; Northland, the; Old Quebec (Vieux-Québec); Parkdale; Place Royale; Prairie Provinces, the; Queen Street West; Ridings, the; Rosedale;

Strip, the, 2; Territories, the; Track, the; White Otter Castle
Canadian Rockies: Rockies, the
Canal Street: Avenue of the Americas; Bowery, the; Chinatown, 1; French Quarter, the; Little Italy; Tribeca
Canary Islands
can-can: Moulin Rouge
Cannes: French Riviera, the; Grand Corniche; South of France, the
Canning, George: Albany
Canning Town: East End
Canongate: Royal Miles, the
Cantab.: Oxon.
Canterbury pilgrims: Borough, the
Canton Street: Chinatown, 2
Cape, the
Cape Ann: Gloucester
Cape Breton Island: Acadia
Cape Cod: Cape, the
Cape Cod Bay: Cape, the
Cape Cod turkey
Cape Comorin: Malabar Coast, the
Cape Hatteras: Graveyard of the Atlantic; Gulf Stream
Cape La Nao: Costa Blanca
Cape Province: Karoo, the
Cape Town: Table Mountain
Cape Verde: Guinea
Cap Ferrat: French Riviera, the
capitalist countries: Iron Curtain, the
Capital of the Highlands, the
Capital of the World, the
Capitol, the: Broadway, 1
Capitol: Capitoline, the
Capitol Building: Hill, the
Capitol Hill: Hill, the
Capitoline, the
Capitoline: Seven Hills, the
Capone, Al: Holy Name Cathedral; Loop, the
Capote, Truman: Tiffany's
Capricornia: Capricornia
Captain Kidd: *Adventure*
Captains Courageous: Gloucester
Cardiff: Coal Metropolis of the World
Carey Street
Carfax, the

Caribbean: Spanish Main, the
Caribbean Sea: Middle Passage, the
Carlisle: Hadrian's Wall
Carlton, the: Clubland, 1
Carlton Club, the
Carlyle, Thomas: Athens of the North, the
Carmelite monastery: Whitefriars
Carnaby Street: King's Road
Caroline Islands: Micronesia
Carpathian Mountains: Transylvania
Carrington, Frank: Paper Mill Playhouse
Carroll, Harry: Blue Ridge Mountains, the
Cartagena, Colombia: blue-light district; Heroic City
Cartagena: Costa Blanca
Carter, Jimmy: Camp David
Cartier: Fifth Avenue; Tiffany's
Casa Oscar Romero
Cascade Mountains: Inland Empire, the
Caspian Sea: Volgograd
Castle Hill: Royal Miles, the
Castle Rock: New Town, the
Castro, the
Cathay
Cathay Pacific: Cathay
Cathedral: Holy Name
Cathedral Parkway: West Side, 1
Catherine the Great: City of Palaces, the
Catskill Mountains: Appalachian Mountains; Borscht Circuit
Cat Street
Causeway Bay
CED: Porton Down
Celebes: East Indies, the; Spice Islands, the
'Celebrated Jumping Frog of Calaveras County, The': Frogtown
Celestial Empire, the
Cellini, Benvenuto: Fontainebleau
cemetery: Forest Lawn
Centennial State, the
Central America: banana republic; Neogaea
Central Criminal Court: Old Bailey
Centralia: Centre, the
Central Park: Columbus Circle; Fifth Avenue; Manhattan; West Side, 1
Central Park South: Plaza, The
Central Park West: Broadway, 1; Columbus Circle; Dakota, the, 2; West Side, 1

Centre, the
Centre Point
Centre Street: Bridge of Sighs, 2; China-
town, 1; Little Italy
Century, the: West Side, 1
Cephissus: Academy, the
Cesarwich: Newmarket
Ceylon
C-47: Gooney Bird
Chad: Sahel, the
chalk cliffs: Seven Sisters
Chalk Farm Road: Camden Lock
Chamberlain, W. J.: Amen Corner
Chambers, William: Kew Gardens
Champlain, Lake: Clinton's ditch
Champs Élysées, the
Champs Élysées: Faubourg St Honoré, Rue
du
Chancellor of the Exchequer: Number 10
Chancery Lane
'Change at Crewe': Crewe
Channel, the
Channel country
Chappaquiddick
Charing: Charing Cross
Charing Cross
Charing Cross Road: Charing Cross;
Shaftesbury Avenue; Tin Pan Alley
Charing Cross Underground station: Em-
bankment, the
Charles Augustus, Grand Duke: Weimar
Charlesbourg-Ouest: D.S.N.C.O.
Charles I: Charing Cross; Queen State
Charles II: Old Dominion
Charles River: Bunker Hill
Charles's Wain
Charleston: Roaring Twenties, the
Charlestown: Bunker Hill
Charlotte, North Carolina: Hornet's Nest
Charlotte Street: Fitzrovia
Charlottetown, Prince Edward Island: Birth-
place of Canada
Charrière, Henri: Devil's Island
Charter Oak City, the
Charus of Lindus: Colossus of Rhodes
Chase, Salmon Portland: Ohio's Jewels
Chatham: Cape, the
Chatsworth, the: West Side, 1

Chattanooga, Battle of: Battle above or in
the Clouds
Chaucer: Borough, the
Checkerboard Lounge: South Side
Checkpoint Charlie
Cheddar
Cheddar Gorge: Cheddar
Chelm: Neasden
Chelsea: Battersea; Earl's Court; Fitzrovia;
Kensington; King's Road; Royal Bor-
ough, the; Sloane Square
Chelsea Arts Club Ball: Chelsea, 1
Chelsea Embankment: Embankment, the
Chelsea Hotel: Chelsea, 2
Chelsea Pensioners: Chelsea, 1
Chelsea Royal Hospital: Chelsea, 1
Cheltenham
Cheltenham Ladies' College: Cheltenham
Chemical Defense Establishment: Porton
Down
Cherokee: Trail of Tears
Cherry Grove: Fire Island; Grand Strand
Chesapeake Bay: Delmarva Peninsula; Tide-
water Virginia
Cheshire: Crewe; Midlands, the; North,
the, 1
Chester: Marches, the, 1
Cheviot Hills: Backbone of England, the
Cheyne Walk: Chelsea, 1
Chiang Kai-shek: Burma Road, the
Chicago, University of: South Side; Stagg
Field
Chicago: a; Aragon Ballroom; Atchison, To-
peka, & Santa Fe; Big Town; Billy Goat
Tavern; Biograph Theater; Bughouse
Square; Cabrini-Green Public Housing
Project; Empire State Building; Fort
Dearborn; Gold Coast; Haymarket
Square; Hog Butcher for the World;
Holy Name Cathedral; Hull House;
Lake Shore Drive; Loop, the; Magnifi-
cent Mile, the; Marshall Field's; Max-
well Street; McCormick Place; Museum
of Science and Industry; Navy Pier;
Near North Side; New Town; North
Side; O'Hare International Airport; Old
Town; Phoenix City; Pilsen; Playboy
Building; Pullman; Rush Street; Sears

Tower; Second City, the; South Side; Staff Field; Toddling Town, That; Union Station; Union Stockyards; Water Tower; West, the, 3; West Side, 2; White City, 1; Wrigleyville

Chicago Circle: West Side, 2

Chicago Cubs: Wrigleyville

Chicago Fire Academy: Mrs O'Leary's Barn

Chicago White Sox: South Side

Chickasaw: Trail of Tears

Chihuahua, Mexico: Camino Real, el

Childe Harold's Pilgrimage: Bridge of Sighs, 1

Chile: Christ of the Andes; Patagonia; South American Alps; Tierra del Fuego

Chiltern Hundreds, Stewardship of: Chiltern Hundreds, the

Chiltern Hundreds, the

Chimneyville

China, Nationalist: Formosa

China, Nationalist Republic of: Formosa

China, People's Republic of,: Formosa; Red China

China: Burma Road, the; Cathay; Celestial Empire, the; Coromandel Coast, the; Far East, the; Forbidden City, the; Formosa; Indochina; Inner Mongolia; Middle Kingdom, the; Mongolia; Red China; Roof of the World, the

Chinatown: Foley Square; Limehouse; South Side

Chinese: Soho

Chisholm, Jesse: Chisholm Trail

Chisholm Trail

chocolate: Bourneville

Chocolate Soldier, The: Paper Mill Playhouse

Choctaw: Trail of Tears

Chomondley's: Greenwich Village

Chopin, Frédéric: Père Lachaise

Christchurch: Four Main Centres, the; House, the; Old North Church

Christiana

'Christian Charity': Piccadilly Circus

Christie, Agatha: Orient-Express

Christie, John: Old Bailey

Christ of the Andes

Chrysler Building: Empire State Building

Chungking: Burma Road, the

Chunnel, the

Churchill, Winston: Camp David; Iron Curtain, the

Church of England: Lambeth

churchyard: God's acre

Cimon: Academy, the

Cincinnati oyster

Cinque Ports, the

Circle Line: London Underground

citadel, Roman: Capitoline, the

City, the

City College, the

'City gent': City, the

City Hall: Foley Square

City of Brotherly Love, the

City of David, the

City of Dreaming Spires

City of Firsts

City of Five Flags

City of Isms

City of Kind Hearts, the

City of Light, the

City of Lilies, the

City of Magnificent Distances

City of Masts, the

City of New York, Museum of: Fifth Avenue

City of Palaces, the

City of Refuge, the

City of Saints, the

City of St Michael, the

'City of the Angels': Los Angeles

City of the Midnight Sun, the

City of the Prophet, the

City of the Seven Hills, the

City of the Sun, the

City of the Sun

City of Witches

City Road: Angel, the

Ciudad Bolívar: Angostura

Clapham: Neasden

Clapham Junction: Clapham

Clapham Sect: Clapham

Clare College: Backs, the

Claremont Avenue: West Side, 1

Clarence Island: Tierra del Fuego

Claridge's Hotel: Grosvenor Square

Cleopatra's Needle: Embankment, the
Clerkenwell Road: Hatton Garden
Cleveland, Grover: Pullman
Cleveland: Northeast, the, 1
clink, in the: Clink Street
Clink Street
Clinton, De Witt: Clinton's ditch
Clinton's ditch
Clock at the Astor/Biltmore
clock tower: Pullman
Cloisters, the: West Side, 1
Club: Newmarket
Clubland: Athenaeum, the; Pall Mall; St
   James's
Clubland circuit: Clubland, 2
Clumber Park: Dukeries, the
Clyde, River: Clydeside; Gorbals, the; Low-
   lands, the
Clydebank: Clydeside
Clydeside
coal: Dusky Diamonds
coal mine: Seven Sisters
coalmining: Ruhr, the
Coat Hanger, the
Cobbett, William: Great Wen, the; Old Lady
   of Threadneedle Street, the
Cobble Hill
Cochin: Native States, the
Cochin China: Indochina
Cockade City
Cockade State, the
Cockney: Lambeth; Old Kent Road, the;
   Petticoat Lane
Cockneys: East End
Cockpit Country, the
Cockpit of Europe, the
codfish: Cape Cod turkey
Cohan, George M.: Broadway, 1; Herald
   Square
Colchester: Naze, the
Coleridge, Samuel Taylor: Lake District, the
Colesberg Hill: Big Hole, the
Colesberg Kopje: Big Hole, the
Colette: Père Lachaise
Coliseum, New York: Broadway, 1
Coliseum: Columbus Circle
Collins Street
Collins Street Grazier: Collins Street

Cologne: Rhineland, the
'Colony, The': Malibu
Colorado: Centennial State; Home of the
   Cheeseburger; Mile High City; South-
   west, the, 1
Colosseum: Domus Aurea
Colossus of Rhodes
Columbia Presbyterian Medical Center: West
   Side, 1
Columbia River: Inland Empire, the
Columbia University: Bloomingdale's;
   Broadway, 1; Rockefeller Center
Columbus, Christopher: Columbus Circle
Columbus: Ohio's Jewels
Columbus Avenue: Broadway, 1
Columbus Circle: Broadway, 1; Hub of New
   York City
Columbus Park: West Side, 2
Combat Zone
Comden, Betty: Greenwich Village
Comiskey Park: South Side
'Committee of 100': Aldermaston
Common Market: European Economic Com-
   munity, the
Commonwealth
Communist bloc: East, the, 2
Communist China: Bamboo Curtain, the
communist countries: Iron Curtain, the
'Community, the': European Economic
   Community, the
Comnena, Anna: Alexiad, the
Comnenus: Alexiad, the
Concord, Massachusetts: Walden Pond
Coney Island: Brooklyn
Confederate flag: Stars and Bars
Confederate prison: Hell Upon Earth
Confederate States: City of Five Flags
Congress: Hill, the
Congress (U. S.): Capitoline, the
Congress Parkway: Loop, the
Congreve rockets: Woolwich
Coniston Water: Lake District, the
Connacht: Province, the
Connaught Hotel: Grosvenor Square
Connecticut: Brother Jonathan; Charter Oak
   City, the; Constitution State; East,
   the, 1; Grand Central; Island, the, 2;

New England; Nutmeg State; Thirteen Original Colonies

Connecticut Avenue

Conrail: Grand Central

Conservative: Shires, the

Conservative Party: Carlton Club, the; Smith Square

Constable, John: Constable Country

Constable Country

Constance Street: Irish Channel

Constantinople: Orient-Express; Stamboul; Sublime Porte, the

Constitution: Old Ironsides

Constitution Hill: Hyde Park Corner

Constitution State, the

Contemporary Art, Institute of: Back Bay

Continent, the

Continental Congress: Birthplace of American Liberty

Continental Divide, the

Continental Divide: Rockies, the

Continental Shelf

Convent Garden: Covent Garden

Cook, Captain: Pig Island

Cook, Captain James: Botany Bay

Cook Islands: Polynesia

Coonskin Library

Cooper's Creek: Channel country

Cooperstown, New York: Birthplace of Baseball

Copacabana

Copenhagen: Christiana; King's City; Sound, the; Tivoli Gardens

Copley Square: Back Bay

Copper Belt, the

Corinth, Gulf of: Aetolia

Corinth, Isthmus of: Peloponnese, the

Corinth: Peloponnese, the

Corio, Ann: Gaiety, the

Cornhill: Bank, the

Corniche: French Riviera, the

Cornish Riviera, the

Cornmarket Street: Carfax, the

Cornwall: Cornish Riviera, the; Land's End to John o' Groat's House; Lizard, the; Southwest, the, 2; Stannaries, the; Tintagel; West Country, the

Coromandel Coast, the

Costa Blanca: Costa Brava, the

Costa Brava, the

Costa Brava: Blackpool

Costa del Crime

Costa del Sol: Blackpool; Costa Blanca; Costa Brava, the

Costa Geriatrica, the

Costa Smeralda

Côte d'Azur: Provence; South of France, the

Côte des Allemands: German Coast

Côte d'Or

Cotswold: Broadway, 3

Cotswolds: Wolds, the

Cottesmore: Shires, the

Cottonopolis

Country of the Thousand Lakes

County Hall: South Bank, the

Courrèges: Faubourg St Honoré, Rue du

Courtauld Institute of Art: Somerset House

Court of Star Chamber: Star Chamber

Court Street: Cobble Hill

Covent Garden: Bow Street; Halles, les

Coventry: West Midlands, the

Coventry Gaol: Coventry

Coward, Noël: Paper Mill Playhouse

Cowes Week: Island, the, 1

Cracker State, the

Cradle of Aviation

Cradle of Civilization, the

Cradle of Liberty, the

Cradle of Liberty: Faneuil Hall

Craig, James: New Town, the

Creek: Trail of Tears

Crescent City

Cretan colony: Atlantis

Crewe

cricket: Hambledon

cricket ground: Lord's

criminal: Bellevue

Crippen, Dr.: Old Bailey

Critias: Atlantis

Croatia: Balkans, the

'Croatoan': Lost Colony, the

Crockern Tor: Stannaries, the

Crockett, Davy: Alamo, the

Crofton: Devils Nest

Cromwell: Coventry

Cromwell Road: Kensington

Cross, the: King's Cross, 2
Croydon: London '
Crystal Palace
Cuba: Queen of the Antilles
C.U.B.S.: Wrigleyville
Cuckold's Point: Pool of London, the
cuckoo clocks: Black Forest, the
Cumberland: Westmorland
Cumberland Gap
Cumberland Mountains: Appalachian Mountains
Cumbernauld: Silicon Glen
Cumbria: Cumberland; Furness; Lake District, the; Northwest, the, 1; Westmorland; Windscale
cummings, e. e.: Minsky's
Curtiss, Glenn Hammond: Cradle of Aviation
Curzon Street: Mayfair
Customhouse Street: Storyville
Cutler's Company: Elephant and Castle
cutlery: Sheffield of Germany
Cymbarka: Hapsburg lip
Cymry: Cambria
Cyrus the Great: Persia
Czechoslovakia: Bohemia; Iron Curtain, the; Sudetenland, the
Côte de Beaune: Côte d'Or
Côte de Nuits: Côte d'Or
D.S.N.C.O.
'Dad and Dave': Snake Gully
Daimaru: Causeway Bay
Dakota, the: West Side, 1
Dakota
Dales, the
Dales: Broad Acres, the; Ridings, the
Daley, Richard J.: South Side
Dallas: Big D; Big Tex; Dallas Book Depository; Silicon Prairie
Dallas Book Depository
'Dallas of the North': Granite City, the
Dalmatia
Dames at Sea: Off Broadway, Off-Off Broadway
Dana, Charles A.: Windy City
Danube River: Orient-Express
Dare, Virginia: Lost Colony, the
Dark and Bloody Ground State, the

Dark Continent, the
Dark Peak: Peak District, the
Darlinghurst: King's Cross, 2
Darling River: Bourke
Dartmoor: Moor, the; Stannaries, the
Darwin: Capricornia; Leaping Lena; Never Never; Track, the
da Serra, José Correa: City of Magnificent Distances, the
David, King: City of David, the
Davies, Marion: Dakota, 2
Davis Park: Fire Island
Davy Jones's locker
Dawson Creek, British Columbia: Alcan Highway
Dawson Island: Tierra del Fuego
Dayton, Ohio: Birthplace of Aviation
DC-3: Gooney Bird
Dead Bastard: Shepheard's Hotel
Dead Heart of Australia, The: Center, the
Dead Sea: Palestine; West Bank, the
Dean, Penny: Channel, the
Dearborn, Henry: Fort Dearborn
Death Valley: Land of Little Rain
Deccan, the
Deccan: Hindustan
Declaration of Independence: Birthplace of American Liberty; Keystone State
Dedham Vale: Constable Country
Deep South, the
Dee River: Offa's Dyke; Wirral, the
Defence, Ministry of: Whitehall
de Gaulle, Charles: Orly
DeKoven Street: Mrs O'Leary's Barn
Delancey Street: Lower East Side
Delaware: Atlantic States; Blue Hen State; Delmarva Peninsula; First State; Mason-Dixon Line; New Sweden; Northeast, the, 2; Thirteen Original Colonies
Delmarva Peninsula: Tidewater Virginia
Demetrius I: Colossus of Rhodes
de Mille, Cecil B.: Grauman's Chinese Theater
Dempsey, William Harrison 'Jack': Jack Dempsey's
Denmark: Christiana; European Economic Community, the; Jutland; King's City;

Scandinavia; Scandinavian Shield, the; Sound, the; Tivoli Gardens
Denmark Street: Tin Pan Alley
Denver: Home of the Cheeseburger; Mile High City
Den vita staden: White City, 2
Derby: Epsom; North, the, 1
Derbyshire: Midlands, the; North, the, 1; Peak District, the
deregulation: Big Bang, the
Derry: Six Counties, the
Derwentwater: Lake District, the
Desborough: Chiltern Hundreds, the
Descent into the Maelstrom, A: Maelstrom, the
Desert Song, The: Paper Mill Playhouse
Desolation Island: Tierra del Fuego
Detroit: Motown; Ren Cen
Deux Magots, les: Left Bank, the
Devil's Island
Devils Nest
Devon: Cornish Riviera, the; Main Line; Moor, the; Southwest, the, 2; Stannaries, the; West Country, the
Devon Riviera: Cornish Riviera, the
Devonshire: Dartmoor; Shires, the; Torquay
Devonshire Place: Baker Street
Diamantina River: Channel country
Diamond City
diamond market: 47th Street; Hatton Garden
Dickens, Charles: Little Britain
Diddy wa Diddy
Dijon: Côte d'Or
Dillinger, John: Biograph Theater
dingoes: Dog Fence, the; wire marvel, the
dinosaur of darkness
Dismal Swamp, the
Disneyland
District of Columbia: City of Magnificent Distances, the; East, the, 1; Foggy Bottom; Great Dismal; Wilderness City
Dix, John A.: Albany Regency
Dixie
Dixieland: Dixie
Dixon, Jeremiah: Dixie; Mason-Dixon Line

Dockland: Chinatown, 2; Isle of Dogs, the; Limehouse; Printing House Square; Ronan Point
Dodge City, Kansas: Boot Hill
dog days
Doges' Palace: Bridge of Sighs, 1
Dog Fence, the
dog pound: Battersea
Dogs, Isle of: Billingsgate; Dockland
Dog Star: dog days
Doldrums, the
dollar: baloney dollar
Dôme, le: Left Bank, the
Domesday Book: Hants
Dominicans: Blackfriars
Domus Aurea
Donald Duck: Disneyland
Doncaster: Ridings, the
Donner, George and Jacob: Donner Pass
Donner Pass
doodlebugs
Doolittle, Gen. James P.: Shangri-La, 2
Dorchester: Park Lane
Doré, Gustave: East End
Doris: Aetolia
Dormitory of New York, the
Dorset: South, the, 2; Southwest, the, 2; Tolpuddle; Wessex; West Country, the
do the Block: Block, the
Doubleday, Abner: Birthplace of Baseball
double nickel
Douglas Park: West Side, 2
Dover, Straits of: Dover
Dover: Cinque Ports, the; Old Kent Road, the; White Cliffs, the
Down: Six Counties, the
Down East
Downing Street: Whitehall
downtown
down under
Doyle, Arthur Conan: Baker Street
Dr. Brighton
Dracula: Transylvania
Drain, the
Drake Hotel: Magnificent Mile, the
Dream Millions: Lasseter's Reef
Drennan, William: Emerald Isle, the
Dreyfus, Alfred: Devil's Island

Driver, William: Old Glory
drought: dust bowl, the
drug traffic: Kowloon City
Drury Lane
Drury Lane Theatre: Drury Lane
Dry Guillotine: Devil's Island
Dubai: Trucial States, the
Duberger: D.S.N.C.O.
Dudley: Black Country, the
Duffy Square: Broadway, 1
Dukeries, the
Dumfries: City of St Michael, the
dundrearies
Dunedin: Four Main Centres, the
Dung: Jamdung
Dunhill: Fifth Avenue
Dunkirk: mosquito armada
Duomo: Giotto's Tower
Durgin Park
Durham: Northeast, the, 1
dusky diamonds
Düsseldorf: Rhineland, the
dust bowl, the
Dutch: Frogland
Dvořák, Anton: New World, the
Dying Bastard: Shepheard's Hotel
Dynamite Decade
Ealing
Earl of Munster: Iron Curtain, the
Earl's Court: Bayswater; Kangaroo Valley
earthenware industry: Potteries, the
East, the: North, the, 3; Orient, the; Spice
    Islands, the; West, the, 1
East Africa
East African Community: East Africa
East and West India Docks: Dockland
East Anglia: Broads, the; Constable Coun-
    try; Midlands, the; Naze, the; South,
    the, 2; Wash, the
East Bengal: Pakistan
East Bergholt: Constable Country
East Berlin: Berlin Wall, the; Unter den Lin-
    den
Eastbourne: Beachy Head; Costa Geriatrica,
    the
Eastchester Bay: Hell Gate

East End: Bow; City, the; Isle of Dogs, the;
    Limehouse; London; Tower Hamlets;
    West End, the; Whitechapel
East Enders: Dockland
Easter Island: Polynesia
Eastern bloc: East, the, 2; West, the, 1
Eastern Desert: Western Desert, the
Eastern Europe: Iron Curtain, the
Eastern Hemisphere: Old World, the; Ori-
    ent, the; West, the, 1
East European Communism: Bamboo Cur-
    tain, the
East Germany: Berlin Wall, the; Brocken;
    Iron Curtain, the; Oder-Neisse Line,
    the; Prussia; Sudetenland, the; Weimar
Easthampton: Hamptons, the
East India: East Indies, the
East India companies: Coromandel Coast,
    the
East India Company: East Indies, the
East India Docks: Isle of Dogs, the
East Indies, the
East Indies: Indies, the; Spice Islands, the
East Midlands, the
East Midlands: Rutland; Soke of Peterbor-
    ough, the
East Midlands Airport: Lincolnshire
East Pakistan: Pakistan
East Prussia: Polish Corridor, the
East Riding: Ridings, the
East River: Brooklyn; Brooklyn Bridge; East
    Side; Hell Gate; Lower East Side; Man-
    hattan; West Side, 1
East Side: Clock at the Astor, Biltmore; Lit-
    tle Italy; Park Avenue; West Side, 1
East Village, the
'East-West talks': East, the, 2
Ebbets Field: Brooklyn
Ebbw River: Valleys, the
Ebbw Vale: Valleys, the
E-boat alley
Ebro River: Iberia
Eclogues: Arcadia
Eddystone Light
Edgbaston
Edinburgh: Athens of the North, the; Auld
    Reekie; Firth of Forth Bridge; Heart of
    Midlothian, the; Highlands, the; Inns of

Court and Chancery; Lowlands, the;
Morningside; New Town, the; North
Britain; Queen of the North; Royal
Miles, the; Silicon Glen; St Andrews
Edinburgh Castle: Royal Miles, the
Edinburgh Tolbooth: Heart of Midlothian,
the
Edward, the Black Prince: Principality, the
Edward I: Charing Cross
Edward III: Principality, the; woolsack, the
Edwards, J. G.: Hawkeye State
Edward VII, King: Royal Borough, the
EEC: European Economic Community, the;
Snake, the
Egypt: City of the Sun, the; Gaza Strip, the;
Middle East, the; Near East, the; North
Africa; Western Desert, the
Egyptian: Barbary Coast, the
Egyptian Theater: Grauman's Chinese Thea-
ter
Eiffel Tower: Blackpool
Eighth Avenue: 42nd Street; Broadway, 1;
Chelsea, 2; Columbus Circle; Garment
District; Hub of New York City;
Madison Square Garden
Eire
Eisenhower, Dwight D.: Camp David; Eisen-
hower Platz
Eisenhower Platz
El Dorado
Eleanor Cross: Charing Cross
Elephant and Castle: Bakerloo; Walworth
Road
El Greco: Prado, the
Ellesmere Port: Wirral, the
Ellice Islands: Polynesia
El Salvador: Casa Oscar Romero
Ely, bishops of: Hatton Garden
Ely: Isle of Ely, the
Ely Place: Hatton Garden
Élysée Palace: Champs Élysées, the
Embankment, the
Embankment: Charing Cross
Embankment Station: Embankment, the
Embarcadero, the
Embassy Row
Emerald Isle, the
Empire City

Empire State, the
Empire State Building: Chrysler Building
Empty Quarter, the
'Empty State Building': Empire State Build-
ing
England: Acemannes burh; Albion; Ashes,
the; Avebury; Backbone of England,
the; Banbury Cross; Beachy Head; Big
Bang, the; Black Country, the; Black
Friday, 2; Blackpool; Bognor Regis;
Bournemouth; Bourneville; Bridge of
Sighs, 4; Broad Acres, the; Broads, the;
Broadway, 3; Bullring, the; Burton
upon Trent; Camberley; Camelot, 1;
Cheltenham; Cinque Ports, the; Cornish
Riviera, the; Costa Geriatrica, the; Cot-
tonopolis; Coventry; Cowes Week;
Crewe; Cumberland; Dartmoor; Dorset;
Dover; East Anglia; East Midlands, the;
Edgbaston; Epsom; Etruria; Fens, the;
Flixborough; Furness; Garden of Eng-
land, the; Geordieland; Glastonbury;
Golden Mile, the; Granta; Green Belt;
Gretna Green; Hambledon; Hand-
sworth; Hants; Hastings; Holland, 2;
Huntingdonshire; Isle of Athelney, the;
Isle of Ely, the; Isle of Thanet, the;
Jarrow; John Bull; Kemp Town; Kes-
teven; Lake District, the; Land's End to
John o' Groat's House; Lanes, the;
Lantern of England; Law Courts, the;
Lindsey; Little Britain; Lizard, the;
Loamshire; Marches, the, 1;
Mayflower; Melton Mowbray; Mercia;
Merseyside; Middlesex; Midlands, the;
Milton Keynes; Moor, the; Mother of
Parliaments, the; Mummerset; Naze,
the; Needles, the; New Forest; Newmar-
ket; Nore, the; North, the, 1; North
Britain; Northeast, the, 1; Northwest,
the, 1; Offa's Dyke; Old Dart, the; Old
Dominion; Old Sarum; Oxbridge; Pan-
tiles, the; Peacehaven; Peak District,
the; Piccadilly, 2; Piltdown man; Pom-
pey; Pool, the, 1; Porton Down; Potteries, the; Principality, the; Ridings,
the; Roedean; Royal Borough, the;
Rugby; Rutland; Salop; Sandringham;

Second City; Seven Sisters; Shambles, the; Shires, the; Soke of Peterborough, the; Solent, the; Southeast, the; Southwest, the, 2; Spaghetti Junction; Stannaries, the; Strawberry Fields; Surrey; Telford; Thames Valley, the; Tintagel; Tolpuddle; Torquay; Tower Bridge; Tunbridge Wells; Tyneside; United Kingdom, the; Wash, the; Weald, the; Wessex; West Country, the; West Midlands, the; Westmorland; White Cliffs, the; Wigan; Windscale; Wirral, the; Wolds, the; woolsack, the
England-Australia test cricket: Ashes, the
English Channel: Channel, the; Chunnel, the; Dover; Eddystone Light; Island, the, 1; White Cliffs, the
English Midlands: Arden
English Rugby Football Union: Twickenham
Enigma: Coventry
Epirus: Aetolia
Epsom
Epsom Downs: Epsom
Epsom salts: Epsom
Equality State, the
Equatorial Guinea: Guinea
Equites: Violet-Crowned City, the
Erechtheum
Ericson, Leif: Vinland
Erie, Lake: Clinton's ditch
Erie Canal: Clinton's ditch; Gateway of the West
Erin: Hibernia
'Eros': Piccadilly Circus
Erzgebirge: Sudetenland, the
Esplanade Avenue: French Quarter, the
Esquiline: Seven Hills, the
Essex: Constable Country; East Anglia; Home Counties, the; Naze, the; Southeast, the
Essex County: Northeast Kingdom
Essex Street Market: Lower East Side
Estonia: Baltic States
Eternal City, the
Ethiopia: Abyssinia; Horn of Africa, the; Ogaden, the
Et in Arcadia ego: Arcadia
Eton

Etruria
eucalyptus: Mallee, the
Eucla: Nullabor Plain
Eucliffe
Euphrates River: Fertile Crescent, the; Hanging Gardens of Babylon; Mesopotamia
Eurasia: Far North, the; Laurasia
Eureka flag: Eureka Stockade
Eureka Stockade
Euroa: Kelly Country
Euromarket: European Economic Community, the
Europe: Anatolia; Arctogaea; Balkans; Black Death, the; Channel, the; Continent; Eurasia; Flanders; German Ocean, the; Low Countries, the; Mauve Decade, the; West, the, 1
European Economic Community, the
European Economic Community: Continent; green pound
European Monetary System: Snake, the
Eu Tong-sen: Eucliffe
Evangeline: Acadia
Evanston: North Side
Everglades: Alligator Alley
executions, public: Tyburnia
Eyre Highway: Nullabor Plain
'Fabian of the Yard': Yard, the
Faculty of Advocates: Inns of Court and Chancery
Fairbanks, Alaska: Alcan Highway
Fairfax Avenue: Miracle Mile; Sunset Boulevard
Falkland Islands, the
Falls Road: Andersonstown; Shankill Road
Falmouth: Cornish Riviera, the
Faneuil Hall: Durgin Park; Freedom Trail; Haymarket, the; Quincy Market
Fannie Mae
Far East, the
Far East: East, the, 2; Honkers; Levant, the; Middle East, the; Orient, the
Farm, the
Far North, the
Far North Side: North Side
Far Southeast Side: Pullman; South Side
Far South Side: Navy Pier; South Side

Foggy Bottom
Foley Square: Chinatown, 1
Folies Bergère
Folkestone: Chunnel, the
Fontainebleau
Fontainebleau Hotel
Fontainebleau Palace: Fontainebleau Hotel
food market: Halles, les
Forbidden City, the
Ford, Henry: tin Lizzie
Ford's Theatre
foreign embassies: Embassy Row
Foreigner State, the
Foreign Ministry, French: Wilhelmstrasse,
    the
Foreign Ministry, German: Wilhelmstrasse,
    the
Foreign Office: Whitehall
Forest Hills: Queens
Forest Hills Tennis Club: Forest Hills
Forest Lawn
Formosa
Forster, E. M.: Bloomsbury
Fort Dearborn
Fort Dearborn massacre: Fort Dearborn
Forth, River: Lowlands, the
Fort Knox
Fort Laramie, Wyoming: Bozeman Trail
Fort Leavenworth, Kansas: Santa Fe Trail
Fort McHenry
Fortnum & Mason: Jackson's of Piccadilly
Fortnum & Mason: Fred's; Piccadilly, 1
Fort Smith, Arkansas: Chisholm Trail
Fort Towson, Indian Territory: Chisholm
    Trail
Fort Tryon Park: West Side, 1
Fort Vancouver: Oregon Trail
Fort William: Black Hole (of Calcutta);
    Glencoe; Glens, the
'Fountainblue': Fontainebleau Hotel
Four Main Centres, the
Fourth Avenue: Park Avenue
42nd Street: 42nd Street
47th Street
foxhunting: Melton Mowbray
France: Camargue, the; City of Five Flags;
    City of Light, the; Cockpit of Europe,
    the; Côte d'Azur; Côte d'Or; European

Economic Community, the; Flanders;
    Fontainebleau; French Riviera, the;
    Frogland; Grand Corniche; Green Ven-
    ice; Landes, the; Languedoc; Little Brit-
    ain; Mississippi Bubble; no man's land;
    Old Dominion; Peninsula, the; Pro-
    vence; South of France, the; Vichy
Francis I: Fontainebleau
Franco, Francisco: Guernica
Frankfurt: Oder-Neisse Line, the
Franklin, Benjamin: Freedom Trail; Gulf
    Stream
Franz Ferdinand, Archduke: accidental war,
    the
Frederick III: Hapsburg lip
Frederick the Great of Prussia: Bayreuth
Fred's
Freedom Trail
Freemantle: Free-O
Free-O
Freeport, Maine: L. L. Bean
Free World, the
Fremantle: Fremantle doctor, the
Fremantle doctor, the
French Foreign Office: Quai d'Orsay, the
French Guiana: Devil's Island
Frenchman Flat: Nevada Proving Grounds
French National Assembly: Quai d'Orsay,
    the
French Quarter, the
French Riviera, the
French Riviera: Cornish Riviera, the; Côte
    d'Azur
Friedrichstrasse: Checkpoint Charlie
friendliness: Main Street
Friendly Confines, the
Friml, Rudolf: Paper Mill Playhouse
Frisco: Los Angeles
Frobisher, Sir Martin: Northwest Passage,
    the
Frogland
Frogtown
'From the New World': New World, the
frost dates: Iron Men of May
Frozen Wilderness, the
Fry, Roger: Bloomsbury
Fuengirola: Costa del Sol
Fujairah: Trucial States, the

Fulham: King's Road
Funfair: Battersea
'fun for all the family': Minsky's
Furness
G. I. Joe: Tommy (Atkins)
Gabba, the
Gaiety, the
Gaiety Delicatessen
Gaiety Theatre: Broadway, 1
Galloping Gertie
Galloway, Mull of: Galloway
Galloway: City of St Michael, the
Gambia: Senegambia
Gambia River: Senegambia
Gamblers Express
Game-cock State, the
Ganges River: Hindustan
gangsters: Roaring Twenties, the
Garden, the: Covent Garden; Madison
　　Square Garden
Garden of England, the
Garden of France, the
Gardiner Bay: Island, the, 2
Garfield, James A.: Mother of Presidents;
　　Ohio's Jewels
Garfield Park: West Side, 2
Garigliano River: Mezzogiorno, the
Garment District: Barbican, the; Fashion
　　Avenue
garment industry: Manhattan
Garnett, David: Bloomsbury
garo: Karoo, the
Garrick, David: Adelphi, the
Garryowen
Gateway Arch
Gateway of the West, the
'gateway to the Highlands, the': Highlands,
　　the
'Gateway to the West': Cumberland Gap;
　　Gateway Arch
Gatwick Airport
gay: Boystown
Gay Nineties, the
Gaza Strip, the
Gdańsk: Polish Corridor, the
Genesis rock
Genghis Khan: Mongolia; Tartary
gentleman in black velvet, the

Geordieland: Northeast, the, 1; Tyneside
Geordies: Northeast, the, 1
George, David Lloyd: Limehouse
George, Lake: Hudson River
George Cross, the: George Cross Island
George Cross Island
George III: Buck House
George IV: Brighton; King's Cross, 1
George V: Bognor Regis
George VI: Sandringham
George Washington Bridge: West Side, 1
Georgia: Atlantic States; Blue Ridge Moun-
　　tains, the; Cracker State; Deep South,
　　the; Iberia; South, the, 1; Thirteen
　　Original Colonies
Georgina River: Channel country
German Coast
German Democratic Republic: Berlin Wall,
　　the
German Ocean, the
German Southwest Africa: Namibia
Germany: accidental war, the; Cockpit of
　　Europe, the; East Indies, the; Oder-
　　Neisse Line, the; Palatinate, the; Polish
　　Corridor, the; Rhineland, the; Sheffield
　　of Germany; Sudetenland, the; Unter
　　den Linden; Weimar
Gerrard Street: Chinatown, 2
Gerry and the Pacemakers: Merseyside
Gershwin, George and Ira: Lower East Side
Gervais: blackthorn winter
Ghan, the
Ghana: Slave Coast, the; Sudan, the
Ghirardelli Square
Gib
Gibraltar: Costa del Sol; Gib; Pillars of Her-
　　cules, the; Rock, the
Gibraltar in the Pacific
Gibraltar of America, the
Gibraltar of the North
Gilbert Islands: Micronesia
Gillespie, Dizzy: Birdland
Gimbels: Filene's Basement; Macy's
Gimbels Basement: Gimbels
Ginnie Mae
Ginza, the
Giotto's Tower

'Girl in the Red Velvet Swing, The':
   Madison Square Garden
Gissing, George: Grub Street
Giurgin: Orient-Express
'Give My Regards to Broadway': Herald
   Square
Gladstone, W. E.: Albany
Glamorous Glennis
Glasgow: Bearsden; Charing Cross, 2;
   Clydeside; Gorbals, the; Lowlands, the;
   Sauchiehall Street; Silicon Glen; Tros-
   sachs, the; Venice of the West
Glastonbury
Glastonbury Tow: Glastonbury
Glencoe, Massacre of: Glencoe
Glencoe
Glendale: Forest Lawn
Glen Eagles: Glens, the
Glenfiddich: Glens, the
Glengarry: Glens, the
Glen More: Glens, the
'Glen of Weeping': Glencoe
Glenrothes: Silicon Glen
Glenrowan: Kelly Country
Glenrowan Hotel: Kelly Country
Glens, the
Glitter Gulch
Globe theatre: Bankside
Gloucester
Gloucestershire: Cheltenham; West, the, 2;
   West Country, the
GNMA: Ginnie Mae
Goa: Malabar Coast, the
Godiva, Lady: Coventry
God's acre
God's Own Country
Goethe, Johann von: Weimar
Golconda
Gold Coast: Cabrini-Green Public Housing
   Project; Lake Shore Drive; Slave Coast,
   the
Golden Chersonese, the
Golden Crescent, the
Golden Gate City, the
Golden Horn, the
'Golden House': Domus Aurea
Golden Mile, the
Golden Mile: Blackpool

Golden Triangle, the
Golden Triangle: Golden Crescent, the, 2
Golders Green
goldmining: Joburg; Rand, the
Goldsmith, Oliver: Liberty Hall
golf: R & A, the; St Andrews
Golgotha
Gómez, Arturo: Big Mac, the
Gomez Object: Big Mac, the
Gondwanaland: Pangaea
gone for a Burton: Burton upon Trent
Gong, the
Gooney Bird
Gorbals, the
Gordon Square: Bloomsbury
Gorki, Maxim: Gorkii
Gorkii
Gotham: Neasden
Gould, Jay: Black Friday, 3
Government Center: Scollay Square
Government National Mortgage Association:
   Ginnie Mae
Governor: Jockey Club
Goya, Francisco de: Prado, the
GP: Jeep
Graceland Cemetery: North Side
Graces: Violet-crowned City, the
Grampian Mountains: Highlands, the
Granada: Alhambra
Grand Banks: Atlantic Provinces, the
Grand Central: East Side
'Grand Central Station': Grand Central
Grand Central Terminal: Grand Central;
   Park Avenue
Grand Corniche
Grand National, the
Grand Strand
Grand Union Canal: Little Venice
Granite City, the
Grant, Duncan: Bloomsbury
Grant, Ulysses S.: Grant's Tomb; Mother of
   Presidents; Ohio's Jewels
Granta
Grant's Tomb: West Side, 1
Grauman, Sidney: Grauman's Chinese Thea-
   ter
Grauman's Chinese Theater
Gravelly Hill: Spaghetti Junction

Gravesend
Graveyard of the Atlantic, the
Gray's Inn: Inns of Court and Chancery
Gray's Inn Road: Printing House Square
Great Australian Bight: wire marvel, the
Great Britain: Britain; Cambria; City of Five
Flags; England; Land's End to John o'
Groat's House; Little Britain; Mistress
of the Seas; North Britain
Great Chicago Fire: Holy Name Cathedral;
Mrs O'Leary's Barn; Water Tower;
West Side, 2
Great Depression: Empire State Building;
Jarrow; Roaring Twenties, the
Great Dismal
Great Dismal Swamp National Wildlife Ref-
uge: Dismal Swamp, the
Greater London: Britain; London
'Greatest Show on Earth, The': Madison
Square Garden
Great Exhibition of 1851: Crystal Palace;
Kensington
Great Expectations: Little Britain
Great Glen: Glens, the
Great Karoo: Karoo, the
Great Ouse River: Fens, the; Wash, the
Great Sandy Desert: Empty Quarter, the
Great Scotland Yard: Scotland Yard
Great South Bay: Fire Island
Great South Beach: Fire Island
Great St Mary's: Golgotha, 2
Great Valley: Appalachian Mountains
Great Wen, the
Great White Way: Herald Square
Great Windmill Street: Windmill Theatre,
the
Greece: Aetolia; Arcadia; Balkans, the; Cra-
dle of Civilization; European Economic
Community, the; Peloponnese, the;
Rumelia; Violet-crowned City, the
Greek Street
Greek Town: West Side, 2
Green, Adolph: Greenwich Village
Green Belt
Greene, Graham: Stamboul
Greenham Common
'Greenham Women': Greenham Common
Greenland: Far North, the

Green Mountains: Appalachian Mountains
Greenock: Clydeside
green pound
green room
Greenstone Church: Pullman
Green Venice
Greenwich: Isle of Dogs, the
Greenwich Mean Time: Greenwich Observa-
tory
Greenwich Observatory
Greenwich Village: Near North Side
Gregory, J. W.: Centre, the
Gretna Green
greyhound racetrack: Harringay
Greymouth: barber, the
Grimethorpe
Grimethorpe Collier Band: Grimethorpe
Grosvenor: Belgravia
Grosvenor House: Park Lane
Grosvenor Square: Berkeley Square; Eisen-
hower Platz; Mayfair
'groupers': Fire Island
Groves of Academe
Grub Street
Guam: Micronesia
Gucci: Fifth Avenue
Guernica
Guerrière: Old Ironsides
Guggenheim Museum: Fifth Avenue
Guiana
Guiana Highlands: Guiana
Guinea, Gulf of: Guinea
Guinea: Guinea; White Man's Grave, the
Guinea-Bissau: Guinea
Guinea Pig State, the
Guinness, Alec: Ealing
Gulf, the
Gulf & Western building: Columbus Circle
Gulf of Carpentaria: Gulf, the
Gulf of Mexico: Gulf, the; Mosquito Coast
Gulf States, the: Gulf, the; Middle East, the
Gulf Stream: Gulf, the
gully winds
GUM: Red Square
gun: big Bertha; peacemaker, the, 1
Gundagai: Snake Gully
gunfights: Boot Hill
Gunga Din: Aldershot

Gunn, Mrs Aeneas: Never Never
gun that won the west, the
Guyana: Guiana
Gwalior: Native States, the
Gwynedd: Snowdonia
gypsy cabs: Pak Pai
Hadrian: Hadrian's Wall
Hadrian's Wall: England
Hague, the: Holland, 1
Haight-Ashbury
half-timbered houses: magpie houses
Haliç: Golden Horn, the
Halifax: Hay, Hell, and Booligal
Hall, Sir Benjamin: Big Ben
Halles, les
Halsted Street: West Side, 2
Hambledon
Hamburg: Reeperbahn, the
Hamlet: Sound, the
Hammacher-Schlemmer
Hammerstein II, Oscar: Ol' Man River
Hammondsport, New York: Cradle of Aviation
Hampshire: Aldershot; Bournemouth; Camelot, 1; Hambledon; Hants; New Forest; South, the, 2; Wessex
Hampstead: Caledonian Market; Camden Town; Golders Green; Highgate; Kilburn
Hampstead Heath: Archway; Hampstead; Highgate
'Hampstead intellectual': Hampstead
Hampton Roads, Virginia: *Monitor* and *Merrimack*
Hamptons, the
Hamtonshire: Hants
Hamtun: Hants
Hanbridge: Five Towns, the
Hancock, Tony: Windmill Theatre, the
Handsworth
Hanford, Washington: First Atomic City
Hanging Gardens of Babylon
Hanging Rock
Hanging State, the
Hanley: Five Towns, the
Hannan, Paddy: Golden Mile, the, 2
Hants.
Hantshire: Hants

Happy Valley
Hapsburg empire: Bohemia
Hapsburg lip
Harbour Bridge: Luna Park
Hardcastle, Squire: Liberty Hall
Harding, Warren G.: Mother of Presidents
Hardy, Thomas: Adelphi, the; Dorset; Wessex
Haringey: Harringay
Harlem: Broadway, 1; Fifth Avenue; Madison Avenue; Park Avenue; Spanish Harlem; Sugar Hill
Harlem River: Broadway, 1; Featherbed Lane; Harlem; Hell Gate; Manhattan; Park Avenue; Sugar Hill
Harley Street: Baker Street; Wimpole Street
Harmon: Hudson River
Harringay
Harringay Stadium: Harringay
Harris and Lewis: Western Isles, the
Harrison, Benjamin: Mother of Presidents
Harrison, William Henry: Mother of Presidents
Harrods: Knightsbridge
Harrogate: Ridings, the
Harrow
Harrow-on-the-Hill: Harrow; Middlesex
Harry Percy of the Union
Harry's American Bar
Hart, Steve: Kelly Country
Hartford, Huntington: Columbus Circle
Hartford: Charter Oak City, the
Hartford College: Bridge of Sighs, 4
Harumi Street: Ginza, the
Harvard College: Harvard Yard
Harvard Hall: Harvard Yard
Harvard Yard
Harz Mountains: Brocken
Hasidic Jews: Brooklyn
Hastings, Battle of: Hastings
Hastings, Rape of: Rapes
Hastings: Cinque Ports, the
Hatteras, Cape: Outer Banks
Hatton Garden
Hausa: Sudan, the
Hausmann, Baron Georges Eugène: Opéra, l'
haute couture: Faubourg St Honoré, Rue du

Hispanic: Barrio, the
Hitler, Adolf: Polish Corridor, the; Sudeten-
land, the; Weimar
HMMWV: Hummer, the
Hog Butcher for the World
Hokonui
Holborn: Camden Town; Chancery Lane
Holborn Circus: Hatton Garden
Holland: Spice Islands, the
Holland Park: Notting Hill
Holliday, Judy: Greenwich Village
Hollywood: Beverly Hills; Broadway, 1;
Grauman's Chinese Theater; Hollywood
and Vine; West, the, 3
Hollywood and Vine
Hollywood Boulevard: Grauman's Chinese
Theater; Hollywood and Vine
Hollywood Road: Cat Street; Ladder Street
Holmes, Oliver Wendell: Old Ironsides
Holmes, Sherlock: Baker Street
Holtby, Winifred: Ridings, the
Holy Grail: Glastonbury
Holy Land, the
Holy Land: Palestine
Holy Mother of the Russians
Holy Name Cathedral
Holy Roman Empire: Holland, 1; Palati-
nate, the; West, the, 1
Holyroodhouse: Royal Miles, the
Holy Sepulchre: Holy Land, the, 1
Home Counties, the
Home Counties: Metroland; Middlesex;
Southeast, the; Surrey
'Home of the America's Cup': State of Ex-
citement, the
Home of the Cheeseburger, the
homosexuals: Boystown; Castro, the; Fire Is-
land
Honduras: Mosquito Coast
hong: Jardine Matheson
Hong Kong: Barefoot Cantonese; Cathay;
Cat Street; Causeway Bay; Eucliffe;
Happy Valley; Hennessy Road; Honk-
ers; Ice House Street; Jardine Mathe-
son; Jockey Club; Kowloon City;
Ladder Street; Macao; Pak Pai;
Rednaxela Terrace; Repulsive Bay;
Wanchai; Yun Yuen Sek

Hong Kong and Shanghai Bank: Jockey
Club
Honkers
honky-tonk: Broadway, 2
Hooker, Thomas: Constitution State
Hoosier State, the
hoozer: Hoosier State
Hope, Anthony: Ruritania
Hore-Belisha, Leslie: Belisha beacon
Horne, Donald: Lucky Country, the
Hornet: Shangri-La, 2
Hornet's Nest, the
Horn of Africa, the
Horse Guards: Whitehall
Horse Latitudes, the
horseracing: Newmarket
House, the
Household Cavalry: Whitehall
House of Burgesses
House of Commons: Westminster
House of Lords: House, the; Westminster
House of Representatives: House, the
Houses of Parliament: Smith Square; Trans-
port House
House That Ruth Built
Houston, General Sam: Alamo, the
Houston Street: East Village, the; Greenwich
Village; NoHo
Hove Albion: Albion
Howard, Eddy: Aragon Ballroom
Howe, Julia Ward: Marseillaise of the
Unemotional Yankee
Hub of New York City
Huddersfield: Broad Acres, the; Ridings, the
Hudson, Henry: Northwest Passage, the
Hudson River: Clinton's ditch; Forty-Second
Street; Gateway of the West; Manhat-
tan; Palisades, the; Rhine of America;
West, the, 3; West Point; West Side, 1
Hudson River Valley: Appalachian Moun-
tains
Hudson Street: Greenwich Village
Hughes, Thomas: Rugby
Hull, Hell, and Halifax: Hay, Hell, and
Booligal
Hull: Ridings, the
Hull House: West Side, 2
Humber estuary: North, the, 1

Humber River: North, the, 1; Northumbria
Humberside: Ridings, the; Wolds, the
Humboldt Park: West Side, 2
Hume, David: Athens of the North, the
hundreds: Chiltern Hundreds, the; Rapes
Hungary: Iron Curtain, the; Transylvania
'hunger marches': Jarrow
Hung Mo Gwai: Jackson Road
Huntingdonshire
Hyannisport: Cape, the
Hyde Park: Belgravia; Crystal Palace; Hyde
   Park Corner; Knightsbridge; Number
   One, London; Paddington; Park Lane;
   Rotten Row; South Side; Speakers'
   Corner; Tyburnia
Hyde Park Corner: Number One, London;
   Park Lane; Piccadilly, 1
Hyderabad: Golconda; Native States, the;
   Sodom of India
'hypersonic' aircraft: Orient-Express
Hythe: Cinque Ports, the
Iberia
Iberian peninsula: Iberia; Peninsula, the
Iberville Street: Storyville
Icebox of the United States, the
Ice House Street
Iceland: Scandinavia
'ice saints': blackthorn winter
Idaho: Bozeman Trail; Inland Empire, the
Idlewild: Brooklyn
Idriess, Ion L.: Lasseter's Reef
Île de la Cité: Latin Quarter, the, 1; Marais,
   the
Îles du Salut: Devil's Island
'I'll be seeing you': Abyssinia
Illinois, University of: West Side
Illinois: Egypt; Midwest, the; Mother of
   States; Sucker State
Imperial City: Forbidden City, the
Imperial War Museum: Bedlam
'In' and 'Out', the
In Darkest Africa: Dark Continent, the
Independence, Missouri: Oregon Trail; Santa
   Fe Trail
Independence Hall: Birthplace of American
   Liberty
India: Bhopal; Black Hole (of Calcutta);
   Blighty; Ceylon; City of Palaces, the;

Coromandel Coast, the; Deccan, the;
   East, the, 2; Eurasia; Far East, the;
   Golconda; Gondwanaland; Hindustan;
   Indies, the; Indochina; Khyber Pass,
   the; Malabar Coast, the; Middle East,
   the; Native States, the; Northwest Fron-
   tier, the; Orient, the; Pakistan; raj, the;
   Rann of Kutch, the; Subcontinent, the
Indiana: Hoosier State; Midwest, the;
   Mother of States
Indian-Appian Way
Indian Ocean: Seven Seas, the
Indian-Pacific Railway: Trans-Australian
   Railway
Indian Removal Act: Trail of Tears
Indian States and Agencies: Native States,
   the
Indian summer
Indian Territory: Trail of Tears
Indies, the: East Indies, the
Indochina: Far East, the; Farther India; In-
   dies, the
Indonesia: East Indies, the; Southeast Asia;
   Spice Islands, the
Indore: Native States, the
Indus River: Sind
Inland Empire, the
Inner City: Forbidden City, the
Inner Hebrides: Western Isles, the
Inner Mongolia: Mongolia
Inner Mongolian Autonomous Region: Inner
   Mongolia
Inner Temple: Inns of Court and Chancery;
   Temple, the
Innsbruck, Austria: Brenner Pass
Inns of Court: Chancery Lane; Temple, the
Inns of Court and Chancery
insanity: Bellevue
Interlaken: Bernese Oberland, the
International Cricket Conference: Lord's
International Falls, Minnesota: Icebox of the
   United States
International Herald Tribune: Harry's Amer-
   ican Bar
International House: West Side, 1
Inverness: Capital of the Highlands, the;
   Glens, the; Highlands, the; Northland,
   the

Inverness-shire: Highlands, the
Ion: Violet-Crowned City, the
Iowa: Hawkeye State; Middle Border, the;
    Midwest, the; Outlaw Country
Ipanema: Copacabana, 1
IRA: Andersonstown; Falls Road
Iran: Golden Crescent, the, 1; Gulf, the;
    Middle East, the; Persia
Iraq: Gulf, the; Mesopotamia; Middle East,
    the
Ireland, Northern: Southie
Ireland, Republic of: Eire; Irish Free State,
    the; Province, the
Ireland: Britain; Emerald Isle, the; Erin; Eu-
    ropean Economic Community, the; Hi-
    bernia; Inns of Court and Chancery;
    Old Dominion; United Kingdom, the
Irish Channel
Irish Free State, the
Irish Free State: Eire
Irish Republican Army: Southie
Iron Bridge: Telford
Iron City
Iron Curtain, the
Iron Curtain: Bamboo Curtain, the; Yerevan
Iron Curtain countries: Iron Curtain, the
Iron Men of May
Irving, Washington: Alhambra; Gotham
Isis
Islam: Golden Crescent, the, 1; Sudan, the
Islamic states: Middle East, the
Island, the
Islas Malvinas: Falkland Islands, the
Islay: Western Isles, the
Isle of Athelney, the
Isle of Dogs, the
Isle of Ely, the
Isle of Thanet, the
Isleworth: Middlesex
Islington: Camden Town
Islington High Street: Angel, the
Israel: Gaza Strip, the; Land of Milk and
    Honey; Levant, the; Middle East, the;
    Palestine; West Bank, the
Istanbul: Golden Horn, the; Orient, the;
    Orient-Express; Stamboul
Italian Riviera, the
Italian Riviera: Cornish Riviera, the

Italy: Brenner Pass; Bride of the Sea; Bridge
    of Sighs, 1; Campagna, the; City of
    Lilies, the; City of the Seven Hills, the;
    Etruria; European Economic Commu-
    nity, the; Italian Riviera, the; Jewel of
    the Adriatic, the; Leghorn; Marches,
    the, 2; Mezzogiorno, the; Naples; Papal
    States, the; Piovro; Rialto; Scylla and
    Charybdis; Seven Hills, the
Ivory Coast: Guinea; Slave Coast, the
jack: Union Jack, the
Jack and Charlie's 21 Club: '21' Club
Jack Dempsey's
Jackson, Mississippi: Chimneyville
Jackson Heights: Queens
Jackson Park: Museum of Science and In-
    dustry; South Side; White City, 1
Jackson Road
Jackson's of Piccadilly
Jackson Square: French Quarter, the
Jack the Ripper: Whitechapel
Jacob's Pillow
Jaggers, Mr: Little Britain
Jamaica: Cockpit Country, the; Jamdung;
    Mo Bay
Jamdung
James I: Addled Parliament; Newmarket
James II: Charter Oak City; Glencoe
James River: Tidewater Virginia
Jamestown, Virginia: House of Burgesses
jammed down: Jamdung
Jammu and Kashmir: Native States, the
Japan: East, the, 2; Far East, the; Land of
    the Rising Sun, the; Third World, the;
    Tidal Basin; West, the, 1
Japung: Japan
Jardine Matheson: Jockey Club
Jarrow
Jarrow march: Jarrow
Java: Coromandel Coast, the; East Indies,
    the; Queen of the Eastern Archipelago
Jeep
Jefferson, Thomas: Billingsgate; Fort Dear-
    born; Mother of Presidents
Jefferson Memorial: Tidal Basin
Jehovah: Adonai
Jenkins, Roy: Limehouse
Jericho

Jericho Street: Jericho
Jerilderie: Kelly Country
Jermyn Street: Simpson's of Piccadilly
Jerome Avenue: Featherbed Lane
Jersey City: Palisades, the
Jerusalem: City of David, the; Holy Land,
    the, 1; Salem; Wailing Wall, the
Jewel of the Adriatic, the
Jih-pun: Japan
Joburg
Jockey Club
Johannesburg: Joburg; Rand, the
John, Augustus: Chelsea, 1; Fitzrovia
John, King: Runnymede
John Bull
John Bull's Other Island: John Bull
John Hancock Center: Magnificent Mile,
    the; Playboy Building; Sears Tower
John Hancock Tower: Back Bay
John Lewis: Oxford Street
John o' Groat's house: Land's End to John
    o' Groat's House
Johnson, Dr: Grub Street
Johnson, Samuel: Happy Valley
Johnstown
Jolly Roger, the
Jolson, Al: Lower East Side
Jones, Inigo: Covent Garden
Jordan: Middle East, the; Trans-Jordan;
    West Bank, the
Jordan River: West Bank, the
Joseph of Arimathea: Glastonbury
Juan-les-Pins: French Riviera, the
Jubilee Market: Covent Garden
Judaism: Wailing Wall, the
Judea: Holy Land, the, 1
Jugoslavia: Dalmatia
Juilliard School: Broadway, 1
Jumbo State, the
Jumping Frog Jubilee: Frogtown
Jungle, The: Union Stockyards
Junkers: Prussia
Jupiter: Capitoline, the; Red Spot, the
Jura: Western Isles, the
Jutes: Jutland
Jutland
Jylland: Jutland

Kalgoorlie: Golden Mile, the, 2; Tea and
    Sugar; Trans-Australian Railway
Kampuchea, People's Republic of: Cambo-
    dia
Kanal, der: Channel, the
Kanem: Sudan, the
Kangaroo Valley: Earl's Court
Kansas: Battleground of Freedom; Bleeding
    Kansas; Kansas Bibles; Navel of the
    Nation; Squatter State; West, the, 3
Kansas Bibles
Kansas City: West, the, 3
Kansas-Nebraska Bill: Battleground of Free-
    dom
Kansas Pacific Railroad: Chisholm Trail
Karelia
Karelia Suite: Karelia
Karoo, the
Kasbah, the
Kashmir: Northwest Frontier, the; Pakistan
Katherine: Big Run, the
Kattegat Strait: Sound, the
Kaufman, George S.: Round Table at the
    Algonquin
Keats, John: Middlesex
Keller, Helen: City of Kind Hearts
Kelly, Ed: South Side
Kelly, Ned: Kelly Country
Kelly Country
Kelly Gang: Kelly Country
Kemp, Thomas: Kemp Town
Kemp Town
Kennedy, Edward: Chappaquiddick
Kennedy, Jacqueline: Camelot, 2
Kennedy, John F.: Camelot, 2; Chappaquid-
    dick; Dallas Book Depository
Kennedy, John F. Airport: Brooklyn
Kennedy, Robert F.: Chappaquiddick
Kennelly, Martin: South Side
Kensington: Chelsea, 1; Shepherd's Bush
Kensington and Chelsea: Royal Borough, the
Kensington Gardens: Bayswater; Kensington;
    Number One, London; Rotten Row
Kensington Palace: Royal Borough, the
Kensington-upon-Thames: Royal Borough,
    the
Kent: Dover; Garden of England, the; Home
    Counties, the; Isle of Thanet, the;

London; Pantiles, the; Rapes; South-
east, the; Tunbridge Wells; Weald, the;
White Cliffs, the
Kentucky: Appalachia; Bible Belt; Bluegrass
State; Commonwealth; Dark and
Bloody Ground State; Fort Knox; Mid-
west, the; Mother of States; South,
the, 1
Kenya: East Africa
Kern, Jerome: Ol' Man River; Paper Mill
Playhouse
Kesteven
Kew Gardens
Key, Francis Scott: Fort McHenry
Key: Kew Gardens
Key City, the
Keynes, John Maynard: Bloomsbury
Keystone State, the
Key West: Boston Post Road
Khmer Republic: Cambodia
Khrushchev, Nikita S.: Camp David
Khyber Pass, the
Khyber Pass: Northwest Frontier, the
Kilburn: Maida Vale
Kilgallen, Dorothy: Stork Club
Kimberley, South Africa: Big Hole, the
kimberlite: Big Hole, the
King, Wayne: Aragon Ballroom
King Arthur: Camelot, 1
King Country, the
King Country: Main Trunk, the
King George V Docks: Dockland
King Kong: Empire State Building
King of Kings: Grauman's Chinese Theater
King's Chapel: Freedom Trail
King's City, the
King's College: Backs, the
Kings County: Brooklyn; Manhattan
King's Cross: Battlebridge; Islington;
Pentonville
King's Cross Station: Battlebridge; King's
Cross, 1; Somers Town
Kingsford Smith
King's inns: Inns of Court and Chancery
King's Road: Chelsea, 1
Kingsway: West End, the
King William Street: London Bridge
Kipling, Rudyard: Gloucester

Kiribati: Micronesia
'Knickerbocker, Cholly': Stork Club
Knightsbridge: Harrods; Hyde Park Corner;
Sloane Square; West End, the
Knightsbridge Barracks: Rotten Row
knights of the shires: Shires, the
Knights Templars: Inns of Court and Chan-
cery; Temple, the
'Knocked 'em in the Old Kent Road': Old
Kent Road, the
Knype: Five Towns, the
Kocourkov
Kodak City
Kokomo, Indiana: City of Firsts
Kola Peninsula: Lapland; Scandinavian
Shield, the
Kongens By: King's City
Kopechne, Mary Jo: Chappaquiddick
Korea: Far East, the
Kowloon City
Kreml: Kremlin, the
Kremlin, the
Kremlin: Red Square
'Kremlinology': Kremlin, the
'Kremlin watchers': Kremlin, the
Krishna River: Coromandel Coast, the
Krupp, Friedrich Alfred: big Bertha
Kurfürstendamm, the
Kuwait: Gulf, the
Kwazulu: Zululand
L.A.: Los Angeles
L. L. Bean
la Botte: Montmartre
Labour Party: Smith Square; Transport
House; Walworth Road
La Brea Avenue: Miracle Mile
La Brea Tar Pits
Lachlan River: Riverina, the
Ladder Street
'Lady in Red': Biograph Theater
Lady of the Lake: Trossachs, the
Lafayette Street: Lower East Side; NoHo;
SoHo
La Guardia, Fiorello H.: Broadway, 1; Gai-
ety, the; Minsky's
La Guardia Airport: Queens
Lake Country: Lake District, the
Lake District, the

Lake District: Furness
Lake Erie: Gateway of the West
Lake Havasu City: London Bridge
Lakeland: Lake District, the
'Lake poets': Lake District, the
Lake Pontchartrain: Florida Parishes
Lakes, the: Lake District, the
Lake Shore Drive: Gold Coast; McCormick Place
Lakeview: Near North Side
Lallands: Lowlands, the
Lamb Cutlets Reform: Reform Club, the
Lambeth: Bedlam; Brixton; Oval, the
Lambeth Conference: Lambeth
'Lambeth degrees': Lambeth
Lambeth Palace: Lambeth
Lambeth Walk: Lambeth
Lammermuir hills: Southern Uplands, the
Lancashire: Blackpool; Cottonopolis; North, the, 1; Northwest, the, 1; Shires, the; Westmorland
Landes, the
Land of a Million Elephants
Land of Cakes
'Land of Fire': Tierra del Fuego
Land of Flowers, the
Land of Little Rain
Land of Look Behind: Cockpit Country, the
Land of Milk and Honey, the
Land of Promise
Land of the Midnight Sun, the
Land of the Rising Sun, the
Land of the Saints, the
Land's End
Lane Crawford's: Causeway Bay
Lanes, the
Languedoc: South of France, the
Languedoc-Roussillon: Languedoc
Lantern of England
Lanvin: Faubourg St Honoré, Rue du
Lanxang: Land of a Million Elephants, the
Laos: Golden Triangle, the, 1; Indochina; Land of a Million Elephants, the; Southeast Asia
Lapland: Land of the Midnight Sun, the
Lapps: Lapland
La Rochelle: Green Venice
Lashio: Burma Road, the

La Spezia: Italian Riviera, the
Lasseter, Henry Lewis Bell: Lasseter's Reef
Lasseter's Last Ride: Lasseter's Reef
Lasseter's Reef
Last Chronicle of Barset, The: Barset
Las Vegas, Nevada: Glitter Gulch; Strip, the, 1
lathe: Rapes
Latin Quarter: Left Bank, the; Old Quebec (Vieux-Québec)
Latin Quarter (Quartier Latin)
Latter-Day Saints: Land of the Saints
Latvia: Baltic States
'Laugh-In': Burbank
Laurasia: Pangaea
Laval University: Latin Quarter, the, 2
Law, John: German Coast; Mississippi Bubble
Law Courts, the
Law Courts: Chancery Lane
Lawnmarket: Royal Miles, the
lawn tennis championships: Wimbledon
Lawrence: Bleeding Kansas
Law Society: Chancery Lane
Lawson, Henry: Bourke
lawyers: Chancery Lane
LAX
Leadbelly: Greenwich Village
Leaping Lena
Lear, Edward: Coromandel Coast, the
Leavenworth, Kansas: Cottonwood City
Lebanon: City of the Sun, the; Levant, the; Middle East, the
Lee, Gypsy Rose: Gaiety, the
Leeds: Broad Acres, the; Dales, the; Ridings, the
Left Bank, the
Left Bank: Deux Magots, les; Latin Quarter, the, 1; Montmartre; Quai d'Orsay, the
Leghorn
Leicestershire: Belgravia; Lincolnshire; Melton Mowbray; Midlands, the; Rutland; Shires, the
Leicester Square
Leinster: Province, the
Le Moyne, Jean Baptiste: French Quarter, the
Lenin, V I: Leningrad

Leningrad
Lenin Mausoleum: Red Square
Lennon, John: Dakota, 2
Lenox Avenue: Harlem
Leofric: Coventry
Leon & Eddie's
lesbian: Boystown
Les Saules: D.S.N.C.O.
Levant, Oscar: Hollywood; Round Table at
    the Algonquin
Levant, the: Near East, the
Lever House: East Side
Lewis, Sinclair: Main Street
Lewis, Wyndham: Fitzrovia
Lewis and Harris: Western Isles, the
Lexington: Birthplace of American Liberty
Lexington Avenue: Chrysler Building
Lexington Commons: Birthplace of Ameri-
    can Liberty
Lexington Hotel: Loop, the
Lhasa: Forbidden City, the
Liberty Hall
Liberty Island: Bedloe's Island
Liberty of the Clink, the: Clink Street
Libya: Maghreb; Middle East, the; Near
    East, the; North Africa
Libyan desert: Western Desert, the
life vest: Mae West, 1
Light, Colonel: Parklands
lighthouse: West Side, 1
Limehouse: Bow; Chinatown, 2; East End;
    Pool of London, the
'Limehouse Four': Limehouse
Lincoln, Abraham: Ford's Theater
Lincoln: Lindsey
Lincoln Center: Broadway, 1; Forty-Second
    Street
Lincoln Center for the Performing Arts:
    West Side, 1
Lincoln Park: Near North Side; North Side;
    Old Town
Lincolnshire: Fens, the; Flixborough; Hol-
    land, 2; Kesteven; Lindsey; Midlands,
    the; Wash, the
Lincolnshire Wolds: Wolds, the
Lincoln's Inn: Chancery Lane; Inns of Court
    and Chancery
Lincoln Square: Broadway, 1; West Side, 1

Lindbergh, Charles A: Bourget, le
Lindesnes: Naze, the
Lindsay, Joan: Hanging Rock
Lindsey
Lindy's
Lisburn: Maze, the
Lithuania: Baltic States
Little Britain: Paternoster Row
Little Cuba
Little Dipper
Littlehampton
Little Italy
Little Karoo: Karoo, the
'Little Red Lighthouse, The': West Side, 1
Little Siberia
Little Venice: Maida Vale
Little Vietnam
Liverpool: Merseyside; North, the, 1; North-
    west, the, 1; Pool, the, 1; Strawberry
    Fields; Toxteth; Wirral, the
Liverpool Street Station: Petticoat Lane
Livingston: Silicon Glen
Livorno: Leghorn
Lizard, the
Llanfairpwllgwyngill:
    Llanfairpwllgwyngillgogerychwyrn-
    droblllllantysiliogogogoch
Llanfairpwllgwyngillgogerychwyrn
Lloret de Mar: Costa Brava, the
Lloyd's
Lloyds Harbor: North Shore, 1
Lloyd's of London: City, the; Lloyd's
Loamshire
Loch Ness: Glens, the; Highlands, the
Locris: Aetolia
Lofoten Islands: Maelstrom, the
Loire River: Garden of France, the
Lombards: Lombard Street
Lombard Street: Bank, the
Lombardy: Lombard Street
London, centre of: Charing Cross
London, City of: Bank, the; Bank of Eng-
    land, the; Barbican, the; Bart's; Bed-
    lam; Billingsgate; Blackfriars; Bow;
    City, the; City College; Derry; Dock-
    land; Drain, the; Fleet Street; Grub
    Street; Little Britain; Lloyd's; Lombard

Street; London; London Bridge; Mansion House, the; Marylebone; Mincing Lane; Old Bailey; Old Lady of Threadneedle Street, the; Paternoster Row; Petticoat Lane; Printing House Square; Smithfield; Square Mile, the; Throgmorton Street; West End, the; Westminster

London, County of: London

London, East: Bethnal Green in the Sun

London, Inner: London

London, Lord Mayor of: Bank, the; Mansion House, the

London, Outer: London

London, Tower of: Billingsgate; Chinatown, 2; Dockland; East End; Tower, the; Tower Hamlets; Whitechapel

London: Abbey Road; Adelphi, the; Albany; Aldermaston; Aldershot; Ally Pally; Angel, the; Archway; Army & Navy Stores; Ascot; Ashes, the; Athenaeum, the; B, the; Bagshot; Baker Street; Bankside; Battersea; Battlebridge; Bayswater; Belgravia; Berkeley Square; Big Bang, the; Big Ben; Billingsgate; Blackfriars; Black Friday, 1; Blackwall Tunnel; Bloomsbury; Bond Street; Borough, the; Bow; Bow Street; Bray; Brixton; Buck House; Burlington House; Bush House; Caledonian Market; Camden Lock; Camden Town; Carey Street; Carlton Club, the; Carnaby Street; Centre Point; Chancery Lane; Charing Cross; Chelsea, 1; Chiltern Hundreds, the; Chinatown, 2; City, the; City College; City of Masts, the; City of the Midnight Sun, the; Clapham; Clink Street; Clubland, 1; Covent Garden; Crystal Palace; Dockland; Downing Street; Drury Lane; Ealing; Earl's Court; East End; Eisenhower Platz; Elephant and Castle; Embankment, the; Eton; Fitzrovia; Fortnum & Mason; Fred's; Gatwick Airport; Golders Green; Golgotha, 1; Gravesend; Great Wen, the; Greek Street; Green Belt; Greenwich Observatory; Grosvenor Square; Halles, les;

Hampstead; Harley Street; Harringay; Harrods; Harrow; Hatton Garden; Heathrow; Henley; Highgate; Holy Land, the, 2; Home Counties, the; Hyde Park Corner; 'In' and 'Out', the; Isle of Dogs, the; Islington; Jackson's of Piccadilly; Jermyn Street; Kangaroo Valley; Kensington; Kew Gardens; Kilburn; King's Cross, 1; King's Road; Knightsbridge; Lambeth; Law Courts, the; Leicester Square; Limehouse; Little Venice; Lord's; Maida Vale; Marylebone; Mayfair; Metroland; Middlesex; Neasden; Newgate Prison; Nine Elms; North, the, 1; Notting Hill; Number 10; Number One, London; Old Kent Road, the; Old Vic, the; Orient-Express; Oval, the; Oxford Street; Paddington; Pall Mall; Park Lane; Paternoster Row; Pentonville; Petticoat Lane; Piccadilly, 1; Piccadilly Circus; Pimlico; Pool of London, the; Portland Place; Portobello Road; RADA; Reform Club, the; Ronan Point; Rotten Row; Royal Borough, the; Runnymede; Sandhurst; Savile Row; Savoy, the; Scotland Yard; Seven Dials; Seven Sisters; Shaftesbury Avenue; Shepherd Market; Shepherd's Bush; Simpson's (in the Strand); Simpson's of Piccadilly; Sloane Square; Slough; Smoke, the; Soho; Somerset House; Somers Town; South Bank, the; Southeast, the; Speakers' Corner; Star Chamber; St James's; St John's Wood; Stoke Mandeville; Strawberry Hill; Surrey; Swiss Cottage; Swone-one; Temple, the; Thames Valley, the; Thorney Island; Thunderer, the; Tin Pan Alley; Tower Hamlets; Transport House; Turnabout, the; Tussaud's Waxworks Museum, Madam; Twickenham; Tyburnia; V & A, the; Vauxhall; Victoria; Wardour Street; Warren Street; Waterloo; Watford; Wembley Stadium; West End, the; Westminster; Whitechapel; Whitefriars; Whitehall; Wimbledon; Wimpole Street;

Windmill Theatre, the; Woolwich;
Yard, the
London Bridge: Borough, the; Clink Street;
Elephant and Castle; Pool of London,
the; Tower Bridge
London County Council: London
Londonderry: Derry
London Dock: Dockland
London Docklands Development Corpora-
tion: Dockland
London Labour and the London Poor: East
End
London Stock Exchange: House, the
London Underground: Archway; Bakerloo;
Drain, the; Metroland; Temple, the
London University: Bloomsbury
London Wall: no man's land
Lone Star of Civilization, the
Lone Star State, the
Long Bay Gaol: Bay, the
Longfellow, Henry Wadsworth: Acadia;
Gloucester
Long Island: Brooklyn; Brooklyn Bridge;
East River; Fire Island; Hamptons, the;
Hell Gate; Island, the, 2; Narrows, the;
Queens; Ridings, the
Long Island City: Queens
Long Island Sound: Hell Gate; Island,
the, 2; North Shore, 1
Long Kesh: Maze, the
Longshaw: Five Towns, the
Longton Potteries, the: Five Towns, the
Looe: Cornish Riviera, the
Lookout Mountain: Battle above *or* in the
Clouds
Loomis, R. S.: Camelot, 1
Loop, the
Loop: Billy Goat Tavern; Holy Name Cathe-
dral; Magnificent Mile, the; Marshall
Field's; McCormick Place; Mrs
O'Leary's Barn; Navy Pier; Near North
Side; North Side; Sears Tower; South
Side; West Side, 2
López de Santa Ana, Antonio: Alamo, the
Lord, Thomas: Lord's
Lord Chancellor: woolsack, the
Lord Mayor: City, the
Lord's: Ashes, the

Lord's Cricket Ground: Ashes, the
Los Angeles: Beverly Hills; Burbank; Forest
Lawn; Grauman's Chinese Theater;
Hollywood; Hollywood and Vine; L.A.;
La Brea Tar Pits; LAX; Malibu; Mega-
lopolis; Miracle Mile; San Fernando
Valley; Second City; Strip, the, 2; Sun-
set Boulevard; Watts
Los Angeles International Airport: LAX
Los Angeles Times: Los Angeles
Lost Colony, the
Lost Horizon: Shangri-La, 1
Lothian: Heart of Midlothian, the
Louisiana: Crescent City; Deep South, the;
Florida Parishes; French Quarter, the;
German Coast; Great South Gate; Gulf,
the; Irish Channel; South, the, 1;
Storyville; Sugar State
Louisiana Avenue: Irish Channel
Louisville: Fort Knox
Louis XIV: Père Lachaise
Louvre, the: Halles, les; Opéra, l'
Low Countries, the
Lower East Side, the: East Village, the
Lower East Side: Five Points
Lower Guinea: Guinea
Lower Lascar Row: Cat Street
Lower Palatinate: Palatinate, the
Lower Pool: Pool of London, the
Lower Regent Street: Piccadilly Circus
Lower Thames River Street: Billingsgate
Lower West Side: Hull House; West Side, 2
Lowlands, the
Lowlands: Highlands, the; Lowlands, the;
Southern Uplands, the
Low Peak: Peak District, the
Low Sellafield: Windscale
Lowther hills: Southern Uplands, the
Lucky Country, the
Ludgate Circus: Fleet Street
Ludgate Hill: Old Bailey
Luna Park
lunatic asylum: Bloomingdale's
Lutine bell
Luxembourg: Benelux; European Economic
Community, the; Low Countries, the
Lynn: North Shore, 2
Lyons, Leonard: Stork Club

Macao
Macaulay, Thomas: Albany
MacDonald, Ballard: Blue Ridge Mountains, the
Macdonalds: Glencoe
MacDowell, Edward Alexander: MacDowell Colony
MacDowell Colony
Macedon: Colossus of Rhodes
Macedonia: Balkans, the
Mackenzie Range: Rockies, the
Macy's: Broadway, 1; Filene's Basement; Gimbels; Herald Square
'Mad Avenue': Madison Avenue
Madeleine, Boulevard de la: Maxim's
Mademoiselle Fifi: Minsky's
Madhya Pradesh: Bhopal
Madison, James: Mother of Presidents
Madison Avenue: Clock at the Astor, Biltmore; Rodeo Drive; Stork Club
Madison Square: Broadway, 1; Madison Avenue
Madison Square Garden
Madrid: Prado, the
Maelstrom, the
Mae West
Mafeking
Mafia: Mezzogiorno, the
Mafikeng: Mafeking
Magdalen College: High, the
Magellan, Strait of: Tierra del Fuego
Magellan: Tierra del Fuego
Maghreb
Magic Valley
Magna Carta: Runnymede
Magnificent Mile, the: Near North Side; Playboy Building; Water Tower
magpie houses
Maida: Maida Vale
Maida Vale
Maidenhead: Thames Valley, the
Maine: Boston Post Road; Down East; East, the, 1; New England; Northeast Corridor
Mainland, the
Main Line
Main Street: Boston Post Road; Camino Real, el; Main Street

Main Street of America, the
Main Trunk, the
Majestic, the: West Side, 1
Majorca: Costa Brava, the
Malabar Coast, the
Málaga: Costa del Sol
Malaya: Indochina
Malay Archipelago: East Indies, the; Far East, the; Oceania; Southeast Asia
Malay Peninsula: Golden Chersonese, the
Malaysia: East Indies, the; Southeast Asia
Mali: Timbuktu
Malibu
Malibu Beach Colony: Malibu
Mall, the: St James's
Mallee, the
Mallee gate: Taranaki
Mallee root: Mallee, the
Malmö: Sound, the
Malory, Sir Thomas: Camelot, 1
Malta: George Cross Island
Maluku: Spice Islands, the
Malvinas, Islas
Mamertus: blackthorn winter
Manche, la: Channel, the
Manchester: Cottonopolis; North, the, 1; Northwest, the, 1; Piccadilly, 2; Wigan
Mandalay: Burma Road, the
M & S
Manhattan: Broadway, 1; Brooklyn; Brooklyn Bridge; brownstone; Dormitory of New York; East River; East Side; Harlem; Harlem River; Hudson River; McAdoo Tubes; NoHo; Off Broadway, Off-Off Broadway; Queens; See also *New York City* in the Index.; SoHo; Third Avenue; Wall Street; West, the, 3
Manhattan Island: Bedloe's Island
'Manhattan Project': Stagg Field
Manila: Pearl of the Orient
man-in-the-street: Wigan
Manitoba: Prairie Provinces, the
Mann's Chinese Theater: Grauman's Chinese Theater
'man on the Clapham omnibus': Clapham
Manship, Paul: Rockefeller Center
Mansion House, the

Mansion House: Bank, the; Mansion House,
the
Maori: Aotearoa; Polynesia
Maoriland: Pig Island
Maoriland Worker: Maoriland
Marais, the
Marais Poitevin: Green Venice
Marbella: Bethnal Green in the Sun; Costa
del Crime; Costa del Sol; Morgue Mo-
torway
Marble Arch: Marylebone; Oxford Street;
Park Lane; Speakers' Corner; Tyburnia
Marblehead: North Shore, 2
Marcantonio, Vito: Harlem; Spanish Harlem
Marches, the
Marches, Welsh: Marches, the, 1
Marcus Vipsanius Agrippa: City of Palaces,
the
Marcy, William L.: Albany Regency
Mare Nostrum
Margate: Isle of Thanet, the
Marguery, the: East Side
Marianas Islands: Micronesia
Maritime Provinces: Atlantic Provinces, the
Market Street: Path of Gold
Marks and Sparks: M & S
Marks and Spencer: Baker Street; M & S;
Oxford Street
Marlborough, Duke of: Blenheim Palace
Marlow: Thames Valley, the
Marmara, Sea of: Golden Horn
Maroons: Cockpit Country, the
Marquesas: Polynesia
Marquette Park: West Side, 2
Marree: Ghan, the
Mars: Red Planet, the
Marseillaise of the Unemotional Yankee
Marseilles: Côte d'Azur; French Riviera, the;
South of France, the
Marsh, Reginald: Minsky's
Marshall Field's
Marshall Islands: Micronesia
Martha's Vineyard: Chappaquiddick
Marx, Groucho: Grant's Tomb
Marx, Karl: Highgate
Maryburn: Marylebone
Maryland: Atlantic States; Camp David;
Cockade State; Delmarva Peninsula;

District of Columbia; Dixie; Fort Mc-
Henry; Mason-Dixon Line; Northeast,
the, 2; Old Line State; Queen State;
Shangri-La, 3; Thirteen Original Colo-
nies
Marylebone
Marylebone Cricket Club: Lord's
Marylebone Road: Tussaud's Waxworks
Museum, Madam
Mascot: Kingsford Smith
Mason, Charles: Dixie; Mason-Dixon Line
Mason-Dixon Line: North, the, 2; South,
the, 1
Massachusetts: Bay Horse; Beantown; Birth-
place of American Liberty; Boston Post
Road; Cape, the; Chappaquiddick; City
of Kind Hearts; Commonwealth; Cradle
of Liberty; East, the, 1; Gloucester; Ja-
cob's Pillow; *Mayflower*; Megalopolis;
Mohawk Trail; New England; Old Col-
ony State; Thirteen Original Colonies
Massachusetts Avenue: Embassy Row
Massachusetts Bay Colony: Old Colony
State
Massachusetts Hall: Harvard Yard
Massachusetts Turnpike: Route 128
Matheson's: Jardine Matheson
Maunee River: Indian-Appian Way
Mauretania: Western Desert, the
Mauve Decade, the
Maxim's
Maxwell Street: West Side, 2
May, Elaine: Second City
Mayfair: Belgravia; Berkeley Square; Gros-
venor Square; Park Lane; Savile Row;
Shepherd Market; Soho; St James's;
West End, the
Mayflower
Mayhew, Henry: East End
Maze, the
McAdoo, William Gibbs: McAdoo Tubes
McAdoo Tubes
McClure, Sir Robert: Northwest Passage, the
McCormick, Cyrus: North Side
McCormick Place
McKim, Mead, and White: Madison Square
Garden
McKinley, William: Mother of Presidents

McOuat, Jimmy: White Otter Castle
Med, the
'Medical Center, the': West Side, 1
Medina: City of Refuge, the; City of the
Prophet, the
Mediterranean coast: Grand Corniche
Mediterranean Sea: Anatolia; Costa Blanca;
Costa Brava, the; Costa del Sol; Costa
Smeralda; Côte d'Azur; Fertile Cres-
cent, the; French Riviera, the; George
Cross Island; Gib; Levant, the; Mare
Nostrum; Med, the; Orient, the; Pales-
tine; Pillars of Hercules, the; Seven
Seas, the; South of France, the; West,
the, 1
Megalopolis: Northeast Corridor
Melanesia: Australasia; Micronesia; Oceania;
Polynesia
Melbourne: Block, the; Capricornia; Collins
Street; Farm, the; Leaping Lena;
Smoke, the; Tullamarine
Melbourne House: Albany
Melbourne University: Shop, the
Melting Pot, the
melton: Melton Mowbray
Melton Mowbray
Melton pad: Melton Mowbray
Mendoza, Argentina: Christ of the Andes
Menton: French Riviera, the; Grand Cor-
niche
Mercia, king of: Offa's Dyke
Mercia: East Anglia
Merion: Main Line
Mersey River: Merseyside; Wirral, the
Merseyside
Mersey sound: Merseyside
Merthry Tydfil: Valleys, the
Mesopotamia: Babylon
Messina, Strait of: Scylla and Charybdis
Met, the: Scotland Yard
Metroland, Margot: Metroland
Metroland
Metropole Hotel: Loop, the
Metropolitan Line: Metroland
Metropolitan Museum of Art: Fifth Avenue;
West Side, 1
Metropolitan Opera: Forty-Second Street
Metropolitan Opera House: Broadway, 1

Metropolitan Police: Scotland Yard
Metropolitan Railway: Metroland
Mexico: Big Bend
Mezzogiorno, the
Miami: Alligator Alley; Little Cuba
Miami Beach: Fontainebleau Hotel
Michigan, Lake: Aragon Ballroom; Gold
Coast; Lake Shore Drive; Navy Pier;
North Side; Old Town; South Side
Michigan: Mother of States; Motown
Michigan Avenue: Magnificent Mile, the
Mickey Mouse: Disneyland
Micronesia: Australasia; Melanesia; Oceania;
Polynesia
Middle Atlantic States: Atlantic States
Middle Border, the
Middle East, the
Middle East: Arabia; East, the, 2; Far East,
the; Near East, the; Orient, the; Pales-
tine; Promised Land, the
Middle Kingdom, the
Middle Passage, the
Middle Rockies: Rockies, the
Middlesbrough: Ridings, the
Middlesex: Home Counties, the; London;
Metroland
Middlesex County Cricket Club: Lord's
Middlesex Street: Petticoat Lane
Middle Temple: Inns of Court and Chan-
cery; Temple, the
Mideast: Middle East, the
Midgetman
Midi, le
Midi, the: South of France, the
Midlands, the: East Midlands, the
Midlands: Five Towns, the; Huntingdon-
shire; Melton Mowbray; Mercia; North,
the, 1; Northeast, the, 1; Potteries, the;
Shires, the; South, the, 2; Watford
Midlothian: Border, the; Heart of Midlo-
thian, the
'Midway, the': South Side
Midway Airport: West Side, 2
Midway Plaisance: South Side; White
City, 1
Midwest, the,
Mies van der Rohe, Ludwig: East Side
Mildura: Sunraysia

Mile End: East End
Mile High City, the
Millburn, New Jersey: Paper Mill Playhouse
Million Dollar Theater: Grauman's Chinese
Theater
Millwall: East End
Millwall Docks: Dockland; Isle of Dogs, the
Milngavie and Bearsden District: Bearsden
Miltiades: Academy, the
Milton, John: Golden Chersonese, the
Milton Keynes
Milton Street: Grub Street
Milwaukee Avenue: West Side, 2
Minch, the: Western Isles, the
minchins: Mincing Lane
Mincing Lane
'Mindy's': Lindy's
Ming Street: Chinatown, 2
Minnenwerfer: moaning Minnie
Minnesota: Middle Border, the; Midwest,
the; Mother of States
Minoan colony: Atlantis
Minsky, Billy, Herbert, Morton, and Abe:
Minsky's
Minsky Brothers' National Winter Garden:
Minsky's
Minsky's
Minster: Shambles, the
Minuit, Peter: Manhattan
Minute Men: Birthplace of American Liberty
Miracle Mile
Mirranpongapongunna Lake:
Taumatawhakatangihangakoauauota-
mateapokaiwhenuakitanatahu
Mississippi: Deep South, the; Gulf, the;
South, the, 1
Mississippi Bubble: German Coast
Mississippi River: Backbone of the Confed-
eracy; Crescent City; dust bowl, the;
Florida Parishes; French Quarter, the;
German Coast; Gibraltar of America;
Irish Channel; Ol' Man River
Mississippi Territory: Mississippi Bubble
Missouri: Bullion State; Gateway Arch; Mid-
west, the; Show Me State
Missouri River: Devils Nest; West, the, 3
Missouri Rockets: Radio City Music Hall
Mistelbach

Mistress of the Seas
Mitchell, David Scott: Mitchell Library
Mitchell Library
Mitsukoshi: Causeway Bay
moaning Minnie
Mo Bay
Mobile: City of Five Flags
model T: tin Lizzie
Mohawk Trail
Mojave Desert: Land of Little Rain
Moldavia: Balkans, the
Moldavian Soviet Socialist Republic: Bessa-
rabia
mole: gentleman in black velvet, the
Moluccas: Spice Islands, the
Monaco: Principality, the
Monash University: Farm, the
Mongolia
Mongolian People's Republic: Mongolia;
Outer Mongolia
Mongols: Mongolia
Monitor and *Merrimack*
Monkey State, the
Monongahela River: Golden Triangle, the, 2
Monopoly: Boardwalk
Monroe, James: Mother of Presidents
Mons: Cockpit of Europe, the
Montana: Bozeman Trail; Inland Empire,
the; Middle Border, the; Northwest,
the, 2
Montauk Point: Island, the, 2
Monte Carlo: French Riviera, the; Grand
Corniche; South of France, the
Monte Cavallo: Quirinal, the
Montego Bay: Mo Bay
Montenegro: Balkans, the
Montmartre: Pigalle
Montparnasse: Left Bank, the
Montreal: City of Saints, the
moonshine: Hokonui
Moor, the
Moore, Henry: Stagg Field
Moorfoot hills: Southern Uplands, the
Moran, Bugs: Loop, the
Morgan, J. P.: Minsky's
Morgue Motorway
Moriches Bay: Fire Island
Moriches Inlet: Fire Island

Mormons: Land of the Saints
Morningside
Morningside Drive: West Side, 1
Morningside Park: Harlem
Morocco: Barbary Coast, the; Kasbah, the;
    Maghreb; North Africa; Pillars of Her-
    cules, the; Western Desert, the
Morris, Edward E: Maoriland
Morris, William: Wardour Street
mortgage belt
Moscow: Gorkii; Holy Mother of the Rus-
    sians; Kremlin, the; Muscovy; Red
    Square; Russia; Siberia
Moses, Robert: Fire Island
mosquito armada
Mosquito Coast
Moss Bros
Moss Brothers: Moss Bros
Mother-in-Law of the Navy
Mother of Parliaments, the
Mother of Presidents
Mother of States
'motor town': Motown
Motown
Mott Haven: Park Avenue
Moulin Rouge: Montmartre
Mount Ebert: Rockies, the
Mount Etna: Atlantis
Mount Everest: Roof of the World, the
Mount Hacho: Pillars of Hercules, the
Mount Helicon: Aganippides, the
Mount Katahdin, Maine: Appalachian Trail,
    the
Mount Snowdon: Snowdonia
Mount Vesuvius: Naples
movie industry: Wardour Street
Mrs O'Leary's barn: West Side, 2
Mt Eden Avenue: Featherbed Lane
Mt Macedon: Hanging Rock
Mt Sinai Hospital: Harlem
Muhammad: Al Borak; City of Refuge, the;
    City of the Prophet, the
Mulberry Street: Little Italy
Mummerset
Municipal Pier: Navy Pier
Munster: Province, the
Murder in the Calais Coach: Orient-Express

Murder on the Orient-Express: Orient-Ex-
    press
Murillo, Bartolomé: Prado, the
Murmansk: Scandinavian Shield, the
Murray River: Riverina, the; Sunraysia
Murray Valley: Riverland, the
Muscle Shoals: Muscle Shoals Area
Muscle Shoals Area
Muscovy
Muses: Aganippides, the; violet-crowned
    city, the
Museum of Science and Industry
music publishing: Manhattan
Muslims: Hindustan
M-X missile: peacemaker, the, 2
Myrtle Beach: Grand Strand
Mysore: Native States, the
Nairn, Ian: subtopia
Nairnshire: Highlands, the
Namib: Namibia
Namibia
Napier, Sir Charles: Sind
Naples, Kingdom of: Mezzogiorno, the
Naples
Napoleon: Peninsula, the; Waterloo
Napoleonic Wars: Maida Vale
Narberth: Main Line
Narmada River: Deccan, the
Narrows, the
Nashville, Tennessee: Natchez Trace
Nassau County: Island, the, 2
Natal: Zululand
Natchez, Mississippi: Natchez Trace
Natchez Trace
National, the: Grand National, the
National Health Service: East Anglia; Wes-
    sex
National Institute of Dramatic Art: NIDA
National Theatre: South Bank, the
National Theatre Company: Old Vic, the
Nation's Most Corrupt State
Native States, the
NATO: Little Siberia
natural gas: Texas Tea
Natural Histories: Albion
Natural History, Museum of: Kensington
Nauru: Micronesia
Naval and Military Club: 'In' and 'Out', the

Navarre: Pamplona
Navel of the Nation, the
Navy Pier
Naze, the
Neal, John: Brother Jonathan
Near East, the
Near East: East, the, 2; Far East, the; Middle East, the; Orient, the
Near North Side: Biograph Theater; Bughouse Square; Cabrini-Green Public Housing Project; Holy Name Cathedral; Lake Shore Drive; Magnificent Mile, the; New Town; North Side; Old Town; Playboy Building; Rush Street; Water Tower; Wrigleyville
Near Northwest Side: West Side, 2
Near Southwest Side: Maxwell Street; Pilsen
Near West Side: Haymarket Square; Hull House; West Side, 2
Neasden
Nebraska: Bad Lands, the; Devils Nest; West, the, 3
Needles, the: Island, the, 1
Neisse River: Oder-Neisse Line, the
Nelson: Woolwich
Nene River: Fens, the; Wash, the
Neogaea
Nepal: Subcontinent, the
Nero: Domus Aurea
Nesbit, Evelyn: Madison Square Garden
Netherlands: Benelux; Diamond City; East Indies, the; European Economic Community, the; Flanders; Holland, 1; Low Countries, the; Venice of the North
Neufchâtel: D.S.N.C.O.
Nevada: Far West, the; Glitter Gulch; Southwest, the, 1
Nevada Proving Grounds
Never Never
New Amsterdam: 42nd Street; Bowery, the; Broadway, 1
Newark, New Jersey: Oranges, the
Newberry, Walter L.: Holy Name Cathedral
New Bond Street: Bond Street
New Brighton: Wirral, the
New Brunswick: Atlantic Provinces, the
New Caledonia: Melanesia
Newcastle, Duke of: Dukeries, the

Newcastle: Hadrian's Wall; Steel City, 1
Newcastle-upon-Tyne: Tyneside
Newcastle-upon-Tyne: Jarrow; Northeast, the, 1
New Covent Garden Market: Nine Elms
New England: Atlantic States; blue laws; Boston Post Road; Brother Jonathan; Cape, the; Iron Men of May
New England Conservatory of Music: Back Bay
New England states: Northeast, the, 2
New England Thruway: Boston Post Road
New Forest
Newfoundland: Atlantic Provinces, the
Newgate Prison: City College; Old Bailey
New Greek Town: West Side, 2
New Grub Street: Grub Street
New Hampshire: Appalachian Mountains; East, the, 1; New England; Thirteen Original Colonies
New Haven, Connecticut: blue laws
New Hebrides: Melanesia
New Holland
New Jersey: Atlantic States; Boardwalk; East, the, 1; Foreigner State; Gamblers Express; McAdoo Tubes; Northeast, the, 2; Palisades, the; Thirteen Original Colonies; West Side, 1
New London Bridge: London Bridge
Newmarket
Newmarket Heath: Newmarket
New Mexico: Rockies, the; Southwest, the, 1; Sunbelt; Sunshine State
New Orleans: Crescent City; French Quarter, the; German Coast; Irish Channel; Storyville
Newport, Rhode Island: America's Cup
New Printing House Square: Printing House Square
New Scotland Yard: Scotland Yard
News of the Screws, the
News of the World: News of the Screws, the
New South Wales: Bananaland; Bondi Beach; Bourke; Dog Fence, the; Gong, the; Hay, Hell, and Booligal; Mitchell Library; NIDA; Premier State, the; Riverina, the; Silver City; Snake Gully; Steel City, 1; Steel City, 2

Noble Square: West Side, 2
NoHo
Nolan, Sidney: Kelly Country
no man's land
non-slave states: Mason-Dixon Line
Nordkalotten: Scandinavian Shield, the
Nore, the
Norfolk, Virginia: Mother-in-law of the
    Navy
Norfolk: East Anglia; Fens, the; San-
    dringham
Norfolk Broads: Broads, the
Norfolk Navy Yard: Mother-in-law of the
    Navy
Norman, Oklahoma: TOTO
Norman: Hastings
Norman Conquest: Wessex
Norman's Woe: Gloucester
North, the: Clubland, 2; Mason-Dixon Line;
    Northeast, the, 1; South, the, 3; West,
    the, 2
North: Midlands, the; North Country, the;
    Northwest, the, 1; South, the, 2;
    Watford
North Adams: Mohawk Trail
North Africa: Black Death, the
North America: Arctogaea; Laurasia; Middle
    Passage, the; Vinland; West, the, 1
Northamptonshire: Lincolnshire; Midlands,
    the; Shires, the; Soke of Peterborough,
    the
North Atlantic: Roaring Forties
North Atlantic Ocean: Herring Pond, the;
    Seven Seas, the
North Auckland: Waitangi
North Britain: Britain
North British Hotel: North Britain
North Carolina: Atlantic States; Dismal
    Swamp, the; Graveyard of the Atlantic;
    Lost Colony, the; Outer Banks; South,
    the, 1; Tarheel State; Thirteen Original
    Colonies
North Country, the
North Dakota: Land of the Dakotas; Middle
    Border, the; Sioux State; West, the, 3
North Downs: Weald, the; White Cliffs, the
Northeast, the
Northeast: Geordieland; Jarrow

Northeast Corridor
Northeast Expressway: North End
Northeast Kingdom
North End
Northern Boulevard: Queens
Northern England: Clubland, 2
northern hemisphere: North, the, 3
Northern Ireland: Andersonstown; Derry;
    Falls Road; Maze, the; Province, the;
    Shankill Road; Six Counties, the
Northern Karoo: Highveld, the; Karoo, the
Northern Rockies: Rockies, the
Northern Territory: Alice Springs; Ayers
    Rock; Big Run, the; Capricornia; Ghan,
    the; Lasseter's Reef; Never Never; Ter-
    ritory, the; Track, the
North Fork: Island, the, 2; North Shore, 1
North Holland: Holland, 1
North Island: King Country, the; Mainland,
    the, 2; Main Trunk, the
Northland, the
North of the Border: Border, the
'north of Watford': Watford
North Pacific Ocean: Seven Seas, the
North Point: Hennessy Road
North Pole
Northport: North Shore, 1
North Rampart Street: French Quarter, the
North Riding: Ridings, the
North River: Manhattan
North Sea: Dales, the; Fens, the; Firth of
    Forth Bridge; German Ocean, the; Jut-
    land; Low Countries, the; Roost, the;
    Wash, the
North Shore: Island, the, 2
North Side: Aragon Ballroom; Gold Coast
*North-South, a program for survival; report
    of:* North, the, 3; South, the, 3
North Uist: Western Isles, the
Northumberland: Northeast, the, 1; North-
    umbria
Northumbria
North Wales: Royal Borough, the
North Wells Street: Old Town
Northwest, the: Crewe; Cumberland; Golden
    Mile, the; Lake District, the; Mersey-
    side; Strawberry Fields; Westmorland;
    Windscale

Old South Meeting House: Freedom Trail
Old State House: Freedom Trail
Old Town: Near North Side; Second City
Old Town School of Folk Music: Old Town
Old Vic, the
Old World, the
O'Leary's barn, Mrs: West Side, 2
O'Leary's cow, Mrs: Mrs O'Leary's Barn
Ol' Man River
Olsen, John: *You Beaut Country*
Oman: Arabia; Gulf, the
One Magnificent Mile: Magnificent Mile, the
Ontario: White Otter Castle
on the wallaby: Wallaby Track
on the wallby track: Wallaby Track
Oodnadatta: Ghan, the
Ootacamund: Deccan, the
OPEC: petro-dollars
Open University: Milton Keynes
Opéra, l'
opera: Covent Garden
opium: Golden Crescent, the, 1; Golden Triangle, the, 1
Orange: Golden Triangle, the, 3
Orange-Green Line: Falls Road
Oregon: Far West, the; Inland Empire, the; Northwest, the, 2; Oregon Trail; Pacific Northwest, the
Oregon Trail: Rockies, the
Öresund: Sound, the
Orient, the: East, the, 2; Levant, the
Oriental Street: Chinatown, 2
Orient-Express: Orient, the; Stamboul
Orient Point: Island, the, 2; North Shore, 1
Orkney Island: Roost, the
Orlando, Florida: Disneyland
Orleans County: Northeast Kingdom
Orly
ortolans: Landes, the
Orwell, George: Wigan
Oswald, Lee Harvey: Dallas Book Depository
Otto I of Bavaria: Disneyland
Ottoman Empire: Bessarabia; Near East, the; Rumelia; Sublime Porte, the
Our American Cousin: dundrearies
'our sea': Mare Nostrum
Outback, the: wire marvel, the

outback: Wallaby Track
Outer Banks
Outer City: Forbidden City, the
Outer Hebrides: Western Isles, the
Outer Mongolia: Mongolia
Outlaw Country
Oval, the
Oval Office
Overend and Gurney: Black Friday, 2
Over South
Ovid: Eternal City, the
Owen, David: Limehouse
Oxbridge
Oxford: Bridge of Sighs, 4; Broad, the; Carfax, the; City of Dreaming Spires; High, the; Isis; Jericho; Thames Valley, the; Turl, the
Oxfordshire: Banbury Cross; Chiltern Hundreds, the; Henley; Midlands, the; Oxon; South, the, 2; Thames Valley, the
Oxford Street: Baker Street; Bloomsbury; Bond Street; Centre Point; Fitzrovia; Mayfair; West End, the
Oxford University: Bodleian Library; House, the; Oxbridge
Oxon.
Oyster Bay: North Shore, 1
Oz
Pacific Northwest, the
Pacific Northwest: Inland Empire, the
Pacific Ocean: Australasia; Northwest Passage, the; Pacific Northwest, the; Russia; Soviet Union, the
Pacific Palisades: Malibu; Sunset Boulevard
Paddington: Bayswater; Little Venice; Paddo; Westminster
Paddington Bear: Paddington
Paddington Green: Paddington
Paddington Station: Maida Vale; Paddington
Paddo
pagoda: Kew Gardens
paille-maille: Pall Mall
Pakistan: Golden Crescent, the, 1; Khyber Pass, the; Native States, the; Northwest Frontier, the; Rann of Kutch, the; Roof

of the World, the; Sind; Subcontinent,
the
Pak Pai
Palace, the: Broadway, 1; Off Broadway,
Off-Off Broadway
palace: Palatine, the
Palace Gardens: Speakers' Corner
Palace of Fine Arts: Museum of Science and
Industry; White City, 1
Palatinate, the
Palatine, Count: Palatinate, the
Palatine, the
Palatine: Seven Hills, the
Palatium: Palatine, the
Palestine, Texas: Homesteader's Paradise
Palestine: Holy Land, the, 1; Near East,
the; Promised Land, the
Palestine Liberation Organization: Palestine
Palisades, the
Palisades: West Side, 1
Pall Mall: Athenaeum, the; Clubland, 1; Re-
form Club, the
Palmer, Potter: North Side
Palmetto Spring: Palm Springs
Palmolive Building: Playboy Building
Palm Springs
Pamirs: Roof of the World, the
Pamplona
Pan Am Building: Grand Central
Pancras: blackthorn winter
Pangaea
Panhandle, the
Pantiles, the
Paoli: Main Line
Paoli Local: Main Line
Papal States, the
Paper Mill Playhouse
Papillon: Devil's Island
Papua New Guinea: Melanesia; Spice Is-
lands, the
Paradise Lost: Golden Chersonese, the
Paramount, the: Broadway, 1
paraplegics: Stoke Mandeville
parfumerie: Faubourg St Honoré, Rue du
Paris: Champs-Élysées, the; City of Light,
the; Deux Magots, les; Dynamite Dec-
ade; Faubourg St Honoré, Rue du; Fo-
lies Bergère; Fontainebleau; George V;

Halles, les; Harry's American Bar;
Latin Quarter, the, 1; Left Bank, the;
Marais, the; Maxim's; Montmartre;
Moulin Rouge; Orient-Express; Orly;
Père Lachaise; Pigalle; Quai d'Orsay,
the; Rodeo Drive
Paris Opera House: Opéra, l'
Park Avenue: East Side; Grand Central;
Harlem; Spanish Harlem
Park Avenue South: Park Avenue
Parkdale
Parker, Charlie 'Bird': Birdland
Parker, Dorothy: Round Table at the Algon-
quin
Parker House, the
Parker House roll: Parker House, the
Parklands
Park Lane: Hyde Park Corner; Mayfair
Park Lane Hotel: Whitefriars
Park Slope: Brooklyn
Park Street Church: Freedom Trail
Parliament, Houses of: Big Ben; Embank-
ment, the; South Bank, the
Parliament: Mother of Parliaments, the;
Westminster
Parliament Square: Downing Street; West-
minster; Whitehall
Parsifal: Bayreuth
Parts of Holland: Holland, 2
Parts of Kesteven: Kesteven
Parts of Lindsey: Lindsey
Pasadena: Crown City of the Valley
passion play: Oberammergau
Passport to Pimlico: Pimlico
Patagonia
Paternoster Row: Little Britain
Paterson, Banjo: Hay, Hell, and Booligal
Path of Gold
Pawleys Island: Grand Strand
Peacehaven
Peace Line: Falls Road
peacemaker, the
Peace People movement: Andersonstown
Peak, the: Peak District, the
Peak District, the
Pearl Harbor: Gibraltar of the Pacific
Pearl of the Orient
Peconic Bay: Island, the, 2

pedestrian crossings: Belisha beacon
Peebles: Border, the
'Peeping' Tom: Coventry
Peers, Edgar Allison: redbrick
Peking: Forbidden City, the
Pekin Street: Chinatown, 2
Peloponnese, the
Peloponnese: Arcadia
Peninsula, the
'peninsula': Golden Chersonese, the
Peninsular War: Peninsula, the
Penn, William: Old Line State; Quaker State
Pennines, the: Backbone of England, the; Dales, the; Peak District, the
Pennsylvania: Appalachian Mountains; Atlantic States; Birthplace of American Liberty; Blue Ridge Mountains, the; City of Brotherly Love, the; Commonwealth; Dixie; East, the, 1; Golden Triangle, the, 2; Johnstown; Keystone State; Mason-Dixon Line; Northeast, the, 2; Quaker State; Rebel Capital; Thirteen Original Colonies
Pennsylvania Station: Grand Central; Madison Square Garden
Pennyfields: Chinatown, 2
Pentagon, the
Pentonville
Pentonville Prison: Pentonville
Pentonville Road: Angel, the; Pentonville
Pepin III, King of the Franks: Papal States, the
Père Lachaise
'perfidious Albion': Albion
Persia
Persian Empire: Persia
Persian Gulf: Arabia; Fertile Crescent, the; Gulf, the; Seven Seas, the; Trucial States, the
Perth, Western Australia: America's Cup; Free-O; Maida Vale
Perth: Fremantle doctor, the; Trans-Australian Railway
Pétain, Marshal Henri: Vichy
Peterborough, New Hampshire: MacDowell Colony
Peters, Bernadette: Off Broadway, Off-Off Broadway

Petersburg, Virginia: Cockade City
petro-dollars
Petrograd: Leningrad
petroleum shortage: double nickel
Petticoat Lane
Philadelphia: Birthplace of American Liberty; City of Brotherly Love, the; Main Line; Rebel Capital
Philippines, the: East Indies, the; Southeast Asia
Philippines: Cat Street; Little Vietnam; Pearl of the Orient
Phoenicia: Fertile Crescent, the
Phoenix: Valley of the Sun, the
Phoenix City
'Physiognomical Haircutting': Columbus Circle
Piaf, Édith: Père Lachaise
Picasso, Pablo: Guernica
Piccadilly: Albany; Bond Street; Fred's; Hyde Park Corner; Knightsbridge; Mayfair; Number One, London; Shepherd Market; St James's; West End, the
Piccadilly Circus: Leicester Square; Piccadilly, 1; Shaftesbury Avenue; Windmill Theatre, the
Piccadilly Street: Burlington House; Fortnum & Mason; 'In' and 'Out', the; Jackson's of Piccadilly; Piccadilly Circus; Simpson's of Piccadilly
Picnic at Hanging Rock: Hanging Rock
Picon, Molly: Lower East Side
Picts: Hadrian's Wall
Piddle: Tolpuddle
Piddlehinton: Tolpuddle
Piddletrenthide: Tolpuddle
Piedmont Region: Blue Ridge Mountains, the; Tidewater Virginia
Piermont, New York: Palisades, the
Pigalle: Montmartre; Moulin Rouge
Pig Island
pig's foot: Cincinnati oyster
Pilgrims: Mayflower
Pillars of Hercules, the
Pillars of Hercules: Atlantis
Pilsen: West Side, 2
Piltdown: Piltdown man
Piltdown man

Pimlico, Ben: Pimlico
Pimlico: Victoria
Pindar: violet-crowned city, the
Pine Gap
'Pines, the': Fire Island
Piovro
'Pirate Coast': Trucial States, the
pirates: Spanish Main, the
pirates' black flag: Jolly Roger
pirate taxis: Pak Pai
Pisco Elqui, Chile: Big Mac, the
Pitcairn Island: Polynesia
Pittsburgh: Golden Triangle, the, 2; Iron
    City; Smoky City; World's Workshop
Pittsfield: Mohawk Trail
Pitt Street
Pitt Street Farmer: Collins Street; Pitt Street
Place de la Concorde: Champs Élysées, the
Place des Armes: French Quarter, the
Place du Tertre: Montmartre
'place of stones': Mafeking
Place Royale: Old Quebec (Vieux-Québec)
Plague: Oberammergau
Plaistow: East End
Plato: Academy, the; Atlantis
Playboy: Gold Coast; Playboy Building
Playboy Building: Magnificent Mile, the
Playboy Mansion: Gold Coast
Plaza, the: Fifth Avenue
Plaza Hotel: Fifth Avenue; Plaza, the
Pleiades: Seven Sisters
Pliny: Albion
PLO: Palestine
plutonium: Windscale
Plymouth: Eddystone Light
Plymouth Colony: Old Colony State
Plymouth of the West, the
Plymouth Rock: *Mayflower*
Poe, Edgar Allan: Maelstrom, the
Pohjoiskalotti: Scandinavian Shield, the
Point Calimere: Coromandel Coast, the
Point o' Woods: Fire Island
poison pill
Poland: Oder-Neisse Line, the; Prussia; So-
    viet Union, the; Sudetenland, the
Polish Corridor, the
Polk Street: Loop, the

'Polly Perkins of Paddington Green': Pad-
    dington
Polo, Marco: Cathay; Orient, the
Polo Lounge: Beverly Hills Hotel
Pol Pot regime: Cambodia
Polynesia: Australasia; Oceania
Pompey
Pompidou Center: Halles, les
Pomponians: Pompey
'Pond, the': Herring Pond, the
Pontalba buildings: French Quarter, the
Pont de la Concorde: Quai d'Orsay, the
Pont de l'Alma: Quai d'Orsay, the
Pool, the
Pool of London, the
Poor Man's Paradise, the
Poplar: East End; Tower Hamlets
popular music: Tin Pan Alley
Porangahau:
    Taumatawhakatangihangakoauauota-
    mateapokaiwhenuakitanatahu
porcelain: Chelsea, 1
Port Arthur: Golden Triangle, the, 3
Port Augusta: Tea and Sugar; Trans-Austra-
    lian Railway
Porte, the
Portillo: South American Alps
Port Jackson: Botany Bay
Port Jefferson: North Shore, 1
Port Kembla: Steel City, 2
Portland Place
Portobello Road
Porto Cervo: Costa Smeralda
Port o' Missing Men, the
Porton Down
Port Pirie: Trans-Australian Railway
Portsmouth, New Hampshire: North
    Shore, 2
Portsmouth: Island, the, 1; Pompey
Portugal: European Economic Community,
    the; Iberia; Peninsula, the; Spice Is-
    lands, the
Portuguese Guinea: Guinea
Port Zodiac: Capricornia
potbanks: Potteries, the
Potomac River: Pentagon, the; Tidal Basin;
    Tidewater Virginia
Potteries, the

Potteries: Etruria
Poultry: Bank, the
Prado, the
prairie oyster
Prairie Provinces, the
prairie schooner
Pratt's: Clubland, 1
prehistoric reptile: dinosaur of darkness
Premier State, the
Presbytre, the: French Quarter, the
presidential retreat: Shangri-La, 3
Preussen: Prussia
Prime Minister (Britain): Downing Street;
    Number 10
Prince Edward Island: Atlantic Provinces,
    the
Princes Street: New Town, the; North Brit-
    ain
Princetown: Moor, the
Principality, the
'Printer's Row': Loop, the
Printing House Square
prison: City College; Moor, the; Wormwood
    Scrubs
Prisoner of Zenda, the: Ruritania
Private Eye: Neasden
Prohibition: '21' Club; Roaring Twenties,
    the
Prometheus: Rockefeller Center
Promised Land, the
pro-slavery partisans: Bleeding Kansas
Prospect Park: Brooklyn
Provençal: Provence
Provence: Midi, the; Province, the; South of
    France, the
Providence, Rhode Island: Beehive of Indus-
    try; Roger Williams City; Southern
    Gateway to New England
Province, the
Provincetown: Cape, the
Prudential Center: Back Bay
Prudential Tower Office: Back Bay
Prussia
Ptolemy: German Ocean, the
'Public Enemy Number One': Biograph The-
    ater
Public Garden: Back Bay
'public schools': Roedean

publishing: Paternoster Row
Pueblo de los Angeles: Los Angeles
Puerto Rican: Barrio, the; Spanish Harlem
Puerto Rico: Commonwealth
puffing billies
Puget Sound: Galloping Gertie
Puke State, the
Pullman, George: North Side; Pullman
Pullman: South Side
Pullman Community: Pullman
Pullman Village: Pullman
Punjab: Pakistan
punks: King's Road
Puritans: blue laws
Pyrenees Mountains: Languedoc
Qatar: Arabia; Gulf, the
Quai d'Orsay, the
Quai d'Orsay: Wilhelmstrasse, the
Quakers: Brother Jonathan
Quaker State, the
Quantrill, William: Bleeding Kansas
quasars: Big Mac, the
Quebec, Canada: Appalachian Mountains
Quebec: City of Saints, the; D.S.N.C.O.;
    Old Quebec (Vieux-Québec)
'Queen of the Angels': Los Angeles
Queen of the Antilles
Queen of the North
Queen of the Sea
Queens: Brooklyn; East River; Forest Hills;
    Hell Gate; Island, the, 2; Manhattan;
    West Side, 1
Queens Boulevard: Queens
Queen's Camel: Camelot, 1
Queen's College: Backs, the; High, the
Queen's Cross: King's Cross, 2
Queensland: Bananaland; Channel country;
    Dog Fence, the; Never Never
Queensland Cricket Association: Gabba, the
Queen State, the
Queen Street: Carfax, the
Queen Street Bushie: Collins Street
Queen Street West
Quincy Market
Quirinal, the
Quirinal: Seven Hills, the
Quirinale, il: Quirinal, the
Quorn and the Pytchely: Shires, the

Quorn hunt: Melton Mowbray
RADA
'Radio City': Rockefeller Center
Radio City Music Hall
Radio Corporation of America: Rockefeller
    Center
radio networks: Manhattan
Radnor: Main Line
Raffles: Albany
raj, the
Raleigh, North Carolina: City of Oaks
Ramillies: Cockpit of Europe, the
Ramses II: Abu Simbel
Ramsgate: Isle of Thanet, the
Rand, Sally: Gaiety, the
Rand, the
R & A, the
Randall's Island: Hell Gate
Randolph Field: West Point of the Air
Rann of Kutch, the
Rapes: Rapes
Rappahannock River: Tidewater Virginia
Ras el Khaimah: Trucial States, the
Rasselas: Happy Valley
Rastafarians: Babylon
RCA Building: Rockefeller Center
Reading: Thames Valley, the
Rebel Capital
Record Office: Chancery Lane
redbrick
Red Centre: Centre, the
Red China
red-light district: Blood Alley; blue-light dis-
    trict; Cat Street; Reeperbahn, the;
    Storyville; Track, the
Rednaxela Terrace
Red Planet, the
Red Sea: Arabia; Seven Seas, the; Western
    Desert, the
Red Spot, the
Red Square
Reef, the: Rand, the
Reeperbahn, the
Reform, the: Clubland, 1
Reform Act of 1832: Old Sarum; Reform
    Club, the
Reformation: Babylon
Reform Club, the

Reform Club: Pall Mall
Regent's Canal: Camden Lock; Camden
    Town; Little Venice
Regent's Park: Baker Street; Camden Town;
    Harley Street; King's Cross, 1; Lord's;
    Marylebone; Portland Place; St John's
    Wood
Regent Street: Carnaby Street; Jermyn
    Street; Savile Row; West End, the
Rego Park: Queens
Reina de los Angeles, la: Los Angeles
Relief of Mafeking: Mafeking
'Remember the Alamo': Alamo, the
remoteness: Mongolia; Timbuktu
Renaissance Center: Ren Cen
Ren Cen
Renmark: Riverland, the
Repeal: '21' Club
Repulse Bay: Eucliffe; Repulsive Bay
Repulsive Bay
Revere, Paul: Freedom Trail
Revolutionary War: Blue Hen State; Faneuil
    Hall; Harvard Yard
Rhineland, the
Rhineland-Palatinate: Palatinate, the
Rhine of America, the
Rhine River: Black Forest, the; Rhineland,
    the; Ruhr, the
Rhode Island: Cape, the; East, the, 1; Na-
    tion's Most Corrupt State; New Eng-
    land; Thirteen Original Colonies
Rhodes: City of the Sun; Colossus of
    Rhodes
Rhondda: Valleys, the
Rhone River: Camargue, the; Languedoc;
    Midi, the
rhyming slang: Khyber Pass, the; Mallee, the
Rhymney River: Valleys, the
Rialto
Rialto Bridge: Bridge of Sighs, 4
Rice, Dan: Uncle Sam
Richmond: Manhattan
Richmond-upon-Thames: Kew Gardens;
    Strawberry Hill; Twickenham
Ridge-and-Valley Province: Appalachian
    Mountains
Ridings, the
Ring, the: Bayreuth

Royal Botanic Gardens: Kew Gardens
Royal Courts of Justice: Law Courts, the
Royal Docks: Dockland
Royal Dockyard: Woolwich
Royal Enclosure: Ascot
Royal Exchange: Bank, the
Royal Festival Hall: South Bank, the
Royal Leamington Spa: Tunbridge Wells
Royal Mile, the
Royal Military Academy: Bagshot;
    Camberley
Royal Military College: Sandhurst
Royal Opera House: Covent Garden
Royal Palace: Unter den Linden
'Royal Road, the': Camino Real, el
Royal Society: Burlington House
Royal Tunbridge Wells: Tunbridge Wells
Royal Victoria Docks: Dockland
Royal Victoria Theatre: Old Vic, the
Royal Yacht Squadron: Cowes Week
Rub' al Khali: Empty Quarter, the
Rue Chu Pao-San: Blood Alley
Rugby
rugby ball: Garryowen
rugby football: Rugby; Twickenham
Ruhr, the
Ruhr River: Ruhr, the
Ruislip: Middlesex
Rumania: Balkans, the
Rumelia
Rumeliotes: Rumelia
rumors: Street, the, 2
Runnymede
Runyon, Damon: Lindy's
Ruritania
Rush Street
Russia: Kremlin, the; Muscovy; Soviet
    Union, the
Russian Empire: Balkans, the
Russians: Tartary
Russian Soviet Federated Socialist Republic:
    Russia; Soviet Russia
Russias, Czar of all the: Russia
Ruth, Babe: House That Ruth Built
Rutland
Rye, England: Cinque Ports, the
Rye, New York: Border Town
Saarinen, Eero: Gateway Arch

Saba: Sheba
Sackville Street: Albany
Sacramento, California: Golden City
Sacré Coeur: Montmartre
Sadat, Anwar el-: Camp David
Sage, Anna: Biograph Theater
Sahara desert: Sudan, the
Sahel, the
Saks Fifth Avenue: Fifth Avenue
Salem, Massachusetts: City of Witches
Salem
Salisbury: Old Sarum
Salisbury-Jones, Sir Guy: Hambledon
Sally Army, the
Salmagundi: Gotham
Salop: Telford
salsa bands: Aragon Ballroom
Saltaire: Fire Island
Salvation Army: Bowery, the; Sally Army,
    the; Strawberry Fields
Samoa: Polynesia
San Angelo, Texas: City of the Angel
San Antonio,Texas: Chisholm Trail
San Antonio: Alamo, the; Alamo City; Cra-
    dle of Texas Liberty; Mission City;
    West Point of the Air
San Benito, Texas: Casa Oscar Romero
Sandburg, Carl: Hog Butcher for the World
Sandhurst: Camberley
San Diego: Plymouth of the West
Sandlapper State, the
Sandringham
Sands Point: North Shore, 1
Sandwich: Cinque Ports, the
San Fernando Valley: Burbank
San Francisco: Alcatraz; Broadway, 2; Cas-
    tro, the; Chinatown, 1; Embarcadero;
    Fisherman's Wharf; Frisco; Ghirardelli
    Square; Golden Gate City; Haight-
    Ashbury; Los Angeles; Over South;
    Path of Gold; Poor Man's Paradise;
    Port o' Missing Men; Silicon Valley
San Gennaro, Feast of: Little Italy
Sangre de Cristo Range: Rockies, the
San Jacinto: Alamo, the
'Sank Roo Doe Noo': Harry's American Bar
San Remo: Italian Riviera, the
Santa Barbara: Queen of the Missions

Santa Claus: North Pole
Santa Fe, New Mexico: Camino Real, el;
    Lone Star of Civilization; Santa Fe
    Trail
Santa Fe Trail: Atchison, Topeka, & Santa
    Fe
Santa Monica Mountain: San Fernando Val-
    ley
Santa Susana Mountain: San Fernando Val-
    ley
Santenay: Côte d'Or
Santiago, Chile: Christ of the Andes
Santorini: Atlantis
Saracens: Barbary Coast, the
Sarajevo: accidental war, the
Sardinia: Costa Smeralda
Sardi's
Sargasso Sea, the
Sargent, John Singer: Chelsea, 1
Sarsaparilla
Saskatchewan: Prairie Provinces, the
Saturnine Hill: Capitoline, the
Sauchiehall Street
Saudia Arabia: Gulf, the
Saudi Arabia: Arabia; City of Refuge, the;
    City of the Prophet, the; Middle East,
    the
Savage, the: Clubland, 1
Savannah, Georgia: Forest City of the
    South; Hilton Head Island
Savile Row
Savoy, the
Savoy Hotel: Savoy, the
Savoy Palace: Savoy, the
Saxons: Broads, the; Isle of Thanet, the
Scafell Pike: Lake District, the
Scandinavia: Far North, the; Lapland
Scandinavian Shield, the
Scarsdale syndrome
Schiller, Johann von: Weimar
School of the Art Institute of Chicago: Gold
    Coast
Schrafft's
Schwab's Drugstore: Sunset Boulevard
Schwartz, Maurice: Lower East Side
Schwarzwald: Black Forest, the
Science and Industry, Museum of: South
    Side; White City, 1

Scollay Square
Scotland: Athens of the North, the; Auld
    Reekie; Backbone of England, the; Bal-
    moral Castle; Bearsden; Border, the;
    Britain; Caledonia; Capital of the High-
    lands, the; Charing Cross, 2; City of St
    Michael, the; Clydeside; England; Firth
    of Forth Bridge; Glencoe; Glens, the;
    Gorbals, the; Granite City, the; Gretna
    Green; Heart of Midlothian, the; High-
    lands, the; Inns of Court and Chancery;
    Land of Cakes; Land's End to John o'
    Groat's House; Little Britain; Low-
    lands, the; Marches, the, 1; Morning-
    side; New Town, the; North Britain;
    Northland, the; Northumbria; Old Do-
    minion; R & A, the; Roost, the; Royal
    Miles, the; Sauchiehall Street; Silicon
    Glen; Silver City by the Sea; Southern
    Uplands, the; St Andrews; Trossachs,
    the; United Kingdom, the; Western
    Isles, the
Scotland Yard: Yard, the
Scots Gaelic: Highlands, the
Scott, Sir Walter: Athens of the North, the;
    Border, the; Heart of Midlothian, the;
    Trossachs, the
Scranton, Pennsylvania: City of Black
    Diamonds
'Scrubs, the': Wormwood Scrubs
Scunthorpe: Flixborough
Scylla and Charybdis
Seagram Building: East Side
Sears Tower: Empire State Building
Seattle, Washington: Skid Row
Seaview: Fire Island
Secombe, Harry: Windmill Theatre, the
Second Avenue: East Village, the; Lower
    East Side
Second City, the
Second City: Old Town
Seeger, Pete: Greenwich Village
'See Naples and die': Naples
Seine River: Halles, les; Latin Quarter,
    the, 1; Left Bank, the; Marais, the;
    Quai d'Orsay, the
Selfridges: Oxford Street
Selkirk: Border, the

Selkirk Range: Inland Empire, the
Seminole: Trail of Tears
send to Coventry: Coventry
Senegal: Senegambia
Senegal River: Senegambia
Senegambia
Senlac, Battle of: Hastings
'Sentinel, The': Leaping Lena
sent to Botany Bay: Botany Bay
Serbia: Balkans, the
Serendip: Ceylon
serendipity: Ceylon
Serra, Father Junípero: Plymouth of the West
Serra, José Correa da: City of Magnificent Distances, the
Seven Dials
Seven Hills, the
Seven Hills: Capitoline, the; Palatine, the; Quirinal, the
Seven Seas, the
Seven Sisters
'Seven Sisters Colliery': Seven Sisters
Seven Sisters Road: Seven Sisters
Seventh Avenue: 42nd Street; Fashion Avenue; Gaiety Delicatessen; Garment District
seventh heaven: Al Borak
Seven Wonders of the Ancient World: Hanging Gardens of Babylon
Seven Wonders of the World: Colossus of Rhodes
Severn: Arden
Severnaya Zemlya: Northland, the
sexual fulfillment: Diddy wa Diddy
Shadwell: Pool of London, the
Shaftesbury Avenue: Piccadilly Circus
Shakespeare, William: Arabia; Arden; Blackfriars
Shambles, the
Shanghai: Blood Alley; Bubbling Well
Shangri-La: Camp David
Shankill Road: Falls Road
Sharjah: Trucial States, the
Shaw, George Bernard: John Bull
Shawn, Ted: Jacob's Pillow
Sheba
Sheerness: Nore, the

Sheffield: Broad Acres, the; Muscle Shoals Area; North, the, 1
Sheffield of Germany
Sheldonian Theatre: Broad, the
Shenandoah Valley: Blue Ridge Mountains, the
Shepheard's Hotel
Shepherd, Edward: Shepherd Market
Shepherd Market
Shepherd's Bush: Wormwood Scrubs
Sheridan, Philip Henry: Ohio's Jewels
Sheridan, Richard Brinsley: Morningside
Sheridan, Thomas: Morningside
Sheridan Square: Greenwich Village
Sherman, William Tecumseh: Ohio's Jewels
Sherwood Forest: Dukeries, the
She Stoops to Conquer: Liberty Hall
Shetland: Thule
Shetland Island: Roost, the
shipbuilding: Clydeside; Furness
Shires, the: Melton Mowbray; Midlands, the
shirtmaking: Jermyn Street
Shop, the
shopping: Oxford Street
Shoreditch: East End
'shot heard round the world': Birthplace of American Liberty
Showboat: Ol' Man River; Paper Mill Playhouse
Show Me State, the
Shrewsbury: Marches, the, 1; Salop
Shropshire: Midlands, the; Salop; Telford; West, the, 2; West Midlands, the
Siam
Sianis, Sam: Billy Goat Tavern
Sibelius, Jean: Karelia
Siberia: Dakota, 1; Far East, the
SICBM: Midgetman
Sicily: Scylla and Charybdis
Sick Man of Europe
Sick Man of the East
Sidney, Sir Philip: Arcadia
Sierra Mountains: Land of Little Rain
Sierra Nevada Mountains: Donner Pass
Sikkim: Native States, the
Silent Service
Silicon Glen
Silicon Prairie

Silicon Valley: Silicon Glen
'Silicon Valley of the East': Route 128
'Silk Stocking District': East Side; Spanish
  Harlem
Silver City
Sim, Alastair: Ealing
Simpson Desert:
  Taumatawhakatangihangakoauauota-
  mateapokaiwhenuakitanatahu
Simpson's (in the Strand)
Simpson's of Piccadilly
Sinatra, Frank: Broadway, 1
Sinclair, Upton: Union Stockyards
Sind
Singapore: Indochina; Southeast Asia
Sinn Fein: Southie
Sioux Indians: Bozeman Trail
Sioux State, the
Sirius: dog days; Dog Star
'sisters of the Bank': Bankside
'Six, the': European Economic Community,
  the
Six Counties, the
1600 Pennsylvania Avenue
Sixth Avenue: 42nd Street; Avenue of the
  Americas; Chelsea, 2; Gimbels; Herald
  Square; NoHo; Rockefeller Center;
  SoHo
Skevington, Sir W.: Skevington's daughter
Skevington's daughter
skid row
Skye: Western Isles, the
skyscrapers: Chrysler Building; Empire State
  Building; Manhattan
slaughterhouses: Shambles, the
Slaughter on Tenth Avenue: Hell's Kitchen
Slave Coast, the
slavery: Middle Passage, the
slaves, fugitive: underground railroad
slave ships: Middle Passage, the
slave states: Mason-Dixon Line
Sleaford: Kesteven
slider
'Sloane': Sloane Square
Sloane Ranger: Sloane Square; Swone-one
Sloane Square: King's Road
Slough: Watford
'slumming': Harlem

small-town life: Main Street
Smith, Betty: Brooklyn
Smith, George 'Brides in the Bath': Old Bai-
  ley
Smith, Jack: Los Angeles
Smith, Seba: Uncle Sam
Smithfield: Bart's
Smith Square: Transport House
Smoke, the
Snake, the
Snake Gully
Snowden, Ethel: Iron Curtain, the
Snowdonia
snuff: anatomist's snuffbox
Social Democratic Party: Limehouse
social work: Hull House
Sodom and Gomorrah
Sodom of India
SoHo: Chinatown, 2; Greek Street; Holy
  Land, the, 2; Seven Dials; SoHo; Tin
  Pan Alley; Wardour Street; West End,
  the
Soho Square: Greek Street; Soho
Soke of Peterborough, the
Solent, the
Solingen: Sheffield of Germany
Solomon, King: Sheba
Solomon, temple of: Wailing Wall, the
Solomon Islands: Melanesia
Somalia: Horn of Africa, the; Ogaden, the
Somerset: Camelot, 1; Cheddar; Glaston-
  bury; Isle of Athelney, the; Southwest,
  the, 2; West Country, the
Somerset House
Somers Town
Songhai: Sudan, the
Sooner State, the
Sorbonne University: Latin Quarter, the, 1
Sothern, Edward A.: dundrearies
Sound, the
sourdough: Fisherman's Wharf
Sousa, John Philip: Stars and Stripes
South, the: Mason-Dixon Line; Midlands,
  the; North, the, 3
South-West Africa: Namibia
South Africa, Republic of: Azania
South Africa: Highveld, the; Joburg; Karoo,
  the; Mafeking; Namibia; Rand, the;

Subcontinent, the; Table Mountain; Third World, the; Zululand
South America, northern coast of: Spanish Main, the
South America: banana republic; El Dorado; Gondwanaland; Guiana; Neogaea; Third World, the; Tierra del Fuego; West, the, 1
South American Alps
Southampton: Hamptons, the; Hants; Island, the, 1; New Forest; Solent, the
South Atlantic Ocean: Seven Seas, the
South Atlantic States: Atlantic States
South Audley Street: Mayfair
South Australia: Ash Wednesdy fires; Dog Fence, the; gully winds; O-bahn; Parklands; Riverland, the
South Bank, the
South Bank: Waterloo
South Boston High School: Southie
South Britain: Britain
South Cadbury: Camelot, 1
South Carolina: Atlantic States; Deep South, the; Game-cock State; Grand Strand; Harry Percy of the Union; Hilton Head Island; Sandlapper State; South, the, 1; Thirteen Original Colonies
South China Sea: Seven Seas, the
South Dakota: Bad Lands, the; Black Hills, the; Middle Border, the; Outlaw Country; Sunshine State; West, the, 3
South Dearborn Street: Loop, the
South Downs: Hambledon; Weald, the
Southeast, the: South, the, 2
Southeast Asia: Cambodia; East Indies, the; Farther India; Golden Triangle, the, 1; Indochina; Land of a Million Elephants, the; Orient, the; Siam
'southern oceans, the': South Seas, the
Southern Uplands, the
Southern Uplands: Lowlands, the
Southey, Robert: Lake District, the
South Fork: Island, the, 2
South Holland: Holland, 1
Southie
South Island: Hokonui; Mainland, the, 2
'South Ken': Kensington
South Kensington: Kensington; V & A, the

South London: Walworth Road
South of England: South, the, 2
South of France, the: Midi, the
South of the Border: Border, the
South Pacific: South Seas, the
South Pacific Ocean: Micronesia; Oceania; Polynesia; Seven Seas, the
South Pass: Oregon Trail
South Pole
South Riding: Ridings, the
South Sea Bubble: South Seas, the
'South Sea Islands': South Seas, the
South Seas, the
South Shields: Tyneside
South Shore, the
South Shore: Hamptons, the; Island, the, 2
South Side: Museum of Science and Industry; North Side; Union Stockyards; White City, 1
South Street: Lower East Side
South Uist: Western Isles, the
South Wabash Avenue: Loop, the
South Wales: Camelot, 1; Valleys, the
Southwark: Borough; the; London Bridge; Old Kent Road, the; Walworth Road
Southwest, the: Isle of Athelney, the; Lizard, the; South, the, 2; West, the, 2; West Country, the
Southwest Side: West Side
South Yemen: Arabia
South Yorkshire: Grimethorpe; Ridings, the
Soviet Russia
Soviet Union, the
Soviet Union: Baltic States; Bessarabia; Iberia; Iron Curtain, the; Karelia; Kremlin, the; Lapland; Mongolia; Polish Corridor, the; Prussia; Red Square; Roof of the World, the; Russia; Siberia; Soviet Russia; West, the, 1
Soyer, Alexis: Reform Club, the
Spaghetti Junction
Spain: Alhambra; Bethnal Green in the Sun; Canary Islands; City of Five Flags; Costa Blanca; Costa Brava, the; Costa del Crime; Costa del Sol; European Economic Community, the; Foreigner State; Gib; Guernica; Hapsburg lip; Iberia; Morgue Motorway; Pamplona;

Peninsula, the; Pillars of Hercules, the; Prado, the; Rock, the; Spice Islands, the

Spanish-American War: Cat Street

Spanish Civil War: Guernica

Spanish Guinea: Guinea

Spanish Harlem: Broadway, 1

Spanish Main, the

Spanish Mainland: Spanish Main, the

Sparta: Peloponnese, the

speakeasies: Roaring Twenties, the

Speakers' Corner

Speck, the

Spence, Basil: Coventry

Spice Islands, the

'Spirit of Progress, The': Leaping Lena

'Spirit of Protest, The': Leaping Lena

Spirit of St Louis: Bourget, le

Spitalfields: East End

Spokane, Washington: Inland Empire, the

Springer Mountain, Georgia: Appalachian Trail, the

Springfield, Missouri: Queen City of the Ozarks

Spuyten Duyvil Creek: Broadway, 1; Harlem River

spy plane: Blackbird

Square Mile, the

Squatter State, the

Sri Lanka: Ceylon; Coromandel Coast, the; Subcontinent, the

Staffordshire: Black Country, the; Burton upon Trent; Five Towns, the; Midlands, the; Peak District, the; Potteries, the; West Midlands, the

Stagg Field

St. Aldate's: Carfax, the

Stalin, Joseph: Volgograd

Stalingrad: Volgograd

Stamboul

Stamboul Train: Stamboul

Standard Oil Building: Sears Tower

St Andrews: R & A, the

Stanley, H. M.: Dark Continent, the

Stannaries, the

'stannary courts': Stannaries, the

Stanton, Edwin McMasters: Ohio's Jewels

Star-Spangled Banner, the: Fort McHenry

Star Chamber

Star Hotel

Starr, Ellen Gates: Hull House

Stars and Bars

Stars and Stripes

Star Wars

State, Department of: Foggy Bottom

Staten Island: Brooklyn; Manhattan; Narrows, the

State of Excitement, the

States of the Church: Papal States, the

State Street: Holy Name

statue: Big Tex

Statue of Liberty: Bedloe's Island

St Augustine: America's Oldest City

St Bartholomew's Church: Park Avenue

St Bartholomew's Hospital: Bart's

St Bartholomew's Medical School: Bart's

St Basil's Cathedral: Red Square

St Charles Parish: German Coast

St Davids: Main Line

Stealth

steam engines: puffing billies

St Edmund Hall: High, the

Steel City

steeplechase horse race: Grand National, the

Steer, Wilson: Chelsea, 1

Steinberg, Saul: West, the, 3

Stepney: East End; Tower Hamlets

Sterling, Captain Edward: Thunderer, the

Stettin: Oder-Neisse Line, the

Stevens, J. C.: America's Cup

St-Germain-des-Prés: Left Bank, the

St Giles: Holy Land, the, 2

St Giles Circus: Oxford Street

Stilton cheese: Melton Mowbray

Stirling: Highlands, the

St James Parish: German Coast

St James's: Clubland, 1; Jermyn Street; West End, the

St James's Palace: Pall Mall; St James's

St James's Park: Westminster

St James's Street: St James's

St John's College: Backs, the; Bridge of Sighs, 3

St John's River: American Nile, the

St John's Wood: Abbey Road; Lord's; Swiss Cottage

St John the Baptist Parish: German Coast
St Joseph Street: Irish Channel
St Katherine's Dock: Dockland
St Laurent, Yves: Faubourg St Honoré, Rue
    du
St Louis: Gateway Arch
St Louis Cathedral: French Quarter, the
St Louis Street: Storyville
St Luke's summer
St Marylebone: Marylebone; Westminster
St Mary-le-bow: Bow; Marylebone
St Mary of Bethlehem: Bedlam
St Michael: City of St Michael, the
St-Michel, Boulevard: Latin Quarter, the, 1
St-Michel: Left Bank, the
St Nicholas Avenue: Sugar Hill
Stock Exchange: Big Bang, the; City, the;
    Manhattan; Throgmorton Street
Stockholm: Sodom and Gomorrah, 2; Ven-
    ice of the North
Stoke: Chiltern Hundreds, the
Stoke Mandeville
Stoke Mandeville Games: Stoke Mandeville
Stoke-on-Trent: Etruria; Five Towns, the;
    Potteries, the
Stoker, Bram: Transylvania
Stone Age: Wolds, the
Stork Club: '21' Club
Story, Sidney: Storyville
Storyville
Stour, River: Constable Country; Isle of
    Thanet, the
St Paul's
St Paul's Cathedral: Bankside; Barbican,
    the; Little Britain; Old Bailey; Paternos-
    ter Row
St Paul's Churchyard: Little Britain; Pater-
    noster Row
St Petersburg: City of Palaces, the; Lenin-
    grad
Strachey, Lytton: Bloomsbury
Strand, the: Adelphi, the; Carey Street; Cov-
    ent Garden; Drury Lane; Fleet Street;
    Golgotha, 1; Law Courts, the; Savoy,
    the; Simpson's (in the Strand); Somerset
    House; West End, the
Strand: Bush House
Strand Bridge: Waterloo

Strand Theatre: Broadway, 1
St Raphael: French Riviera, the
Strategic Defense Initiative: Star Wars
Strawberry Fields
Strawberry Hill
Streatham: Lambeth
Street, the
'Street of Ink, the': Fleet Street
'Street of Shame, the': Fleet Street
Strip, the: Sunset Boulevard
Stromboli: Atlantis
St Tropez: French Riviera, the; South of
    France, the
Stuart, Charles Edward: Black Friday, 1
Stuart Highway: Track, the
Subcontinent, the
Sublime Porte, the
submarine: boomer
submarine service: Silent Service
subtopia
suburban housing estate: subtopia
Sucker State, the
Sudan, the
Sudetenland, the
Sudeten Mountains: Sudetenland, the
Suetonius: City of Palaces, the
Suffolk: Constable Country; East Anglia;
    Newmarket
Suffolk County: Island, the, 2
Sugar Hill
Sugar Loaf Mountain: Copacabana, 1
Sulawesi: East Indies; Spice Islands, the
Sullivan, Anne Mansfield: City of Kind
    Hearts
Sullivan, Ed: Stork Club
Sullivan, Louis: North Side
Sultan's Palace: Sublime Porte, the
Sumatra: East Indies, the
Sumeria: Fertile Crescent, the; Mesopotamia
Sumner, John: Minsky's
Sun Also Rises, the: Pamplona
Sunbelt
'Sunken Forest': Fire Island
Sunraysia
'sunrise, orient': Japan
Sunset Boulevard: Beverly Hills Hotel; Sun-
    set Boulevard
Sunset Strip: Strip, the, 2

Ten, the: European Economic Community, the

Tennessee: Appalachia; Appalachian Mountains; Bible Belt; Deep South, the; South, the, 1

Tennessee River: Muscle Shoals Area

Tenth Avenue: Broadway, 1; Chelsea, 2; Hell's Kitchen; Third Avenue

Terra Australis

terra sancta: Holy Land, the, 1

Territories, The

Territory, the

test cricket: Ashes, the

Texas: Alamo, the; Bible Belt; Big Bend; Big D; Big Inch; Dallas Book Depository; Golden Triangle, the, 3; Gulf, the; Jumbo State; Lone Star State; Panhandle, the; Rio Grande Valley; Silicon Prairie; Southwest, the, 1; West, the, 3

Texas State Fair: Big Tex

Texas Tea

Thailand: Golden Triangle, the, 1; Indochina; Siam; Southeast Asia; Venice of the East

Thames River: Adelphi, the; Alsatia; Bankside; Battersea; Bedlam; Bermondsey Market; Blackfriars; Blackwall Tunnel; Bray; Caledonian Market; Chelsea, 1; City of Masts, the; Clink Street; Dockland; East End; Embankment, the; Gravesend; Henley; Isis; Isle of Dogs, the; Lambeth; London Bridge; Nine Elms; Nore, the; Pimlico; Pool of London, the; Runnymede; Savoy, the; South Bank, the; Temple, the; Thames Valley, the; Tower, the; Tower Bridge; Vauxhall; Waterloo; West End, the; Whitefriars; Woolwich

Thames Valley, the

Thames Valley: Wessex

Thaw, Harry K: Madison Square Garden

theatre: green room

Theatre Royal, Drury Lane: Drury Lane

theatres: Leicester Square

Theocritus: Arcadia

Thera: Atlantis

Thessaly: Aetolia

Third Avenue: Bowery, the

Third World, the

Third World: Free World, the

Thirlmere: Lake District, the

thirteen colonies: Rebel Capital

Thirteen Original Colonies

Thomas, Dylan: Fitzrovia

Thompson sub-machine gun: Tommy gun

Thoreau, Henry David: Walden Pond

Thoresby Hall: Dukeries, the

Thorney Island

Thousand Guineas race: Newmarket

Thrace: Balkans, the

Thracian peninsula: Golden Chersonese, the

Threadneedle Street: Bank, the; Old Lady of Threadneedle Street, the; Throgmorton Street

'Three Princes of Serendip, The': Ceylon

Throggs Neck Bridge: Hell Gate

Throgmorton Street

Throg Street: Throgmorton Street

Through Bolshevik Russia: Iron Curtain, the

Through the Dark Continent: Dark Continent, the

Thule

Thunderer, the

'Thyrsis': City of Dreaming Spires

Tibet: Forbidden City, the; Roof of the World, the

Tibullus: Eternal City, the

Tidal Basin

Tidewater Virginia

Tiergarten: Unter den Linden

Tierra del Fuego

Tiffany: Fifth Avenue

Tiffany's

Tigris River: Fertile Crescent, the; Mesopotamia

Tilbury: Dockland

Timaeus: Atlantis

Timbuktu

Time, Incorporated: Rockefeller Center

Time-Life Building: Rockefeller Center

Times, The: Dockland; Printing House Square; Thunderer, the; Turnabout, the

Times Square: Broadway, 1; Clock at the Astor, Biltmore; Gaiety, the; Great White Way; Herald Square; Jack Dempsey's; Strip, the, 2

'Times Square of the West, the': Hollywood and Vine

Timor: East Indies, the

tin Lizzie

Tin Pan Alley

'Tinseltown': Hollywood

Tintagel

Titusville, Pennsylvania: Oil Dorado

Tivoli Gardens

Todd, Sir Charles: Alice Springs

Toddling Town, That

Todd River: Alice Springs

Todd River Regatta: Todd River

Tokyo: Ginza, the; Megalopolis; Orient-Express

Toledo, Ohio: Corn City

Tolpuddle

'Tolpuddle Martyrs': Tolpuddle

Tom Brown's Schooldays: Rugby

Tombs, the: Bridge of Sighs, 2

Tommy (Atkins)

Tommy gun

Tompkins Park: East Village, the

Tondo Foreshore: Little Vietnam

'Tonight Show': Burbank

Tonkin: Indochina

Toothpick State, the

Topanga Malibu Sequit land grant: Malibu

Top End, the

Toronto: Bay Street; Parkdale; Queen Street West; Rosedale; Strip, the, 2; Track, the

Torquay: Cornish Riviera, the

Torremolinas: Costa del Sol

Torrio, Johnny: Holy Name Cathedral; Loop, the

torture: Skevington's daughter

Tory: Turnabout, the

Totable Tornado Observatory: TOTO

TOTO

Tottenham: Seven Sisters

Tottenham Court Road: Centre Point; Fitzrovia; Warren Street

Toulouse-Lautrec, Henri de: Montmartre; Moulin Rouge

Touraine: Garden of France, the

Tower, the: Blackpool; Tower Bridge

Tower Bridge: Bermondsey Market; Caledonian Market; London Bridge

Tower Hamlets

Tower of London: Tower Bridge

Town That Moved Overnight, the

Toxteth

toy business: Chelsea, 2

Track, the

Trafalgar Square: Aldermaston; Charing Cross; Number 10; Pall Mall; Soho; Whitehall

Trail of Tears

Trail of the Lonesome Pine, the: Blue Ridge Mountains, the

Trans-Australian Railway: Nullabor Plain; Tea and Sugar

Trans-Jordan

Transport and General Workers' Union: Transport House

transportation: Botany Bay

Transport House: Smith Square; Walworth Road

Trans-Siberian railway: Siberia

Transvaal: Highveld, the; Joburg; Rand, the; Zululand

Transylvania: Balkans, the

Travancor: Native States, the

Travellers Club: Pall Mall

Travis, William Barret: Alamo, the

Treasury: Whitehall

Treaty of Waitangi: Waitangi

Tredegar: Valleys, the

Tree, Beerbohm: RADA

Tree Grows in Brooklyn, A: Brooklyn

Tremont Street: Combat Zone

Trent: Arden

Trent River: Backbone of England, the; Burton-upon-Trent

Treorchy: Valleys, the

Tribeca

Triboro Bridge: Harlem; Hell Gate

Tribune Company: Wrigleyville

Tribune Tower: Magnificent Mile, the

Trinity Church: Back Bay

Trinity College: Backs, the; Broad, the

Triple-headed Monster

Tripolitania: Barbary Coast, the

Trollope, Anthony: Barset

Upper Palatinate: Palatinate, the
Upper Peninsula, Michigan: Land of Hiawatha
Upper Pool: Pool of London, the
Upper Regent Street: Piccadilly Circus
Upper West Side: West Side, 1
uptown: Aragon Ballroom; North Side
Ural Mountains: Siberia
Ursa Major: Big Dipper; Charles's Wain
Ursa Minor: Little Dipper
U. S.: East, the, 1; House, the; Main Street of America, the; South, the, 1; Tin Pan Alley
'Use of Sarum': Old Sarum
U. S. Military Academy: West Point
U. S. Open: Forest Hills
Uspallata Pass: Christ of the Andes
U. S. S. R., the
USSR: Gorkii; Land of the Midnight Sun, the; Leningrad; Volgograd
U. S. Treasury: Uncle Sam's Crib
Utah: Land of the Saints; Southwest, the, 1
Utrecht, Treaty of: Acadia
Valentine State, the
'Valley, the': Rio Grande Valley; San Fernando Valley
'Valley girls': San Fernando Valley
Valleys, the
vampires: Transylvania
Van Buren, Martin: Albany Regency
Van Cleef and Arpels: Tiffany's
Van Cortlandt Park: Broadway, 1
Vancouver, George: Northwest Passage, the
V & A
Van Diemen's Land
Vandiver, Willard D.: Show Me State
Varna, Bulgaria: Orient-Express
Vauxhall
Vauxhall Gardens: Vauxhall
Velásquez, Diego de Silva y: Prado, the
Venezuela: Angostura; Guiana
Venice: Bride of the Sea; Bridge of Sighs, 4; Jewel of the Adriatic, the; Orient-Express; Rialto
Venice of the East
Venice of the North
Venice of the West

Venice Simplon Orient-Express: Orient-Express
Ventnor: Boardwalk
Ventura: Malibu
Vermont: Appalachian Mountains; East, the, 1; Mohawk Trail; New England; Northeast Kingdom
Verne, Jules: Reform Club, the
Versailles, Treaty of: Polish Corridor, the
Vesuvius: Atlantis
Via Condotti: Rodeo Drive
vicar of Bray: Bray
Vichy
Vichy France: Vichy
Vicksburg, Mississippi: Gibraltar of America; Key City
Victoria, Queen: Island, the, 1; Royal Borough, the; St James's; Tunbridge Wells; Victoria
Victoria: Ash Wednesdy fires; Cabbage Patch, the; Eureka Stockade; Hanging Rock; Hanging State, the; Kelly Country; Mallee, the; Pimlico; Scotland Yard
Victoria and Albert museum: Kensington; V & A, the
Victoria Embankment: Embankment, the
Victoria River Downs: Big Run, the
Victoria Station: Orient-Express
Vienna: Mistelbach
Vietnam: Indochina; Southeast Asia
Vikings: Vinland
'Village, the': Greenwich Village
Village Vanguard, the: Greenwich Village
Villanova: Main Line
Ville, the
Viminal: Seven Hills, the
Vine Street: Hollywood and Vine
Vineyard Sound: Cape, the
Vinland
Vinland Map: Vinland
Violet-crowned City, the
Violet-Crowned City
Virginia, General Assembly of: House of Burgesses
Virginia: Atlantic States; Blue Ridge Mountains, the; Commonwealth; Delmarva Peninsula; Dismal Swamp, the; District of Columbia; Mother of Presidents;

Mother of States; Old Dominion; Outer Banks; South, the, 1; Thirteen Original Colonies
Virginia City, Montana: Bozeman Trail
Virginian: Monitor and *Merrimack*
Vistula: Polish Corridor, the
Vizcaya: Guernica
Vladivostok: Siberia
Volga River: Volgograd
Volgograd
Wabash River: Indian-Appian Way
Waco, Texas: Athens of Texas; Queen of the Brazos (River)
Wagga Wagga: Riverina, the
Wagner, Richard: Bayreuth
Waikiki: Banzai Pipeline
Wailing Wall, the
Waitangi
Waitangi Day: Waitangi
Walden, or Life in the Woods: Walden Pond
Walden Pond
Waldorf-Astoria Hotel: East Side; Park Avenue
Waldorf Towers: East Side
Wales, Prince of: Brighton; Principality, the
Wales: Britain; Cambria; Coal Metropolis of the World; England; Lake District, the; Law Courts, the; Little Britain; Llanfairpwllgwyngillgogerychwyrndrobllllantysiliogogogoch; Marches, the, 1; Paddington; Principality, the; Royal Borough, the; Seven Sisters; Snowdonia; United Kingdom, the
'Wales and the West': West, the, 2
Wallaby Track
Wall Street: Broadway, 1; Manhattan; Street, the, 1
Walpole, Horace: Strawberry Hill
Walpurgisnacht: Brocken
Walsall: Black Country, the
'Waltz King, the': Aragon Ballroom
Walworth: Old Kent Road, the
Walworth Road: Transport House
Wanchai
Wanchai Burberry
Wantsum, River: Isle of Thanet, the
wapentakes: Rapes

Wapping: Dockland; Pool of London, the; Printing House Square
Warden, the: Barset
Wardour Street
'Wardour Street English': Wardour Street
War of the Spanish Succession: Blenheim Palace
Warren Street
Warwickshire: Arden; Coventry; Midlands, the; Rugby; West Midlands, the
Warwickshire County Cricket Club: Edgbaston
Wash, the: Fens, the
Washington, D. C.: Camp David; Connecticut Avenue; Embassy Row; Foggy Bottom; Ford's Theater; Hill, the; Megalopolis; Northeast, the, 2; Northeast Corridor; Pentagon, the; Tidal Basin
Washington, George: Brother Jonathan; Bunker Hill; Featherbed Lane; Mother of Presidents
Washington: District of Columbia; Far West, the; Galloping Gertie; Inland Empire, the; Northwest, the, 2; Pacific Northwest, the
Washington Heights: Broadway, 1; Featherbed Lane; West Side, 1
Washington Park: South Side
Washington Square Park: Bughouse Square; Fifth Avenue; Greenwich Village
Washington Street: Combat Zone
Wastwater: Lake District, the
'watchtower': Barbican, the
waterfront: Embarcadero; Fisherman's Wharf
Waterloo: Bakerloo; Cockpit of Europe, the; Old Vic, the
Waterloo and City Line: Drain, the
Waterloo Bridge: South Bank, the; Waterloo
Waterloo Place: Athenaeum, the
Waterloo station: Drain, the
Water Tower: Magnificent Mile, the
Water Tower Place: Magnificent Mile, the
Watford: Bakerloo
Watson, Dr.: Baker Street
Watts
Waugh, Evelyn: Azania; Metroland

Wayne: Main Line*
Weald, the
Wealden oaks: Weald, the
Weavers, the: Greenwich Village
Webb, Captain Matthew: Channel, the
Webster, Daniel: Great Dismal
Wedgwood, Josiah: Etruria
Wednesbury: Black Country, the
Weimar
Weimar Republic: Weimar
Weiss, Hymie: Holy Name Cathedral
Welfare Island: Manhattan
Welland River: Fens, the; Wash, the
Wellbeck Abbey: Dukeries, the
Wellington, Duke of: Number One, London;
　Peninsula, the; Waterloo
Wellington: Four Main Centres, the; Main
　Trunk, the
Wellington Museum: Number One, London
Wellington Place: Hyde Park Corner
Wells, H. G.: Burton upon Trent
'Welshmen': Cambria
Wembley Stadium
Wensleydale: Dales, the
We of the Never-Never: Never Never
Wessex: Dorset; East Anglia
Wessex Region: Wessex
West, the: Bamboo Curtain, the; Chelten-
　ham; Free World, the; Iron Curtain,
　the; North, the, 3; Paddington; V & A,
　the; West Country, the
West: East, the, 2; Midlands, the
West Africa: Guinea; Middle Passage, the;
　Senegambia; Slave Coast, the; Tim-
　buktu; White Man's Grave, the
West Bank, the
West Berlin: Kurfürstendamm, the
West Britain: Britain
West Bromwich: Black Country, the
West Bromwich Albion: Albion
Westchester County: Grand Central; Scars-
　dale Syndrome
West Country, the
West Country: Mummerset; Southwest,
　the, 2; West, the, 2
West End, the

West End: Albany; Belgravia; Berkeley
　Square; Bond Street; Bow Street; Car-
　naby Street; City, the; Clubland, 1;
　Drury Lane; Eisenhower Platz; Fitz-
　rovia; Harley Street; Islington; Jermyn
　Street; Knightsbridge; Leicester Square;
　London; Mayfair; Oxford Street; Pall
　Mall; Park Lane; Portland Place; Re-
　form Club, the; Savile Row; Seven Di-
　als; Shepherd Market; Soho; St
　James's; Tyburnia; Wardour Street;
　Warren Street; Wimpole Street
Western Australia: Albany doctor, the;
　Golden Mile, the, 2; Lasseter's Reef;
　State of Excitement, the; Trans-Austra-
　lian Railway
Western Desert, the
western frontier: Wild West, the
Western Hemisphere: New World, the;
　West, the, 1
Western Isles, the
Western Ocean, the
Western Sahara: Western Desert, the
Western Samoa: Australasia
West Germany: Berlin Wall, the; European
　Economic Community, the; Prussia;
　Reeperbahn, the; Ruhr, the
West Glamorgan: Seven Sisters
West Ham: East End
Westhampton: Hamptons, the
West Hollywood: Boystown
West India Docks: Billingsgate; Isle of Dogs,
　the
West Indies: Indies, the
West Midlands, the
West Midlands: Black Country, the;
　Bourneville; Bullring, the; Burton upon
　Trent; Edgbaston; Etruria; Hand-
　sworth; Lincolnshire; Salop; Second
　City; Spaghetti Junction
Westminster, monks of: Covent Garden
Westminster, Palace of: Star Chamber;
　Westminster
Westminster: Lambeth; Mother of Parlia-
　ments, the; Smith Square; Thorney Is-
　land; Vauxhall; Whitehall
Westminster Abbey: Thorney Island; West-
　minster

Westminster Bridge: London Bridge
Westminster chimes: Big Ben
Westminster College: Iron Curtain, the
Westmorland
West Pakistan: Pakistan
West Point
West Riding: Ridings, the
West Side: Chelsea, 2; Tribeca
West Village, the: East Village, the; Green-
wich Village
West Virginia: Appalachia; Atlantic States;
Mason-Dixon Line; Mother of States
Westwood: Sunset Boulevard
West Yorkshire: Ridings, the
Wharfedale: Dales, the
Wheeling, West Virginia: Nail City
Whig: Turnabout, the
whirlpool: Maelstrom, the
Whistler, James McNeill: Chelsea, 1
White, Patrick: Sarsaparilla
White, Stanford: Madison Square Garden
Whitechapel: East End
'Whitechapel murders': Whitechapel
White City
White Cliffs, the
Whitefriars: Alsatia
Whitehall: Charing Cross; Downing Street;
Number 10; Scotland Yard
White House: 1600 Pennsylvania Avenue;
Camelot, 2; Oval Office
white man's burden
White Man's Grave, the
White Mountains: Appalachian Mountains
White Otter Castle
White Otter Lake: White Otter Castle
White Peak: Peak District, the
White's: Clubland, 1
White Sea: Karelia
Whitestone: Queens
White Tower: slider; Tower, the
Whittington, Dick: Highgate
Wicker Park: West Side, 2
Wieland, Christoph: Weimar
Wigan: Neasden
'Wigan Pier': Wigan
Wight, Isle of: Island, the, 1; Needles, the;
Solent, the
Wilberforce, Bishop: Timbuktu

Wilcannia shower: Bourke
Wilcox, Horace: Hollywood
Wilde, Oscar: Père Lachaise
Wilder, Billy: Sunset Boulevard
Wilderness City
Wild West, the
Wilhelm (William II), emperor of Germany:
Sick Man of Europe
Wilhelmstrasse, the
Willamette Valley: Oregon Trail
William III: gentleman in black velvet, the;
Glencoe
Williams, Shirley: Limehouse
Williamsburgh: Brooklyn
Wilmington: Chemical Capital of the World;
New Sweden
Wilshire Boulevard: Beverly Hills; Miracle
Mile
Wilson, Edmund: Minsky's
Wilson, Woodrow: Mother of Presidents
Wilson Dam: Muscle Shoals Area
Wiltshire: Avebury; Old Sarum; Porton
Down; South, the, 2; Wessex; West
Country, the
Wimbledon
Wimpole Street
Winchell, Walter: Stork Club
Winchelsea: Cinque Ports, the
Winchester: Barset; Camelot, 1
Winchester rifle: gun that won the west
Windermere: Lake District, the
Windmill Girls: Windmill Theatre, the
Windmill Theatre, the
Windscale
Windsor: Royal Borough, the; Runnymede
Windy City
wine trade: Mincing Lane
Wirral, the
Wisconsin: Midwest, the; Mother of States
Witham, Riber: Fens, the
Witwatersrand: Rand, the
Wizard of Oz, the: TOTO
Wolds, the
Wollongong: Gong, the; Steel City, 2
Wollsend: Hadrian's Wall
Wolverhampton: Black Country, the
Wong Nei Chong Valley: Happy Valley
Woods Hole: Cape, the